READINGS IN MUSIC LEARNING THEORY

Edited by

Darrel L. Walters
Temple University

and

Cynthia Crump Taggart
Case Western Reserve University

with a Foreword by Edwin E. Gordon

G-3302

G.I.A. Publications, Inc.
7404 S. Mason Ave.
Chicago, IL 60638

1989

GIML 1989

The Gordon Institute for Music Learning (GIML) endorses these materials and certifies that they are authentic, correct, and representative of the philosophy and principles underlying Gordon Music Learning Theory.

GIML
4501 Spruce St.
Philadelphia, PA 19139

Readings in Music Learning Theory
Edited by Darrel L. Walters and Cynthia Crump Taggart
©Copyright 1989, G.I.A. Publications, Inc.
7404 S. Mason Ave., Chicago, IL 60638
International copyright secured
Library of Congress Catalog Card Number: 89-84093
ISBN: 941050-17-3
Printed in U.S.A.

FOREWORD

Perhaps the last thing to enter my mind when I was developing Music Learning Theory, if I thought of it at all, was the actual application of the theory in the classroom. I found the challenge of dealing with Music Learning Theory itself to be so compelling and overwhelming that I never thought that I would have the energy or the time to direct my thoughts to practical considerations. That I would eventually have to concern myself with the reality and the demands of education and become dependent upon the interest and knowledge of my colleagues and peers should not have come as a surprise. I am grateful to them, and I accept and recognize the value of their contributions with humility. Without involvement on the part of those who contributed papers to this book, as well as many others, I am certain that the fruits of my endeavors would have remained a private love affair between me and the research.

It all began in the late 1960's after the <u>Musical Aptitude Profile</u> was published and was well established. As you know, the primary purpose of the test battery is to assist teachers in teaching to the individual musical differences among students. It was found that after the scores for the seven subtests were derived, the majority of the teachers were not sure of how to adapt instruction to the individual musical needs of their students. In other words, they were in a quandary about how we learn when we learn music. The suggestions given in the test manual apparently were not sufficient. At about the same time I was invited to write the book <u>The Psychology of Music Teaching</u>. I took that opportunity to begin to explore Music Learning Theory so that I could be more precise in explaining to teachers how they might teach music more appropriately and efficiently. I eagerly engaged in systematic reading and experimental and observational research. With those activities, the seeds of Music Learning Theory took root, and the concept has been flowering ever since. Whereas the most up-to-date theoretical aspects of Music Learning Theory can be found in the Fifth Edition of <u>Learning Sequences in Music: Skill, Content, and Patterns</u>, and the materials for implementing Music Learning Theory in the classroom can be found in <u>Jump Right In: The Music Curriculum</u>, suggestions of those who have successfully used Music Learning Theory activities in their day-to-day teaching can be found in this book.

During the mid 1970's, Edward Harris, president of G.I.A., became aware of my work in Music Learning Theory and invited me to write a book on the subject. That resulted in the first comprehensive edition of Music Learning Theory. Neither he nor I was aware that eventually it would become my responsibility to oversee the compilation of materials for the practical application of Music Learning Theory in the classroom. In collaboration with David G. Woods, eight years were devoted to designing, field testing, and publishing Jump Right In: The Music Curriculum. With that monumental task behind me, I am more vigorously than ever conducting research in audiation, the basis of Music Learning Theory, Music Learning Theory itself, music aptitudes, and other related subjects. I hope that by continuing my research and writing that in some small measure I will be expressing my appreciation to those who believe in Music Learning Theory, especially to the contributors to this book. I realize, of course, that I will never be able to adequately express my gratitude to and admiration for Darrel Walters and Cynthia Crump Taggart for serving as editors of this book. I have only a small inkling of the time and effort that they devoted to the project. I will be forever grateful to them.

The breadth of knowledge of the authors of the papers and the practical information based upon practical experience offered is, in my estimation, unparalleled in music education. The papers exude careful independent thinking, but nevertheless, an awareness of responsibility. A perusal of the Table of Contents will indicate that the writings cover the span of early childhood music guidance to music instruction in the college and university, for non-music majors as well as music majors. In all, there are more than twenty-five authors and more than thirty topics.

The one unanticipated specific result of the book is something that only I can enjoy and uniquely reflect upon. It is the opportunity to gain some insight into how my professional thoughts are extensively interpreted by others, by those who are sincere and single-minded and who share many of my beliefs. I learn more and more from every reading of each paper. In a word, I am fortunate to be able to see myself through the eyes of others and to hear myself through the ears of others. I am not sure that I will ever again experience such an awesome and profound experience. I do not take the privilege and responsibility that accompany such a delight lightly.

Edwin E. Gordon
April, 1989

PREFACE

Edwin Gordon's early research led to his developing the Musical Aptitude Profile (MAP) in 1965, recognized as the best test of its kind on the market. In MAP, music educators had a powerful tool by which to obtain important information about students, but there was widespread uncertainty about how to make use of that information. Upon hearing those uncertainties expressed repeatedly, Gordon decided that it was incumbent upon him to investigate the question of how music instruction might be improved, in part, by use of knowledge about music aptitude.

The question that Gordon pursued was "how do children learn when they learn music?" By asking that question, and by pursuing its answer tirelessly, he acquired information that led to the development of his Music Learning Theory. (The term is capitalized throughout this book so that it can be identified easily as an entity rather than as a generic phrase.) Music Learning Theory is unique in several ways. First, it is based upon a student view rather than upon a teacher view, i.e., it is based upon the premise that the nature of learning must dictate approaches to teaching. Second, it is supported by substantial educational research. Third, it has incorporated into it the collective wisdom of previous music educators and educational theorists. And fourth, Music Learning Theory is conceived by Edwin Gordon to be subject to constant growth and revision.

We should elaborate on the fourth point. While Gordon laments the interruption of learning that occurs when effective music learning sequences are ignored, or when they are befouled by the interjection of changes based upon notions and whims, he acknowledges that there is danger in thinking of Music Learning Theory as complete and adequate in its present form. In his mind, proponents of Music Learning Theory, whether now or fifty years from now, should never view Music Learning Theory as static. Simply put, teachers who base their teaching upon evidence of how learning takes place should never close their eyes and ears to new evidence if that new evidence is well-founded. That attitude of openness is needed so that Music Learning Theory can be preserved as a "theory" rather than as an "ism," and consequently remain effective and up-to-date indefinitely.

The purpose of this book is to bring together a wide spectrum of thought about Music Learning Theory as it exists in 1989, and specifically as it is being applied to the teaching of music to children and adults in a variety of settings. Part I, "Theory," is intended to provide the uninitiated with important information about Music Learning Theory, introductory information that will make the articles in Part II much more understandable and useable. Nonetheless, the reader who considers himself "initiated" will do well to also read Part I before partaking of segments from Part II, as the theoretical articles in Part I have been written expressly for this book and may contain insights that will add to previous learning.

The articles in Part II have been contributed, without exception, by teachers who have some understanding of Music Learning Theory, and who have applied that understanding to the teaching of music. There is diversity among the authors with regard to the type of teaching experience they have had and the type and amount of contact they have had with Music Learning Theory. Some authors (including Gordon) might disagree with others on specific points, but all have one experience in common: they have found that Music Learning Theory is an indispensable source of insight for the teacher who wants to guide students to an optimal level of understanding, competency, and appreciation in music.

Note that the pronoun "he" is used throughout the articles without any predisposition toward one gender or another. The decision to use "he" in a generic sense was made simply to avoid the awkwardness and distraction from content that occurs for most persons when they have to read through "s/he," "he or she," or "she or he" repeatedly.

We need to thank the authors for contributing their expertise to this endeavor, and for their forbearance throughout an editing process that at times seemed interminable to all of us. And we need to thank Nadine Cernohorsky, Dick McCrystal, and Bob Schilling, for their help on the editorial committee in the early stages of the book. We need also to thank Temple University's Boyer College of Music, and particularly Roger Dean, Chair of the Music Education and Music Therapy Department, for help and support in many small, and some not-so-small, ways. An indispensable Temple resource was Steven Estrella, who so ably waved his computer wand over the many discs submitted and turned them into a physical book. And most of all, editors, authors, and readers alike need to thank Edwin E. Gordon for a lifetime of intensely committed work that has provided both the inspiration and the substance for this book.

The Editors

vi

CONTENTS

PART ONE

THEORY

AUDIATION: THE TERM AND THE PROCESS

Darrel L. Walters

Introduction

A concept or process is sometimes thought about and discussed for generations without being given an adequate label. Until recently, a prime example was the aural-mental process by which humans assimilate music. Several terms have been applied to that process over time - aural perception, silent singing, aural imagery, inner hearing - but not one of them adequately labels that which occurs. "Aural perception" implies the presence of sound (because one can perceive only that which is present), but the aural-mental process that facilitates the assimilation of music needs to account also for the "hearing" of music that is not sounding. "Silent singing" and "aural imagery" address the issue of hearing music that is not sounding, but they too are flawed terms. "Silent singing" connotes a limitation to vocal music, and further to a single melodic line, because that is all that anyone can sing at a given time. "Aural imagery" is a confusing oxymoron, as the term "image" is for most persons irrevocably attached to the visual realm of their life-long, connotation-building experiences.

"Inner hearing" is perhaps more acceptable than any of the three preceding terms, but it does not bring clarity and focus to the aural process in the way that visual terms bring clarity and focus to the visual process. The antithesis of "inner hearing" would be "outer hearing," which is awkward if not nonsensical. To draw an analogy, one would never speak of "inner seeing" and "outer seeing." "Outer seeing" is simply visual perception, and "inner seeing" is identified with the label "visualization." That single, unambiguous term facilitates clarity of thought and focused discussion about the visual-mental process by which visual stimuli are assimilated. Similarly, "inner hearing" needs to be replaced with a single, unambiguous term analogous to the term "visualization," which will facilitate clarity of thought and focused discussion about the aural-mental process by which aural stimuli are assimilated. Edwin Gordon has responded to that need by coining the term "audiation" (1976, p. 2).

The term "audiation" is gaining acceptance, but is still without definition and connotation for many persons. One of the purposes of this article is to provide the reader with a definition and a connotation for the term "audiation," and for its derivations, e.g., "audiating" and the verb "to audiate." Familiar frames of reference are used to help the reader more easily incorporate the new terms into his working vocabulary. A second purpose of this article is to describe the process of audiation as theorized by Edwin Gordon. That description is given in general terms, leaving a more detailed account of the stages of audiation to Gordon (1988).

The Term "Audiation"

Visual parallels are helpful in constructing a definition and connotation for the term "audiation," because visual terms and visual processes are common and familiar to us. We know, for example, that to be capable of visualizing objects, one must have previously seen those objects and acquired a degree of visual understanding of them. Nearly everyone in our culture can visualize an automobile; relatively few can visualize the inside of a transmission. The greater the frequency with which one sees an object, and the greater the understanding that accompanies that seeing, the more completely and accurately will that person be able to "see" when the image is not actually present - that is, the greater will be his powers of visualization.

Following the same line of thought, to be capable of audiating sounds one must have previously heard those sounds and acquired a degree of aural understanding of them. In terms of music, nearly everyone in our culture can audiate hard-driving duple meter with an accented upbeat; relatively few can audiate a variety of rhythm pattern functions in triple meter or unusual meter. The greater the frequency with which one hears sounds, and the greater the understanding that accompanies that hearing, the more completely and accurately will that person be able to hear when the sound is not actually present - that is, the greater will be his powers of audiation.

The following four pairs of definitions will add clarity to the visual/aural comparison. The first of each pair relates to a visual experience, and the second to a parallel aural experience.

Pair One:

To visually perceive is to see that which is before the eye.
To aurally perceive is to hear that which is before the ear.

Pair Two:
>   To visually recall is to visualize sights that we have previously seen.
>   To aurally recall is to audiate sounds that we have previously heard.

Pair Three:
>   To visually predict is to visualize sights that we anticipate seeing.
>   To aurally predict is to audiate sounds that we anticipate hearing.

Pair Four:
>   To visually conceive is to visualize (or envision) sights that we create
>   or improvise.
>   To aurally conceive is to audiate sounds that we create or improvise.

A clear definition of the term visualization and a clear definition of the term audiation can be synthesized from those four pairs of statements. Visualization is the seeing of sights that are not before the eye at the moment, through recall, prediction, or conception. Similarly, audiation is the hearing of sounds that are not before the ear at the moment, through recall, prediction, or conception. That definition of audiation will be the working definition for purposes of this article.

The working definition of audiation is not meant to imply that the absence of sound is a prerequisite to the exercising of audiation skill. We are perfectly capable of, and in fact are bound to, audiate as we listen to music. The important distinction is that we are not, at any given moment, audiating the music of that moment. The music of the moment is being aurally perceived, while we concurrently audiate in recall music heard moments before and audiate in prediction music that we expect to hear in moments to come. The audiation process is complicated, and is understood most readily in relation to the types of audiation and stages within those types.

The Types of Audiation

Edwin Gordon (1988) has identified seven types of audiation, each of which may be thought of as a specific situation in which audiation skills are needed if one is to be successful. In their most brief form, the types of audiation are as follows.

1. Listening to music.
2. Reading music (silently or in performance).
3. Writing music from dictation.
4. Recalling music (silently or in performance).
5. Writing music from recall.
6. Creating or improvising music (silently or in performance).
7. Writing music as it is created or improvised.

In short, all "types" of experiences related to music are dependent for their quality upon the ability of the person involved to audiate, i.e., to hear sounds that are not present at the moment. The sounds audiated during a given experience may have been heard recently or not so recently, and they may have been "triggered," i.e., brought to conciousness, by either an external source or an internal source.

Refer again to Gordon's seven types of audiation. Notice that Types 3, 5, and 7 are written applications of Types 1, 4, and 6, respectively. In Figure 1, Gordon's seven types of audiation are combined with information about audiation triggers and their sources, and with options for the practical application of each type of audiation. Viewed in this way, the seven types of audiation may be thought of as four general audiational processes, each of which may be applied to any one of two or three specific music activities.

Trigger	Audiational Process	Application Options
external: the sound of music	listening to music	— think about music — write music (from dictation)
external: the sight of music notation	reading music	— think about music — perform music
internal: thought (memory traces)	recalling music	— think about music — write music — perform music
internal: thought (variations on memory traces)	creating/improvising music	— think about music — write music — perform music

Figure 1. A Unique View of the Types of Audiation

The degree to which one is able to participate in the activities cited in Figure 1 will depend upon the level of his audiation skill. Everyone possesses some level of ability to recall and predict sounds, and thus some ability to hear sound that is not present, i.e., to audiate. There are many elements involved in the audiation of music, however, and some are more fundamental to music understanding and music performance than are others. To audiate a piece of music to be loud as opposed to soft, or fast as opposed to slow, or to audiate a specific sound to be a saxophone as opposed to a violin, is elementary. Little music understanding is needed to engage in such "surface" audiation. On the other hand, to audiate the tonality of a piece of music to be minor as opposed to major, or to audiate the meter to be triple as opposed to duple, requires music understanding. Further, to audiate specific tonal patterns and rhythm patterns and their functions within identified tonalities and meters requires not only a degree of understanding, but an acquired music vocabulary as well. Therefore, the elements of music that are fundamental to the development of skill in music audiation are a sense of meter and the consequent ability to discriminate among meters, a sense of tonality and the consequent ability to discriminate among tonalities, a vocabulary of rhythm patterns, and a vocabulary of tonal patterns. While the audiation of dynamics, timbre, expression, etc. are indispensable to the complete picture of music audiation, one who aspires to be skillful in music beyond "listening for pleasure" first needs to acquire audiation skills that are fundamental to music understanding.

To examine further the information shown in Figure 1 as it relates to skill in audiation, let us assume two hypothetical cases. The first is a minimally skilled audiator and the second a highly skilled audiator.

The minimally skilled audiator can recall music in an elementary way that brings to mind non-fundamental characteristics, such as volume and timbre. He may recall a few fundamental characteristics, such as rhythm patterns or tonal patterns, if they are simple and repetitive. He can also make associations with nonmusical elements, such as lyrics or the visualization of the performing group. However, his powers of music recall are extremely limited. Also, he is unable to read, write, create, or improvise music. Therefore, the minimally skilled audiator is limited to listening as his only musical experience, and he is limited further to surface listening because of his inability to identify important musical characteristics of the sound.

Unlike the minimally skilled audiator, the highly skilled audiator gives syntactical meaning to the music that he hears, much as he gives syntactical meaning to language. Meaning in language is derived from an understanding of words and phrases, applied in a variety of functions, so that the same parts arranged in different orders result in different "wholes" that are understood (through language syntax) for their uniqueness. Meaning in music is derived from an understanding of tonality, meter, tonal patterns, rhythm patterns, etc., applied in various functions and arranged in different orders to create different "wholes" that are understood (through music syntax) for their uniqueness. The highly skilled audiator is capable of recognizing familiar parts of musical sound, he is capable of identifying the functions of unfamiliar parts on the basis of their relationship to familiar parts, and he is capable of giving meaning to the whole on the basis of his recognition, identification, and understanding of the parts. He is also capable of retaining his understanding of musical sound over time, and can draw on his understanding to recall, create, and improvise music.

Incidentally, it is possible for individuals to possess high-level skills in music audiation without knowledge of how to read or write music notation. One endowed with high music aptitude often develops a "good ear" with little or no formal music instruction. Many outstanding performers, particularly jazz musicians, have demonstrated extraordinary abilities in what Gordon calls "basic audiation" without having learned to read and write music. Of course, one whose audiation skill is limited to basic audiation will be excluded from all reading and writing activities shown in the center column and the right-hand column of Figure 1. Still, it can be seen that the exclusion of those items does not preclude accomplishment in music. On the other hand, one who can name the symbols used in music notation and produce a corresponding sound on a music instrument, but who cannot "audiate" the sound represented by those symbols, will produce unmusical results.

The ideal for comprehensive musicianship is skill in basic audiation coupled with the ability to read and write music. That union produces another skill, which Gordon has labeled "notational audiation." Skill in notational audiation allows the reader of music to use notation to visually trigger aural impressions, and the writer of music to record mentally triggered aural impressions via music notation. A reasonable supposition would be that advanced skill in audiation is more necessary for success in notational audiation than for success in basic audiation. That is true to the extent that basic audiation serves as a readiness for notational audiation. However, the appearance that a greater audiational challenge exists for one engaged in notational audiation than for one engaged in basic audiation is due partially to the fact that a person can more easily feign basic audiation than he can feign notational audiation. Simple imitation - parroting sounds without giving syntactical meaning to them - will sometimes pass for skill in basic audiation. No such opportunity for "fudging" is available to a person asked to sing a piece of music from notation without accompaniment or any other aural cues.

It should be mentioned that imitation is an important early step toward acquiring skill in audiation, but imitation is not audiation. To use the visual parallel again, music performance by imitation is to music performance through audiation as drawing a picture by tracing is to drawing a picture through visualization.

It can be said that one who has fully acquired the skill of notational audiation has learned to hear with his eyes and see with his ears. In other words, he can see notation and audiate the sound it represents, and he can audiate sound and visualize the notation needed to represent it.

The Stages of Audiation

An important and difficult question to answer is "how does the process of audiation actually occur?" That is, what kind of interplay transpires between the ear and the mind as one engages in the audiation of music? A correct answer, but an evasive one, is that the process of audiation is never quite the same for one individual as for another. The interplay between ear and mind is necessarily influenced by individual aptitudes, backgrounds, personalities, preferences, retention skills, and other characteristics. However, as important as those individual differences are to an educator or a therapist, they need to be ignored for purposes of conveying a technical description of the basic process of audiation.

The process of audiation, as it has been analyzed to date by Edwin Gordon, appears to consist of a series of six stages.[1] For one who is engaged in listening to music, those stages potentially involve, among other things, the organization of perceived sounds into meaningful patterns, the comparing of those patterns with other currently-heard sounds, the comparing of those patterns with previously-heard sounds, and the prediction of imminent sounds. A comprehensive analysis of the stages of audiation can be found in Gordon's Learning Sequences in Music: Skill, Content, and Patterns, G.I.A. Publications, Inc., 1988.

The reader will enhance his understanding of the stages of audiation, and of the interrelationships among the stages, if he is conscious of two additional facts while reading Gordon's description of the stages. First, the stages of audiation are chained so tightly that they overlap. While one pattern of sounds is being aurally processed at an advanced stage of audiation, a pattern of sounds perceived a fraction of a second later is simultaneously being processed at a less advanced stage of audiation. A description of the stages of audiation amounts to a slow-motion tour of aural/mental processes that overlap and occur within seconds and fractions of seconds. Second, the stages of audiation are hierarchical, but all six stages will not necessarily be completed each time audiation is begun. That is, the audiation process always begins with the most elementary stage (retention of sound), but the most advanced stage (prediction of sound) may or may not be reached, depending upon whether the audiator has a sufficient combination of aptitude and experience to participate through all six stages. If the ability of the audiator is insufficient, the audiation process will be "short-circuited," and the audiator will continually return to the first stage of audiation without completing the audiation process.

A narrative statement describing the complete process of audiation as theorized by Gordon and embodied in his stages of audiation is by nature complex. Still, a compact description is worth reading for the concept of the whole that it offers. To this end, one might say that a person fully and competently engaged in a music listening experience will perceive sounds and retain an aural impression of them, organize those sounds into tonal and rhythm patterns based upon a sense of tonality and a sense of meter, retain those patterns for reference as the process continues, recall patterns from other music previously audiated to serve as further reference, and predict patterns to come based on all previous information perceived and assimilated. Because the preceding statement contains a large amount of complex information compressed into a small space, the reader is encouraged to study it several times and to compare it with Gordon's more detailed explanation.

Perspective

As a practice, music audiation is age-old; as a subject of scientific investigation, music audiation is new and incomplete. Additional thought is needed, and observable aspects of audiation need to be researched. Meanwhile, the music educator needs to recognize the fact that audiation skill is central to all achievement in music. Once that fact is accepted, the music educator, if he is operating in good conscience, can do no less than to give the development of audiation skill a central role in his teaching.

NOTES

[1]Until very recently, Gordon cited five stages of audiation. He has rethought and reconstructed the stages of audiation, and cites six stages in the 1988 edition of Learning Sequences in Music, which was released a few months prior to the publication of this collection.

REFERENCES

Gordon, Edwin E. (1976). Learning Sequence and Patterns in Music. Chicago: G.I.A Publications, Inc.
Gordon, Edwin E. (1988). Learning Sequences in Music: Skill, Content, and Patterns. Chicago: G.I.A. Publications, Inc.

SKILL LEARNING SEQUENCE

Darrel L. Walters

Introduction

Learning involves two fundamental elements: content and skill. Content consists of characteristics of the material being learned. In the case of music learning, some examples of content are minor tonality, triple meter, and tonic function. Skill is the action that the learner applies to the material being learned. In the case of music learning, some examples of skill are the association of tonal syllables with tonal patterns or rhythm syllables with rhythm patterns, or at a more advanced stage, the interpretation of symbols found in music notation.

Of course content in music cannot be studied without applying some specific level of skill, nor can skill be exercised in relation to music except as it is applied to specific content. The two are as interdependent as a lock and key, neither able to function meaningfully without the other.

The efficiency and the thoroughness of music learning are affected by the order in which pieces of content are learned and by the order in which skills are learned. In recognition of the importance of order, or sequence, in relation to both content learning and skill learning, Edwin Gordon has established "content levels" and "skill levels" within his Music Learning Theory. On the basis of extensive research, Gordon has constructed three learning hierarchies, two for content learning and one for skill learning. Knowledge about each of those hierarchies is invaluable to music educators who want to employ what is known about learning sequence to improve the efficiency and thoroughness of their own teaching. Gordon has labeled his hierarchies "Tonal Learning Sequence," "Rhythm Learning Sequence," and "Skill Learning Sequence." The subject of this article is Skill Learning Sequence.

Gordon's skill learning hierarchy is shown in Figure 1. By itself, the hierarchy tends to be confounding and intimidating, but given adequate explanation, the music educator will see logic in the hierarchy and will begin to acquire insights that will have a profound influence upon his teaching. The remainder of this article is devoted to providing that explanation.

DISCRIMINATION LEARNING

AURAL/ORAL

VERBAL ASSOCIATION

PARTIAL SYNTHESIS

SYMBOLIC ASSOCIATION
Reading – Writing

COMPOSITE SYNTHESIS
Reading – Writing

INFERENCE LEARNING

GENERALIZATION
Aural/Oral – Verbal – Symbolic

CREATIVITY/IMPROVISATION
Aural/Oral – Symbolic

THEORETICAL UNDERSTANDING
Aural/Oral – Verbal – Symbolic

Figure 1. Gordon's Skill Learning Hierarchy

The hierarchy shown in Figure 1 is divided into two sections, labeled "Discrimination Learning" and "Inference Learning." Within each section is a series of learning levels written in capital letters and sequenced from top to bottom. Below each of the learning levels from symbolic association to the end of the hierarchy is a series of subparts of levels, written in upper and lower case letters and sequenced from left to right.

Discrimination Learning

Discrimination learning is rote learning. The teacher gives the student all of the information that he will need to learn to categorize the many pieces of content that he perceives and to learn to discriminate among them. Students engaged in discrimination learning learn to recognize a given piece of content on the basis of what it is not as well as on the basis of what it is.

Music students perceive content, sensate that which has been perceived by singing, moving, etc., and finally audiate that which has been sensated.[1]

In the study of music, all content is perceived aurally until the student encounters music notation, and that should not occur until aural readinesses have been acquired. The role of visual perception will increase with an increase in the use of music notation, but aural discrimination processes must always predominate over visual discrimination processes at all levels of music learning and music performance.

Discrimination learning needs to be of primary concern to the teacher for two reasons. First, only at discrimination levels of learning does the teacher have control of (and consequently responsibility for) the learning that takes place. Second, the quality of the student's inference learning will be no better than the quality of his discrimination learning.

Inference Learning

Inference learning takes place in the study of music when a student encounters content that is unfamiliar to him, that is, content that he has not specifically learned by rote at discrimination levels of learning. To learn by inference, the student must identify and give meaning to unfamiliar material on the basis of its similarities to and differences from familiar material. During the process of learning by inference, the learner often does not know what he has learned, and he is commonly unaware even that learning has taken place. The sensation for the learner is likely to be one of having put together, in a flash, pieces of learning that he has acquired previously.

For obvious reasons, the teacher has less control over inference learning than he has over discrimination learning. The teacher can teach the student how to make inferences, he can guide the student to materials and circumstances that will induce inferences, and he can recommend alternative approaches to problems when students fail to make inferences, but the teacher cannot teach the student what to infer. If a student is consistently unsuccessful at making inferences, the teacher can only return that student to a discrimination learning sequence that will equip him to make those inferences.

The Discrimination/Inference Relationship

The use of categorizations such as "discrimination learning" and "inference learning," as important as those categorizations are to an analysis of the learning process, tends to oversimplify concepts and create misconceptions about how discrimination and inference function in the world of practical application. The reader should be continuously aware of two important truths while reading the specific information to follow regarding the individual levels of Gordon's skill learning hierarchy.

First, discrimination learning and inference learning are never wholly separated in practice. For example, while the teacher is consciously teaching at a discrimination level of learning, students are making inferences within that discrimination learning experience. The amount of inference learning that coexists with discrimination learning is greater among students who have a high music aptitude and among students who have benefited from prior experiences with music. The amount of inference learning that coexists with discrimination learning becomes greater also as the levels of discrimination learning become more advanced, that is, as the learning process advances toward the bridge between discrimination learning and inference learning. Once that bridge has been crossed, inference learning becomes dominant, but discrimination learning continues to occur as needed. In short, the difference between discrimination learning and inference learning is more a matter of degree than of type.

Second, the levels of learning shown in Gordon's skill learning hierarchy are not merely progressive; they are accumulative. Once a given piece of content has been learned at a particular skill level, that skill is carried forward to and becomes a part of the next skill level in relation to the same content. In effect, the partial synthesis level of learning, for example, is actually the aural/oral-verbal association-partial synthesis level of learning.

The remainder of this article will be devoted to a series of explanations, one for each of the levels of learning shown in Gordon's skill learning hierarchy. The explanations are oriented to learning sequence activities, with only incidental reference to classroom activities.[2]

The Aural/Oral Level of Learning

At the aural/oral level of learning, the student hears music (aural) and performs some form of music (oral) in response to what he hears. The oral side of the equation may take the form of singing, moving in response to rhythm, chanting, or some combination of the three.[3] The aural/oral level of learning is the only level that, for a period of time, is engaged in isolation from all other levels of learning. That period of isolation extends for months, if not years. The explanation is that aural/oral learning begins in an informal way at or before birth. That informal learning continues for years, with only incidental, chance contact with other levels of learning, until a child has worked his way through the music babble stage.[4]

While all informal learning is aural/oral, all aural/oral learning is not informal. Once the child has finished with the music babble stage, which usually occurs no later than about age five if experiences with music are optimal, he is ready for what Gordon refers to as "formal" music instruction. Formal music instruction involves the presentation of specific material by the teacher with expectations of specific achievement on the part of the student. The child engaged in formal music instruction at the aural/oral level is developing a sense of meter, a sense of tonality, and the beginning of a vocabulary of rhythm patterns and a vocabulary of tonal patterns. The teacher of music must not underestimate the importance of the aural/oral level of learning to formal music learning. Formal aural/oral learning is the foundation upon which all other formal music learning is built. To neglect the aural/oral level of learning during formal music instruction is to sabotage the efficiency and thoroughness of all subsequent formal music learning.

Solo performance, using a neutral syllable, is important to learning and to the evaluation of learning at the aural/oral level. Rhythm patterns must be heard and performed in solo without melody and tonal patterns must be heard and performed in solo without rhythm if a child is to learn to audiate the patterns with precision and if he is to be well prepared later to generalize. The ability to audiate a vocabulary of rhythm patterns and a vocabulary of tonal patterns is dependent upon, and at the same time provides reinforcement for, the ability to audiate meter and tonality.

The singing of rote songs in classroom activities is also important to the solidification of a sense of meter and a sense of tonality. Children first perceive the songs as wholes, and later become aware that songs are composed of patterns. As a result of that awareness, they are able to give more meaning to both songs and patterns. Songs and patterns should be pursued as independent activities, patterns being selected on the basis of content objectives and relative difficulty rather than because they appear in a song. Coordination of the two will occur naturally as a child's vocabulary of patterns and repertoire of songs increases, but there are specific actions that the teacher can take as well that increase the level of the interaction.[5]

(Iconic)

The Verbal Association Level of Learning

Just as children recognize objects around them and discriminate one from another with the help of the names of those objects, so must they associate names with elements of music if they are to readily recognize those elements and discriminate efficiently among them. Two types of names are used at the verbal association level of music learning, as shown in Figure 2.

Type of Name	Examples
Proper Name	**major** tonality **triple** meter **tonic** function **macro** beat
Vocabulary Name	**do re mi** (tonal syllables) **du da di** (rhythm syllables)

Figure 2. Types of Names Used for Verbal Association

Verbal associations solidify patterns in audiation, and they make recall simpler. Without the help of verbal associations, the number of elements of music that one could store and accurately recall would be greatly reduced.

At the verbal association level of learning, the teacher performs rhythm patterns using rhythm syllables or tonal patterns using tonal syllables, and the student chants rhythm syllables in echo or sings tonal syllables in echo. That process solidifies the association of vocabulary names (syllables) with sounds. The teacher also helps the student to associate proper names with specific elements of music, such as tonality or meter.

As was true at the aural/oral level of learning, rhythm patterns must be heard and performed without melody and tonal patterns must be heard and performed without rhythm. Also, students must perform in solo for effective learning and for an accurate evaluation of learning to take place.

The Partial Synthesis Level of Learning

To synthesize is to combine parts into a whole that is different from the sum of the parts and interpretable on the basis of the syntax that is created. At the partial synthesis level of music learning, series of rhythm patterns and series of tonal patterns are used in learning sequence activities, and students are taught to recognize characteristics of the series on the basis of what they have learned previously about characteristics of the individual patterns. The combining of familiar patterns in unfamiliar order enables students to gain insight into the possibilities for creating wholes out of parts, similar to the way in which phrases and sentences are formed out of series of familiar words. Students learn that the wholes take on characteristics by which they can be given meaning, e.g., tonality and meter. Students are taught to employ rhythm syllables and tonal syllables at the partial synthesis level as they hear, perform, and audiate series of patterns. Use of syllables not only helps students to give meaning to the whole, but it also helps them to appreciate the inherent logic of the rhythm syllables within and among rhythm patterns and tonal syllables within and among tonal patterns.

To use an analogy, students learning at the partial synthesis level of learning have spent time at previous levels of learning examining the trees, and now they are beginning to examine, if not the forest, at least clumps of trees. Of course the examinations are all aural rather than visual. The term "partial" specifically refers to the fact that the synthesis takes place only aurally, the visual being held in abeyance until after the introduction of notation.

It should be noted that many teachers tend to omit or severely limit learning at the partial synthesis level in favor of proceeding directly to the symbolic association level of learning. There are probably two reasons for that. One is that teachers generally do not understand and appreciate the partial synthesis level of learning. Another is that audiation skill is less easily demonstrated than is reading and writing skill, which means that symbolic association learning can lead more quickly to impressive demonstrable results. Teachers should know that partial synthesis learning is too important to subsequent learning to be neglected or treated lightly.

The Symbolic Association Level of Learning

At the symbolic association level of learning the student graduates from the use of basic audiation skills alone to the addition of notational audiation skills, commonly known as music reading and music writing. At the symbolic association-reading level of learning, the student learns to associate the notation of patterns with vocabulary names and proper names and to audiate the corresponding sounds. At the symbolic association-writing level of learning, the student learns that the sequential process for writing is the reverse of the sequential process for reading. The music reading process begins when a person sees symbols in music notation. The person associates those symbols with a system of syllables, and finally associates the syllables with sound and audiates the sound. The music writing process begins when a person audiates sound that he wants to notate. The person associates those sounds with a system of syllables, and finally associates the syllables with symbols and writes the symbols to create music notation. Both the music reading process and the music writing process draw heavily upon skills acquired at previous levels of learning.

To learn to read and write music is typically thought of as a rigorous process. That perception is due principally to the fact that music notation is so often engaged prematurely. If the proper aural readinesses are in place, symbolic association learning can be accomplished with surprising ease.

The Composite Synthesis Level of Learning

At the composite synthesis level of learning, partial synthesis learning (and hence aural/oral and verbal association learning) and symbolic association learning are combined. Stated another way, all levels of discrimination learning are synthesized into a whole at the composite synthesis level of learning. Assuming that a background of well-sequenced and effective learning has been acquired throughout the other levels of discrimination learning, composite synthesis learning will enable the student to notationally audiate (hear what is seen; write what is heard) series of familiar patterns, in familiar or unfamiliar order. The student will also acquire the ability to notationally audiate familiar songs read or written in the course of classroom activities. Included in the process of notational audiation will be the ability to recognize the meter and the tonality of series of familiar patterns or familiar songs and to recognize the functions of tonal patterns and rhythm patterns within those series and those songs. During classroom activities, patterns, meter, and tonality are all synthesized at the same time, along with form, style, dynamics, timbre, and possibly harmony. The precise audiation process that occurs while a complete piece of music is being assimilated is extremely complex, and is impossible to fully explain. It is because of those complexities that the wholistic nature of classroom activities does not allow the teacher to design, administer, and evaluate sequential music learning without the companion activity that Gordon refers to as learning sequence activities.

The Generalization Level of Learning

The inference learning half of Gordon's skill learning hierarchy is more complex within and among levels and subparts than is the discrimination learning half of the hierarchy. Generalization, for example, the lowest level of inference learning, has three subparts. Accomplishments within each subpart are dependent upon readinesses from among prior levels and subparts. It is difficult to describe in narrative form the various ways in which unfamiliar material is identified and assimilated at the generalization level of learning. For that reason, the explanation is given here in the form of a set of sample tasks that a student might be expected to perform at the generalization level of inference learning. Those tasks are shown in Figure 3, where they are categorized by generalization subpart. Prior levels and subparts that serve as readinesses have been cited for each case. It should be understood that all generalization tasks include unfamiliar patterns.

Teachers should understand and remember that unless a student can read familiar patterns at the symbolic association level of learning and series of familiar patterns at the composite synthesis level of learning, he should not be expected to sight-read at the generalization-symbolic level of learning. Unfortunately, teachers who ask that of students, and then witness the inevitable failure, often respond by teaching theoretical understanding as a substitute for the aural and symbolic discrimination learning that was neglected. That only compounds the problem.

Generalization Subpart	Sample Tasks	Readiness
Generalization – aural/oral	1. Identify two series of patterns as same or different.	Aural/Oral
	2. Echo patterns in solo, using a neutral syllable.	Aural/Oral
Generalization – verbal	1. Echo in solo, using rhythm or tonal syllables, patterns performed by the teacher, using neutral syllables.	Verb. Assoc., General. – aural/oral
	2. Echo in solo, using rhythm or tonal syllables, a series of patterns performed by the teacher, using neutral syllables.	Part. Synth., General. – aural/oral
Generalization – symbolic	1. Read or write patterns performed by the teacher, using tonal or rhythm syllables.	Symb. Assoc., General. – verbal
	2. Read or write a set of patterns performed by the teacher, using tonal or rhythm syllables.	Comp. Synth., General. – verbal

Figure 3. Sample Tasks and their Readiness for Each Subpart of the Generalization Level of Learning.

The Creativity/Improvisation Level of Learning

In creativity/improvisation-aural/oral learning, the student does not echo what the teacher performs, but rather he engages in dialogue with the teacher. It is important that all rhythm patterns are void of melody and that all tonal patterns are void of rhythm. The response in tonal dialogue must include the same number of patterns as the teacher's dictation, and all pitches must be of the same duration to avoid incorporating rhythm. Once the student has established skill in creativity and improvisation with rhythm patterns and tonal patterns separately in learning sequence activities, he may combine the two by creating and improvising music in classroom activities.

The two subparts of creativity/improvisation (aural/oral and symbolic) might be thought of as three, because the aural/oral subpart can function either with or without the use of verbal association. Verbal association, rather than functioning as a subpart of the creativity/improvisation level of learning, functions as a technique for creating and improvising with those patterns, meters, and tonalities previously solidified at the verbal association level of discrimination learning. Stated another way, verbal association, which had previously been viewed as an end in itself at lower levels of learning, functions at the creativity/improvisation level of learning as a means to an end. That is reflective of the fact that verbal association actually has no meaning apart from music (just as the name of an object has no meaning apart from the object). Verbal association at the creativity/improvisation level of learning "explains" to the mind what is being audiated, and explains through the mind - to the fingers and other muscular systems - how to execute or notate what is being audiated.

Teaching creativity/improvisation without verbal association limits the teacher to requesting improvisatory responses that "sound like" the patterns used by the teacher. Teaching creativity/improvisation with the use of verbal association is easier, because the student can be directed with the use of proper names, (major, duple, etc.) and with the use of rhythm syllables and tonal syllables. Consequently, fewer spoken directions are necessary when verbal association is used.

The symbolic subpart of creativity/improvisation includes only the writing of music. While the act of reading music does leave room for individuality of interpretation, typical creative and improvisatory activities are not possible within the process of reading music. Accomplishments within each subpart of the creativity/improvisation level of learning, as with

the generalization level of learning, are dependent upon readinesses from among prior levels and subparts of levels.
It should be noted that individual differences will be more pronounced at the creativity/improvisation level of learning than at any previous levels. High music aptitude is a prerequisite to success in creativity and improvisation.

The Theoretical Understanding Level of Learning

Theoretical understanding (commonly referred to as music theory) is to music as grammar and linguistics are to spoken language. To introduce a student to music theory before he can sing, move, and audiate makes as little sense as to introduce a child to parts of speech before he can speak and think in that language. Theoretical understanding should be attempted only after the student has achieved all previous levels of discrimination and inference learning to the extent that his music aptitude will allow. Some teachers (especially instrumental teachers) believe that music theory should be taught as a readiness for music reading. When that is done, students engage in the solving of music crossword puzzles and the memorizing of symbols and rules, none of which has useful meaning to one who has not first developed audiation skills. An opposite approach to the teaching of music, also unfortunate, is to drill discrimination learning (rote learning) for years to the exclusion of inference learning. Inference learning is necessary if the true role of the school is to help students think for themselves and make their own choices.
Three thoughts need to be added in reference to the subject of theoretical understanding.

1. Music theory follows the establishment of form and style in music. That is, music theory does not create form or style; it simply functions as an explanation of what is perceived, sensated, audiated, notated, and performed.
2. Although theoretical understanding is an inference learning level, rote information must be taught at that level, e.g., verbal associations for pitch-letter names, time-value names, accidentals, key signatures, measure signatures, etc. The reader will recall the earlier statement that all learning processes entail a combination of discrimination learning and inference learning, and that a given learning process is identified by which type of learning is dominant.

3. While all other levels of learning function as readiness for theoretical understanding, theoretical understanding functions as a readiness for group performance, where one will be expected to communicate in theoretical terms with the conductor and with other musicians.

Perspectives on Skill Learning Sequence

The most dependable way for a teacher of music to align his teaching with Gordon's skill learning hierarchy is to use published materials based upon Music Learning Theory. But even then, the teacher will use the materials as they are intended to be used only if he has some knowledge of the learning hierarchies on which the materials are built and some commitment to adhere to appropriate learning sequence. On the other hand, given that knowledge and commitment, a music teacher will increase the efficiency and the thoroughness of the learning process for his students regardless of the materials and literature being used.

The greatest temptation to ignore the wisdom of Gordon's skill learning hierarchy stems from the perceived need for theoretical understanding in the every-day world of group rehearsals. There are at least two solutions to that problem that are more sensible than violating skill learning sequence.

The first solution is to begin instruction early. If students are taught in accordance with Gordon's skill learning hierarchy from the time they begin attending school, they will have ample readiness for the playing of an instrument and for the learning of theory by the time they are in the upper elementary grades. On the other hand, if students are taught in accordance with Gordon's skill learning hierarchy for the first time as upper-elementary beginning instrumentalists, compromises will undoubtedly need to be made in learning sequence (but fewer compromises than one would think).

The second solution is to compromise on demands for the need for music theory. Demands for upper elementary and early junior high school instrumentalists and vocalists to understand music theory are more arbitrary than functional. Long-term music learning is better served by a delay of music theory learning than by the premature interruption of properly sequenced aural learning for the purpose of teaching music theory.

The articles in this book that explain rhythm learning sequence and tonal learning sequence are natural companions to this article. It is important that the teacher of music coordinate the teaching of specific skills and the teaching of specific content. Gordon's <u>Learning Sequences in</u>

Music (1988), other articles in this book, and other related books, articles, and manuals should all be read by music teachers interested in incorporating Music Learning Theory into their teaching. The additional insight to be gained into learning hierarchies, their coordination, and other issues relevant to efficient and thorough music teaching, will be translated into valuable benefits to students.

NOTES

[1]Within this book, see "Audiation: The Term and the Process" for more information about audiation.

[2]Learning sequence activities are designed to occupy the first five to ten minutes of each class period, and classroom activities are the traditional activities that occupy the remainder of each class period. Within this book, see the articles by Robert Harper and Linda Jessup for details about the implementation of learning sequence activities.

[3]In relation to rhythm learning, the aural/oral level of learning might be thought of as the aural/oral-kinesthetic level of learning.

[4]Within this book, see "Informal Music Instruction as Readiness for Learning Sequence Activities" for more information about the music babble stage.

[5]Within this book, see "Coordinating Learning Sequence Activities and Classroom Activities" for more information.

REFERENCES

Gordon, Edwin E. (1988). Learning Sequences in Music: Skill, Content, and Patterns. Chicago: G.I.A. Publications, Inc.

RHYTHM LEARNING SEQUENCE

James M. Jordan

While most music educators agree upon the importance of teaching rhythm skills, perhaps no aspect of music education has been subject to such confusion. Attempts have been made to develop a pedagogy for the teaching of rhythm, but that pedagogy lags far behind the pedagogy for teaching tonal skills. Most music education curricula limit rhythm content to relatively few patterns in duple and triple meters, and even then there is confusion about whether to teach those rhythm patterns using numbers, e.g., "1-e-and-a" (for four sixteenth notes), or using mnemonic devices, e.g., "Mississippi," for the same pattern.[1] Whatever system is used, terminology is inconsistent, leaving a chasm of illogic for students between what is audiated and what is written.[2] While the teacher has probably suffered through and eventually reconciled those inconsistencies of rhythm notation, children and adults who have limited experiences with music are hopelessly confused by those same inconsistencies.

Natural Body Response to Rhythm:
The Basis of Rhythm Content in Music Learning Theory

Between birth and age three, children learn without biases (and without notation). Their bodies move and respond to rhythm in a natural way. They play with and experience rhythm and movement without inhibition. If teachers of music are to work with the rhythm dimension of music in accordance with Music Learning Theory, they must try to learn as a child learns. They must audiate as a child audiates, i.e., they must constantly seek to understand how a child hears and learns music. If they succeed, they will find that their rhythm skills improve by leaps and bounds. More important, they will gain insight into the proper teaching of rhythm, and their students will develop rhythm skills at an even faster rate. Perhaps for the first time, those teachers will begin to sense the power of rhythm as children experience it.

In short, the essence of rhythm according to Music Learning Theory is movement. Rhythm classifications are organized on the basis of natural body responses to rhythm. Consider the following controversial example. Audiate "My Country 'tis of Thee." Music theorists describe that as being in three-four time with three beats in a measure and a quarter note representing one beat. That is visually correct. However, there is a conflict between the measure signature and how the music is audiated. Audiate "My Country 'tis of Thee" again, but this time move to the music. Do you move on each quarter note? You probably do not. Do you step or move once each measure? You probably do. Is it amusical to step to each quarter note? Yes. Would children step to each quarter note? They most likely would not.

The organization of rhythm according to Music Learning Theory is based upon the body's response to audiated rhythm, free of notation. Rhythm learning should be rooted not in the theory of music, but in its audiation. While the theory of music is important to the explanation of the common practice of a given period, it is not necessary for the learning of rhythm. In the same way that the reading of individual letters and the theory of grammar is not necessary for speaking or reading a language, the knowledge of note values and the theory of meter signatures does not directly bear upon the beginning stages of rhythm learning. However, a body that responds naturally to rhythm is a necessary prerequisite for the learning of rhythm, and for the establishment of consistent tempo.

Explanation of Rhythm: Audiation Layers

In this article I will present a unique approach to the understanding of Gordon's explanation of rhythm. Remember to move to the rhythm in question rather than analyze its mathematical relationship to the beat or its appearance on the staff. Consider Figure 1.

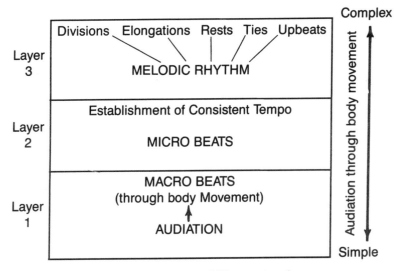

**Figure 1. The Fundamental Elements of
Rhythm Audiation: Layering of
the Elements of Rhythm**

Rhythm, when audiated with understanding, is heard at three different levels concurrently. For the purpose of this explanation, consider the three levels as layers of audiation. That is, rhythm is audiated in relation to three separate elements. To audiate rhythm, one must organize rhythm patterns either consciously or unconsciously (unconscious organization pertains only to high aptitude students, and only after they have overcome the organizational problems associated with patterns that are new and unfamiliar). The three elements of rhythm are pictured in figure 1. The macro beat, the largest unit of pulse to which the body can move comfortably, is at the bottom of the chart, indicating that it is fundamental to rhythm audiation. While the macro beat is fundamental to rhythm audiation, consistent tempo cannot be established without the concurrent audiation of macro beats and micro beats. The macro beats and the micro beats must be audiated separately and then combined in audiation. If macro beats and micro beats are not audiated separately before being combined, each loses its fundamental character and relationship to the other; hence inconsistent tempo is the result. Micro beats are the principal subdivisions of the macro beat; the macro beat is divisible into either two or three micro beats (except in the rare case of an intact macro beat).

Melodic rhythm is the third layer of rhythm audiation. Melodic rhythm cannot be audiated with meaning and with consistency of tempo unless the previous two layers of rhythm are being audiated concurrent to it. Melodic rhythm is superimposed over the micro beat layer, which has in turn been superimposed over the macro beat layer. Melodic rhythms can be categorized according to one or a combination of two or more of the following descriptive terms: divisions, elongations, rests, ties, and upbeats. Combinations of those functions constitute the rhythm of the melody, which is superimposed over the audiation of the macro beats and micro beats. Rhythm audiation is therefore a three-fold hearing process. Of the three layers of rhythm "hearing," the most crucial, if not the most fundamental, is the middle layer. Without the ability to accurately place micro beats, one will know only unusual meter, and will never experience the feeling of a consistent tempo.

Let us consider some practical application of the principles cited above. They are principles that can lead to effective rhythm learning for the student while they provide constant feedback for the teacher. Contemplate a student performing the following rhythm: two eighths, two eighths, four sixteenths, two eighths. The student performs the rhythm, but rushes the sixteenth notes. Consider the three fold layering of rhythm audiation. What should be the instructor's corrective instruction? First, the student should move his body to macro beats at a consistent tempo while chanting micro beats (eighth notes), emphasizing an equal subdivision of the beat. The student should continue that procedure until he senses consistent tempo. When consistent tempo has been established, the third layer of rhythm, the melodic rhythm, may be added. The teacher must be aware that a student's sense of consistent tempo is the strongest indicator of correct rhythm audiation. Each student must move to chanted rhythm alone, using a neutral syllable, before the teacher can assume that the student has learned consistent tempo. For any rhythm activity, if a consistent tempo is not present, the teacher must remove each layer of rhythm audiation, beginning with melodic rhythm, until the problem is resolved. He can rebuild the layers back through melodic rhythm, so long as consistency of tempo is maintained. The strength of Gordon's approach to the teaching of rhythm is that it separates the audiation of rhythm into three distinct layers, and reveals that melodic rhythm is superimposed over two more fundamental rhythm elements, which together provide a foundation for consistent tempo.

Meter Classifications

Pairing of Macro Beats

Gordon has used the concept of the pairing of macro beats in establishing his rhythm classifications. That concept causes some confusion among music educators whose concept of meter classifications is based upon notation. The pairing of macro beats is not an objective process. Consider Figure 2.

Figure 2. An Example of Micro Beats Superimposed Over Paired Macro Beats

In performance and audiation, the group of two eighth notes and the group of three eighth notes are heard as a pair. Some might expect the first group (two eighth notes) to receive a stronger accent than the second group (three eighth notes). What is most important, however, is that the pairing occurs naturally as a result of the organization of rhythm in audiation. The process is analogous to the kind of pairing that occurs in language. For example, read the following sentence: "My mother and father encouraged me to enter college." When reading that sentence, one naturally groups words together to give the sentence a pleasing sound. "My mother and father" will form one group and "encouraged me to enter college" will constitute a second group. Pairing macro beats when hearing and reading words is a natural approach to the process of organizing language for recitation. Similarly, the pairing of macro beats is a natural approach to the process of rhythmically organizing music. Those who have difficulty understanding that concept may find an explanation for their difficulty in the way that they were taught rhythm. One who has been taught isolated note values, i.e., eighth note, quarter note, etc, may have a difficult time understanding pairing. An analogous approach to the teaching of language would be to teach the individual letters of words rather than the complete words. Single note values cannot exist alone with meaning, any more than individual letters can exist alone with meaning. Moreover, groups of notes are combined into phrases in music in the same way that groups of words are combined into phrases in language, each case resulting in a whole that has a more complex meaning of its own. Considering the earlier example, one could speak the phrase "mother and father" without connecting the words, but it would lack a natural flow. Students who lack an understanding of pairing in music performance, due to inadequate rhythm training, experience a similar unnaturalness in musical phrasing. To correct the problem, students should move to every rhythm. Their bodies will suggest a natural pairing.

In figure 3, one of the macro beats is unpaired. Which macro beat is unpaired? That depends upon the grouping chosen by the performer. That is, one might pair the first group (two eighth notes) with the second group (three eighth notes), leaving the third group unpaired. Another listener might pair the second and third groups, leaving the first group unpaired. Either pairing is acceptable.

Figure 3. An Example of Micro Beats Superimposed Over Unpaired Macro Beats

Description of the Meter Classifications

Once the logic of Gordon's meter classification system is understood, one will understand meter in greater detail. While other systems of meter classification may help one to understand meter, they do little to encourage or facilitate audiation. Gordon's meter classifications are rooted in audiation and natural body movement to rhythm. By learning meter through audiation, not through notation, one will be able to hear, perform, and organize meter, and consequently teach and learn efficiently.

Gordon's meter classification is based upon the relative length of macro beats and the division of macro beats into micro beats. If the meter is characterized by macro beats of equal length, the meter is usual. If the meter is characterized by macro beats of unequal length, the meter is unusual. Usual meter is either duple, triple, or combined, depending upon the way in which macro beats are divided into micro beats. Because an understanding of meter is basic to rhythm learning, there is no advantage in teaching students any other information concerning rhythm until they can audiate macro beats and micro beats in a consistent tempo.

Let us now assume that you (and your students) can audiate macro and micro beats in consistent tempo. Let us also assume that you have taught those concepts through movement. Consider the following two charts for the purpose of understanding and organizing the rhythm classification system. Included in Figures 4 and 5 are notated examples so that you can quickly organize past rhythm learning into the new meter classifications. Remember that macro beats can be divided in one of two ways, in twos or threes, and that an intact macro beat is one that cannot be subdivided. Pictured for each meter is an example of macro beats, micro beats, and a melodic rhythm.

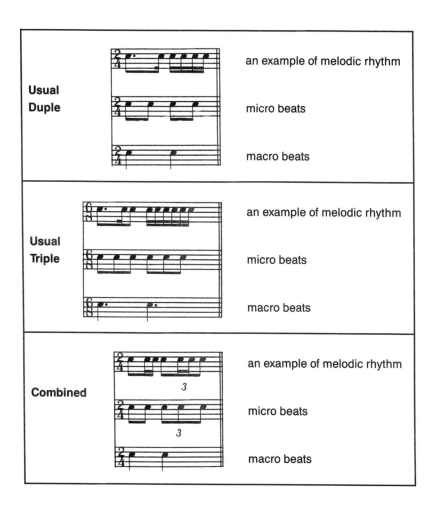

Figure 4: Meter Classifications: The Usual Meters

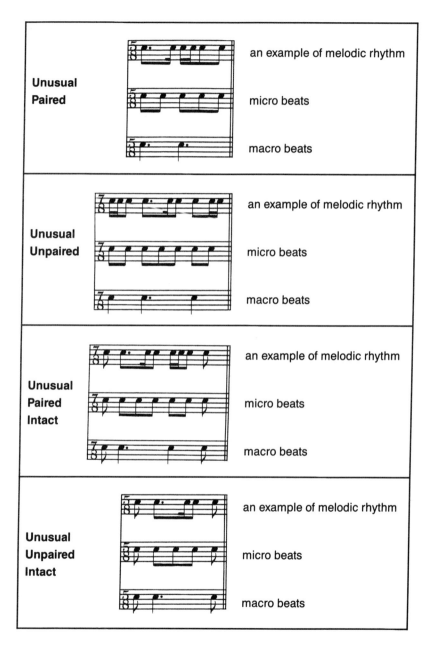

Figure 5: Meter Classifications: The Unusual Meters

Rhythm patterns consisting of macro beats, micro beats, melodic rhythm, rests, ties, and upbeats (as seen in figure 1) can be performed or notated in any meter. With the concept of either equal or unequal macro beats in mind, audiate rhythm patterns and then classify them. Do not attempt to classify the patterns visually. Instead, audiate and move to the rhythm patterns that you are classifying. You will begin to discover that each meter has a distinctly different body feeling. All usual meters, because of the equal length of the macro beats, have in common similar body feelings. All the unusual meters, because of the unequal length of the macro beats, have in common similar body feelings. It is important in initial stages of rhythm learning that the difference between the two feelings, one of equal length macro beats and the other of unequal length macro beats, be stressed by the teacher. Now consider figures 6 and 7.

MULTITEMPORAL	Two or more tempos are used alternately in a piece of music.
MULTIMETRIC	Two or more meters are used alternately in a piece of music.

Figure 6. Classification for Changes of Meter and Tempo: One Part Music

POLYTEMPORAL	Two or more tempos are used simultaneously in a piece of music by superimposing one over the other via two or more parts.
POLYMETRIC	Two or more meters are used simultaneously in a piece of music by superimposing one over the other via two or more parts.

Figure 7. Classification for Changes of Meter and Tempo: Multi-voiced Music

Once one can audiate rhythm in usual and unusual meter, it becomes relatively simple for that person to understand the multi and poly classifications. It has been the author's experience that most persons do not understand the poly and multi classifications because they do not understand the basic meter classifications. One who cannot audiate a consistent tempo in usual and unusual meter technically audiates all music as multitemporal or multimetric, hence leading to a great amount of audiational confusion.

It is important to learn rhythm through audiation, without picturing notation. Those who continually try to picture notation as they learn the rhythm classifications will become confused and frustrated. It is also important to recapture the sensation of moving like a child and learning like a child. The truly great music teachers and musicians of our age and ages past have known that secret, perhaps having discovered it either by accident or as a result of high aptitude.

The elegance of Gordon's work is that it is rooted in movement. One who has difficulty understanding the rhythm concepts presented by Gordon should seek movement instruction, because without the experience of free movement, one will never organize the rhythm experience and will consequently never achieve rhythm accuracy. Without a body free to experience movement, there can be no organizing of the rhythm experience. One having problems with rhythm may need to return to informal movement instruction. Music Learning Theory knows no chronological age. It is for all ages. Those who have worked with Music Learning Theory, both with students and with colleagues, have experienced its benefits. Other teachers who honestly assess their own abilities may well find a need to learn the art of teaching by first teaching themselves.

NOTES

[1]Within this book, see "Rhythm Syllables: A Comparison of Systems."

[2]Within this book, see "Audiation: The Term and the Process" for more information about audiation.

REFERENCES

Gordon, E.E. (1988). Learning Sequences in Music. Chicago: G.I.A. Publications, Inc.

TONAL LEARNING SEQUENCE

Richard F. Grunow

Consider the following interaction between two individuals upon hearing a performance of Dvorák's "New World Symphony." After singing the opening theme (in minor tonality) from the last movement, the first individual makes the following comments: "That was a splendid performance. I have never heard the orchestra sound better...and the English Horn solo in the second movement...what he does with a simple melody in major tonality." Following a vocal rendition of the English Horn solo by the first individual, the second person responds, "Yes, I remember studying that work. The melodies are reminiscent of American folk songs and spirituals. The work is so uplifting at times; at other times, it sounds so melancholy. Dvorák must have been experiencing mixed emotions about being in America when he wrote that symphony."

The conversation between the two individuals suggests that each is attending to different aspects of the performance. The first individual is giving intrinsic meaning to the music as evidenced by his ability to recall and sing melodies from the music just heard. The second individual is giving extrinsic meaning to the music by relating emotional, programmatic, and historical aspects of the music.

Fundamental meaning in music is intrinsic. It is given to the music by an individual through audiation.[1] Intrinsic meaning in music is based upon an understanding of tonality and meter. One who cannot audiate is forced to give extrinsic meaning to the music in various forms, e.g., by an emotional response or by the relating of programmatic and historical facts surrounding the composition or composer. Extrinsic meaning, while not unimportant, takes on greater importance when founded upon intrinsic meaning. A fundamental goal of music education is to enable individuals to give intrinsic meaning to music.

Research in Music Learning Theory has resulted in the development of a tonal learning sequence for teaching intrinsic tonal understanding. The primary purpose of this paper is to discuss the role of tonality as the framework for syntax in tonal learning sequence. A second purpose is to promote greater understanding of the terminology necessary to the understanding of tonal learning sequence.[2]

Music has a syntax similar to that of language. Just as groups of letters form words in language, groups of pitches form tonal patterns in music. Tonal patterns are grouped into phrases in music in the same way that words are grouped into phrases and sentences in language. Syntax in language allows the reader to give meaning to what is said. For example, if the first statement in this paragraph were stated, "Language that similar a music of to syntax has," the meaning of the statement would be lost. Although music does not have a specific meaning, as does language, it does have a syntax that allows the listener to give musical meaning to what is heard. In order for the first individual in the opening sketch of this article to have recalled and sung major and minor melodies from the "New World Symphony," it was necessary for that individual to give syntax to the music being heard. Among the elements of music associated with tonal learning sequence, a sense of tonality is most fundamental to a syntactical approach to listening to, performing, recalling, and creating or improvising music.

Traditionally, the term "tonality" refers to major and minor tonal systems, and the term "modality" refers to the other tonal systems that have evolved from church modes. All of those tonal systems are referred to as "tonalities" in tonal learning sequence to provide a common term for all tonal systems sharing the characteristic of being audiated in relation to a resting tone. The seven tonality classifications in tonal learning sequence are major, harmonic minor, dorian, phrygian, lydian, mixolydian, and aeolian. Tonal syllables are associated with each tonality. For example, "do" is the resting tone in major; "la" is the resting tone in harmonic minor; "re" is the resting tone in dorian, and so on. One has acquired a sense of tonality when he can audiate a resting tone. For example, when one has acquired a sense of dorian tonality he can audiate the resting tone "re" and sing in dorian tonality. The greater the sense of dorian tonality, the more secure one will be when singing in solo, when singing in harmony, and when improvising and creating in dorian tonality. The ability to locate dorian tonality at a keyboard, e.g., dorian is "D" to "D" on the white keys, or identify it theoretically from a music score does not constitute a sense of that tonality.

When listeners agree on the resting tone of a piece of music, the music has objective tonality. When listeners do not agree on the resting tone of a piece of music, the music has subjective tonality. For example, phrygian tonality may be a subjective tonality to listeners who can audiate resting tones and sing only in major and minor tonalities. Given the opportunity to achieve, those persons may develop a sense of tonality in phrygian. As a result, that which was subjective becomes objective.

Many listeners give subjective tonality to much of the contemporary music that they hear. Traditionally that music is called "atonal." If it were truly atonal, i.e., without tonality, no one could give meaning to the music through the use of tonal syntax. What is traditionally called "atonal" is really "multitonal" if viewed in terms of the research supporting tonal learning sequence. Multitonal music contains many tonalities that may alternate and last for only short periods of time. When two or more tonalities are sounded simultaneously, e.g., aeolian and dorian, a piece of music is said to be polytonal. One finds it easier to give intrinsic meaning to music that is unitonal, i.e., music that has one tonality sustained for a long period of time or perhaps the entire piece, than to music that is multitonal or polytonal. However, the larger the vocabulary of tonal patterns that an individual possesses, the easier it is for him to give meaning to multitonal and polytonal music.

When a person can name the key, e.g., D, F, Bb, of a piece of music through music notation, absolute pitch, relative pitch, or audiation, he is aware of the keyality of that piece of music. The fifteen common keyalities are C, G, D, A, E, B, F#, C#, F, Bb, Eb, Ab, Db, Gb, and Cb. Keyality does not affect tonality. A piece of music in D keyality could be in any tonality. It is also true that a piece of music in major tonality could be in any keyality. Resting tone is associated with tonality; tonic is associated with keyality. A piece of music in G Major has "do" for the resting tone and the tonic is G. A sense of keyality (tonic) does little to promote intrinsic musical understanding, while a sense of tonality (resting tone) is fundamental.

Just as music can be unitonal or multitonal, it can also be unikeyal, i.e., having one keyality sustained throughout the music, or multikeyal, having many alternating keyalities sustained only for short periods of time during the piece. Music may also be polykeyal, i.e., it may have two or more keyalities sounding simultaneously.

Key signatures as used in a traditional sense do not define tonality or keyality. For example, the key signature with one flat may be F major, D harmonic minor, G dorian, A phrygian, B lydian, C mixolydian, or D aeolian. Regardless of tonality or keyality, however, F is "do." The traditional key signature is in fact a "do" signature. It tells one where "do" is located on the staff. Traditionally, F major and D minor are considered relative tonalities. In tonal learning sequence, F major, D harmonic minor, G dorian, A phrygian, B lydian, C mixolydian, and D aeolian are all considered relative tonalities; they all share the same "do." Of course, given enough accidentals, any tonality or keyality is possible regardless of the "do" signature. Ultimately tonality is determined through audiation, and not by the "do" signature.

An important aspect of a musician's tonal development is the acquisition of a tonal vocabulary, a concept best understood by comparing music acquisition with language acquisition. Whereas words represent vocabulary in language, tonal patterns represent a tonal vocabulary in music. Tonal patterns function within the context of tonality, and each tonal pattern serves a specific function, e.g., tonic, dominant, subdominant, within that tonality. In traditional terminology, tonal patterns are labeled according to the intervallic structure of the pattern, e.g., major chord, minor chord, minor third, major sixth, etc. In tonal learning sequence, tonal patterns are labeled by the function they serve. A major tonic pattern contains any combination of "do," "mi," and "so." A major dominant pattern contains any combination of "so," "ti," "re," and "fa." A major subdominant function contains any combination of "fa," "la," and "do."

It is important to remember that tonal patterns are labeled by function in all tonalities. For example, in dorian tonality any combination of "re," "fa," and "la" is a tonic pattern. The same tonal pattern may be associated with more than one tonality. For example, in major tonality any combination of "do," "mi," and "so" is a tonic pattern; in dorian tonality, that same combination is a subtonic pattern. It is audiated with different syntax as a subtonic pattern in dorian than as a tonic pattern in major, even though both patterns contain a combination of "do," "mi," and "so."

Following is a list of tonal classifications and pattern functions in tonal learning sequence.[3]

TONALITY CLASSIFICATION AND PATTERN FUNCTION OUTLINE

Tonality	Patterns	Tonality	Patterns
Major	Tonic Dominant Subdominant	Minor	Tonic Dominant Subdominant
	Modulatory Chromatic Cadential Multiple Expanded		Modulatory Chromatic Cadential Multiple Expanded
Dorian	Tonic Subtonic Subdominant	Phrygian	Tonic Subtonic Supertonic
	Cadential Characteristic Tone		Cadential Characteristic Tone
Lydian	Tonic Dominant Supertonic	Mixolydian	Tonic Subtonic Dominant Subdominant
	Cadential Characteristic Tone		Cadential Characteristic Tone
Aeolian	Tonic Subtonic Dominant Subdominant		
	Cadential Characteristic Tone		

In the preceding chart, each tonality classification is accompanied by the pattern functions in that tonality. The most characteristic or basic functions of each tonality appear first, e.g., tonic, dominant, and subdominant in major and harmonic minor; tonic, subtonic and subdominant in dorian; and tonic, subtonic and supertonic in phrygian. Additional pattern functions include modulatory, chromatic, cadential, multiple, expanded, and characteristic tone. An explanation of those functions can be

found in Gordon's <u>Learning Sequences in Music</u> (Chicago: G.I.A.
Publications, 1988).

The importance of singing tonal patterns to the development of a sense
of tonality and to the acquisition of a tonal vocabulary cannot be overstated.
In learning to sing tonal patterns it is important initially to incorporate two
tonalities so that they may be compared to each other. Major tonality and
relative harmonic minor tonality are taught first. Harmonic minor is taught
rather than natural minor because, like major, harmonic minor includes the
half-step leading tone relationship that facilitates the development of a sense
of resting tone. As other tonalities, e.g., mixolydian, are taught, they will be
given musical meaning through comparisons with major and harmonic
minor.

Pentatonic is not found in the tonality classification. Because of the
lack of half steps in pentatonic, any one of the five pitches of the pentatonic
scale may be audiated as the resting tone. As discussed earlier, if there is no
objective resting tone, the tonality is subjective. However, many listeners
will audiate a resting tone in the pentatonic tonal system because of their
familiarity with major, minor, or other tonalities. Although pentatonic may
serve an effective role at the tonal babble stage with young children, it
should be introduced in tonal learning sequence only after exposure to
objective tonalities, e.g., major and minor. The same is true of the whole-
tone and chromatic scales.

In practice, tonal content learning sequence is combined with skill
learning sequence.[4] For example, at the aural/oral level of skill learning
sequence a student sings songs in major and minor tonalities. He also sings,
using a neutral syllable, tonic and dominant patterns in those same
tonalities. At the verbal association level of skill learning sequence he sings
those same tonal patterns using tonal syllables, in addition to learning to
recognize and label tonic and dominant pattern functions. That kind of
combining of skill learning sequence and tonal content learning sequence
provides efficient instruction in the intrinsic tonal understanding of music.[5]

Following is a suggested order (top to bottom and left to right) in which
the seven tonality classifications and corresponding pattern functions can be
effectively introduced to students.

MAJOR AND MINOR TONALITIES
Resting Tone

MAJOR AND MINOR TONALITIES
Tonic and Dominant Functions

MAJOR AND MINOR TONALITIES
All Functions

MIXOLYDIAN TONALITY
Tonic and Subtonic Functions

DORIAN TONALITY
Tonic, Subtonic, and Subdominant Functions

LYDIAN TONALITY
Tonic and Supertonic Functions

PHRYGIAN TONALITY
Tonic, Supertonic, and Subtonic Functions

AEOLIAN TONALITY
Tonic and Dominant Functions

MIXOLYDIAN, DORIAN, LYDIAN, PHRYGIAN, AND AEOLIAN
TONALITIES
All Functions

NOTES

[1] Within this book, see "Audiation: The Term and the Process" for more information.

[2] When considering tonal learning sequence, the reader is reminded to think aurally. The terminology associated with tonal learning sequence applies specifically to the aural interpretation of music.

[3]For the purposes of this discussion the listing does not include multitonal, polytonal, or harmonic tonal classifications and patterns. For further information regarding multitonal, polytonal, and harmonic patterns, read Edwin E. Gordon, Learning Sequences in Music: Skill, Content, and Patterns (Chicago: G.I.A. Publications, Inc., 1988).

[4]Within this book, see "Skill Learning Sequence" for more information.

[5]For further information regarding the combining of content learning sequence and skill learning sequence read Edwin E. Gordon and David Woods, "Reference Handbook for Using Learning Sequence Activities," from Jump Right In: The Music Curriculum (Chicago: G.I.A. Publications, Inc., 1985).

THE MEASUREMENT AND EVALUATION OF MUSIC APTITUDES AND ACHIEVEMENT

Cynthia Crump Taggart

Introduction

If group music instruction is to be completely effective, it must meet the needs of each student. In order for that to occur, the music teacher must know the potential for achievement of each student. He also must know how each student is achieving in relation to that potential. Only when that is the case can a teacher plan instruction so that he can teach to the individual differences among his students.

Often a music teacher will ignore differences in potential among students. Such a teacher focuses his teaching upon some of the students within his classroom while ignoring the needs of the rest. He may focus upon the students who are achieving the most, and frustrate the average and low achievers; he may focus upon the average students, and bore the high achievers and frustrate the low achievers; he may focus upon the low achievers, and bore everyone else. Discipline problems will arise in each of those cases, and the student drop-out rate will be high in elective classes as a result of either boredom or frustration. More important, none of the students will learn as much as if the teacher had taught all of the students effectively.

The purpose of this article is to explain how to teach to the individual differences among students. Music aptitude and music achievement will be defined. Also, tests of music aptitude and tests of music achievement will be discussed. Finally, information will be given to help music teachers incorporate the results of those tests into music instruction for the benefit of students.

Music Aptitude and Music Achievement: A Description

Music teachers are often unclear about the differences between aptitude and achievement. Consequently, they use words such as "talent" or "ability," which can mean both aptitude and achievement. Stated simply, music aptitude is the potential for one to achieve in music, and music achievement is the level of skill that one has acquired as a result of his aptitude and his experience with music. Unless a teacher understands the difference between aptitude and achievement, he will not know what to expect of each student. Therefore, he will be unable to meet each student's instructional needs.

One cannot reliably estimate a student's music aptitude on the basis of that student's music achievement. Although a student who is achieving at a high level necessarily has high music aptitude, a student who is achieving at a low level does not necessarily have low music aptitude. It is possible that a student who is a low achiever may have high aptitude, and may be failing to achieve at a higher level by choice or for some other reason. He might, for example, be uncomfortable in the classroom environment as a result of boredom, shyness, peer pressure, or dislike of the teacher. Many students who have the potential to achieve in music are never labeled as such by their music teacher, and thus never are encouraged to participate in music. Forty percent of children with high music aptitude are never identified throughout their school career (Gordon, 1987, pp. 98-99).

Just as each person is born with some level of intelligence, each person is born with some level of music aptitude. In fact, as with IQ, music aptitude is distributed normally throughout the population at birth. Although music aptitude is innate, it is not hereditary. In other words, the level of music aptitude that one is born with cannot be predicted on the basis of the level of music aptitude of his parents.

After birth, the level of a person's music aptitude fluctuates. Until a person is nine years of age, the level of music aptitude that he was born with is affected by the quality of his environment. Although the level of a person's music aptitude can never be higher than it was at birth, it can be lower. Unless a person's music environment is rich and varied, the level of his music aptitude will continually decrease until age nine, at which time it stabilizes (Gordon, 1987, p.9). After age nine, a person can still achieve in music, but he will be able to achieve only to the level that his stabilized aptitude will allow. In light of that, the importance of early instruction becomes clear.

Therefore, there are two stages of music aptitude. Developmental music aptitude can be affected by the environment, while stabilized music aptitude cannot. A person's music aptitude is developmental from birth (or possibly even as early as nine months before) until he is approximately nine years of age. A person's music aptitude is stabilized after he is approximately nine years of age.

To speak of a single music aptitude is misleading. In fact, Gordon (1987) has found more than 20 dimensions of stabilized music aptitude (p. 36). The two dimensions of music aptitude that have the greatest bearing on music learning are the tonal dimension and the rhythm dimension. Those two dimensions are not significantly related to one another. In other words, it is possible for a person to have a high tonal aptitude and an average or low rhythm aptitude, or a low tonal aptitude and an average or high rhythm aptitude. Rarely will a person have a high level or a low level of both tonal aptitude and rhythm aptitude.

The Measurement of Music Aptitudes and Achievement

Without the use of a valid music aptitude test, the best that one can do is to guess the level of a student's aptitude based upon that student's level of achievement. Fortunately, there are readily-available, published music aptitude tests that have been proven valid for students who are in kindergarten through high school.[1] Because there are two types of music aptitude, developmental and stabilized, there must be two types of aptitude tests. Also, because there is more than one important dimension that must be measured within each type of music aptitude, there must be subtests within each aptitude test that are designed to measure each of those dimensions.

Two tests are available that can be used to measure developmental music aptitude. Those tests are the Primary Measures of Music Audiation (PMMA) and the Intermediate Measures of Music Audiation (IMMA), both written by Edwin Gordon. The formats of PMMA and IMMA are the same, but IMMA is more difficult than PMMA. The tests were designed to be used with two different types of students. PMMA is designed for use with students in kindergarten through grade three. IMMA is designed for use with students in grades one through four, or for any students who, as a group, score exceptionally high on PMMA.

PMMA and IMMA each consist of two subtests, the Tonal subtest and the Rhythm subtest. For each of those subtests, students are asked to listen to a pair of tonal phrases or a pair of rhythm phrases, each phrase consisting of a single-line, synthesized sound, and determine whether the phrases in the pair are the same or different from one another. The phrases in the Tonal subtest are performed without rhythm; the phrases in the Rhythm subtest are performed without melody.[2] The students are told to circle a pair of smiling faces if the phrases sound the same and to circle a pair of faces, one of which is smiling and the other of which is frowning, if the phrases sound different. Students are not required to read or to know numbers in order to take PMMA or IMMA.

Because the level of a student's developmental aptitude fluctuates depending upon the quality of his music instruction and music environment, the scores from PMMA or IMMA for a given student can quickly become outdated. Therefore, it is necessary to administer PMMA and IMMA at regular intervals in order for test scores to remain accurate. Gordon (1986) recommends that PMMA or IMMA be given to all appropriate students once each semester (p. 29).

The Musical Aptitude Profile (MAP), also developed by Edwin Gordon, is a test of stabilized music aptitude. It is designed to be used with students in grades four through twelve. Because the level of a person's music aptitude usually has stabilized by the time that he is in fourth grade, it is necessary to administer MAP to each student only once during his school career. Although the number of items on MAP that the student answers correctly will increase as the student grows older, his percentile ranking, i.e., his standing in relation to other students, will remain the same. Therefore, a single administration of MAP is sufficient.

Gordon (1987) found that, in addition to tonal aptitude and rhythm aptitude, style preference is an important dimension in the measurement of stabilized music aptitude (pp. 36-37). Therefore, MAP has three main sections: Tonal Imagery, Rhythm Imagery, and Musical Sensitivity. The Tonal Imagery section and the Rhythm Imagery section each have two subtests, Melody and Harmony, and Tempo and Meter, respectively. The Musical Sensitivity section has three subtests, labeled Phrasing, Balance, and Style.

Gordon (1987) also found that, unlike developmental aptitude, stabilized music aptitude is best measured in a musical context (p. 37). Therefore, rhythm, melody, musical expression, and other elements of music are present in each test item. Stringed instruments, instead of a synthesizer, are used to play all of the examples and all of the test items.

Students are asked to perform a variety of tasks when taking MAP. For example, in the Tonal Imagery subtests, Melody and Harmony, they are asked to compare two short phrases and decide whether one is a variation of the other. Of course, the word variation is not used, because an understanding of the word "variation" requires music achievement. In the Rhythm Imagery subtests, Tempo and Meter, students are asked to identify whether two musical phrases are the same or different from one another. In the Tempo subtest, all other music elements remain the same while the tempo either does or does not vary between phrases. In the Meter subtest, all other music elements remain the same while the meter either does or does not change between phrases. When taking the Musical Sensitivity subtests, Phrasing, Balance, and Style, students are asked to decide which of two performances of the same melody they like better.[3]

Music aptitude is measured best by use of a published music aptitude test, because developing, researching, and validating an aptitude test is beyond the financial means and knowledge of most music teachers. However, music achievement can be measured using teacher-made tests. In fact, depending upon the situation, teacher-made achievement tests usually are preferable to published achievement tests. A teacher who knows what and how his students have been taught is able to tailor the content of a test so that it can appropriately measure what those students have achieved, whereas a test author who is unfamiliar with those students and their instructional background cannot. However, published, standardized music achievement tests are useful when comparing a given group of students to other students throughout the country.

Any one of a number of test formats might be applied to the measurement of cognitive music learning. Well-written multiple choice tests, assuming that the test author accommodates all of the validity requirements necessary for a good test, are perhaps the most efficient and most objective of the options.

The most valid way, and therefore the best way, to measure achievement in music performance is through the use of a rating scale. Following is an example of a rating scale. It would be used to rate the tonal aspect of a student's performance of a given song, etude, or musical example. Additional rating scales could be constructed to rate the rhythm aspect, or any other aspect, of that student's performance.

The student plays

1. the resting tone in tune.
2. a tonic pattern in tune.
3. a dominant pattern in tune.
4. a subdominant pattern in tune.
5. a multikeyal pattern in tune.

The kind of rating scale that is most useful for measuring music performance skills is the continuous rating scale. In a continuous rating scale, 1 is the easiest to achieve and 5 is the most difficult to achieve. Therefore, a student should not be able to perform 3, for example, unless he also can perform 1 and 2. However, a student who can perform 3 will not necessarily be able to perform 4 or 5. Similarly, if a student performs 5, he should be able to perform 1, 2, 3, and 4.

The Use of Music Aptitude and Music Achievement Test Scores to Improve Instruction

A music teacher who has reliable music aptitude scores for each of his students can adapt his music instruction so that it meets the needs of each of those students. He will know which students are capable of the highest level of achievement in a tonal or a rhythm activity, and he can challenge those students by giving them more difficult tasks to perform. Also, he will know which students are going to need more help, and he can give those students the help that they need without embarrassing them in front of their peers by repeatedly asking them to perform tasks that are beyond their capabilities.

Learning sequence activities, a part of instruction according to Music Learning Theory, are an excellent example of the adaptation of instruction based upon music aptitude scores. During learning sequence activities, a music teacher uses music aptitude scores to teach to the individual differences among students and to make his instruction more efficient. The use of the register books and pattern cards from Jump Right In: The Music Curriculum facilitate such instruction.

Learning sequence activities consist of the teaching of tonal patterns or rhythm patterns at different skill levels.[4] Tonal patterns are taught without rhythm and rhythm patterns are taught without melody. The two types of patterns are never taught on the same day.[5]

Before teaching learning sequence activities, the teacher should list his students' names in descending order according to their aptitude levels, and those lists should be transferred to the Achievement Record Sheets in the appropriate register book. Tonal aptitude scores should be used to formulate the list of students for the Achievement Record Sheet in the tonal register book, and rhythm scores should be used to formulate the list of students for the Achievement Record Sheet in the rhythm register book.

Since a student's tonal aptitude is not related to his rhythm aptitude, separate lists are necessary in order to adapt instruction appropriately.[6]

When teaching learning sequence activities, the music teacher should refer constantly to his list of students in order to choose appropriate patterns for individuals to perform. All students learn the same skills, but the difficulty level of the patterns that each student learns varies according to his aptitude level. All students are taught the easy patterns. While the low aptitude students are still learning the easy patterns, the average and the high aptitude students begin learning the moderately difficult patterns. Finally, while the low aptitude students continue·to learn the easy patterns and the average aptitude students continue to learn the moderately difficult patterns, the high aptitude students advance to learning the difficult patterns. If a low-aptitude student quickly masters the easy patterns, he is given the opportunity to learn the moderately difficult and then the difficult patterns. However, the teacher does not hold the class back until all students learn all of the patterns. Rather, as soon as most of the students learn the patterns that are appropriate to their level of aptitude, the teacher moves the class either to new patterns or to a more advanced skill level. Thus, the class never stagnates at a level where the high aptitude students are bored and the low aptitude students are frustrated; learning is as efficient as possible.

If a low-aptitude student is able to perform the moderately difficult and the difficult patterns consistently, it is possible that his aptitude score is inaccurate. Perhaps he was ill on the day of the aptitude test or perhaps he was not paying attention as the test was being administered. That student should be retested. On the other hand, if a high-aptitude student consistently fails to perform the difficult patterns, the teacher should continue to challenge him. High scores on aptitude tests rarely occur by chance, so it is likely that that student simply is not performing up to his potential.

Teaching to the individual needs of students based upon their levels of music aptitude is especially important when students are in the developmental music aptitude stage. A teacher should compare each student's tonal aptitude score with his rhythm aptitude score, and focus the instruction for that student on the dimension for which the student received the lower test score. If instruction is appropriate, the student's aptitude level for that dimension will increase, and therefore the student will acquire the potential to become a better all-around musician. The opportunity to increase a student's aptitude is available for only a limited time, so it is important that the music teacher take advantage of the opportunity while it exists.

Gordon (1987) identifies several other ways that music aptitude scores can be used to individualize instruction (pp. 133-134 and 145-146). Aptitude scores can be used to identify those students who would benefit from special instruction. For example, students with high aptitude scores could be encouraged to participate in a special choir or instrumental ensemble. They also could be encouraged to study an instrument privately. However, one must remember that students should never be denied instruction in music as a result of low aptitude scores. Everyone has some potential to achieve in music, and each person should be given the opportunity to achieve to the extent that his potential will allow.

Music aptitude scores can be used also to provide parents with objective information about their child's potential for achievement in music. Given that objective information, parents will know whether their expectations for their children's music achievement are realistic. Knowing a child's potential could prevent parents of children with low music aptitude from forcing their child to participate in extra-curricular music activities at the expense of other activities for which they have more potential. Knowing could also prevent parents from expecting the same level of achievement from each of their children; it is probable that siblings will have different levels of music aptitude. And of course, knowing a child's potential could give parents of children with high levels of music aptitude incentive to encourage their children to participate in music activities.

Stabilized music aptitude scores can be used to help a student decide upon a career. A student who has only an average level of music aptitude and excels in other subjects should be encouraged to choose music as an avocation rather than as a vocation. A student with only an average level of aptitude will probably compare poorly with most college music majors. Such a student often grows discouraged and quits music school. That student could have pursued other career interests while remaining active in music as an avocation through community performance organizations. On the other hand, a student whose music aptitude scores are high, especially if other measures of his aptitude are comparatively low, should be encouraged to consider music as a realistic career option.

Conclusion

The proper use of music achievement and music aptitude test scores can help a teacher to improve music instruction greatly. A music educator who does not make use of aptitude scores can only guess at the potential of his students. Such guessing is often inaccurate. Through the use of music aptitude test scores, the music teacher can develop realistic expectations for the achievement of his students, and thus can teach them more efficiently and guide them more wisely.

NOTES

[1]Edwin Gordon is currently completing a music aptitude test for children who are three and four years of age. It will measure both the tonal and the rhythm dimension of aptitude, and is designed to be administered by parents in the home. That test will be published in 1989 by G.I.A. Publications, Inc., Chicago, Illinois.

[2]A more complete description of PMMA and IMMA, as well as test administration procedures and rationale for the test content, can be found in the Manual for the Primary Measures of Music Audiation and the Intermediate Measures of Music Audiation (Gordon, 1986).

[3]A more complete description of MAP, as well as test administration procedures and rationale for test content, can be found in the Manual for the Musical Aptitude Profile (Gordon, 1988).

[4]Within this book, see "Skill Learning Sequence" for more information about Gordon's levels of skill learning.

[5]Within this book, see the two articles by Robert Harper for more information about techniques for teaching learning sequence activities.

[6]For more information about the use of the register books, see the "Reference Handbook for Using Learning Sequence Activities," from Jump Right In: The Music Curriculum (Gordon and Woods, 1985).

REFERENCES

Gordon, Edwin E. (1986). Manual for the <u>Primary Measures of Music Audiation</u> and the <u>Intermediate Measures of Music Audiation</u>. Chicago: G.I.A. Publications, Inc.

Gordon, Edwin E. (1987). <u>The Nature, Description, Measurement, and Evaluation of Music Aptitudes</u>. Chicago: G.I.A. Publications, Inc.

Gordon, Edwin E. (1988). Manual for the <u>Musical Aptitude Profile</u>. Chicago: Riverside Publishing Company.

Gordon, Edwin E. and Woods, David G. (1985). "Reference Handbook for Using Learning Sequence Activities," from <u>Jump Right In: The Music Curriculum</u>. Chicago: G.I.A. Publications, Inc.

RHYTHM SYLLABLES: A COMPARISON OF SYSTEMS

Cynthia Crump Taggart

Introduction

Although many persons learn music without the use of rhythm syllables, the learning process could be made more efficient and effective by the correct use of an appropriate rhythm syllable system. Instruction according to Music Learning Theory correctly uses such a system. In instruction according to Music Learning Theory, rhythm syllables are associated with rhythm patterns that have been learned aurally, kinesthetically, and orally. In other words, once students have heard, moved to, and performed rhythm patterns without rhythm syllables, they associate appropriate rhythm syllables with those patterns. The purpose of this article is to discuss the purpose and characteristics of an appropriate rhythm syllable system, and to examine the rhythm syllable systems currently in use in light of those purposes and characteristics.

The Purpose of Using a Rhythm Syllable System

Rhythm audiation is improved when rhythm syllables are included as a part of the music learning process.[1] That is because the use of rhythm syllables enables students to remember (retain in audiation) a larger vocabulary of rhythm patterns than would be possible without the use of those syllables. Without providing labels for rhythm patterns by associating them with rhythm syllables, most students would be able to retain only a small number of distinct rhythm patterns in their audiation. In the same way that words serve as labels that help one to classify and remember things in the environment, rhythm syllables serve as labels that help one to classify and remember rhythm patterns in his audiation.

The use of an appropriate rhythm syllable system facilitates the rhythm audiation process in other ways. When students are using an appropriate rhythm syllable system to associate rhythm syllables with the music that they are experiencing, they have also in those syllables a guide to recognizing the meter of the music and the functions of the rhythm patterns within that music. Those recognitions enable them at least to partially organize the music that they are experiencing, so that in the future they can meaningfully compare that familiar music with unfamiliar music, and thus better understand the unfamiliar music.

Requisites of an Appropriate Rhythm Syllable System

A rhythm syllable system must have several specific characteristics in order to be used to facilitate rhythm audiation and consequently the rhythm learning process. Unless a rhythm syllable system has those characteristics, not only will its use not facilitate the rhythm learning process, but it may hinder it.

First, if appropriate music learning sequence is to be followed, syllables must be associated with how music is audiated rather than with how music is notated. The most efficient way to learn music is to experience it first aurally, orally, and kinesthetically, and only then to experience it visually in the form of music notation.[2] In Music Learning Theory terminology, aural/oral learning should precede verbal association learning, which should precede symbolic association learning. Only then is appropriate learning sequence observed.

When a person audiates as he listens to or performs music, he is either overtly or covertly moving to the rhythm of that music. In other words, the most basic level at which one learns rhythm is kinesthetic. Therefore, rhythm syllables must relate in a meaningful way to how one moves to music.

When one moves to music, he moves to the macro beats and the micro beats, not to the melodic rhythm.[3] Therefore, the organization of a rhythm syllable system should be based upon how beats function within music rather than upon the note values that are a part of melodic rhythm. All macro beats should be associated with the same syllable, because all macro beats function rhythmically in the same way within a piece of music, regardless of whether they coincide notationally with a quarter note, an eighth note, or any other written note value. In the same way, all micro beats within a given meter should be associated with the same syllables as the other micro beats within that meter, regardless of their note values. Only when rhythm syllables are assigned in that way can one learn the rhythm syllables without seeing music notation. Conversely, when syllables are assigned according to note values, one needs to know exactly how each note is written in order to know what syllable to chant. The same pattern notated with two different measure signatures, such as 3/4 and 6/8, would be associated with different rhythm syllables, even though that pattern would sound exactly the same for each of the measure signatures. Such a system would be based upon notation rather than upon audiation.

Second, a rhythm syllable system should provide a means by which one can discriminate among meters and, to some extent, among the functions of rhythm patterns within those meters. When one moves to music, each meter has its own characteristic and unique "feel." Therefore, each meter should have its own characteristic and unique set of rhythm syllables. A rhythm syllable system that uses the same syllables for all meters cannot be used as a tool to help one discriminate among meters, because many rhythm patterns that feel different due to differences in meter will be associated with the same syllables. Only when each meter has its own syllables can those syllables be used as a tool to help one recognize a meter. That means that a thoroughly effective rhythm syllable system must have provisions for all meters, including unusual meter.

Similarly, not all rhythm patterns function in the same way within each meter. A rhythm syllable system also should be organized so that it helps one to discriminate among the different functions within each meter.

Finally, a rhythm syllable system must have internal logic; the syllables within the system must be comprehensive and must relate in a meaningful and logical way to each other. If a rhythm syllable system has internal logic, the rhythm syllables from that system will be generalizable to all rhythm patterns, regardless of how complicated they are. Unless syllables from a rhythm syllable system can be associated logically with all rhythm patterns that occur in music, that system is of limited value.

A Comparison of the Rhythm Syllable Systems Currently in Use

There are countless rhythm syllable systems currently in use, so it would be impossible to discuss all of them. The purpose of this section of the article is to analyze critically the more commonly used rhythm syllable systems.

The use of time value names is one of the least appropriate systems in use. According to the time value name system, the actual name of a note should be chanted, regardless of the function of that note as a rhythmic duration. For example, if one were to see an eighth note, one would chant "eighth," if one were to see a quarter note, one would chant "quarter," and so on.

In order to know what words from the time value name system to associate with each duration, one must see that duration in notational form. That means that the learning of music notation must precede the learning of rhythm syllables. In other words, symbolic association learning would necessarily precede verbal association learning. That is a serious violation of learning sequence and an inefficient and ineffective way to learn music.

A person learning rhythm by use of the time value name system is forced to focus upon the notational value of each duration rather than upon how each duration functions within a pattern. Consequently, the syllables of the time value name system do not relate in a meaningful way to movement. For example, one might be moving to macro beats and chanting a different syllable for one macro beat than for another, depending upon the notational value that coincides with each. The syllables would then contradict what is being experienced kinesthetically.

The time value name system also fails to help the learner discriminate among meters. The same syllables are used regardless of meter. Sixteenth notes are chanted as "sixteenth," whether those sixteenth notes are a part of a pattern in duple meter, triple meter, or unusual meter. Consequently, those syllables cannot be used as a tool to help one to recognize the meter of the music.

In addition, time value names cannot be successfully associated with all rhythm patterns. First, some notations, such as quarter-note triplets, do not have one-word time value names. Second, some durations are so short that it would be impossible to chant time value names in the rhythm of the pattern. The following patterns could not be chanted in rhythm, even if they were to be performed at a moderate tempo.

Finally, some of the time value names, such as "quarter," are polysyllabic. To associate a two-syllable word with one duration is problematic. The chanted syllables create a new rhythm that differs from the original rhythm with which the syllables are being associated. Following are two rhythms to serve as an illustration. The first is a melodic

rhythm. The second is the new melodic rhythm that would be created by
the articulation of the time value names associated with the first.

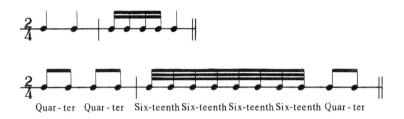

Words other than time value names are often associated with rhythm
patterns. Those words either can be based upon body movement, e.g., the
word "walking" could be associated with macro beats in duple meter and the
word "running" could be associated with micro beats duple meter, or they
can be mnemonic, e.g., the word "pineapple" could be associated with a
triplet. There are problems with the association of words with rhythm
patterns, whether those words are based upon movements or are mnemonic.

Words such as "galloping" or "running" relate to labels for movement
rather than to movement as it is experienced. The syllables that coincide
with the macro beat depend solely upon what word is used to label the
movement that is being performed.

It is possible to use such words to discriminate between meters.
Because there are so few movement words, students can be taught by rote
which words are associated with each meter. For example, repeatedly
chanting the word "galloping" creates a feeling of triple meter. Students can
be taught that whenever they are chanting "galloping," the music is in triple
meter. Similarly, they can be taught that whenever they are chanting
"walking" or "running," the music is in duple meter. Unfortunately, the use
of those words is useful only in discriminating among and recognizing
meters. The words cannot be associated with melodic rhythm that contains
anything other than macro beats and micro beats in duple meter and micro
beats in triple meter. Therefore, those words are limited in value because
they cannot be associated with most patterns that have been learned at the
aural/oral level of learning.

Associating mnemonic words with rhythm patterns also is of limited
value to the process of music learning. First, as with movement labels,
mnemonic words do not relate in a meaningful way to movement. Second,

mnemonic words relate only to specific patterns and not in any way to how those patterns function within a meter. In fact, the words are not related to meter in any way. As a result, the words cannot be used to discriminate among meters. Finally, although the use of a mnemonic word can be helpful in remembering a specific rhythm pattern, that word cannot be generalized in a meaningful way to any other pattern. Because there is an unlimited quantity of rhythm patterns in music, it is essential to have a system in which the associations with one pattern can be generalized in some degree to other patterns. For that to occur, the syllables in the system must relate in a meaningful way to each other. There is no relationship between words that are arbitrarily assigned to rhythm patterns.

One of the most widely used rhythm syllable systems is part of the Kodály method of teaching music. Students using that system are asked to associate specific syllables with specific note values. Following are the note values and the syllables that are associated with those values.

The syncopated pattern is associated either with note-value-based syllables or with the mnemonic word "syn-co-pah," depending upon the preference of the teacher using the system.

The Kodály system is better than the syllable systems that have been discussed previously, because the way in which the syllables are used gives it a higher degree of internal consistency. Still, the Kodály syllables are based upon note value rather than upon beat function, and consequently do not relate to movement. A macro beat, the fundamental unit of movement to music, is chanted using a variety of syllables, depending upon notational circumstances. Again, because one must know the note value in order to know what syllable to chant, one must see the rhythm in notation before associating syllables with that rhythm.

When the Kodály rhythm syllable system is employed, the same syllables are used for all music, regardless of meter. For example, eighth notes are chanted using the syllable "ti," regardless of whether those eighth notes are in duple meter, triple meter, or unusual meter. Consequently, those syllables cannot be used as a tool for metric discrimination.

The Kodály rhythm syllable system has another distinct advantage over the systems that have been discussed previously. Syllables can be associated with most of the rhythm patterns that are found in music. However, there are no provisions for sixty-fourth notes, duplets, and other less common rhythmic occurrences.

There are additional problems with the Kodály syllable system. First, the syllables "syn-co-pah" are not consistent with the rest of the syllable system, because that is the only instance in which a mnemonic association is used instead of a note value association. That problem can be avoided by using "ti ta ti" instead of "syn-co-pah." Finally, stressing the second macro beat in "ta-ah" is not musical. One would never perform a half note with a breath accent on the second beat. If the feeling of macro beat had been internalized at the aural/oral level of learning through kinesthetic experience, that accent would not be necessary.

Perhaps the most commonly used rhythm syllable system among instrumental teachers is the "1-e-and-a" system. Following are examples of rhythm patterns and their associated rhythm syllables in the "1-e-and-a" system.

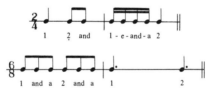

The "1-e-and-a" system is the first system discussed so far that is based upon beat function rather than upon note value. Macro beats are always associated with a number, micro beats in duple meter are associated with "and," and micro beats in triple meter are associated with "and-a." In that way, the "1-e-and-a" system relates to music as it is kinesthetically experienced.

Unfortunately, the "1-e-and-a" system violates appropriate learning sequence in other ways. Students must see rhythm in notation in order to associate the appropriate numbers with the macro beats. Two 2/4 measures of quarter notes would be chanted "1-2-1-2," while one 4/4 measure of quarter notes would be chanted "1-2-3-4," even though those examples would sound the same and feel the same kinesthetically. The association of numbers is based upon the placement of the measure lines. Thus, as with other inadequate rhythm syllable systems, notation is taught before rhythm syllables, which is in violation of appropriate learning sequence.

The most serious shortcoming of the syllable system based upon "1-e-and-a" is that it was originally intended for use with duple meter only. The syllables that are used for triple meter merely duplicate the duple meter syllables. The use of the same syllables for duple meter and for triple meter is confusing to the learner. Following are two patterns, one in duple meter and one in triple meter, that would be chanted using the same rhythm syllables.

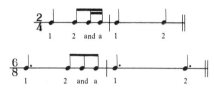

When the same syllables are associated with two different rhythms, those syllables lose their associational meaning. Students must use notation in addition to the syllables in order to recognize those rhythms. Also, it becomes impossible to discriminate among meters on the basis of syllables if the same syllables are used for all meters.

The "1-e-and-a" system is inappropriate for use with triple meter for other reasons as well. There are no provisions for division patterns in triple meter. Clearly, if the syllables used in triple meter are "1-and-a," the use of "a" for a subdivision is confounding. Therefore, the "1-e-and-a" system cannot be associated with many of the patterns that occur frequently in music. Thus, its value is limited.

Finally, the "1-e-and-a" system forces the learner to count. Counting requires intelligence, and intelligence is not closely related to music aptitude. Therefore, the "1-e-and-a" system will lower potentially high achievement in students who have low intelligence but high music aptitude.

The French time name syllable system was first presented in the Elementary Method of Vocal Music, written by Nanine Paris and Emile Chéve in 1844, making it one of the first known rhythm syllable systems. The French time name system is used less today than are the rhythm syllable systems that have been discussed previously, but it is the foundation upon which many of the other syllable systems have been built. It is also better than those syllable systems, and consequently, it deserves discussion. Following are examples of rhythm patterns and the French time name syllables that are associated with them.

The French time name syllables relate meaningfully to movement. Every macro beat is chanted using the syllable "ta." The micro beats are associated with the syllable "té" in duple meter and the syllables "té" and "ti" in triple meter. Because the syllables relate in a meaningful way to movement, music notation is not required in order to learn the syllables. Therefore, appropriate learning sequence is not violated.

Unfortunately, duple and triple meter are confounded in the French time name syllable system. The triple syllables are an extension of the duple syllables. That is inappropriate, because triple meter is not experienced kinesthetically as an extension of duple meter; triple meter "feels" completely different than duple meter. Therefore, the syllables that define triple meter should be different from those that define duple meter. Unless the syllables are different for the two meters, one cannot reliably discriminate between duple meter and triple meter on the basis of rhythm syllables.

One of the strengths of the French time name syllable system is that its syllables can be associated with most usual-meter patterns that occur in music. Its internal logic extends to more rhythm patterns than any of the systems that have been discussed so far. Unfortunately, it does not have provisions for rhythm patterns in unusual meter.

The final rhythm syllable system to be discussed is one that has been developed by Edwin Gordon. That is the rhythm syllable system that is currently used in instruction according to Music Learning Theory. Following are examples of rhythm patterns and the syllables that would be associated with those patterns by students using the Gordon rhythm syllable system.

The structure of the Gordon rhythm syllable system is based upon music audiation rather than upon music notation. Therefore, it is possible to learn the Gordon rhythm syllable system without first being familiar with music notation; appropriate music learning sequence can be followed. Also, because syllables are assigned to rhythm patterns on the basis of how music is audiated, i.e., according to beat function rather than note value, those syllables can be associated meaningfully with movement. All macro beats are associated with the same syllable, regardless of meter, because macro beats function in the same fundamental way in all meters.

Because a different set of syllables is used for duple meter, for triple meter, and for unusual meter, Gordon's rhythm syllable system can be used to help one discriminate among meters and among functions within those meters. If one is audiating rhythm syllables and knows which rhythm syllables are associated with each meter, he will be able to recognize correctly the meter based upon the rhythm syllables that he is audiating. The same holds true for pattern function. If one is audiating rhythm syllables and knows which rhythm syllables are associated with each pattern function, he will be able to recognize correctly the function based upon the rhythm syllables that he is audiating. For example, a pattern containing the syllable "ta" is a division pattern.

Finally, unlike the other rhythm syllable systems that have been discussed so far, Gordon's system has a provision for unusual meters as well as for duple meter and triple meter. Gordon's rhythm syllable system can, therefore, be logically associated with every rhythm pattern that can be found in music.

Summary and Conclusion

The use of rhythm syllables is an important part of an appropriate music-learning process. However, in order for the use of those syllables to optimally facilitate music learning, they must be (a) based upon how music is audiated, (b) structured so that they can be used as a tool in the discrimination of meter and pattern function, and (c) structured so that they can be generalized logically to all patterns that are found in music.

The use of such a rhythm syllable system will enable one to remember a large vocabulary of rhythm patterns and will help one to discriminate among meters and among pattern functions. Also, because it reinforces the audiation of meter and the audiation of groupings within that meter, its use will help one to become a more expressive musician.

NOTES

[1]Within this book, see "Audiation: The Term and the Process" for more information about audiation.

[2]Within this book, see "Skill Learning Sequence" for more information.

[3]Within this book, see "Rhythm Learning Sequence" for more information about macro beats, micro beats, and melodic rhythm.

REFERENCES

Choksy, Lois (1981). The Kodály Context: Creating an Environment for Musical Learning. Englewood Cliffs, N.J.: Prentice-Hall, Inc.
Gordon, Edwin E. (1988). Learning Sequences in Music. Chicago: G.I.A. Publications, Inc.
Szönyi, Erzsébet (1973). Kodály's Principles in Practice. London: Boosey & Hawkes.

TONAL SYLLABLES: A COMPARISON OF PURPOSES AND SYSTEMS

Edwin E. Gordon

Introduction and Definitions

There are different reasons for associating names with pitches and there are different systems by which the associations can be made. The two purposes of this paper are 1) to explain the importance of audiation as the part of the process of associating names with pitches and 2) to clarify the superiority of the movable "do" tonal syllable system when it is used with "do" as a resting tone in major and with "la" as the resting tone in minor, as compared with a numbers system, with the immovable "do" system, and with the movable "do" system when it is used with a "do" based minor (tonic sol fa).[1]

As an introduction, the following words and terms must be defined: "audiation," "tonality," "keyality," "key signature," "resting tone," and "tonic." More comprehensive discussions of those words as well as additional words may be found in Edwin E. Gordon, Learning Sequences in Music: Skill, Content, and Patterns, Chicago: G.I.A. Publications, 1988.

Audiation

When we are hearing in our minds music for which the sound is no longer or never has been physically present, we are audiating. When we are hearing music for which the sound is physically present, we are perceiving. We may audiate while we are listening to music, while we are reading and writing notation, while we are performing music through recall, and while we are creating and improvising music. There are several stages of audiation. While we are listening to music, for example, we are audiating 1) what we have just perceived in the music that we are hearing, 2) what we expect to perceive and audiate in the music that we are hearing, and 3) what we have perceived and audiated in other pieces of music that we have heard at previous times. Moreover, musicians audiate at least a pitch center and a tempo as they audiate a melody.

Tonality and Keality

The word "tonality" is best understood by comparing it with the word "keality." If a piece of music is in A major, it is in major tonality and in A keality. If a piece of music is in D minor, it is in minor tonality and in D keality. The different tonalities are major, minor, dorian, phrygian, lydian, mixolydian, and aeolian. A keality may be C, C#, D, D#, or any other of the twelve pitches in a diatonic scale. Minor·tonality, technically harmonic minor, differs from aeolian tonality in that minor tonality has a leading tone, which is a half step below the resting tone (for example, G# in A keality); aeolian tonality has a subtonic, which is a whole step below the resting tone (for example, G in A keality).

The word "tonality" is synonymous with the word "modality." The word "tonality" is used instead of the word "modality" because the word "mode" is often used imprecisely and becomes confused with the word "modal." Major and minor are modes, but they are not modal. Dorian, phrygian, lydian, mixolydian, and aeolian are modes and they are modal.

Keality and Key Signature

A keality is audiated. In comparison, a key signature is observed; it is seen in notation at the beginning of a piece of music. It is not possible to audiate a key signature, because a key signature does not indicate any specific keality. For example, the key signature of one sharp may indicate G keality in major tonality, E keality in minor or aeolian tonality, A keality in dorian tonality, B keality in phrygian tonality, C keality in lydian tonality, or D keality in mixolydian tonality. Using movable "do" syllables with a "la" based minor, a key signature simply indicates where "do" is found on the staff, and thus, at best, it can only assist in identifying the keality of a piece of music. Actually, a key signature can be said to represent a keality only when a piece of music is audiated.

Resting Tone and Tonic

A tonality has a resting tone and a keality has a tonic. In the movable "do" system with a "la" based minor, "do" is the resting tone in major tonality, "la" is the resting tone in minor tonality and in aeolian tonality, "re" is the resting tone in dorian tonality, "mi" is the resting tone in phrygian tonality, "fa" is the resting tone in lydian tonality, and "so" is the resting tone in mixolydian tonality. C is the tonic in C keyality, C# is the tonic in C# keyality, D is the tonic in D keyality, and so on.

A piece of music in a tonality must be in a keyality. That is, the resting tone (for example, "do") must be associated with a tonic (for example, C). A piece of music in a keyality, however, need not be in a tonality. That is, a tonic (for example, C) does not necessarily have to be associated with a resting tone (for example, "do").

Purposes of Associating Names with Pitches

In the eleventh century, Guido d'Arezzo associated tonal syllables with lines and spaces of the staff in order to teach monks how to read notation. To facilitate communication among teachers, conductors, composers, singers, and instrumentalists, and to make the pronunciation of letters and accidentals simpler, tonal syllables began to be used sometime later in conservatories in Europe as pitch name substitutes for the names of lines and spaces of the staff. In the nineteenth century, tonal syllables were used by Sarah Glover and John Curwen to teach persons how to listen to music with understanding as well as how to read notation. Professors used numbers to teach students music theory. It was not until the late twentieth century, during research in the psychology of music, that the primary and most important purpose for using tonal syllables became clear: to teacher persons how to audiate.

Unless one can audiate, he cannot truly read notation. That is, unless one can audiate what is seen in notation before it is performed, he is not reading notation; he is simply following notation and giving music no more meaning than he would a manuscript in a language unknown to him. Notation cannot teach one what to hear or what to audiate. Notation can serve only to help one recall what he already hears and audiates. Stated another way, if one can audiate, notation becomes a pictorial representation of what is audiated. If one cannot audiate, sound becomes merely a realization of what is seen in notation.

Music is audiated, whereas notation is read. To try to teach one who cannot audiate music how to read notation makes little sense.[2] Moreover, to try to teach one how to audiate music and how to read notation at the same time makes even less sense. What makes least sense, and the "drop-out" rate in beginning instrumental music classes verifies it, is to try to teach a student how to audiate music, how to read notation, and how to develop instrumental technique at the same time.

Simply stated, audiation is a prerequisite for all music endeavors. Unless one can audiate, he cannot listen to music with understanding; he cannot meaningfully read or write notation with creativity or from dictation; he cannot meaningfully improvise music; and he cannot meaningfully perform music, either vocally or instrumentally. Artists audiate; artisans do not.

Tonal meaning, and consequently understanding, are derived from music by continually audiating a resting tone as music is being heard and performed. The reason is that syntactical meaning is given to music by relating all tonal patterns to a resting tone and to the tonality that that resting tone represents. By audiating movable "do" tonal syllables, one finds that the tonality (and tonalities) of a piece of music becomes obvious.

Syllable Systems for Associating Names with Pitches

In addition to numbers, there are three tonal syllable systems used to associate names with pitches. They are movable "do" syllables with a "la" based minor, movable "do" syllables with a "do" based minor, and immovable "do" syllables.

Movable "do" syllables with a "la" based minor are most appropriate and efficient for associating names with the audiation of tonal patterns. A given tonal pattern (for example, "do mi so") is associated with the same movable "do" syllables in every keyality. When letter names or immovable "do" syllables are used, twelve verbal associations are required to represent the same tonal pattern in each of the twelve keyalities.

The resting tone used with the movable "do" syllables with a "do" based major and a "la" based minor indicates the tonality of the music and not the keyality of the music. The tonic used with the immovable "do" syllables indicates the keyality of the music and not the tonality of the music. For example, with movable "do" syllables, "do" is always the resting tone in major tonality, "la" is always the resting tone in minor tonality, and "re" is always the resting tone in dorian tonality, and so on, regardless of keyality. With immovable "do" syllables, however, "do" is always the tonic in "C" keyality, "re" is always the tonic in "D" keyality, and "mi" is always the tonic in "E" keyality, and so on, regardless of tonality. The resting tone used with the movable "do" syllables with a "do" based major and a "do" based minor indicates, of course, neither the tonality of the music nor the keyality of the music. The number system, assuming that it can be either fixed or movable, suffers the same limitations as the immovable "do" system and the movable "do" system with a "do" based minor when "1" is always used as the first degree of the scale regardless of tonality.

There are syllable names for every chromatic alteration within the movable "do" system. That is not so for immovable "do" syllables or for numbers. Although the movable "do" chromatic syllables may be used in conjunction with immovable "do" syllables, natural and altered pitches ("F" and "F#", for example) typically are sung with the same syllable in the immovable "do" system. Because, among other things, the same syllable must be used with different pitches, one must be able to audiate before using immovable "do" syllables. In contrast, one is taught to audiate by using movable "do" syllables. There seems to be no logical solution for associating numbers with chromatic alterations.

The use of movable "do" (and immovable "do") syllables is unique to music. Because numbers are used in arithmetic, it is difficult, particularly for younger students, to learn to skip numbers when singing an arpeggio and to learn to use numbers backward when singing a descending diatonic or intervallic pattern. Because they have been taught to use numbers for counting, it is difficult for them to associate the number "6" with the resting tone in minor tonality and then to sing, for example, the number "1" as the mediant. Moreover, if numbers are associated with tonal patterns for the purpose of learning to audiate those tonal patterns, confusion arises when numbers are used also for teaching fingering of an instrument and for counting "time." Numbers, like interval names, may serve a useful function in the teaching of music theory, but they do not serve a useful function in developing audiation skills. Moreover, the ability to recite numbers either consecutively or with skips is related more to one's general intelligence than to his music aptitude or music achievement.

Some persons believe that the use of immovable "do" syllables teaches a student to develop "perfect" pitch. To the knowledge of the writer, there is no evidence to support that conclusion. Other persons believe that movable "do" syllables are useful for audiating only unitonal and unikeyal music. They believed that movable "do" syllables cannot be used to audiate multitonal and multikeyal music. Such a belief is unwarranted. A piece of multitonal and multikeyal music may be audiated with movable "do" syllables in the same way as traditional music, which includes fewer tonality and keyality modulations. All that need be done is to change the syllable name of the resting tone with each tonality modulation, regardless of keyality. Or, if one still insists that the audiation of resting tones is inappropriate to "atonal" music, after he has learned the movable "do" system he can easily assign "do" to "C," regardless of the tonalities and keyalities found in the music.

To identify the tonal syllable system that is most appropriate for teaching audiation, the teacher must be concerned primarily with the answers to the following two questions when comparing the systems. 1) Does the syllable name of the resting tone change with a change in tonality? 2) Does the syllable name of the tonic change with a change in keyality? An appropriate tonal syllable system is one in which the syllable name of the resting tone changes with a change in tonality and the syllable name of the tonic does not change with a change in keyality. That is the movable "do" system with a "do" based major and a "la" based minor. A system in which the syllable name of the tonic changes with a change in keyality and the syllable name of the resting tone does not change with a change in tonality is an inappropriate system. That is the immovable "do" system. Another inappropriate tonal syllable system is the one in which the syllable name of the tonic does not change with a change in keyality and the syllable name of the resting tone does not change with a change in tonality. That is the movable "do" system with a "do" based major and a "do" based minor.

It is unfortunate that the name "movable 'do'" was given to the most appropriate tonal syllable system, for it is not "do" that moves in the movable "do" system; it is the keyality that moves. If a better descriptive name had been given to the system, such as "changeable resting tone," the superiority of "do" based major and a "la" based minor over "do" based major and "do" based minor would be more easily comprehended.

NOTES

[1]Within this book, see "Audiation: The Term and the Process" for more information about audiation.

[2]Some teachers even attempt to collapse the aural/oral, verbal association, and symbolic association levels of music skill learning sequence into a single level, and to skip partial synthesis and composite synthesis altogether.

PART TWO

PRACTICE

INFORMAL MUSIC INSTRUCTION AS READINESS FOR LEARNING SEQUENCE ACTIVITIES

Lili Muhler Levinowitz

The music educator who has realized the logic of and the acute need for Music Learning Theory is eager to <u>Jump Right In</u> (Gordon and Woods, 1985) and implement Music Learning Theory in his music classes. A common problem, however, is that the students are often not ready for formal learning sequence activities. That is, they can not sing tonal patterns in tune, and/or they can not perform rhythm patterns with a consistent tempo or sense of meter.

Why can't students sing in tune or keep a consistent tempo? What can the music educator do to remediate that problem? Furthermore, what can he look for as signals that students are ready to begin learning sequence activities? The purpose of this article is to answer those questions.

Until a person can sing in tune or move with a consistent tempo he is considered to be in the music babble stage (Gordon, 1988). Most children outgrow the music babble stage between the ages of five and seven, while some leave the music babble stage as early as two. Some adolescents, as well as adults, however, are still in the music babble stage. The discrepancy is due to individual differences in music aptitude and to the quality of the music environment to which they were exposed (Gordon, 1988).

One might say that the babble stage in music is analogous, in some respects, to the babble stage in language. The child in the language babble stage learns the semantics and the syntax of his mother tongue by being spoken to directly and by being privy indirectly to others' conversations. The child is not taught formally to speak as an adult; rather, he teaches himself by experimenting with the language. Although those experimental utterances are considered a form of communication, they are often unintelligible, albeit often interpretable to the adult.

Like the language babble stage, the music babble stage is of paramount importance to a child's development. The tonal syntax and rhythm syntax of music of the culture are formed during that time (Holahan, 1987; Gordon, 1988.) The person in the music babble stage teaches himself the tonal and rhythm syntax of music by experimenting with the information that he has gathered from his music environment. He may sing parts of familiar songs and create his own short songs; he may recite familiar chants and create his own chants; he may also express himself rhythmically with his body. Those early music performances, like early language utterances, are difficult for the adult to understand and to interpret because the music syntax of those performances is unlike the music syntax of most adult performances.

Why the music syntax of a person in the music babble stage is unlike the music syntax of an adult has only been theorized (Holahan, 1987; Gordon, 1988; Moorhead and Pond, 1977). It is reasonable to suggest that the musical mind of the person in the music babble stage is qualitatively different from the musical mind of the adult. Perhaps that is why the "music babbler" is unconcerned that his performances are incorrect by adult standards.

The music babble stage comprises a tonal dimension (tonal babble) and a rhythm dimension (rhythm babble). A person may be babbling rhythmically but he may be out of the tonal babble stage; he may be babbling tonally but he may be out of the rhythm babble stage; he may be babbling both rhythmically and tonally; he may be out of the tonal babble stage as well as the rhythm babble stage. That is, for most persons, rhythm achievement is not strongly related to tonal achievement.

Researchers and music psychologists have begun to classify the sequence of tonal development and rhythm development through which persons in the music babble stage progress. The developmental sequence for the acquisition of tonal syntax and rhythm syntax does not vary among persons.

Evidence of primitive tonal performances occur soon after birth. Often, in the presence of a music stimulus such as singing or recorded music, the baby will coo or hum on a prolonged pitch. That pitch remains relatively consistent from day to day. It seems reasonable to suggest that the baby remembers that pitch kinesthetically. That is, he recalls the pitch center by remembering the placement of the pitch in his vocal mechanism (Levinowitz, 1985). At that stage of development, it is unlikely that he can represent musical sounds mentally through audiation.[1]

The young child continues to favor one pitch in a song. He may perform small and large deviations from that pitch center, but that single pitch dominates his singing performance (Gordon, 1988). A different pitch center may be apparent for each different song among the child's repertoire of songs. The pitch center for any one song will remain consistent from one performance to the next. Audiation in a primitive form has begun at that time.

As the person progresses through the tonal babble stage, he sounds less and less like a monotone singer. More advanced tonal performances of persons in the tonal babble stage include patterns of disjunct intervals away from and returning to the audiated pitch center. When the person performs in that pentatonic-like manner he has developed a sense of keyality (Gordon, 1988).

One is nearly out of the tonal babble stage when he can sing parts or all of familiar songs, but not unfamiliar songs, in tune. He has left the tonal babble stage when he can sing both familiar and unfamiliar songs in tune. At that time, he is audiating the tonal syntax of the music of his culture. That is, he has a sense of tonality (Gordon, 1988).

When a person who is in the rhythm babble stage moves to music, his movements are often unrelated to that music. Initially, a consistent pattern of body motion occurs with a music stimulus. That consistent pattern of body motion, however, does not have an underlying consistent tempo. That is, one can not predict when the next consistent pattern of body motion will be performed. Eventually, a repertoire of consistent patterns of body motion develops. Combinations of different consistent patterns of body motion are also performed with and without a music stimulus. When a person can perform combinations of different consistent patterns of body motion in a predictable manner over a period of time, he has developed a consistent tempo (Gordon, 1988). For example, a person may march or clap with a consistent tempo to music that he is singing himself or that is being played or sung for him. His footsteps or clapping, however, may not coincide with the beat of the music.

Another characteristic of a person in the rhythm babble stage is the manner in which he performs rhythmically a familiar or unfamiliar song. He may perform familiar and unfamiliar songs without a consistent tempo. He may perform some or most discrete rhythm patterns of a familiar or unfamiliar song incorrectly. He may sing the song and perform motions that seemingly have little to do with his singing performance. A person has left the rhythm babble stage when his body movements consistently coincide with the beat of the music and when he can perform correctly the rhythm of familiar and unfamiliar songs.

As was aforementioned, persons in the music babble stage teach themselves the music syntax of their indigenous music by experimenting with the information acquired from their music environment. Music instruction for persons in the music babble stage should therefore be informal.

Informal Music Instruction

When a person listens to and speaks his language, he is informally establishing an aural/oral sense of that language. The aural of his language is collected by listening to his language. The oral of his language is acquired by speaking his language. The aural/oral sense represents the person's fundamental understanding of language; it is the foundation upon which he will base a theoretical understanding of his native language when he gets older. That additional information about language is taught formally to persons in school.

A person should also informally establish an aural/oral sense of the music of his culture. The aural of his music is collected by listening to music. The oral of his music is acquired by performing songs and chants and by moving or dancing to music. The aural/oral represents the person's fundamental understanding of music; it is the readiness for formal instruction in music such as learning sequence activities and instrumental instruction, and is the foundation upon which he will base a theoretical understanding of music later on. Furthermore, the aural/oral sense of music provides a person with the basis for audiation. The skill of audiation is basic to all types of music thinking.

In general, persons are not exposed to music as much as they are exposed to language. If the person in the music babble stage is not exposed to the music of his culture, he will have only a limited aural vocabulary of music with which to orally experiment. As a result, he cannot effectively teach himself the music syntax of his culture, and thus leave the music babble stage.

A person's aural/oral sense of music can be enhanced by his participation in informal music activities. A music activity is informal when it takes place in an environment where no expectations for formal achievement are placed upon the child. For example, when the young child first utters a word that sounds like "ball," the attending adult does not usually correct the pronunciation nor expect the young child to know that "ball" is a noun. At that time, it is unnecessary for the child to demonstrate achievement with formal concepts about language.

Some formal concepts about music are the following: (a) high and low, (b) up and down, (c) loud and soft, and (d) step, skip, and leap. A person should not be expected to demonstrate achievement of formal concepts of music until he can perform music successfully, both rhythmically and tonally. Moreover, a person should not be expected to achieve in learning sequence activities until he has had sufficient informal music instruction, and until he has left the music babble stage.

Informal music activities should meet both the tonal and rhythm needs of the person who is in the music babble stage. In general, the more time spent with informal music activities and the more varied those activities are during that developmental stage, the more the person will profit. Moreover, there is a direct correspondence between the quality, quantity, and diversity of rhythm and tonal activities that the young person receives and the extent to which his rhythm and tonal music aptitudes develop (Gordon, 1988).

There is much to consider if informal music instruction is to be successful. Herein is presented a guide for comprehensive informal music instruction based on an aggregation of past and current research in the psychology of music learning.

A curriculum for comprehensive informal music instruction should include the following: (a) song instruction, (b) coordination and movement instruction, (c) chant instruction, (d) tonal pattern instruction, (e) rhythm pattern instruction, and (f) listening.

Song Instruction

Song instruction should include songs with words and songs without words. The repertoire of songs should represent all tonalities. Furthermore, those songs should represent not only duple and triple meters, but also unusual meters. The repertoire of songs should represent various tempi. Those persons receiving song instruction should be given the chance to sing alone as well as in a group.

When teaching a song, the teacher should first establish the tonality. That is, he should play the appropriate harmonic progression or sing the appropriate melodic sequence. He should sing the song more than once in its entirety, and then allow the children to choose what portions of the song they want to sing. The song should always be sung in the same key, tonality, meter, and tempo. If an accompaniment instrument is used, the teacher should not play the melody of the song; he should play only the harmony.

Coordination and Movement Instruction

Children and adults often do not have fine coordination of their bodies. If persons do not have that rhythm competency, they should not be expected to achieve in organized rhythm activities such as learning sequence activities, circle games, and folk dancing. Therefore, it is important to include instruction that will provide children with body coordination. The following coordination sequence is based upon the work of Phyllis S. Weikart (1982).

Coordination instruction comprises the following levels:

1. Single Coordinated Motion of the Arms - the children move both arms together.
2. Single Coordinated Motion of the Legs - the children move both legs together.
3. Alternating Single Motion of the Arms - the children move their arms alternately.
4. Alternating Single Motion of the Legs - the children move their legs alternately.
5. Single Coordinated Motion of the Arms and the Legs Together - the children move simultaneously both arms together and both legs together.
6. Alternating Single Motion of the Arms and the Legs Together - the children move their arms alternately and their legs alternately.

Students should be seated when any level of the coordination sequence is taught. Until the students have executed a level of the sequence accurately, no external beat should be supplied by using either a drum, song, or recorded music. After students have mastered a level, as evidenced by a number of successful executions, the teacher should ask them to perform that step to recorded music, to a song, or to the beat of a drum. He should not expect, however, that the movements will coincide with the beat of the music. Opportunity should be given to perform each level to different tempi.

Concurrent with coordination instruction, students should receive instruction leading to basic comfort with movement. That is, students should be provided the opportunity to perform locomotor and nonlocomotor activities by themselves and in conjunction with a partner and a group. Those movement activities may be performed with or without music.[2]

Chant Instruction

Nursery rhymes, finger-plays, and rhythmic poems constitute a portion of the genre referred to herein as chant. That is, chants are metered, rhythmic recitations. They may or may not have words. Chants with and without words should comprise duple, triple, and unusual meters. Among the repertoire of chants, varying tempi should be represented. Students who receive chant instruction should be given the opportunity to chant alone and in a group.

The meter of the chant should be established prior to its performance. That may be accomplished by the teacher performing the first line of the chant in solo, by chanting macro and micro beat patterns in the appropriate meter, or by playing macro and micro beat patterns in the appropriate meter on an instrument. A given chant should always be performed in the same meter and tempo.

Tonal Pattern Instruction

Tonal pattern instruction should consist primarily of successive two-tone and three-tone tonic and dominant patterns in major and minor tonalities.[3] Patterns in other tonalities may also be included, but to a lesser extent.

The tonality for the sequence of patterns should be established first by playing the appropriate harmonic progression or singing the appropriate melodic sequence. Tonal patterns should be performed using a neutral syllable such as "bum." The teacher should separate the tones of the individual patterns and should leave a space after each pattern to allow students to echo if they so desire. It is not necessary for students to echo the teacher in informal instruction if they do not so choose. The teacher should not perform tonal patterns with melodic rhythm or in a meter.

Rhythm Pattern Instruction

Rhythm patterns that are taught informally to students should be four macro beats in length and they should be in duple or triple meters.[4]

The teacher should establish the tempo and the meter of the patterns first by chanting or playing two micro beat patterns in the appropriate tempo and meter. Rhythm pattens should be performed using a neutral syllable, such as "bah." The teacher should perform two patterns in succession, and then leave a space for students to echo if they so desire. The patterns may be performed with movement of the arms or legs. The teacher should not perform the patterns with melody.

Listening

Adult records are appropriate for use in listening instruction. Classical music from the Renaissance through the twentieth century, ethnic music from various cultures, avant-garde music, contemporary popular music, jazz, and music composed specifically for students in the music babble stage may be used. Instrumental music is more beneficial than vocal music because the words in vocal music may distract the students' attention from the music itself. Foremost, recordings should be chosen because they exemplify good tone quality. Following are additional considerations for choosing recordings: (a) frequent changes in timbre, (b) contrasting dynamic sections, (c) rhythmic drive, and (d) melodies in unusual tonalities, such as dorian, phrygian, lydian, and mixolydian. Beyond those factors, the teacher should choose music that he himself finds enjoyable.

Music may be played for students during the class or as they enter or leave the classroom. Listening activities may also be combined with relaxation, coordination, and movement activities.

Finally, how much informal music instruction is appropriate? What are some signals that students are ready to begin learning sequence activities? Unfortunately, the answers to those questions are not concrete. Therefore, the following should be considered only guidelines that must be adapted to the needs of the individual classes within a music program.

No musical harm will come to students if they are exposed to more, rather than less, informal music instruction. Evaluate solo performances to decide whether to start learning sequence activities; a group performance can be misleading.

A teacher who works in an elementary music program, kindergarten through grade three, or in any grade level where previous music instruction is unknown, should begin with informal music activities. Informal activities may continue for several months, e.g., approximately from September through December. During that time, the teacher can observe the individual differences in music achievement among his students. Once the majority of students are singing rote songs in tune and are moving to the micro and macro beat of music with a consistent tempo, the teacher should start formal tonal and rhythm pattern instruction. He should continue to use informal instruction throughout the general classroom activities to facilitate leaving the music babble stage for those students who are still in it.

If the music educator knows his students well and believes that they are ready to engage in learning sequence activities, he should proceed accordingly. If he subsequently finds during learning sequence activities that the majority of the solo performances are out of tune or lacking a consistent tempo, he should discontinue learning sequence activities and return to informal music instruction for as long as necessary to prepare the class for formal instruction.

NOTES

[1]Within this book, see "Audiation: the Term and the Process" for more information about audiation

[2]For more detailed information, consult P. Weikart, Teaching Movement and Dance. Ypsilanti, MI: High/Scope Press,. 1982.

[3]For a taxonomy of patterns, consult E. Gordon. Learning Sequences in Music. Chicago: G.I.A. 1988.

[4]For a taxonomy of patterns, consult E. Gordon. Learning Sequences in Music. Chicago: G.I.A. 1988.

REFERENCES

Gordon, E.E. (1979). Primary Measures of Music Audiation. Chicago: G.I.A. Publications, Inc.

Gordon, E.E. (1988). Learning Sequences in Music: Skill, Content and Patterns. Chicago: G.I.A. Publications, Inc.

Holahan, J. M. (1987). "The Development of Music Syntax: Some Observations of Music Babble in Young Children." in J. Craig Peery, I. W. Peery and T. W. Draper, (Eds.) Music and Child Development. New York: Springer-Verlag.

Levinowitz, L. M. and Edwin E. Gordon (1987). Preschool Music Curricula. Philadelphia: Temple University.

Levinowitz, L. M. (1986). "Music Lessons -- The Sooner the Better?" Tempo. November, pp. 16-18; 19.

Levinowitz, L. M. (1985). "Song Instruction for the Young Child in the tonal Music Babble Stage". Bulletin of Research in Music Education, 16, 19-21.

Moorhead, G. E. and D. Pond (1977). Music for Young Children. Santa Barbara, California: Pillsbury Foundation for Advancement of Music Education.

Moog, H. (1976). The Musical Experiences of the Pre-School Child (C. Clarke, trans.) London: Schott and Co. Ltd.

Weikart, P. S. (1987). Round the Circle. Ypsilanti, MI: High/Scope Press.

Weikart, P. S. (1982). Teaching Movement and Dance. Ypsilanti, MI: High/Scope Press.

TEACHING A ROTE SONG

Gail Waddell

The singing of rote songs is important to the development of a student's musical understanding. Rote song instruction is a basic ingredient of aural/oral learning, which is essential to all other levels of discrimination learning and which forms the foundation for all levels of inference learning. The repertoire of rote songs that a student acquires becomes a bank of information to draw upon when making inferences at a later time. In addition, the singing of rote songs can help develop a student's singing voice and can serve as a link between the student and the musical heritage of his culture.

The purpose of this article is to offer specific suggestions for the music teacher who wants to make maximum use of rote songs within the implementation of Music Learning Theory in the music curriculum. The teaching of rote songs should take place during classroom activities. Through informal singing of rote songs, a child develops the readiness to formally study tonal patterns and rhythm patterns in learning sequence activities by becoming acquainted with a variety of tonalities, meters, styles, and forms. For example, if dorian tonality is taught in learning sequence activities after the student has sung songs in dorian tonality, the successful audiation of patterns in dorian tonality will be more readily achieved.[1]

While rhythm and tonal content are being introduced through rote songs as part of classroom activities, care must be taken to avoid introducing skills that should be taught in learning sequence activities. For example, if students are functioning at the aural/oral level of skill learning sequence, the teacher should not use terms that will be introduced at the verbal association level of learning. Similarly, if students are functioning at the verbal association level of skill learning sequence, to use music notation would be incorrect, as it should be introduced in learning sequence activities only after the students have achieved readiness for symbolic association learning.

Time constraints in most music programs force the teacher to choose song material judiciously. Therefore, before presenting a rote song to a class or group of children, the teacher should thoroughly examine the merits of that song.   To ensure that students experience a variety of tonalities, meters, styles, and forms, teachers should include the following.

1.   New tonalities or tonalities infrequently heard.
2.   New meters or meters infrequently heard.
3.   A variety of styles.
4.   A variety of forms.

Teachers should also consider range and tessitura of the song, its musical merit, its long term appeal, and its appropriateness for use outside of school.

A song's debut performance is primarily an opportunity for the teacher to "plant seeds" that will stimulate interest and initiate the audiation process. Several repetitions of the song (in total, never in part) will be beneficial and will be enjoyed by the students. If the song has more than one verse , only the first verse should be taught initially. Additional verses should be added at a later time. Informal comments or discussion about the song may arise and should be encouraged to the extent that it piques interest but does not detract from the presentation of the song itself. If the song is presented carefully, audiation will begin to occur and will continue, consciously or unconsciously, while the students are away from the music class and are involved in other activities. Careful attention to phrasing, balance, and style on the part of the teacher will preserve the spirit and vitality of the song and will help students develop musical sensitivity. When the song is reviewed in subsequent lessons, it should always be performed in the same keyality and tonality as in its initial presentation. That will help students to sing in tune. The success of the initial presentation will become evident in the students' degree of involvement and their eagerness to participate.

Patience and time in combination with an excellent initial performance by the teacher usually results in successful and pleasurable singing. Asking students to sing immediately after a song is presented tends to frustrate both the students and the teacher. If students are not given sufficient time to audiate, the result will be poor singing, which leads to inaccurate audiation. That type of negative experience dampens the enthusiasm of the class.

Teachers and parents can help a student learn as much from a rote song as is possible by providing cues and information that will insure meaningful listening. The more accurately students audiate the tonality, keyality, meter, and tempo of a song before being asked to sing, the more quickly they will understand the music. Tonal preparatory sequences, tune-ups, and cues provide tonal, rhythmic, and stylistic information and serve as powerful catalysts in the audiation process. A tonal preparatory sequence and a tune-up provide tonality and key orientation a few moments prior to listening or singing. A cue adds tempo and meter orientation, and is given immediately prior to either the teacher's or the students' performance. For example, to establish major tonality for the listener, the teacher should sing a tonal preparatory sequence such as "So, Mi, Do" or "So, La, So, Fa, Mi, Re, Ti, Do." [2] The keyality of the tonal preparatory sequence should be the same as the keyality of the rote song to be sung. A corresponding tonal preparatory sequence for harmonic minor tonality would be "Mi, Do, La" or "Mi, Fa, Mi, Re, Do, Ti, Si, La." For dorian tonality it would be "La, Fa, Re," or "La, Ti, La, So, Fa, Mi, Do, Re." As alternatives to those tonal preparatory sequences, tune-ups consisting of tonic patterns alone or tonic and dominant patterns in alternation can be sung in any of the tonalities. The objective is simply to have students audiate a tonality and resting tone that corresponds to the tonality of the rote song to be heard or sung. If the class is not yet functioning at the verbal association level in skill learning activities, tonal preparatory sequences or tune-ups should be sung using neutral syllables.

After singing the tonal preparatory sequence or tune-ups, the teacher should audiate the opening phrase of the song in order to prepare himself to deliver the cue to listen or to sing. In major tonality and duple meter, the cue for students to begin listening to a song that begins on "So" should be sung by the teacher as follows.

The parallel cue to listen to a song in triple meter is as follows.

If the song begins on "Mi", the cue is as follows.

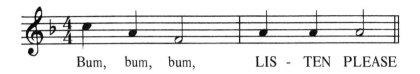

Bum,   bum,   bum,   LIS - TEN PLEASE

Cues can be adapted to fit any combination of tonality and meter. For example, in unusual paired meter, a cue to listen to a song that begins on "So" is as follows.

Bum, bum, bum, bum, bum, WILL YOU LIS - TEN NOW

If the cue involves sustained sounds, care must be taken to audiate the micro beats so that the rhythm is performed accurately. An example in unusual unpaired meter follows.

Bum,   bum,   bum,   bum,   HERE'S THE SONG NOW

After presenting a song and allowing time for audiation, the teacher will want to use tonal preparatory sequences and cues to help students perform accurately, through audiation, all or part of the song. In major tonality and duple meter, the cue for students to begin to sing a song that begins on "So" should be sung by the teacher as follows.

Bum,   bum,   bum,   READ - Y   SING

The parallel cue for students to begin singing a song in triple meter is as follows.

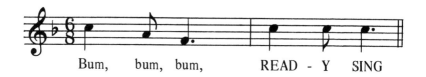

Bum,   bum, bum,   READ - Y   SING

After the teacher performs the cue, "READ-Y SING," the students should begin singing on the macro beat that immediately follows the word "SING." If there is an upbeat, the students will begin singing immediately before the next macro beat. An example follows.

Bum, bum, bum,   READ - Y SING (Students begin)

If well prepared, the students will be audiating the tonality, keyality, beginning pitch, meter, and tempo of the song at the moment they begin to sing. They will also be audiating and singing the dynamic level, style, etc. demonstrated by the teacher through the tonal preparatory sequence and cue.

Teachers will find that children have fewer "pitch problems" when they have been given such a thorough opportunity to audiate before being asked to sing. When children are audiating tonally and rhythmically in conjunction with singing, they will automatically adjust their physical actions in order to achieve their musical goals. Breathing, posture, articulation, tension, and relaxation will be subconsciously adjusted to permit the external production of that which is being audiated. If a student is unable to give tonal syntax to a melodic pattern, cannot audiate it, and is having difficulty singing in tune, talking about posture and breathing will be of little value. The primary emphasis should be placed on the audiation process. If that is done, rote songs can be used to good advantage to help the young singer use his voice more skillfully. Properly used, rote songs constitute the oral experience that is necessary for building aural skills.

Problems or difficult phrases of a song can often be mastered by isolating them and working with tonal and rhythm elements independently.

Difficult tonal patterns can be sung using neutral syllables without any rhythmic context. Short rhythm patterns, freed from melodic constraints, can be chanted using neutral syllables. If a class is functioning at the verbal association level, tonal syllables and rhythm syllables may be used.

While the use of tonal syllables and rhythm syllables helps to clarify tonal patterns and rhythm patterns, Gordon states the following:

> Songs should not be sung from beginning to end with tonal syllables, rhythm syllables, numbers or any other technique substituted for the text. When the text is taught independently, however, the entire text should be presented in the melodic rhythm of the song. That is, the text should be chanted. If that is not done, the children will tend to add and omit macro beats and change meters when the teacher tries to apply the music to the text. (Gordon, 1986, p.81.)

Accompaniments should be used sparingly, if at all. Unaccompanied singing will help develop audiation skills more effectively than will providing children with the aural crutch that an accompaniment offers. If some accompaniment is desired, it should not duplicate the melody. Also, the teacher should stop singing with the students as soon as possible. If the students cannot perform a song completely, the weak phrases or sections that have been learned incorrectly should be reviewed starting at the troublesome section. The song can then be performed from the beginning.

Repetition is an important element of rote learning. Low-aptitude children will need to hear a rote song several more times than will high-aptitude children before they can experience success in audiation and performance. Following are several techniques that might be used.

Neutral syllables, e.g., "loo," "bum," "mah," are delightful vehicles for varying the presentation of a song. An initial presentation of a song, using only neutral syllables, can sometimes stimulate the student's curiosity about the text. Neutral syllables are also an effective way to teach the melody of a rote song, because students will focus more keenly on the melody when the text does not distract them. Pronunciation problems are avoided as well, and the quality of the sound increases dramatically with the increased emphasis on vowel sounds. The use of different syllables affects the style and mood of the music differently, and consequently can enhance its dramatic quality or can inject a humorous twist. In a short time, five or six repetitions of a song are possible as students and teacher take turns suggesting new syllables. Neutral syllables can be used also when reviewing a familiar song. By isolating difficult phrases and having students sing them on a neutral syllable, the teacher can correct performance problems.

Another approach to making repetition palatable is to have students sing for each other. Singing in small ensembles appeals to those who feel confident about performing but enjoy some support. Girls quintets, boys quartets, and mixed octets are examples of ensembles that help the teacher to hear individuals more clearly and help children to hear themselves more clearly. A conductor's podium can serve as a "stage" for singers who are ready to perform in a small ensemble. An antiphonal effect can be created by separating groups of singers over a large area and having them sing back and forth.

Repetitions of a rote song can also be varied by adjusting the environment. Changing the physical surroundings, e.g., turning off the lights, lighting a candle, sitting in a circle, or sitting in parallel lines can change or reinforce the mood and style of a song. Accompaniments of a song can be modified or eliminated. Adding or subtracting tone colors or adding movement can also enhance listening. Bringing in a tape recorder to tape students and letting them listen to themselves sing will guarantee enthusiastic repetition and focused listening.

The importance of repetition applies not only to rote songs, but also to tonal preparatory sequences and tune-ups. If children become accustomed to hearing them often, tonal preparatory sequences and tune-ups will do much to promote the audiation of tonality. The more musically and imaginatively tonal preparatory sequences and tune-ups are performed, the more they will enhance the total musical experience. They should not be imposed, nor should they be perceived as something that is good "medicine" for the students but unnecessary for the teacher. In fact, the teacher might want to request a few moments of class time to "tune up." Singing quietly, as if to himself, the teacher should model tonic and dominant patterns for the class. While the students humor their "confused" teacher, they will hear exactly the tonal and rhythm information needed to audiate the next song. Tonal preparatory sequences and tune-ups can also be sung quietly and privately into several individuals' ears, just loud enough so that neighbors will certainly overhear. Gathering several students into small groups to share a "secret message" is another technique that can be used to focus attention on the tonal preparatory sequence.

Another guise under which tune-ups can be repeated is dramatic play, in which students and teacher assume new roles while performing tune-ups. The "quarterback" (teacher) can secretively reveal a "game plan" by singing tonic and dominant patterns to the team (students) while huddling together.

A nervous singer is warming up before a performance by singing tonic and dominant patterns. A mechanical toy sings tonic and dominant patterns. The teacher can ask the students to assume a new shape or posture while they listen. If approached positively, discreetly, and artfully, tune-ups will soon become familiar sounds that are associated with pleasant experiences.

Repetition that is spontaneous and voluntary is, of course, the ultimate goal. Songs that are shared at home, at assemblies, and on the playground are songs that help to develop accurate, confident, enthusiastic, and musical singing. Building a repertoire of songs that can be shared by all age levels also ensures repetition. While children from each grade level should learn some rote songs that are uniquely appropriate to children of their age, other rote songs should be learned by the entire school population to encourage a sharing of songs outside of the classroom.

Rote songs can provide more than an opportunity for pleasure and joy through music-making. They also can provide a wealth of musical experiences that will be the basis for developing tonal and rhythm skills as well as for developing musical sensitivity, and ultimately, music understanding.

NOTES

[1]Within this book, see "Audiation: The Term and the Process" for more information about audiation.

[2]Tonal preparatory sequences must be sung devoid of rhythm and meter, i.e., with every tone of the same duration.

REFERENCES

Gordon. Edwin E. (1988). Learning Sequences in Music. Chicago: G.I.A. Publications, Inc.

Gordon, Edwin E. (1985). "Reference Handbook for Using Learning Sequence Activities," from Jump Right In: The Music Curriculum. Activities Chicago: G.I.A. Publications, Inc.

Gordon, Edwin E. (1986). Manual for the Primary Measures of Music Audiation and the Intermediate Measures of Music Audiation. Chicago: G.I.A. Publications, Inc.

TEACHING CHILDREN OF ALL AGES TO USE THE SINGING VOICE, AND HOW TO WORK WITH OUT-OF-TUNE SINGERS

Betty Bertaux

Well-tuned singing is important not only to the satisfaction of aesthetic ends, but to the development of music understanding as well. Research supports the conclusion that the "musical ear" develops best when singing is an integral part of both vocal and instrumental music instruction. Unfortunately, poor singing in varying degrees of imprecision and for any number of reasons is at present a common enough problem that serious attention needs to be given to its remediation.

In her paper The Child Voice, Anna Langness (1983) reports conclusions drawn by researchers studying the issue of "monotonism." The consensus was that "much poor pitch discrimination arises from poor vocal control, and that gaining control of the voice leads to improvement in pitch discrimination in many cases" (p. 1). The author's experience confirms Langness's opinion. The number of out-of-tune singers is greatly reduced as awareness and control of the operation of the vocal instrument increases.

The following are steps that a teacher might take in approaching the teaching of singing to students. He might (a) become aware of the aural/kinesthetic feedback loop, (b) become familiar with the nature of the voice, its registers, and the student's singing range, and (c) apply techniques that encourage tuned singing.

Singing and the Feedback Loop

Singing is a learned skill. Two kinds of aptitude are required for successful in-tune singing: music aptitude and vocal-kinesthetic aptitude, the second of which may be independent of any of the tonal aptitudes.[1]

Edwin Gordon (1979) offers the opinion that "The ability to use the singing voice has no more to do with music aptitude than the ability to speak has anything to do with intelligence" (p. 56). Without a high tonal aptitude, a student who can produce a singing quality with his voice may not be able to sing accurately; also, without a high vocal-kinesthetic aptitude, an otherwise tonally apt student may not sing accurately. Howard Gardner (1985) states, "A competent musical performer will certainly exhibit musical intelligence but must equally exhibit some bodily kinesthetic skills" (p. xii).

Tuned singing involves vocal-kinesthetic sensation that the individual has learned to associate with an aural perception of tone. Mary Goetze's succinct definition of singing is comprehensive.

> The act of singing is a complex skill involving cognitive, psychomotor and affective components. Pitch discrimination, tonal memory, a responsive vocal mechanism, self-monitoring of vocal pitch based on aural and kinesthetic sensations, attention to one's own voice and motivation have been cited as essential elements in tuneful singing" (Goetze, 1985, pp.15-16).

"Accurate singing involves continual evaluation of the singing pitch," writes Goetze (1985), citing a process similar to what Mysak (1966) describes in relation to speech as an "intricate 'feedback loop.' " Goetze explains that "the singer listens to his own vocalizations and applies a recognition process to the sounds he himself is making." The process is a continual "monitoring in order to adjust for errors" (p. 13, 14). In terms of Music Learning Theory, the description of a feedback loop as a mechanism for the self-monitoring of vocal production is, in part, a description of the audiation process and the stages of audiation.[2] In order for an individual to make the appropriate adjustment to his vocal mechanism, he must have auditory information. Researchers have found that without auditory information, singing will be inaccurate (Goetze, 1985, p. 15). In order for the feedback loop to be completely effective, the child must have "a responsive vocal mechanism" or a high vocal-kinesthetic aptitude, as well as a high tonal aptitude. Without a high vocal-kinesthetic aptitude, the student will be unable to make the adjustments that his ear demands. Low vocal-kinesthetic aptitude may account for the factor of inattention in singing. Goetze (1985) cites a study by Bently (1969) that "suggests that attention is another essential element upon which both pitch discrimination and tonal memory are dependent." "One would assume," she notes, "that the use of feedback requires attention, at least for the correction or monitoring of errors. Inattention to one's singing voice may result in a singing response which is similar to singing without auditory feedback..." (1985 p. 15).

In effect, a singer who is low in vocal-kinesthetic aptitude and inattentive to his own voice, and who is consequently unable to exercise precise control over his vocal mechanism, may fail to associate kinesthetic sensation with the music that is audiated. Such a singer may develop habits of kinesthetic disassociation when singing, causing singing to become a sensory experience exclusive of the auditory dimension. Conversely, one may perceive music as an auditory experience exclusive of singing. If an individual who is low in vocal-kinesthetic aptitude but high in tonal aptitude never learns to make the aural/kinesthetic connection, singing may actually interrupt and interfere with his aural perception, and he may never develop accurate audiation. He certainly will not learn to sing.

Voice Registers

The terms "register" and "range" have been mistakenly used interchangeably. "Range" refers to the number of tones between the lowest and highest notes that a person can sing. "Register" has to do with timbre and sensation, and it involves muscular action that affects the vocal folds.

Registers seem to function in part to regulate the mechanism and protect the vocal folds from damage. The modal register or heavy mechanism (formerly referred to as "chest voice"), is used primarily in speech, low pitches, and loud singing. Designed for loud sounds, its timbre could be described as "yell-like," "heavy," "reedy," or "coarse," especially at higher pitches. Voice projection and sensation are great in the modal register, but so is vocal fold collision, especially when a singer is straining at the higher or lower limits of his modal register's pitch range. If the modal register is consistently used for singing or for loud, pressed speaking, there is great risk of vocal damage and the development of vocal nodules.

Cautions about the over-use of the heavy mechanism are common. Appleman (1986) reports Manuel Garcia's opinion that the female chest voice "should not be used above the notes E-flat and E-natural [a third above middle C], for to do so would abuse it"(p. 88). Vennard (1967) makes an even stronger statement. With underscoring, he says that "forcing the female chest voice upward is dangerous if not actually malpractice" (p. 76). The same may be said for children's voices.[3] For a child, the suggested upper limit for the use of the heavy mechanism is G' or A', somewhat higher than that of an adult female.

Because there is little vocal fold collision in the loft register, or light mechanism (formerly referred to as "head voice"), it is the most vocally restful register and the one that offers the most protection from vocal damage. Having a light, thin, flute-like, or sweet quality, it is used primarily for higher pitches, soft singing, and soft, high speech and sounds. There is an effortlessness in loft register production. Kinesthetically, the singer feels little sensation. While there is less projection in the lower pitch range than in the upper pitch range of the loft register, as the pitch level ascends and breath intensity is added, the sound becomes louder. Like the modal register, the loft register has a physiological pitch range limit. The intoning of low pitches will be impossible without adjusting the vocal mechanism.

Points at which one register must give way to the next are "register breaks." At those points, if not controlled, the vocal quality and intensity will make a dramatic alteration. Experienced as a kind of "gear shifting," the break might be defined as that point at which tension is either too great for the vocal folds to endure or not great enough for them to produce sound. They are points in mid-range at which one can neither strain higher nor sing lower. Ideally, both adult and child singers should try to develop the skill of blending the registers in mid-range. When that is accomplished, the audible break from the modal register to the loft register will be avoided, the best aural and physiological properties of both registers (maximum projection with minimum collision) will be exploited, and a wide range of pitches can be sung.

If either register is used significantly more than the other, the less used register, lacking in muscle strength, will be underdeveloped and inefficient. With use, either or both registers will develop to their potential. The adult pitch range in each register varies with voice types, but can generally be said to encompass about an octave and a fourth with overlapping or blending of registers in mid-range (Vennard, 1967).

The Child's Singing Range

When approaching the question "What is the child's singing range?" it should now be understood that an appropriate response must be "In what register?" One might add, "And at what age?"

Goetze (1985) carefully examined fourteen studies made of the child's singing range. "Many studies," she tells us, "begin vocal range evaluation by having the child select a so-called 'comfortable' pitch level. In nearly all of the studies, this chosen pitch is near to the mean of the speaking voice as well. This mean has been found to be within a step above or below C' (middle C)" (p. 49). The child is probably singing in the register with which he has the most experience, the modal register.

Generally, studies of children ranging from age three to age eleven indicate that range begins with an interval of about a second or third around middle C and extends outward almost two octaves from A to F' by age eleven. The average pitch range in young children tends to be smaller and the tessitura lower (D' to A'), perhaps because the loft register was not engaged. While registration was not taken into consideration by a number of the researchers in their studies, Goetze (1985) cites several who mention it as a possible factor in determining the child's vocal range. "Vocal registration," she writes, "poses questions about the assessment techniques used to determine vocal range and has implications for methods of teaching singing as well" (p. 55). Her conclusion is that a range "should be chosen which should be singable by the largest number of [children]" (p. 55).

A recommended average pitch range relative to registration is from around C' to A' in the modal register and A' to E' and beyond in the loft register with overlapping(blending) from F' to C', or possibly higher. For developing singers, songs and tonal patterns of short range (a fourth to a sixth) should be chosen and pitched either high, above the break (the key of G, for example) or low, below the break (in the key of C or D). Pitching songs in a key that requires the vocally unskilled singer to negotiate the voice break may encourage out-of-tune singing.

Techniques for Developing Skill in Voice Use

Physiologically, singing is "natural," and the only way it can be done "wrong" is through the development of poor habits or as the result of instructional misconceptions. Every child, without instruction, does everything required to sing; he breathes, utters sound, and articulates words. The objective for out-of-tune and tuned singers alike should be to learn to refine the way in which to do those things. That refinement comes through a growing personal awareness of the voice and one's skill in using it to satisfy the ear. Awareness comes best within the framework of self-discovery in an emotionally safe environment created and directed by the teacher.

The traditional approach to the teaching of singing is "instructional" or "telling." That approach can prompt a student to engage muscles in ways that restrict singing efficiency and encourage inhibiting and restrictive habits.

The recommended approach is that of "discovery" or "asking." In this approach, the teacher functions as a facilitator for self-discovery by setting up a vocal task, listening for the desired sound, watching for the appropriate physiological response, and suggesting alternatives. After the vocal task is performed, the teacher encourages discussion about what was felt as opposed to suggesting what should have been felt. For example, "Was any part of your body moving when you did that? What was moving? What was it doing? Did you notice any feeling (sensation)? Can you describe that feeling? Was anything else moving? Did you have any other feeling? Where was it?" Discussion is an integral part of this approach in that it helps the student to become more aware of the sensation that he is experiencing. There is no right or wrong way to experience sensation. While efficient singing is relatively free of laryngeal sensation, whatever muscular and resonating sensations are felt may be somewhat different for each individual. Those individual differences should be acknowledged and accepted.

Students who are not participating vocally at any given time are participating aurally. Questions about sound should be directed toward them. For example, "What animal do you think Johnny was imitating? Was it large or small? Did his voice sound at a high or low pitch? Did it sound loud or soft? Did it sound rough, smooth, pushy, breathy, pressed, or relaxed?" Other descriptive terms can be created by the students, but the ones to be avoided are "good," "bad," "right," and "wrong."

To encourage the engagement of the singer's aural/kinesthetic feedback loop, the teacher might ask similar questions of him, but with a variation. For example, "When you made your 'big dog' (or 'kitten') imitation, did your voice sound loud or or did it sound soft? Was the sound high or was it low? Was it rough, smooth, pushy, breathy, pressed, or relaxed? Do you have more feeling (sensation) when your voice sounds loud or when it sounds soft? When it sounds pressed or when it sounds breathy? When it sounds like a mewing kitten or when it sounds like a barking dog?" Focusing on what is sensated during routine vocal production helps the student to become aware of what happens in his body without his having to manipulate or contort any part of it in order to "sing correctly." It also helps him to know what to engage when the teacher, or his own audiation, asks for something specific.[4]

There is a hierarchy of technical skills and a suggested sequence of activities designed to help students develop control of their vocal instrument. The hierarchy is as follows: (a) breath management, (b) connecting breath to sound, (c) exploring vocal registers, (d) controlling pitch levels of sound, (e) producing a specific pitch, (f) exercising the muscles of articulation and tone modification, and (g) producing specific pitches in time while articulating vowels, selected words, or a song text. The skills (a) through (e) are so basic that they are often ignored by teachers working with unskilled singers. In reality, those skills are vital in the remediation of out-of-tune singing. Because techniques applied to the development of skills (f) and (g) are better known (vocalizing and warm-ups), attention will be given only to the first five points

A. Breathing: Because successful voice use depends on the right combination of breath management and the adjusting of the vocal mechanism for the appropriate register, skill in using the breath efficiently is of primary importance. In his vocal methodology "Teaching Kids to Sing," Kenneth H. Phillips (1986) emphasizes the importance of implementing a program of exercises that systematically develops breathing skill. Graded levels of exercises to encourage awareness and control should be begun in the early years and continued throughout childhood.

The most effective methods for teaching breathing skills begin with body awareness in various natural breathing situations. The teacher could present a variety of routine and easy tasks involving breathing. For example, Phillips recommends that the teacher have students lie horizontally on their backs and breathe naturally and quietly. With a hand resting gently on the soft area just below their ribs, students should notice the gentle rise and fall of the thorax ("stomach" or "belly"). Then, so that students pay attention to the natural abdominal expansion during inhaling, the teacher should ask them to yawn, taking a slow and slightly fuller breath than usual.

Another activity designed to encourage the students' awareness of expansion in inhaling is to have them explore the difference between "a long sip of air through an imaginary straw" and "a sudden gasp for air," or between "yawning," or "taking little sniffs to find the scent." To draw the students' attention to the process of exhaling, the teacher could ask them to respond to such actions as blowing up a balloon, keeping imaginary bubbles afloat, or blowing out birthday candles. It is especially important that students notice the diaphragmatic sensation of squeezing when exhaling the "last possible ounce of air" from their lungs, and that they notice the automatic inhaling that occurs when those muscles are relaxed after exhaling.[5] Those sensations ultimately will be refined and used extensively in vocal production.

To promote additional awareness, the teacher could ask the students, "Do you inhale or exhale when gently blowing through your nose? When preparing to jump into a swimming pool? When acting surprised? When sneezing? When blowing a bubble? When panting?"

   To practice coordinating the various components of the breathing mechanism, the class might participate in activities such as "Simon Says," with the following being commands from Simon: "take three short sniffs; blow out four candles; take two short and one long sip; blow up a balloon with two strong breaths; etc."

B. Breath to Sound: Still directing the students' attention to breathing, the teacher could ask the students,"When you sigh, do you inhale or exhale?" In investigating that task, students will automatically pay attention to breathing, and not to the involvement of the larynx in phonating. Next, the teacher could ask the students to repeat the sigh and try to decide where the sound came from. Because the engagement of the light mechanism creates little sensation, it is likely that the source of the sound will be unclear, especially to young children. If that is the case, the teacher might have the children go on a "voice hunt" by touching different points on their body in search of their voice. Ultimately they will find that the movement (vibration) is in the "Adam's apple." The teacher should instruct the students that the "real name" for the Adam's apple is "larynx" and that it is the "home of the voice." The students should sigh again and notice the sensation (or lack of sensation) without touching the larynx.

C. Exploring Voice Registers: Having called attention to the voice itself, the teacher should direct attention to ways in which the voice is used. Students will undoubtedly develop a list that includes such things as speaking, laughing, crying, whining, and maybe even singing! The students should engage in voice play. For example, the teacher might say to the students, "Use your voice to talk like a teacher, a baby, a famous actor, an old man, etc.," or "Change the way you laugh," or "Use your voice to make animal sounds (dog, cat, chicken, pig, bird, mouse, lion, etc., or even the imaginary 'pushmepullme' and' omanoggin')."
   In subsequent lessons, the teacher should direct attention to the amount of sensation experienced in the larynx with each sound made. It will be especially important to compare the sensations of imitating a barking or growling dog to those of mewing like a cat, for example, or to compare the sensations of "fussing at a naughty pet" compared to "praising an obedient pet." When it is apparent that the students recognize a greater and lesser degree of sensation relating to low, loud sounds or high, soft sounds, the teacher should explain that "when you can feel your voice the most and it sounds low and loud, you are using your voice's modal register (or heavy mechanism); when you can feel your voice the least and it sounds high and

soft, you are using your voice's loft register (or light mechanism)." The teacher can subsequently use those terms to direct the student to engage either register as desired.

After the registers have been identified and labeled, activities can be generated that serve to develop skill in regulating breath flow and registration in relation to the desired sound. For example, the teacher might ask the students, "What happens when you use your loft register to mew like a kitten (or whoo like an owl) but use your breath the same way you would to quickly blow out a candle?" (The desired response: "It makes a short, or staccato sound.") "Now make several high staccato sounds with your voice in the loft register. Make several low staccato sounds with your voice in the modal register. Now jump the sounds around from the loft register to the modal register." The teacher could ask the students to describe what happens to the pitch in a sigh. (Possible responses might be: "It gets lower." "The pitches slide into each other." "It gets softer.") Then the teacher might ask the students to begin a sigh but let the pitch slide as low as possible. Next, still using the loft register, the students should let the slide happen slowly and make it last until there is no more breath, then stop. Following that, the teacher might ask the students to let the voice slide low and then slide high, alternating slides until there is no more breath. Then the students should do the same thing using the modal register.

To help students become aware of the vocal break, the teacher should ask if anyone had to make a change in order to go higher when beginning in the modal register or to go lower when beginning in the loft register. The break probably will be more obvious from the modal register to the loft register, but the teacher should not be surprised if some children do not sensate one. Some students may already have learned to blend registers without a break. However, it is possible that some children may also have learned to extend the modal register to pitches as high as E' or higher. Careful listening to voice quality and intensity will help the teacher to determine which is the case. The teacher should reassure those who, after time, still do not sensate the break and may be successfully blending the registers, that not everyone feels the break clearly. He should point out that for some, the registers may blend into each other and that where one ends and the other begins may hardly be noticeable. The teacher should encourage those who may not have changed the mechanism to sing with a soft, breathy quality in a high pitch range, and continue to explore the voice in voice modification games until the two registers are clearly defined. Register blending can be encouraged further by engaging the loft register to begin a descending passage, such as a scale, and by making a crescendo as the passage descends. Conversely, it can be encouraged by beginning an ascending passage in the modal register and by making a diminuendo as it ascends.

D. Controlling Pitch Levels of Sound: As students become adept at voice sliding, they might create aleatoric sound paintings with directional signals such as "high: to the student's right," "low: to the student's left," "mid-range: in the center," indicated with a wave of the arm.[6] Small adjustments of the mechanism will be exercised as small right or left movements are made. The teacher should use activities such as rhymes, stories that require voice inflection, e.g., "The Three Bears," and dramatizations varying the pitch level of the voice, or counting to ten while changing and sustaining the pitch of each number at will.

E. Producing a Specific Pitch: All activities up to now have been primarily independent of tuned sound. The main aural concepts have been the pitch directions of higher and lower. The awareness of kinesthetic sensation and the skills developed have been those of breath management for the general production of sound, the identification and engagement of the loft and the modal registers, and the controlling of the pitch direction of sound. The students are now ready to focus attention on producing specific pitches, a skill that requires a greater degree of tonal aptitude. Using the "voice slide" or "counting to ten" techniques, the teacher could have individual students stop their sliding or counting at any time they choose and listen to the pitch made at that point. He could have them notice voice sensation while listening and attempting to repeat the pitch. Then the students should continue the activity, stopping from time to time to listen, repeat, and sensate. Next, the teacher could challenge the students individually to repeat the same sounding pitch or, even better, patterns of pitches as they were performed by the teacher.[7] (The belaboring of matching random pitches is a technical rather than a musical skill and therefore is not recommended. The teacher should not delay in applying technical achievement in singing skills to the singing of tonal patterns and songs.) The teacher should follow up with such questions as "Did you sing the same sounds that I did?" If not, he might ask, "How were they different?" "Was your pattern (or your starting pitch, ending pitch, second tone, etc.) higher or lower than mine?" or "Try singing softer this time and see if you can correct it." Once precise pitch or pattern matching is expected, voice sliding should not be allowed. Gordon (1979) says that "under no circumstances should a tonal pattern be sung with a slur or glissando" (p. 59). The

objective is for the student to eventually be able to adjust his vocal
mechanism in order to produce specific pitches instantaneously in any
vocal register.

Several suggestions for working with out-of-tune singers have been
found to be helpful. (a) Discontinue the use of piano accompaniments.[8] (b)
Encourage individual singing.[9] (c) Do not sing along with students. (d)
Match group singing to the pitch range and key of the unskilled singer.

Of all of the techniques mentioned above, the two that have been the
most frequently cited by teachers as effective in the remediation of out-of-
tune singing is the student's discovery of the loft register and individual
singing. It is not uncommon for a student with a history of "monotonism" to
begin singing in tune upon discovering the loft register, especially when
singing alone. However, for some young students, dramatic improvements
might not be noticed until as late as fourth or fifth grade. If the student, with
instruction, has not learned to sing in tune by the sixth grade, he probably
never will. On the other hand, most children trained to sing since early
childhood learn to do so successfully.

NOTES

[1]For more information on bodily-kinesthetic aptitude, refer to Frames
of Mind, Chapter 9, (Gardner, 1983).

[2]Within this book, see "Audiation: The Term and the Process" for more
information.

[3]At the 1988 National Conference of the Organization of American
Kodaly Educators, Kenneth H. Phillips cited a study that revealed that an
estimated 20% of public school children have vocal nodules. If such a
condition is suspected, parents should be informed and a recommendation
made for an examination by a laryngologist.

[4]Refer to A Responsibility to Voices: Exercises for Awareness
(Bennet, 1985) and The Child Voice (Langness, 1983).

[5]It is impossible to rid the lungs entirely of air; there is always residual
air remaining.

[6]It is preferable for young music students to develop an understanding
of "high" and "low" as an aural skill. In an effort to reinforce that aural
concept, it is often taught in relationship to the visual concept of "high" (up)

and "low"(down). The preferred reinforcement of the aural concept is not visual but kinesthetic.

[7]Goetze (1985) cites studies that indicated that the best timbre for voice modeling in the training of children to sing was the adult female voice. (pp. 56-57) The male falsetto has reportedly also been used successfully.

[8]Gordon (1979) supports the judicious use of a well-tuned piano, guitar, ukulele, or autoharp to provide appropriate harmonic support. He says, however, that "the melody of the tonal pattern should never be played as the child is singing" (p. 59).

[9]One aspect of Goetze's study related to "the presence of other voices in unison singing when compared with individual singing." In testing children in grades K-3, she found that "the subjects sang more accurately when singing individually than when singing in unison." More third grade students in general sang accurately than did the younger subjects; girls sang more accurately than boys, especially in unison singing; and "the difference between boys' individual and unison responses was greater than that of the girls.' " The implication is that young children, especially boys, will sing more accurately when singing alone than when singing in a group. However, the child who sings correctly when singing alone may not be developmentally ready to succeed with unison singing before the third grade.

REFERENCES

Applemen, D. Ralph (1986). The Science of Vocal Pedagogy: Theory and Application (First Midland Book edition). Bloomington: Indiana University Press.

Bennet, Peggy (1985, Summer). "A Responsibility to Voices: Exercises for Awareness." Texas Sings, 1 (3), 4-12.

Ehmann, Wilhelm, & Frauke Haasemann (1981). Voice Building for Choirs. Chapel Hill: Hinshaw.

Gardner, Howard (1983). Frames of Mind. New York: Basic Books.

Goetze, Mary (1985). "Factors Affecting Accuracy in Children's Singing". Dissertation Abstracts International, 46, 2955A.

Gordon, Edwin E. (1979). Manual for the Primary Measures of Music Audiation. Chicago: G.I.A. Publications, Inc.

Gordon, Edwin E. (1981, 1983, 1984, Summer). Music Learning Theory Seminars. Temple University: Philadelphia.

Howard, Francis D. (1898). The Child-Voice in Singing. New York: Novello, Ewer, & Co.

Langness, Anna (1983). The Child Voice. The Richards Institute of Music Education and Research, Portola Valley, California.

Phillips, Kenneth H. (1986). Teaching Kids to Sing. Unpublished
   manuscript, University of Iowa: Iowa City.
Phillips, Kenneth H. (1988, March). Lectures on developing voice skills in
   children. Organization of American Kodaly Educators National
   Conference, Fort Worth.
Thurman, Leon (1985, Summer) Voice Skills in Choral Conducting and
   Classroom Music. University of Texas: Arlington.
Vennard, William (1967). Singing: The Mechanism and the Technic
   (Revised Edition, Greatly Enlarged). New York: Carl Fischer.

GENERAL TECHNIQUES FOR TEACHING LEARNING SEQUENCE ACTIVITIES

Robert Harper

A young autistic student improvises a syncopated pattern using rhythm sticks...

A second grade student proudly announces that the song that the class just sang is in minor tonality...

A class of elementary students performs a complex piece on barred instruments with good ensemble in response to the statement, "Let's all audiate this macro beat..."

These are but a few of the benefits realized by knowing what to teach and in what order. Music Learning Theory functions as a guide to what and when to teach, leaving open only the question of how to teach. That is, each teacher must determine what techniques to use in order to most effectively apply Music Learning Theory, and specifically learning sequence activities, to the teaching of music. The purpose of this article is to provide the elementary school music teacher with techniques that have been proven effective when applied to the teaching of learning sequence activities.

There are two prerequisites for using learning sequence activities as a part of music instruction. First, in order for a student to benefit from learning sequence activities, he must be out of the music babble stage.[1] Second, an appropriate music aptitude test must be given to obtain a tonal aptitude score and a rhythm aptitude score for each student.[2]

Audiation

Audiation is as important to music as thinking is to language.[3] Because children who are being taught according to Music Learning Theory will constantly be asked to audiate, they must have a clear understanding of the concept of what audiation is in order to know what they are being asked to do. For children in grade two and above, a simple definition and demonstration of audiation will probably be sufficient. The class should be asked to sing a well-known melody such as "Happy Birthday to You" or "Twinkle, Twinkle Little Star." Next, they should be told to sing only the first phrase of the song aloud, to continue singing the rest of the song silently, and to raise their hands when they reach the end of the song. The teacher should then explain that when one silently hears music in that way, he is audiating. Subsequently, frequent use of the term audiation in class will help children to become familiar with it and to incorporate it into their own vocabularies.

Younger children may need more concrete, non-musical examples to understand what is meant by audiation. For example, the teacher may hold up several familiar objects, such as a ball, spoon, and pencil, and ask the student to think the name of each object without saying its name aloud. The objects should then be put away, and the teacher should ask questions about them, such as, "What did I show you that was round? What did I show you last? Which was the biggest?" The students will realize that by thinking about the objects, they can answer questions about those objects without seeing them. Once the idea of thinking about something that is not there is understood, the teacher can introduce musical examples in the same way. For example, the teacher can ask the students to think the song "Happy Birthday to You" and count how many times they hear the word "you." The teacher can then explain that silently thinking music is called audiating.

Seating

Assigning each student in a class to a tonal seat and to a rhythm seat based upon tonal aptitude scores and rhythm aptitude scores makes it easier for the teacher to locate students of high, average, and low aptitude during learning sequence activities, and consequently to teach to individual differences. Also, having assigned tonal and rhythm seats can provide a sense of consistency within classroom instruction. When students know exactly what to expect upon entering the classroom, no time is wasted in explaining what to do. The class simply comes in and instruction begins.

The specific way of seating children for learning sequence activities should be determined by the style and the individual needs of the teacher. Teachers with a relatively small number of students may find it easy to remember each child's aptitude group, making assigned seats unnecessary. In that circumstance, high aptitude students can be distributed throughout the room so that others can hear them and learn from them.

Another way of seating students is to designate three areas, one for high aptitude students, one for average aptitude students, and one for low aptitude students. The high aptitude students should be seated in the middle area with students of average aptitude on one side and students of low aptitude on the other. A neutral name may be given to each group, such as the "Red group," the "Blue group," and the "Yellow group." On days when tonal learning sequence activities will be taught, a certain symbol, e.g., a triangle, can be displayed in a prominent location in the room. Each child should be taught where to sit whenever the triangle is displayed. On days when rhythm learning sequence will be taught, a different symbol, e.g., a circle, can be displayed. Each child should be taught where to sit whenever the circle is displayed. After the students learn the two seating arrangements, all that is needed is to display the appropriate symbol at the start of class. Consequently, no instructional time is lost in seating students by either tonal aptitude or rhythm aptitude.

An alternative to having children memorize their place in the two seating arrangements is to make a chart for each class. On the front of the chart, the teacher can list all of the students' names by tonal seating arrangement. On the back of the chart, the teacher can list all of the students' names by rhythm seating arrangement. The teacher can then display the appropriate side of the chart at the beginning of each class period, depending upon the learning sequence activity unit to be studied that day.

A similar seating arrangement can be achieved by numbering chairs or places and assigning each child to a tonal seat number and to a rhythm seat number based upon his aptitude level. Again, a chart can be used listing all students' names by tonal seat number and by rhythm seat number, with tonal numbers and rhythm numbers written in different colors. A piece of paper of the appropriate color displayed at the front of the room can indicate to the students which seat number to use.

Preparation

Before teaching a group of patterns to a class, the teacher should learn all of those patterns as thoroughly as possible. The teacher must be able to improvise similar patterns without having to stop and think. Knowing the patterns completely allows the teacher to maintain eye contact with the students rather than with the pattern card, resulting in a smoother, more controlled learning sequence activity session. [4] Style and dynamics should be incorporated into the delivery of all patterns to keep the class interested and focused upon the task at hand, and to teach musicianship.

The teacher attempting to apply learning sequence activities to music instruction for the first time should perhaps use only class patterns initially in order to become familiar with the patterns and with the routine for delivering them. Once the teacher is comfortable having the entire class echo patterns, individual patterns should be used. At that time, class tonal patterns are used to reinforce, maintain, and re-establish tonality; class rhythm patterns are used to reinforce, maintain, and re-establish meter. The evaluation of individuals should not be attempted until the teacher is comfortable with the use of both class and individual patterns.

Teaching Patterns

Because a large part of the time spent on learning sequence activities is devoted to class performances and individual performances of patterns in response to the delivery of patterns by the teacher, it is necessary for the teacher to devise hand gestures that cue the students to audiate, to respond as a class, or to respond individually. Gestures should be simple and unambiguous. For example, the teacher might wave an open hand back and forth as the signal for the class to audiate without responding. That gesture would be used when the teacher establishes tonality or meter before teaching class patterns and individual patterns. To indicate that it is the teacher's turn to sing or chant and that a response will be expected, the teacher might hold both hands to his chest. The teacher might invite the group to respond by extending both hands outward, palms up, and he might invite an individual to respond by using the same gesture with one hand only. That is much less threatening to a student than is pointing. Before inviting an individual to respond, the teacher should establish eye contact with him at the last moment and then gesture to him. The longer a child knows that it is his turn, the more anxious he will become. For young children, a pop-up puppet can be used in place of the gestures. The teacher might sing or chant when the puppet is down and the class might respond when the puppet pops up. Once a class has been taught how to respond, the teacher should talk as little as possible, if at all.

Accuracy in individual responses should be expected, especially from high aptitude students. A precise response is a sign of precise audiation. While it is not necessary for the teacher to acknowledge a correct response, students in need of positive reinforcement might be given a nod or a smile. Incorrect responses do not need to be acknowledged either, and should, in fact, be downplayed. However, the teacher needs to remember to give that child another chance to respond correctly at a later time.

At all levels of discrimination learning, students should be taught by rote. This means that the teacher should tell the student how to respond and/or should respond with the student. Once a student has responded with the teacher's help, he should be asked to respond without the teacher's help, and should be evaluated on the basis of that solo response. It is important that the teacher remain conscious of the fact that an individual must be taught how to respond before he is asked to respond in solo for evaluation. It is not necessary to teach all of the students in a class how to respond before any one student is evaluated. As some students are being taught, others who have already been taught can be evaluated. Once an individual has successfully sung or chanted a pattern in solo, that pattern should be considered by the teacher to be a familiar pattern to that student.

General Tonal Techniques

Because pitch accuracy is important when singing tonal patterns, it is recommended that the teacher use a small hand-held keyboard.[5] It should be used only as a tonal center reference. It should not be used to play the patterns, because children respond much better to the sound of the human voice than to any other sound.

The teacher should establish tonality and keyality to provide a context for the patterns to be taught by singing the appropriate preparatory sequence from among those shown below.

Major sequence (M) - so la so fa mi re ti do
Minor sequence (m) - mi fa mi re do ti si la
Mixolydian sequence (MIX) - re mi re do ti la fa so
Dorian sequence (DOR) - la ti la so fa mi do re

If the particular criterion being taught calls for the teacher to teach patterns using a neutral syllable, tonality should be established using a neutral syllable such as "bum." If the teacher is to teach patterns using tonal syllables, movable "do" syllables should be used to establish tonality.[6] The sequence of tones should be sung twice as fast as the actual tonal patterns, and all the tones should be of equal length. After singing the sequence of tones to establish tonality, the teacher should pause to allow the class to audiate that tonality. The teacher should then teach class and individual patterns. The keyality used can be the one on the card, or the patterns can be transposed if deemed appropriate. However, the same keyality should be used for that entire section (card).

The register book with the achievement record sheet should be used to record which students correctly performed which patterns. It can be held in one hand, or laid on a music stand or table for easy access. During the class, the teacher may find it easier to mark the register book for only those students who do not respond correctly. After class, he can mark for those who responded correctly. Regardless, the teacher's focus of attention should be predominantly on the students and not on the register book.

When teaching tonal patterns, a silent beat should be placed between the teacher's pattern and the class or individual response. The teacher should conduct the response with an upbeat and a downbeat. Students should be taught to breathe on the upbeat and to sing on the downbeat. If a criterion calls for singing two or more patterns, patterns should be separated by a silent beat. Tonal patterns should be kept free of meter. That is accomplished by keeping all tones equal in length and by varying the number of tones in the patterns.

Occasionally a student or a group of students may be reluctant to respond. For young children, simple hand puppets can be constructed for each child in the class. The children can then "make the puppet sing," which takes the focus from the child. An older child who is reluctant to respond can be paired with a more confident classmate. A length of pool hose or PVC piping can also be used to encourage the reticent singer. The hose can be used as a "telephone," creating a sense of privacy. The child sings in one end and the teacher listens at the other. Reversing the procedure, the teacher can hold the hose to the student's ear and sing directly to him. Also, placing one end of the hose by the child's ear and the other by his mouth will make it possible for the child to hear his own voice more accurately.

Children with low tonal aptitude may have difficulty responding correctly. Those children may benefit from being placed next to a student with high tonal aptitude. The two can occasionally be asked to sing together, or the high aptitude student can be cued to sing the same pattern immediately before the low aptitude student is asked to sing it. The same purpose can be served by having the class sing a particular pattern immediately before a low aptitude student is asked to sing it.

General Rhythm Techniques

All of the rhythm patterns in a section should be performed at the same tempo. A metronome can be used to establish the appropriate tempo. While individual teachers may have their own preference for tempo, triple meter should be performed at a slower tempo than duple meter (macro beat in duple = approximately 76; macro beat in triple = approximately 72).

Once the teacher has decided upon a tempo, the appropriate meter should be established to provide a context for the patterns to be taught by chanting the appropriate preparatory sequence from among those shown below.

Usual duple sequence (D) - du de du I du de du I
Usual triple sequence (T) - du da di du I du da di du I
Usual combined sequence (C) - du de du da di I du de du da di I
Unusual paired sequence (UP) - du be du ba bi I du be du ba bi I
Unusual unpaired sequence (UU) - du be du ba bi du be I
  du be du ba bi du be I
Unusual unpaired intact sequence (UUI) - du be du du be I
  du be du du be I
Unusual paired intact sequence (UPI) - du du be du du ba bi I
  du du be du du ba bi I

If the particular criterion being taught calls for the teacher to teach patterns using a neutral syllable, meter should be established using a neutral syllable such as "bah." If the criterion being taught calls for the teacher to teach patterns using rhythm syllables, meter should be established using rhythm syllables.[7] After chanting the sequence to establish meter, the teacher should pause for two macro beats to allow the class to audiate the meter, and then should proceed to teach class and individual patterns. The pause of two macro beats helps to ensure that the class will be superimposing macro and micro beats over the class patterns. Once the teacher has started teaching class and individual patterns, there should be no pause between teacher and student response. The teacher should conduct individual and group responses by giving an upbeat and a downbeat. Students should be taught to breathe on the upbeat and to chant on the downbeat.

Rhythm patterns should be chanted softly, easily, and musically, but without pitch. The register book and achievement record sheet should be used as they were with tonal learning sequence activities. Again, it is of utmost importance to maintain eye contact with the students. Most students are more willing to respond to rhythm patterns than to tonal patterns. However, if a teacher encounters a reticent student, the same techniques suggested in the section on general tonal techniques may be used.

NOTES

[1]Within this book, see "Informal Music Instruction as a Readiness for Learning Sequence Activities" for more information about music babble.

[2]Within this book, see "The Measurement and Evaluation of Music Aptitudes and Achievement" for more information about music aptitude measurement.

[3]Within this book, see "Audiation: The Term and the Process" for more information.

[4]Jump Right In Tonal and Rhythm Pattern Cassettes are available from G.I.A. Publications for those teachers who would like help in developing their own tonal pattern and rhythm pattern vocabularies.

[5]The Casio PT-1 is a compact battery operated unit that is small enough to be held in one hand and can be fine-tuned if needed. With the volume control at its minimum, it is loud enough for the teacher to hear, yet barely audible to the students.

[6]Within this book, see "Tonal Syllables: A Comparison of Purposes and Systems" for more information about tonal syllables.

[7]Within this book, see "Rhythm Syllables: A Comparison of Systems" for more information about rhythm syllables.

SPECIFIC TECHNIQUES FOR TEACHING LEARNING SEQUENCE ACTIVITIES BY LEVEL OF LEARNING

Robert Harper

The music teacher using learning sequence activities for the first time should not expect to know all of the techniques presented in this article. Knowledge of general techniques and techniques for teaching the aural/oral level of learning will be enough to see a teacher through one full year of successful teaching.[1] As higher levels of learning are approached in subsequent years, the teacher can study the applicable techniques.

Aural/Oral

Tonal

Tonal learning at the aural/oral level entails the delivery of tonal patterns by the teacher, using a neutral syllable, and a response by the students. Children will perceive the individual tones of a tonal pattern and audiate the complete pattern better if the teacher slightly separates the tones.[2]

The first criterion of units 1, 4 and 7 of Jump Right In: The Music Curriculum requires the student to sing only the first tone of the pattern or set of patterns sung by the teacher. The concept of first tone, which is often confusing to young students, can be demonstrated using concrete, non-musical examples. For example, groups of shapes, familiar objects, animals, etc., can be named for the class. The teacher then can ask, "Which of the group was mentioned first?" Having demonstrated the concept of first sound through the use of familiar words, the teacher can demonstrate the same concept using tones. The teacher then can show the students how the first tone sounds by singing "What's the first tone?" on the pitch of the first tone before the class or individual responds. At first, the teacher should sing the first tone of the pattern along with each student. In that way, rote learning occurs. Once an individual has been taught by rote, he can be evaluated in solo.

Units 1, 4, 7, 44, and 48 contain criteria that require the student to sing the resting tone in response to the complete pattern or patterns sung by the teacher. In preparation, verbal games can be played in which the answer to the teacher's question is always the same. Following those games, the resting tone can be demonstrated to the class by showing that, within those learning sequence activities, the resting tone is always the same regardless of what patterns the teacher performs. At first, the teacher can show the class what the resting tone sounds like by singing, "Sing me this tone," on the pitch of the resting tone. The teacher should sing the resting tone with each student. After each student has been taught by rote, he should be evaluated in solo. The teacher should take into account that a quicker tempo will enable the students to better retain the resting tone in audiation.

The remaining criteria of the aural/oral units require the student to echo the entire pattern sung by the teacher. Class patterns of a function different from the individual patterns must be interspersed among the patterns in order to maintain tonality. For example, if students are singing dominant patterns, and if no tonic patterns are included as class patterns, tonality is lost. In that case, the teacher should include a tonic class pattern between every two dominant patterns that are performed. Again, the teacher should sing along with each student before they are evaluated in solo.

Rhythm

At the aural/oral level of rhythm learning, students hear rhythm patterns chanted by the teacher using a neutral syllable, then chant and/or move to those patterns. Because a student may be out of babble in one meter and in babble in another, every time a new meter is introduced the class must develop a syntax for that meter.[3] The units in which a new meter is introduced (1, 11, 16, 24, 37, 42, and 48) begin by having students move informally in response to rhythms chanted in the appropriate meter by the teacher. Informal movement should be guided by the teacher, but the teacher should allow students to respond naturally and spontaneously. Students should be encouraged to respond in different ways with different parts of their bodies, but should not be expected to respond in the given meter. The students should not chant. Once the students have developed a sense of syntax for a meter through informal movement, they should be asked to respond formally.

When responding formally, students first should be asked to move to macro beats while the teacher continuously chants rhythm patterns in the appropriate meter. Most students will move best when seated in a chair, in a comfortable, non-restricting position. Large muscle movement is easier to perform than small muscle movement. Macro beats can be performed with the legs by raising both heels off the floor, keeping the tocs on thc floor. Both heels should drop to the floor on the macro beat. If chairs are not available, the students can stand and alternately tap their heels on the floor, shifting their weight while pivoting slightly at the hips. In all cases, the teacher should provide a visual model for the class.

Next, the students should move to micro beats using their arms, and to macro beats using their legs while the teacher chants rhythm patterns in the appropriate meter. If students are seated at desks or tables, the micro beats should be performed by tapping the forearms on the desk or table top while the elbows stay anchored on the same surface. If students are seated in chairs without desks or tables, or if they are standing, they can pat to micro beats on the sides of their legs, moving both arms together.

Many students do not have the necessary coordination to move to macro beats and micro beats simultaneously. If needed, time should be taken to develop that skill, because in order to audiate meter, one must simultaneously feel macro and micro beats. A technique that is helpful in getting students to feel both macro and micro beats is to have the class sit and move to or chant the macro beat. Then, the teacher should chant micro beats and tap the micro beat on the shoulders of individual students. The procedure can be reversed by having the students chant and/or move to micro beats while the teacher chants macro beats and taps the macro beat on the shoulders of individual students. Pairs of students can perform a variation of that procedure. One child in each pair should move his feet to the macro beats, while the second child, standing behind the first, taps the micro beats on the first child's shoulders. The teacher should move his feet to the macro beat and tap his shoulders to the micro beat, directing the first child to copy his feet and the second child to copy his hands. Then, the partners should change places so that the second child can experience the simultaneous macro and micro beats.

Whenever students are asked to move to macro and micro beats simultaneously, the larger of the two movements should be the macro beat. Walking, swaying, or tapping the heels are appropriate movements for macro beats. Tapping hands on the sides of the legs is appropriate for micro beats.

Once students can move formally to macro beats, and to macro and micro beats simultaneously within a meter, they can begin to learn a vocabulary of rhythm patterns in that meter by echo-chanting patterns performed by the teacher. Patterns are taught to the class using a neutral syllable. When chanting rhythm patterns, the teacher should give all notes their proper value. If macro beats and elongations of macro beats are not sustained for their full value, the students will tend to rush the tempo. After an initial vocabulary of patterns has been learned, the students should move to the macro beat while they chant those patterns. Younger students can be asked to walk to the macro beat while they echo-chant. All students should move to macro beats continuously, during teacher, class, and individual patterns.

Next, the initial vocabulary of patterns should be learned with movement to micro beats. This is best done by having students move their arms or hands while in a seated position. The teacher must be sure that individuals are not moving to the melodic rhythm. Initially, a metronome that allows the students to hear the micro beats may prove helpful.

Finally, the familiar patterns should be learned with movement to the macro and micro beat together. The teacher should provide a visual model. The pairing techniques for teaching students to move to macro and micro beats might be used again at this point. The more automatic the movement becomes, the easier it will be for students to move and chant simultaneously. The overt movement later becomes covert as students imperceptibly move to (audiate) macro and micro beats.

Verbal Association

Tonal

At the verbal association level of tonal learning, students should be taught how to recognize the tonality and function of tonal patterns. For example, for the verbal association unit used to teach tonic and dominant patterns in major tonality, the teacher first should establish tonality by singing the appropriate sequence of tones[4] using tonal syllables.[5] Then, the teacher should ask the class to listen for the last tone, "do," and to sing that tone using its syllable. Students should be taught that this final sound is called the "resting tone." Then the teacher should sing the sequence several more times and ask the class to sing the resting tone in response. Next, the class should be taught that when the resting tone is "do," the patterns sung after it are "major patterns," and conversely that if patterns are major patterns, the resting tone is "do." This circular reasoning should satisfy any need for further explanation. Constant rote repetition will help every student to understand.

Once the connection has been established between "do" as the resting tone and major tonality, students can be taught to recognize major tonic patterns. First the teacher should establish major tonality by singing the appropriate tonal sequence using tonal syllables, and should emphasize that the pattern or patterns to follow will be in major tonality because "do" is the resting tone. Next, students should be told that they are going to hear a special kind of major pattern. The teacher should sing "do mi so" and the students should echo that pattern. After the students have successfully echoed the first tonic pattern, the teacher should sing another tonic pattern using the same tones, such as "so mi do," and ask the class if the second pattern used the same tones as the first pattern. In that way, students are led to discover that the tones were the same, but that the order of the tones was different. At that point, a game can be played with the students to see whether they can recognize the "special pattern," even when its tones are rearranged. Students can answer "yes" or "no" to the question, "Was that the special pattern?" earning the class a point for each correct response. The use of a variety of tonic patterns keeps the game interesting. The teacher must include patterns that are not tonic function in order to maintain a sense of tonality and to create opportunities for function comparisons. The idea of major tonic can be expanded by including examples that use only two of the three tones. The description "major tonic" should be introduced as the name of the special pattern, along with the rule that if a major pattern has at least two of the tones "do mi so" in any order, it is called a major tonic pattern.

The rote learning can be reinforced by following a correct individual response with a statement of the reason why it was correct. For example, the teacher might say, "That's correct. That was a major tonic pattern because it had at least two of the tones 'do mi so.'" When students are evaluated, they can be asked why they answered as they did. Major dominant, minor tonic, and minor dominant should be taught in a similar fashion.

At the verbal association level of tonal learning, students also are asked to echo patterns sung by the teacher using tonal syllables. The patterns are familiar, having been taught at the aural/oral level of learning, and the same techniques that were used at the aural/oral level of learning can be used. While students echo tonal patterns using tonal syllables, the teacher can continue to help students recognize tonality and pattern function.

Rhythm

At the verbal association level of rhythm learning, students are taught by rote to recognize the meter and function (proper names) of familiar patterns, i.e., patterns learned at the aural/oral level of learning. They then learn to associate rhythm syllables with those patterns by echoing the teacher's performance of the patterns.[6] Rhythm syllables should always be chanted, never spoken. Each verbal association unit begins with a section in which students are to recognize the meter and function of the patterns without chanting them, followed by sections in which students chant the patterns using rhythm syllables.

For sections requiring students to recognize the meter and function of rhythm patterns, the class must be taught by rote how to recognize them. For demonstration purposes, the verbal association unit used to teach macro and micro beats in usual duple meter and usual triple meter will be used. The procedure for other meters and functions is the same.

Students should begin by learning to recognize macro beats in usual duple meter. The teacher should chant macro beats, using the syllable name "du," as the class moves to that beat. The name "macro beat" should be associated with the syllable name "du." The teacher should teach the students by chanting a pattern for each child and asking whether that pattern is all macro beats. The teacher should answer "yes" or "no" with the student. After each student has been taught, he can be evaluated in solo.

Next, the class should be taught to recognize successive micro beats in usual duple meter. The teacher should chant micro beats in duple meter, using the syllables "du de," as the class moves to the micro beats. The name "micro beat" should be associated with the syllables "du de." Some children may question why one of the micro beats is called "du," which is the macro beat name. By performing macro beats and micro beats together, the class can be shown that the first micro beat and the macro beat occur simultaneously. Since that beat can not be called "du" and "de" at the same time, a choice must be made.

The students should be taught that rhythm patterns using the syllables "du" and "du de" are duple meter patterns. The teacher should chant patterns that consist solely of micro beats in duple meter and patterns that do not. The patterns that do not consist solely of micro beats in duple meter may consist of macro beats, micro beats in triple meter, or macro and micro beats in duple or triple meter. Each student should respond by answering "all micro beats in duple meter" or "no," first with the teacher for teaching purposes and then in solo for evaluation. Younger children can simply answer "yes" or "no."

Next, the same procedure should be followed for the teaching of triple meter patterns. The patterns that are not all micro beats in triple meter may be given a "no" response, as before, or they may be recognized by name, depending upon whether those patterns have been taught previously, i.e., macro beats and micro beats in duple meter.

Once the students can recognize patterns that consist of all macro beats and patterns that consist of all micro beats in duple meter and in triple meter, they should be taught to recognize patterns containing macro beats and micro beats combined in duple, and then in triple meter. The teacher should establish duple meter by chanting the preparatory sequence using rhythm syllables, and explain to the class that the meter is duple because they are audiating combinations of "du" and "du de." The class should be taught that patterns containing "du" and "du de" are called macro and micro beat patterns because they contain both macro beats and micro beats. The teacher should chant macro and micro beat patterns as well as other patterns. Individuals can answer "macro and micro beats in duple meter" or "no." Patterns that are not macro and micro beat patterns may or may not be recognized by name, depending upon whether those patterns have been taught previously. Finally, the same procedure should be followed for macro and micro beat patterns in triple meter.

The remaining verbal association sections of the rhythm units require students to chant rhythm patterns using rhythm syllables by echoing those patterns as performed by the teacher. The patterns used are familiar, having been taught at the aural/oral level of learning, and the same techniques can be used. While students echo rhythm patterns using rhythm syllables, the teacher can continue to help them recognize meter and pattern function.

Partial Synthesis

At the partial synthesis level of learning, students learn by rote how to distinguish between two sets of patterns in terms of tonality or in terms of meter. Those sets of patterns are sung or chanted by the teacher using a neutral syllable.

For example, a class may be learning to distinguish between a set of patterns in major tonality and a set of patterns in minor tonality. The teacher should sing the first set of patterns using a neutral syllable, and the class should be asked to audiate and sing the resting tone of that set of patterns. Then, the teacher should sing, using tonal syllables, the sequence of tones used to establish major tonality and the sequence used to establish minor tonality. He should help the students decide which sequence "fits" the first set of patterns. If the sequence ending on "do" fits, then the resting tone is "do" and the set of patterns is in major tonality. If the sequence ending on "la" fits, then "la" is the resting tone and the set of patterns is in minor tonality. The same process should be used to determine the tonality of the second set of patterns. Other tonalities should be taught in a similar fashion.

Rhythm syllables should be used to teach students how to recognize meter. After a set of rhythm patterns has been chanted by the teacher, the class should be asked to audiate and move to macro beats, then to micro beats, and finally to both at once. The students should be told that if they are audiating "du de" for micro beats, the meter is duple. If they are audiating "du da di" for micro beats, the meter is triple. Other meters should be taught in a similar fashion.

Before being evaluated, students must hear many sets of patterns. The teacher should tell the class the tonality or meter of each set of patterns and how to recognize that tonality or meter. If an individual responds correctly before the teacher can simultaneously respond, the student should be told why his answer is correct.

When evaluating students at the partial synthesis level of learning, the teacher should sing or chant using a neutral syllable without first establishing tonality or meter. Tonal patterns may be sung or may be played on an instrument. The teacher should say "First," and perform the first set. Then the teacher should say "Second," and perform the second set. When singing tonal patterns, the teacher should pause between individual patterns within a set. Students should respond by naming the tonality or meter of the set.

Symbolic Association

Reading

At the symbolic association level of learning, students learn to associate music notation with familiar patterns. When learning tonal notation, students should become familiar with the staff, clef signs, note heads, and accidentals. Key signatures should be referred to as "do" signatures, because they indicate where "do" can be found on the staff. All other syllables can be found in relation to "do." When teaching the relationships of the syllable names on the staff, the teacher can use a "hand staff" with the five fingers extended to represent the five lines of the staff. Letter names are not necessary when teaching tonal notation.

When learning rhythm notation, students should become familiar with measure signatures, stems, and beams. Measure signatures need be associated only with a meter rather than with what type of note gets a beat and with how many beats there are in a measure.

Students are taught by rote to associate music notation with familiar patterns. Rote learning is reinforced when the teacher reads the patterns along with individuals. After each student has been taught by rote, he can be evaluated. When evaluating students, the teacher should establish tonality or meter, using tonal or rhythm syllables, and individuals should be asked to read the familiar patterns, also using tonal or rhythm syllables.

Writing

Once students are able to read familiar patterns, they can learn how to write them. When learning to write tonal notation, students should practice drawing clef signs, accidentals, and note heads on staff paper. Students must be taught by rote how "do" signatures are written, how to find where other syllables are located on the staff, and how to notate familiar patterns before they are asked to notate patterns sung by the teacher.

When students are learning to write rhythm notation, they should be taught by rote how to draw stems and beams, how to write measure signatures, and how to notate familiar patterns. Students can be taught in groups based upon their aptitudes. Each child can keep a "dictionary" of patterns that he can notate.

When evaluating students, the teacher should establish tonality or meter using tonal or rhythm syllables, and then should sing or chant an appropriate pattern to an individual or group. The students should notate that pattern.

Composite Synthesis

Reading

At the composite synthesis-reading level of learning, students are asked to read sets of familiar patterns and to determine the tonality and function of sets of tonal patterns or the meter and function of sets of rhythm patterns. Before students are asked to read sets of familiar tonal patterns, using a neutral syllable, the teacher should review the "do" signature, the location of "do" on the staff, and the location of other pitches on the staff. Before students are asked to read familiar sets of rhythm patterns using a neutral syllable, the teacher should review measure signatures and the meters that they are associated with and how individuals patterns are notated.

When teaching students at the composite synthesis-reading level of learning, the teacher, using a neutral syllable, should establish tonality or meter before each set of patterns is read. The teacher should read the patterns along with each student. The tonality or meter of the set should be identified by both the teacher and the student, using the same techniques that were used at the partial synthesis level of learning. Then students should be reminded how to recognize the function of each pattern in the set, based upon the syllables that they audiate when the patterns are read. Because there are no class patterns, the teacher should ask questions about tonality or meter and the function of patterns to keep individuals involved.

Once the teacher is satisfied that each student has been taught how to sing or chant the appropriate set or sets, how to recognize the tonality or meter of the set or sets, and how to recognize the function of each pattern in a set, evaluation can begin. Individuals should be asked to read an appropriate set in solo using a neutral syllable, and to name the tonality or meter of the set and the function of each pattern within the set. The teacher should avoid consecutive readings of the same set. Once the high aptitude students have been evaluated reading the easy set, the moderate set and later the difficult set can be interspersed among other students' readings of the easy set so that different sets are read successively. That forces students to audiate rather than simply imitate. When the same set must be evaluated successively, the teacher can separate the readings by re-establishing tonality or meter, or by asking questions about individual patterns in the set.

Writing

At the composite synthesis-writing level of learning, students are taught how to write familiar sets of patterns sung or chanted by the teacher using a neutral syllable. The teacher should use the same techniques as at the symbolic association-writing level of learning.

After all students have been taught how to notate the easy set of patterns, the students of average and high aptitude can begin notating the moderately difficult set of patterns. During that time, the teacher should work with the low aptitude students, checking their work, and helping them to recognize the tonality or meter of the set that they notated and recognize the function of each pattern. Once the moderate set has been notated, by the high aptitude students, the teacher should help the low and average aptitude students with their work while the high aptitude students go on to notate the difficult set.

Generalization

Aural/Oral

The sets of patterns used at the generalization-aural/oral level of learning include both familiar and unfamiliar patterns. The teacher should establish the tonality or meter of the first set using a neutral syllable. Then, the teacher should say, "First," and sing or chant the first set of patterns, using a neutral syllable, pausing between each pattern. Next, the teacher should say, "Second," and sing or chant the second set of patterns in the same way. Finally, the teacher should ask the students whether the two sets are the same or different. The teacher needs to decide which aural/oral skills the students can use and how much of the set the student should perform in order to demonstrate knowledge that the sets are different. Tonally, those skills include singing back the first pitch of any pattern in the set, singing the resting tone of a particular set, or singing one pattern of a set. Rhythmically, those skills include moving to macro beats and/or moving to micro beats, or chanting any pattern in a set. By guiding each student's response in the presence of the class, the teacher teaches all of the students how to tell the difference between the sets. No class patterns are used at the generalization-aural/oral level of learning. Again, the teacher should try to avoid using the same sets consecutively. The first and second sets can be reversed for variety, or any one set can be sung or chanted twice by the class as a group, making the answer "same."

Verbal

The teacher should use neutral syllables to establish tonality or meter and to perform patterns at the generalization-verbal level of learning. Students should be asked to respond, depending upon the section, by performing the patterns using tonal syllables or rhythm syllables, or by identifying the tonality or meter and function of the patterns.

In sections requiring the students to respond by naming the tonality or meter and function of the patterns, students should not echo the patterns. The students should identify the tonality by audiating the resting tone using its syllable name. The students should identify the meter by audiating and moving to macro and micro beats using their syllable names. The students should identify the function of the patterns in a set by audiating the tonal or rhythm syllables for a pattern. Patterns should be delivered initially as sets, but a given pattern in a set can be presented individually to facilitate discussion of pattern function. Students should be asked why they answer as they do to determine whether they are audiating or guessing. Individual responses can be alternated with class patterns or with a preparatory sequence of tones to keep the whole class involved and to encourage audiation rather than imitation.

The remaining generalization-verbal sections require students to sing or chant, using tonal or rhythm syllables, patterns that were performed by the teacher using a neutral syllable. When teaching tonal units, the teacher should sing the entire pattern and ask the students to audiate and then to sing the first tone, using its tonal syllable. In that way, the students are guided in deciding which tonal syllable goes with that first tone. The same should be done for each tone in the pattern until the student can sing the entire pattern using tonal syllables. When teaching rhythm units, the teacher can ask the students to echo the patterns two macro beats at a time. In that way, the teacher guides the students in deciding which rhythm syllables go with the pattern. The same should be done for each two beat pattern in the set until the student can chant the entire set using rhythm syllables.

Symbolic - Reading

At the generalization-symbolic (reading) level of learning, students are asked to read familiar and unfamiliar patterns from notation and to identify the tonality or meter, and the function of those patterns. When one tonal pattern or a rhythm pattern of four macro beats is to be read, the teacher should establish tonality or meter using tonal or rhythm syllables and the students should read the patterns using tonal or rhythm syllables. If more than one pattern is to be read, the teacher should establish tonality or meter using a neutral syllable and the students should read the patterns, also using a neutral syllable.

Symbolic - Writing

At the generalization-symbolic (writing) level of learning, students are asked to write familiar and unfamiliar patterns performed by the teacher. Again, if one tonal pattern or a rhythm pattern of four macro beats is to be written, all singing or chanting should be done using tonal or rhythm syllables. If more than one pattern is to be written, all singing or chanting should be done using a neutral syllable.

Before performing a tonal pattern or patterns for the class, the teacher should select a "do" signature and should establish tonality (see composite synthesis-writing). Once students have successfully notated a pattern or set of patterns, they can be guided in identifying the tonality and function of that pattern or set of patterns. Before performing a rhythm pattern or set of patterns for the class, the teacher should select a measure signature. Once a group has successfully notated a pattern or set of patterns, they can be guided in identifying the meter and function of that pattern or set of patterns. Students can be grouped by tonal or rhythm aptitude.

Creativity/Improvisation

Aural/Oral (without verbal association)

Because creativity and improvisation are largely a re-ordering of the familiar, the larger an individual's audiational vocabulary, the better he will create and improvise. One cannot improvise without a vocabulary of patterns from which to choose. Creativity is less restricted than is improvisation. When creating, an individual is bound by no restrictions other than those that are innate or of his own making. When one is improvising, restrictions are externally imposed. Therefore, creativity is less difficult than (and may serve as a prerequisite for) improvisation.

For sections requiring a created response, the class should be told to sing or chant a response that is different from the pattern delivered by the teacher. Tonality, or meter should be established by the teacher using a neutral syllable, and then the teacher should perform a pattern or a set of patterns for the class. The students should be asked to audiate their responses first and then to perform them together. The fact that the class response is dissonant does not matter.

When evaluating the created responses of individuals, the teacher must decide whether the response is musical and whether it is sufficiently related to the delivered pattern or patterns. Tonal responses must have a sense of tonality. A student can be asked to sing the resting tone if his response appears to be tonally unrelated to the teacher's pattern. Students who have a difficult time creating a different tonal pattern can begin by simply re-ordering the tones of the teacher's pattern. Rhythm pattern responses must have a sense of meter. If a student's rhythm response appears to be unrelated to the teacher's pattern, the student can be asked to move to the macro beat and/or the micro beat. Students who have a difficult time creating a different rhythm pattern can re-order the durations of the teacher's pattern.

When an improvised response is called for, the teacher should impose restrictions on the student's response by asking the student to perform patterns of specific functions within a tonality or meter. For example, a student might be asked to sing a dominant pattern followed by a tonic pattern in major tonality in response to the teacher's pattern or patterns. The student would respond by singing a dominant and tonic pattern of his choice, using a neutral syllable. Rhythmically, a student might be asked to chant a division and elongation pattern in duple meter in response to the teacher's pattern or patterns. Again, the student would respond with an appropriate pattern of his choice, using a neutral syllable.

Class patterns can be used also when improvising. They will sound better than class patterns used when creating because most students will be singing or chanting patterns of the same function at the same time.

Aural/Oral (with verbal association)

Tonal and rhythm syllables used in creating and improvising are functioning as a technique. One does not create the syllables, but rather uses them to create. The techniques used at this level are the same as at creativity/improvisation-aural/oral (without verbal association), except that all singing or chanting is done using tonal syllables and rhythm syllables.

Symbolic

Students create or improvise patterns and then notate them at the creativity/improvisation-symbolic level of learning.   Students may or may not be asked to perform their response before notating it. When evaluating, the teacher must again decide whether an individual's response is musical and whether it is sufficiently related to the delivered pattern. If a student changes the tonality or keyality of his tonal response or the meter or tempo of his rhythm response, the teacher must be sure that the change was intentional. Any student having difficulty creating a different pattern can simply re-order the tones or durations of the teacher's pattern.

For improvised responses, the tonality or meter name and function names are used to guide the student's responses. Individuals must respond using a neutral syllable within the limitations given by the teacher.

NOTES

[1]Within this book, see "General Techniques for Teaching Learning Sequence Activities."

[2]Within this book, see "Audiation: The Term and the Process" for more information about audiation.

[3]Within this book, see "Informal Music Instruction as Readiness for Learning Sequence Activities" for more information about the music babble stages.

[4]Within this book, see "General Techniques for Teaching Learning Sequence Activities" and "Teaching a Rote Song" for more information about the preparatory sequence of tones.

[5]Within this book, see "Tonal Syllables: A Comparison of Purposes and Systems" for more information.

[6]Within this book, see "Rhythm Syllables: A Comparison of Systems" for more information.

BEGINNING LEARNING SEQUENCE ACTIVITIES: TECHNIQUES FOR TONAL UNIT 1 AND RHYTHM UNIT 1 OF JUMP RIGHT IN: THE MUSIC CURRICULUM

Linda L. Jessup

A music teacher who wants to implement learning sequence activities typically is hesitant about making the transition from theory to practice. Although the skill and content to be taught during learning sequence activities are well-defined by the levels of learning and their associated sequential objectives, shown in the printed materials of Jump Right In: The Music Curriculum, many questions naturally arise about how to begin teaching the initial units.[1] Among the questions that may be of concern are: 1) must instruction begin with Unit 1? 2) why are Tonal Unit 1 and Rhythm Unit 1 not similar? 3) should the tonal and rhythm units be taught synchronously? and 4) how many sections and criteria should be covered within a given period of time? The following paragraphs will address those questions. Then appropriate techniques will be suggested for teaching Tonal Unit 1 and Rhythm Unit 1.

Regardless of the chronological age, grade level, or previous level of musical experience of students, the teacher should begin instruction with Unit 1 for both tonal and rhythm learning sequence activities. The curriculum is designed to be used sequentially, so that skill level and content for each unit serve as a readiness for the skill level and content of the next unit. If instruction were to begin with Unit 2, for example, a verbal association unit, students would lack the aural/oral foundation for the verbal associations that they must learn to make. It is wrong to assume that children (even older children) innately possess aural/oral skills simply as a result of environmental exposure to music. Therefore, if teachers erroneously begin instruction with Unit 2, the syllables that are sung or chanted will tend to become labels that carry minimal aural meaning. In that case, the process of imitating sound unfortunately will substitute for the musical process of audiating sound. Although students will perform tonal and rhythm patterns using tonal syllables and rhythm syllables,[2] their inability to audiate those same patterns and to use the syllables as tools of verbal association will impede learning.[3] In that case, as the content progresses and the number of patterns taught and learned increases, the development of audiation skills will become increasingly problematic.

There is no timetable for the completion of the first tonal unit and the first rhythm unit. The teacher should take as much time as needed to teach those units completely. In some circumstances a class may need the entire school year to complete Tonal Unit 1 and Rhythm Unit 1. In general, it will take longer to complete Unit 1 if: (a) students are young, (b) classes meet only once a week, or (c) there is a large number of students in each class.

Tonal and rhythm units should not be taught synchronously. In other words, it is not desirable (and probably not possible) to teach equal numbers of criteria, sections, and units for both tonal and rhythm units within the same period of time. Neither is it desirable to teach tonal and rhythm learning sequence activities within the same class period. Tonal and rhythm learning sequence activities should be alternated from one week to the next, regardless of the number of times per week that classes meet.

Many teachers do not understand Rhythm Unit 1 Sections A and B, and therefore are reluctant to teach those sections. They see a logical association between Rhythm Unit 1 Sections C and D and Tonal Unit 1 Sections A and B, but may assume that Rhythm Unit 1 Sections A and B are not necessary because students have already engaged in a sufficient amount of informal movement. What they do not realize is that many students, because they are not coordinated, do not audiate while they move. Also, most students' previous experience with movement is unrelated to tempo and meter. Sections A and B of Rhythm Unit 1 are designed to teach students to coordinate their large and small muscle movement with audiation of tempo and meter. In a similar way, the first two criteria of Tonal Unit 1 Sections A and B are designed to teach students to coordinate their vocal mechanism with the audiation of keyality and tonality.

Tonal Unit 1

It is important for the teacher always to perform the tonal patterns in the same tonalities indicated on the pattern cards. In some circumstances (particularly with older children) the keyalities for the tonal patterns may be transposed. In that case, all patterns on the same card must be systematically transposed so that the keyal relationships among patterns and criteria are maintained (Gordon and Woods, 1985, p. 35). If a teacher transposes patterns, the keyalities selected for those transpositions should be used whenever patterns from that card are taught. In other words, the teacher should not arbitrarily transpose all patterns on the same card to one set of keyalities one day, then transpose the patterns on that same card to a different set of keyalities on a different day. However, different transpositions may be desirable for different classes, depending upon age and other factors.

Some teachers are concerned that students may have difficulty audiating tonal patterns that are sung by a male teacher, whose vocal range would be an octave below the students' singing range. There is no evidence that compensating by singing in a falsetto voice is beneficial. The normal voice is preferred because it is more natural and more musical.

Because verbal instructions waste time and interfere with audiation, the teacher should develop a consistent system of gestures to indicate whether students are to listen only, sing as a group, or sing as individuals (Gordon and Woods, 1985, p. 38). Consistent gestures minimize inappropriate and premature responses. The gestures selected should feel comfortable and natural to the teacher, and should not imply rhythm or meter.[4]

The skill level of Tonal Unit 1 is aural/oral. There are four sections within the unit. The response asked of students and the content for Sections A and B are similar to each other, except that the patterns in Section A are in major tonality and the patterns in Section B are in minor tonality. A corresponding relationship exists between sections C and D, making it permissible to teach Tonal Unit 1 in the section order A, B, C, D or B, A, D, C.

Sections A and B, Criterion 1: First Tone

For the first criterion, students are asked to sing only the first tone of a tonic or dominant pattern that is sung first by the teacher. The teacher must teach the meaning of "first tone," especially for younger students, to avoid having them sing the entire pattern. The teacher might say, "Please listen carefully. I am going to sing a pattern and I would like you to sing only the first tone of the pattern back to me. The first tone of the pattern is the first sound that you hear." When demonstrating the response to young children, the teacher might cup one or both hands over his mouth immediately after singing the first tone to emphasize the point. The easy pattern for Criterion 1 should be used as a model, because that pattern will be used to evaluate all students.

Other types of verbal explanations may be necessary to help students understand the concept of first tone. Letters, numbers, or short word phrases may be used. The teacher might say, "I am going to say three words for you. After I finish I will ask you to say the first word that you heard," etc.

It is probably helpful to have young children sing several class patterns in their entirety before teaching the first-tone response (Gordon and Woods, 1985, p.39). Children then will be able to compare the two types of responses and will be able to distinguish between an entire pattern and the first tone only.

It is sometimes helpful to hold up fingers corresponding to the number of tones and their ordinal position in a pattern. While the teacher sings alone, one, two, and then three fingers can be held up for a three-tone pattern. When indicating a first-tone-only response, the teacher can hold up one finger only. Holding up one finger then provides a visual reminder to respond with only the first tone.

Sections A and B, Criterion 2: Resting Tone

Students are able to understand the concept of resting tone more easily than they are able to understand the concept of first tone. The concept of resting tone should be introduced as it relates to the sequence of tones that is used by the teacher to establish tonality and keyality, a sequence whose final tone should always be the resting tone.[5] In association with that sequence, an explanation of the resting tone can be given effectively if the explanation is sung, without meter, on the resting tone. For example, a sequence for major tonality in the keyality of D should be sung, using a neutral syllable, several times in succession for Criterion 2 of Section A. Then the teacher might sing on the resting tone, "Listen to my special pattern." The teacher should then sing the sequence again, and continue to sing the verbal explanation on the resting tone, e.g., "Whenever you hear my special pattern, the last note has a special name. It is called the resting tone. Would you please sing the resting tone with me." The teacher then should sing the resting tone, using a neutral syllable, gesture for the students to also sing the resting tone, and subsequently continue singing, "That is correct. Whenever I ask you to sing the resting tone you should sing ..." and the teacher sings the resting tone again using a neutral syllable.

As was true for teaching the concept of first tone, visual and kinesthetic cues can be used to help reinforce the concept of resting tone. One technique that can be used to encourage constant audiation of the resting tone is to have students cross their arms and hold them against their chest, as though holding the resting tone silently inside their bodies. Then, when the resting tone response is requested, students can unfold their arms and sing the resting tone, as though releasing it from audiation.

Sections A and B, Criteria 3, 4, and 5: Echo Using a Neutral Syllable

For Criteria 3, 4, and 5, students are asked to echo entire patterns, using a neutral syllable. One pattern is echoed for Criterion 3 and for Criterion 4, and two for Criterion 5.

After students have become accustomed to responding with a single tone for Criteria 1 and 2, it is not uncommon for them to respond initially with one tone only, rather than with the entire pattern, for Criterion 3. The teacher then should explain to students that they are to sing all the tones. Brief echo games can be played with words if students still need help in understanding how to echo an entire tonal pattern.

There are many points to consider when teaching complete tonal patterns. Patterns should be performed musically, with as clear a tone quality as possible, and at a moderate dynamic level. The tones within a pattern should be equal in length, and should be sung with a slight separation between them. Also, the teacher must guard against inadvertently developing a style that might imply rhythm and meter. One way to lessen the chances of introducing rhythm and meter into tonal patterns is to avoid singing several consecutive patterns that contain the same number of tones. Many consecutive two-note patterns can develop into triple meter if the pause between the pattern and the response is the same length as each tone in the pattern. Similarly, many consecutive three-note patterns can develop into a feeling of duple meter (Gordon, 1988).

The teacher should practice the tonal patterns for each criterion of each section before performing them for and with the students (Gordon and Woods, 1985, p. 35). When patterns are memorized the teacher has greater freedom to perform in a musical manner and to observe responses.

Sections C and D, Criteria 1 through 5: Echo Using a Neutral Syllable

Sections C and D parallel Sections A and B. The only difference is that the students' audiation is challenged by increasing the number of patterns that must be listened to and audiated before responding. Specifically, each criterion in Sections C and D is one pattern longer than its counterpart from Sections A and B. The teacher should pause briefly between patterns when series of patterns are sung. However, the length of the pause should not be metronomic (Gordon and Woods, 1985, p. 37).

Rhythm Unit 1

Whereas a keyality is specified for the tonal patterns to be sung within each tonal unit, no tempo is specified for the rhythm patterns to be chanted within each rhythm unit. When chanting rhythm patterns in usual duple meter, the teacher should use a tempo in which the macro beat is equal to approximately M.M.=76. When chanting rhythm patterns in usual triple meter, the teacher should use a tempo in which the macro beat is equal to approximately M.M.=72. (Gordon, 1988). It is important for the teacher always to perform the patterns from a given section in the same tempo and meter each time that section is taught. Also, it is essential that the teacher always perform rhythm patterns devoid of melody.

The skill level of Rhythm Unit 1 is aural/oral. The responses asked of students and the content for Sections A and B are similar to each other, except that the patterns in Section A are in usual duple meter and the patterns in Section B are in usual triple meter. A corresponding relationship exists between Sections C and D, making it permissible to teach Rhythm Unit 1 in the section order A, B, C, D or B, A, D, C.

Sections A and B, Criterion 1:
Informal Large and Small Muscle Movement

For the first criterion, students are asked to move informally in a steady beat to rhythm. It is suggested that the teacher chant (using a neutral syllable), play an instrument, or play a recording to accompany students' movement. Pre-recorded music may elicit the best response, and it allows the teacher the greatest freedom to simultaneously participate with and observe students. Students will be reluctant to engage in movement if the teacher is not an equal participant. Therefore it is recommended that the teacher chant using a neutral syllable or play an instrument only if the teacher can move with freedom and ease while chanting or playing. When using pre-recorded music, the teacher should include instrumental music from various style periods. Music with extensive tempo rubato should not be selected, as consistency of tempo is important to the activity.

Since the publication of Jump Right In: The Music Curriculum (Gordon and Woods, 1985), Gordon has elaborated upon his recommendations for instruction at the beginning stages of rhythm development. He has consequently developed a ten-step sequence designed to facilitate the development of coordination. Those steps, constructed in response to the child's need to experience a feeling of weight in conjunction with specific body movements, are shown in Figure 1. Note that the movements progress from the upper half of the body to the lower half of the body. Gordon believes that students will not be able to audiate rhythm unless they can feel their bodies move, and that, to be felt, movement must have weight (Gordon, 1988).

In light of recent changes in Gordon's emphasis, the initial sections for rhythm learning sequence activities may require revision and expansion. Each current criterion for Sections A and B of Unit 1 may need to become a section, with each of the new sections containing a new set of criteria. For example, Gordon now believes that students must precede rhythm learning with learning how to sustain the flow of body movement to music. Flow might best be described as a state of continuous movement in which there are no clearly defined borders to the motions, but rather a continuous fluidity to the movement.[6] Of course the teacher must be able to sustain flow and serve as a model for the students. There are several types of motions that might help students to develop a feeling of flow, e.g., pretending to swim in a relaxed manner, pretending to be a tree with flexible branches blowing in a steady wind, and maintaining constant flow with a long but light-weight piece of fabric, such as a scarf, in each hand. In the last case, the manipulation of the objects also will help distract reticent students from their own self-consciousness about movement.

It may take several weeks or months for students to develop ease of movement. Meanwhile, the teacher should never judge a particular observed movement to be incorrect for Criterion 1. To do so would discourage movement entirely. The teacher should accept any form of movement, even if awkward and rigid at first. Teacher modeling, creative suggestions, and patience are necessary for the gradual development of sustained flow movement in students.

STEP	POSITION	MOVEMENT
1	Seated, elbows resting on a table	Drop forearms as a unit on the table; the hands should be included as part of the forearm unit, and the wrists should be straight.
2	Seated, elbows resting on a table	Alternate the forearm drop movement described in step 1 (one arm at a time).
3	Standing, knees slightly bent and heels free	Swing arms forward and back as a complete unit; the hands should be included as part of the full arm unit, and the wrists should be straight.
4	Seated	Sway from side to side.
5	Seated	Drop heel to the floor; toes remain in contact with the floor, while only the heels move up and down.
6	Seated	Alternate the toe-to-heel movement described in step 5 (one heel at a time).
7	Seated	Combine the forearm drop movement described in step 1 with the toe-to-heel movement described in step 5.
8	Standing, knees slightly bent	Generate a side-to-side, toe-to-heel movement, using the balls of the feet as pivot points (similar to making ski turns).
9	Standing, knees slightly bent	While executing step 8 to macro beats, tap the arms as a unit against the sides of the body to micro beats; perform in duple meter and in triple meter as two separate exercises.
10	Seated	Perform the toe-to-heel movement described in step 5 to macro beats while performing the forearm drop movement described in step 1 to micro beats; perform in duple meter and in triple meter as two separate exercises.

Figure 1. Gordon's Ten Steps to Coordination

Sections A and B, Criteria 2, 3, 4 and 5:
Performing Macro and Micro Beats with Body Response

Problems arise in implementing Criteria 2 through 5 of Sections A and B as they are written in the Rhythm Register Book, primarily because the types of leg, arm, and hand movements to be used are not specified.[7] In general, what should probably replace Criteria 2 through 5 is weighted movement to macro beats and then to micro beats, first in the upper body, then in the lower body, and finally progressing to macro and micro beats in the upper and lower body together. The following list of possible criteria revisions for Rhythm Unit 1, Sections A and B, is based upon Gordon's ten steps to coordination. The sequence is not necessarily correct; ultimately its appropriateness will need to be determined by future research.

Rhythm Unit 1, Section A (Duple) and B (Triple):
While in a seated position, the student performs in a consistent tempo to

1   macro beats, using a forearm movement in which the elbows are placed on a flat surface and the weight of the arms is dropped to the table.

2   micro beats, using the same movement as in Criterion 1.

3   macro beats, using a toe-to-heel movement in which the toe remains in contact with the floor and the weight of the heel is dropped to the floor.

4   micro beats, using the same movement as in Criterion 3.

5   macro beats, using the forearm movement and the toe-to-heel movement, simultaneously.

6   micro beats, using the forearm movement and the toe-to-heel movement, simultaneously.

7   macro and micro beats, using the forearm movement to macro beats and the toe-to-heel movement to micro beats.

8   macro and micro beats, using the toe-to-heel movement to
     macro beats and the forearm movement to micro beats.

It may be desirable to add another pair of sections in which students are
asked to perform corresponding movements in a standing position in duple
and triple meters. The forearm movement to the table might be replaced
with full arm movement against the sides of the body, and the heel
movement might be either a parallel or a variation of the seated heel
movement, depending upon the technique preferred by the teacher. Those
new sections would be taught after Sections A and B but before Sections C
and D.

Sections C and D, Criterion 1:
Echo using a Neutral Syllable

For Criterion 1 the student is asked to echo two familiar macro and
micro beat patterns without movement, using a neutral syllable. Criterion 1
is a readiness for Criteria 2 through 5, in which students echo patterns and
imitate movement simultaneously.

Style is of great importance in the performance of rhythm patterns
(Gordon, 1988). Unfortunately, many teachers believe that macro beats and
micro beats should be accented in performance, ignoring the fact that
constant use of accent contradicts musicality and results in students learning
a vulgar musical style. It is important that the teacher vary stylistic
elements when performing rhythm patterns for students. There should be
tasteful, musical variations in dynamic levels, articulation, and inflection
among rhythm patterns and within the same rhythm pattern.

When students echo rhythm patterns, their response should begin on the
next macro beat after the teacher's performance of the pattern (Gordon and
Woods, 1985, p. 55). To encourage a timely response, the teacher should
conduct the final macro beat of the dictated pattern (upbeat) while chanting,
that macro beat functioning as a springboard for the student's response, and
then conduct the first beat of the student's response (downbeat) so that the
student has a clear indication of the precise moment at which the response
should begin (Gordon, 1988). Students whose responses begin between
macro beats probably are not audiating the correct meter. Students whose
responses begin on the second macro beat probably are audiating the correct

meter, but do not understand that the response should begin on the macro beat immediately following the dictated pattern.

Sections C and D, Criteria 2 through 5: Echo, Using a Neutral Syllable, with Movement

The previous sections and criteria were used to teach students how to coordinate the body and the voice separately. Criteria 2 through 5 in Sections C and D are used to teach students how to coordinate the two with each other. If sufficient time has been spent teaching students all the criteria in Sections A and B, there should be little difficulty coordinating the chanting voice with body movement.

Conclusion

Tonal Unit 1 and Rhythm Unit 1 of <u>Jump Right In: The Music Curriculum</u> can be used to build the foundation for a lifetime of musicianship. It is the fault of our culture that performing by the use of the body and the singing voice tends not to be socially acceptable among older children. The taboo against singing and moving, once established, becomes more firmly ingrained with each passing year of a child's life. If music learning sequence activities are taught regularly and correctly at an early age, the act of engaging in musical conversation eventually may become as natural as engaging in spoken conversation.

An excellent way to discover our strengths and weaknesses as teachers is to observe ourselves by standing in front of a mirror, or to study an audio or video tape of ourselves teaching. As musicians we should approach the challenge of learning to teach music learning sequence activities in the same way that we approach the challenge of learning to perform new literature on our instruments. We should be able to audiate the polished musical performance before it is realized, and then refine our technique in pursuit of that musical goal through practice. Neither teacher nor student can expect musicianship to just happen; it is achieved. That applies to teacher and student alike.

NOTES

[1]Within this book, see "Skill Learning Sequence," "Rhythm Learning Sequence," and "Tonal Learning Sequence" for more information about skill levels and content levels.

[2]Within this book, see "Tonal Syllables: A Comparison of Purposes and Systems," and "Rhythm Syllables: A Comparison of Systems" for more information about the use of tonal syllables and rhythm syllables.

[3]Within this book, see "Audiation: The Term and the Process" for more information about audiation.

[4]Within this book, see "General Techniques for Teaching Learning Sequence Activities" and "Specific Techniques for Teaching Learning Sequence Activities" for recommendations about specific gestures, how they should be used, and other technical details related to the delivery of patterns during learning sequence activities.

[5]Within this book, see "Teaching a Rote Song" for specific information about preparatory sequences and their use.

[6]Within this book, see "Laban Movement Theory and How it Can Be Used in Music Learning Theory" for additional insight into the concept of flow and other elements of movement.

[7]Perhaps hand movements will be excluded from future editions, as they are not a part of Gordon's ten steps to coordination; muscle movements associated with the hands do not give a strong feeling of weight.

REFERENCES

Gordon, Edwin E. (1988) Learning Sequences in Music. Chicago: G.I.A. Publications, Inc.
Gordon, Edwin E. (July 3 - 8, 1988). 1988 Music Learning Theory Seminar I (unpublished proceedings). Philadelphia: Temple University Conference Center.
Gordon, Edwin E. and David G. Woods (1985). Reference Handbook for Using Learning Sequence Activities. Chicago: G.I.A. Publications, Inc.

COORDINATING LEARNING SEQUENCE ACTIVITIES AND CLASSROOM ACTIVITIES

Darrel L. Walters

The two components of music teaching that are the subject of this article, learning sequence activities and classroom activities, each will be described here. After those descriptions, an overview will be given of the model learning process that occurs when learning sequence activities and classroom activities are effectively coordinated using the principles of Music Learning Theory. Finally, examples will be given of specific actions that general music teachers, vocal music teachers, and instrumental music teachers can take to facilitate effective learning through the coordination of learning sequence activities and classroom activities.

Learning Sequence Activities and Classroom Activities: A Description

Learning sequence activities are part of a concept that is relatively new to the music education community. Classroom activities, on the other hand, are familiar to all music teachers. Because it is easier for the reader to progress from the familiar to the unfamiliar, classroom activities will be described first.

Classroom activities are essentially those kinds of activities that music educators everywhere employ when they teach music. For the general music teacher, typical classroom activities are movement games, the singing of songs, and the playing of simple instruments. For the vocal music teacher, typical classroom activities are the use of vocalises and the rehearsing of choral literature. For the instrumental music teacher, typical classroom activities are the use of instrumental warm-up exercises and the rehearsing of band or orchestral literature. One of the refreshing aspects of Music Learning Theory is that its integration into an established approach to music teaching does not necessitate the abandonment of classroom activities that are already in place and that the teacher and students have found to be effective and enjoyable. Therefore, materials and techniques developed by Dalcroze, Orff, Kodaly, Suzuki, and individual teachers of general, vocal, and instrumental music, can be preserved and used in the context of the classroom activities component of instruction that is designed in accordance with the principles of Music Learning Theory. Gordon's insight into learning sequence often can be tapped to increase the effectiveness of existing approaches to classroom activites simply by re-ordering those activities to conform to the natural learning tendencies of children. Existing classroom activities can be enhanced also by adding to them the complementary component developed by Gordon, that component being learning sequence activities.

Learning sequence activities are designed to exploit the power of sequential learning that Edwin Gordon has brought to the attention of music educators through his Music Learning Theory. Properly used, learning sequence activities occupy only the first five to ten minutes of each music class period or ensemble rehearsal. The remainder of the time is devoted to classroom activities.

The many dimensions of music that interact with each other during the course of classroom activities are treated separately during learning sequence activities. More accurately, the two principal dimensions of music, the tonal dimension and the rhythm dimension, are each made an object of specific, sequential learning. The other dimensions of music (dynamics, form, style, timbre, etc.) are not specifically accounted for within learning sequence activities. For that reason, the materials that are a part of learning sequence activities do not constitute "music," any more than the vocabulary words taught by an English teacher constitute "literature." What learning sequence activities do constitute is an opportunity to develop in children, in a sensible and effective way, the basic skills needed to successfully understand, appreciate, and produce music, just as the learning of English vocabulary words constitutes an opportunity to develop in children the basic skills needed to successfully understand, appreciate, and produce literature.

Students engaged in tonal learning sequence activities begin by hearing tonal patterns sung by the teacher, and respond by singing those patterns or designated pitches related to those patterns. Students engaged in rhythm learning sequence activities, after moving to macro beats and micro beats in duple meter and in triple meter, begin by hearing rhythm patterns chanted by the teacher, and respond by chanting those patterns.[1]

Gordon's skill learning hierarchy provides the organizational framework for learning sequence activities.[2] Consequently, learning sequence activities lead logically from the aural/oral activities of hearing, singing, and chanting, to verbal association activities that entail the use of proper names and tonal syllables and rhythm syllables, through partial synthesis activities that include the identification of meters and tonalities, through symbolic association and composite synthesis activities that entail the reading and writing of tonal patterns and rhythm patterns, and through the generalization and creativity/improvisation levels of inference learning that are composed of appropriate tonal and rhythm activities.

The choices of content for learning sequence activities are made on the basis of Gordon's content learning hierarchies.[3] Consequently, the teacher teaching tonal learning sequence activities begins with tonic patterns and dominant patterns in major tonality and in minor tonality, and the teacher teaching rhythm learning sequence activities begins with macro and micro beat patterns in duple meter and in triple meter. Throughout the process of teaching learning sequence activities, the teacher takes individual differences among students into account and keeps careful records of individual achievement so that appropriate subsequent instruction can be carried out.[4]

Classroom activities used alone would dwell upon the Gestalt of music, and consequently neglect a systematic acquisition of skill on the part of individuals. Learning sequence activities used alone would be mechanical and wearing, and would deprive students of musical experiences. The interaction of learning sequence activites and classroom activities produces a true method of learning, a "method" being a path that leads clearly to an objective. Through the application of that method, teachers of music may find that they can elevate individual and group achievement in music to heights never before realized.

A Model Learning Process for Music

A universally respected approach to learning, whatever the subject being learned, is the whole-part-whole approach. The rationale for that approach is that students will learn most efficiently if they are given a general view of the whole followed by a specific study of parts within that whole, and finally followed by a more enlightened view of the whole. Some learning theorists refer to the whole-part-whole learning model as "introduction, application, and reinforcement."

Music teachers can create a whole-part-whole approach to learning for their students by treating learning sequence activities and classroom activities as complementary parts of the total learning process. The teacher who manipulates that total learning process skillfully will see the light of insight shine in the eyes of students every day, and he will have the year-to-year satisfaction of knowing that his students are deriving maximum value from both learning sequence activities and classroom activities.

Look at Figure 1 to see the role of learning sequence activities and classroom activities in the whole-part-whole model as applied to music learning.

I (Introduction)	II (Application)	III (Reinforcement)
CLASSROOM ACTIVITIES	LEARNING SEQUENCE ACTIVITIES	CLASSROOM ACTIVITIES
Overview of the Whole	Specific Study of the Parts (but not parts specific to the whole)	Greater Understanding of the Whole

**Figure 1. A Three-Part Learning Process Resulting from the
Coordination of Learning Sequence Activities
and Classroom Activities**

Step II of the learning model shown in Figure 1 is qualified with the words "not parts specific to the whole." That is because the teacher does not extract rhythm patterns and tonal patterns from literature sung or played during Step 1 and then teach those patterns during Step II. Instead, he chooses the patterns to be taught during Step II on the basis of appropriate learning sequence and difficulty level. That is done because learning sequence and difficulty level are of paramount importance to learning efficiency. The fact that the "specific parts" studied within Step II of the total learning process are not extracted directly from the literature performed in Step I of the process does not in any way invalidate the process as an example of the whole-part-whole model. That is because the rhythm patterns and tonal patterns taught during Step II are of the same content as the literature performed during Step I, e.g., they are in the same meter, tonality, etc. It might be helpful to think of the rhythm patterns and tonal patterns studied in Step II of the total learning process as being specific to "the type of literature" performed during Step I, rather than as being specific to "the literature" performed during Step I. Nevertheless, many of the patterns studied at Step II will correspond exactly with patterns found in the literature performed during Step I.

By the time students participate in Step III of the whole-part-whole learning process, they will have acquired enough of a vocabulary of patterns to enable them to make generalizations. When students generalize, they learn unfamiliar patterns by comparing and contrasting them with familiar patterns. In effect, they are teaching themselves. The self-teaching of those patterns not specifically studied at Step II may occur either in the classroom or in a setting apart from formal learning. Stated another way, the understanding of the whole attributed to Step III of the whole-part-whole learning process is acquired through repeated exposures to music, some of which occur in the controlled environment of the classroom (classroom activities or subsequent learning sequence activities) and some of which occur as a part of "real life" experiences. That is a natural learning process. Music Learning Theory, supported by extensive field and experimental research, amounts to an approach to the learning of music that recognizes and makes maximum use of natural learning tendencies.

Having become familiar with Gordon's content learning hierarchies and skill learning hierarchy, the reader is aware of the important interaction between content and skill within the music learning process. Content is the "material" contained in the songs or patterns (minor tonality, tonic function, triple meter, etc.) and skill is the action that the student applies to that material (associate syllables with patterns, interpret symbols in notation, etc.). The guiding rule for a teacher who is creating a whole-part-whole approach to learning may be thought of in two parts relative to content and skill.

1. The teacher must present a given content, e.g., sing a song in major tonality, in Step I (Introduction) before he applies that content, e.g., to the learning of tonal patterns in major tonality, in Step II (Application).

2. The teacher must teach a given skill, e.g., the association of tonal syllables with tonal patterns, in Step II (Application) before he asks students to use that skill, e.g., sing tonal syllables as an aide to understanding a particular tonal pattern within a song, in Step III (Reinforcement).

Teachers reading this article may gain a better understanding of the learning process described here by studying a hypothetical account of a teaching/learning relationship between a general music teacher and a class of elementary music students. Assume that the teacher and the class are getting to know each other for the first time at the beginning of a new school year.

The teacher decides to use only classroom activities for the first few class sessions. That gives the students experience with specific content at the Step I level of learning. The content chosen by the teacher is duple meter and major tonality. The teacher has the students move to songs in duple meter and sing rote songs in major tonality and duple meter. One of the songs learned is "Ally Bally," shown in Figure 2.

Figure 2. "Ally Bally," a Song Learned by Rote in Classroom Activities.

After a few sessions of classroom activities involving duple meter and major tonality, the teacher can choose to engage the students in learning sequence activities, using either rhythm patterns in duple meter or tonal patterns in major tonality, at Step II of the learning process. The teacher will teach the first learning sequence activities at the most elementary skill level, which is aural/oral (hearing and then chanting or singing). Also, the teacher will employ only elementary pattern functions during the first learning sequence activities, i.e., macro beat and micro beat rhythm patterns or tonic and dominant tonal patterns.

If the teacher were to choose to teach rhythm learning sequence activities, he might use patterns similar to those from Rhythm Unit I of the Jump Right In curriculum, shown in Figure 3. If the teacher were to choose to teach tonal learning sequence activities, he might use patterns similar to those from Tonal Unit I of the Jump Right In curriculum, shown in Figure 4. (A vocal music teacher or an instrumental music teacher would use similar patterns if the students had no previous experience with learning sequence activities. If the vocal music teacher or instrumental music teacher were teaching students who had been taught <u>Jump Right In</u> learning sequence activities as general music students, that foundation could be built upon with more advanced patterns.)

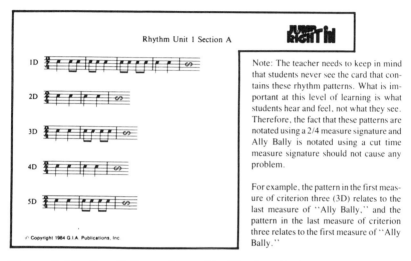

Figure 3. Rhythm Patterns Found in Rhythm Unit 1, Section A.

Figure 4. Tonal Patterns Found in Tonal Unit 1, Section A.

The classroom activities that follow the first learning sequence activities may be limited to more duple meter and major tonality, or they may incorporate triple meter or minor tonality. Their content will determine the number of options available to the teacher for the next learning sequence activities session. During the next learning sequence activity session, probably the teacher would choose to either continue the learning sequence activities content begun at the first learning sequence activities session or teach the alternate dimension (tonal or rhythm) from the one taught at the first session. That is, even if minor tonality, for example, had been introduced through classroom activities during the previous class session, the teacher would probably wait until the students had accumulated a series of experiences with minor tonality in classroom activities (Step I) before beginning to teach tonal patterns in minor tonality in learning sequence activities (Step II).

Assume that after a few sessions of learning sequence activities the teacher were to have the students sing "Ally Bally" again, and work with them to improve their performance. Even though many of the rhythm patterns and tonal patterns found in "Ally Bally" (Figure 2) are different from the specific rhythm patterns and tonal patterns learned aurally in learning sequence activities (Figures 3 and 4), the focused experience that the students have had with rhythm patterns in duple meter and tonal patterns in major tonality will enable them to bring a slightly greater understanding to "Ally Bally" (Step III).

It is important to note that Step III learning is not necessarily limited to literature that has been performed previously. Just as the "specific parts" studied in Step II are specific to "types" of literature rather than to the literature itself, those specific parts and the skills applied to them can be generalized to "types" of literature rather than to specific literature. Therefore, skill and content applied to learning sequence activities can be reinforced for greater understanding in relation to either literature being reviewed/rehearsed or to literature being performed for the first time.

A summary perspective on the relationship of the three parts of the whole-part-whole learning process to each other might be helpful. Step II of the process as illustrated above, chanting rhythm patterns in duple meter and singing tonal patterns in major tonality at the aural/oral skill level, would have been more difficult for one who had not felt macro beats and micro beats in duple meter and heard tonic and dominant sounds in major tonality while singing songs during Step I. Further, to have studied those patterns at Step II would have become a useless and easily-forgotten exercise if that learning had not been subsequently applied to a greater understanding of the whole at Step III. Of course the "pay-off" for having studied patterns at Step II can theoretically come from any one of a number of Step III experiences, including many possibilities outside the teacher's influence, but if the teacher neglects to offer that experience directly he is leaving the acquisition of "greater understanding" by the student to fate. Even more important, the Step III experience provided by the teacher prepares the student to recognize and take advantage of informal learning opportunities that will come along later. In short, the formal Step III experience functions as a catalyst for informal Step III experiences, and consequently sets into motion a multiplication of the effect of the formal learning generated by the teacher.

The preceding whole-part-whole illustration is of course an oversimplification of the total learning process as it occurs over time. In practice, the steps recycle and reinforce each other many times over in order to produce truly effective learning. Still, several important principles have been illustrated.

1. Content is first experienced in classroom activities.
2. Skill is first taught in learning sequence activities.
3. Either the rhythm dimension or the tonal dimension is taught in learning sequence activities, but never the two together.
4. The rhythm dimension and the tonal dimension are combined in classroom activities.
5. Introductory Overview (Step I) and Reinforcement (Step III) are both the province of classroom activities.
6. Specific Study of the Parts (Step II), related to skill, content, and patterns, is the province of learning sequence activities.
7. Learning sequence activities ensure that repeated music experiences (classroom activities and other music experiences) become sequentially higher levels of experience rather than mere repetitions of the same experience.

Specific Actions that Enhance Step III Learning by Reinforcing Step II Learning

The reader will need to understand the skill learning hierarchy of Edwin Gordon in order to make sense of the remainder of this article. The article

"Skill Learning Sequence," which can be found earlier within this book, will be helpful.

General music teachers, vocal music teachers, and instrumental music teachers who are conscious of the specific learning that has taken place among their students during learning sequence activities will find opportunities to reinforce that learning constantly while teaching classroom activities or rehearsing an ensemble. The purpose of the last section of this article is to provide the reader with a few examples that can either be applied directly to the classroom situation or used as catalysts for the creation of other specific approaches to the reinforcement of learning.

At the aural/oral level of learning, the teacher can help students to reinforce the tonality or meter of a piece of music being sung or played by having them sing the resting tone, using a neutral syllable, or by having them move to macro and micro beats and chant macro and micro beats, using a neutral syllable. The teacher can also help students to reinforce the audiation of the beginning of a song by having them sing the first pitch, using a neutral syllable, or by having them move to and chant the opening rhythmic figure. Individual tonal patterns and rhythm patterns can be reinforced in the same way. Also, elements of form can be reinforced by having students sing or chant, using neutral syllables, patterns that reveal relationships among elements of the piece (such as repetitions) and consequently reveal information about the design of the piece as a whole.

At the verbal association level of learning, the teacher can help students to further reinforce all of the aspects of the piece of music cited in the preceding paragraph. The only difference is that the teacher and the students will use tonal syllables or rhythm syllables in place of neutral syllables when reinforcing the verbal association level of learning. Additional reinforcement of verbal associations is accomplished when the teacher guides the students to recognize tonality, meter, pattern functions, and other aspects of the piece of music by use of proper names learned during learning sequence activities (minor tonality, triple meter, tonic function, etc). It should be noted also that the correct recognition of such characteristics of a piece of music as tonality, meter, and form is a reinforcement of skills learned by the student at the partial synthesis level of learning during learning sequence activities.

At the symbolic association level of learning, the teacher can help students to reinforce the reading and writing of rhythm patterns and tonal patterns that prove troublesome during the process of reading or writing a piece of music. The teacher can simply isolate the troublesome spot, either as a rhythm pattern or as a tonal pattern, depending upon the nature of the problem, and then have the student audiate the pattern by use of the appropriate syllables. Further, similar reinforcement can occur at the composite synthesis level of learning when series of patterns rather than individual patterns are involved.

At the generalization level of learning, the teacher can help students to identify characteristics of an unfamiliar piece of music being sung or played by guiding them to compare and contrast those characteristics with characteristics of familiar music. For example, students can audiate and identify the tonality or meter of an unfamiliar song being sung, using text or neutral syllables, by recognizing the resting tone or micro beats in association with the appropriate tonal syllable or rhythm syllables. Similarly, specific tonal patterns and rhythm patterns can be isolated and identified. The identification can be purely aural (generalization-aural/oral), it can be related to tonal syllables or rhythm syllables (generalization-verbal), or it can be related to notation (generalization-symbolic). Students who are ready to function at the generalization level of learning will have acquired a great amount of understanding and skill and a large tonal vocabulary and rhythm vocabulary, all in relation to both basic audiation and notational audiation. That background will make it possible for the student, with the guidance of the teacher, to identify many characteristics about literature being heard, sung, or performed, including elements of form, tonal modulations, metric modulations, and other information that is generalizable by use of the more basic information about tonal and rhythm characteristics of music as learned at discrimination levels of learning.

At the creativity/improvisation level of learning, teachers can guide students to use the same skills and understanding cited in the paragraph above to improvise on a piece of music, e.g., re-write the beginning or the end of the piece, write a variation, etc., and to create their own music. To have a student, for example, create an ostinato for a piece of music being performed in classroom activities is an entirely different experience for a student who has acquired specific skills through learning sequence activities than for a student whose experience with music has been limited to classroom activities. The former will be truly improvising as he draws upon his reservoir of skill and understanding to bring about a pre-meditated, pre-audiated musical result. The latter will simply explore possibilities on the spot in a trial-and-error fashion until an acceptable result has been attained. The possibilities for successful and satisfying experiences in creativity and improvisation in the music classroom or ensemble may be the single greatest benefit gained from the systematic application of learning sequence activities to the music curriculum.

The activities cited here are described in general terms. For more specific instructions, the reader might consult the booklet, <u>Coordinating Classroom Activities and Learning Sequence Activities</u> (Walters, 1987). That booklet contains much of the information given in this article, but also describes step-by-step techniques that the teacher can apply to the reinforcement of learning at Step III. It is important for the teacher to realize, however, that neither that booklet nor this article is a definitive source of information on this topic. Different teachers will and should pursue different approachs to the coordination of learning sequence activities and classroom activities. Once a teacher understands the principles of coordinating the two, and once that teacher values the power of those principles to promote efficient learning among students, the form that the coordination takes is bound to become increasingly personal. Ultimately, the techniques applied to coordinating learning sequence activities and classroom activities will become specific to the teaching style of the teacher and to the needs of the students with whom the teacher works.

NOTES

[1]Macro beats refer to the beats represented by quarter notes in music written using a 2/4 measure signature and by dotted quarter notes in music written using a 6/8 measure signature. Micro beats refer to the beats represented by groups of two eighth notes in music written using a 2/4 measure signature and by groups of three eighth notes in music written using a 6/8 measure signature.

[2]Within this book, see "Skill Learning Sequence" for more information about Gordon's skill learning hierarchy.

[3]Within this book, see "Rhythm Learning Sequence" and "Tonal Learning Sequence" for more information about Gordon's content learning hierarchies.

[4]Within this book, see "The Measurement and Evaluation of Music Aptitudes and Achievement" for more information about detecting individual differences for purposes of improving instruction.

REFERENCES

Gordon, Edwin E. (1988). Learning Sequences in Music: Skill, Content, and Patterns. Chicago: G.I.A. Publications, Inc.

Gordon, Edwin E. and David G. Woods (1985). Jump Right In: The Music Curriculum. Chicago: G.I.A. Publications, Inc.

Walters, Darrel L. (1987). Coordinating Classroom Activities and Learning Sequence Activities. Chicago: G.I.A. Publications, Inc.

THE APPLICATION OF MUSIC LEARNING THEORY TO THE TEACHING OF MIDDLE SCHOOL GENERAL MUSIC

Coletta M. Wierson

This article contains rhythm and tonal readiness activities, techniques for using learning sequence activities, and suggested classroom activities. Those activities are designed for students in grades six through nine who have not been taught using principles of Music Learning Theory. Those students are expected to have a wide range of music aptitudes and performance skills. They will probably be a mix of non-singers, out-of-tune singers, and in-tune singers. Some will be uncoordinated and will fear movement, while others will be comfortable with movement. Some will even be experienced in dance, skating, or gymnastics.

Because teenage students are keenly aware of their peer relationships, music instruction for that age group should be presented in a way that will avoid any embarrassment or ridicule for the student. Marple (1975) believes that,

> Music classes for upper grades of the junior high school should consider more of the "masculine" traits in approach to organization, teacher personality, and the literature used or the activities developed. The teacher should be physical in behavior, a bit loud, friendly, outgoing, daring, and with an easy humor (p.192).

Trust, cooperation, discipline, and especially humor are essential characteristics for teachers who intend to use the activities presented here.

Readiness for Formal Learning: Rhythm

Heterogeneously grouped students will be in various stages of rhythm development. Some middle school students will still be in the rhythm babble stage.[1] Those students must be brought out of rhythm babble before they can benefit from formal instruction. Emergence from rhythm babble depends upon motor coordination. Until students have motor coordination skills, they will not achieve beat competency (the ability to match their movement to an external beat).[2]   Until students have achieved beat competency, they cannot be expected to audiate macro beats, micro beats and rhythm patterns in a consistent tempo, and consequently they cannot be expected to perform musically.[3] To be brought out of rhythm babble, the student must experience body movement in time and space through a variety of enjoyable movement activities. The rhythm learning process must proceed from kinesthetic experience to audiation because "when a student is audiating rhythmically, he is moving imperceptibly" (Gordon, 1984, p. 23). Further, because "motor skills are the direct result of experience and practice" (Weikart, 1987, p. 3), the parent, the music teacher, and the physical education teacher must provide experience and practice in movement.

Students who can move synchronously in a repeated pattern to an external beat in duple and triple meter are out of rhythm babble. However, the coordination and movement activities described here are of value to students who are in any stage of rhythm development.

An important issue for one teaching general music to middle school students, in addition to the issue of music babble, is the issue of rhythm aptitude. The Musical Aptitude Profile (MAP) will yield rhythm aptitude scores upon which teachers can base decisions about how students should be taught and what skill level can be expected from each student.[4] An alert teacher will pair a high aptitude student with a low aptitude student, will encourage the babbling student by accepting his movement without criticism, and will expect more complex and accurate movement from the high aptitude student than from students of average or low aptitude.

During the middle school years, the music teacher can take advantage of activities that tend to be attractive to young teens to help them acquire coordination skills. Motivation to participate in movement activities and discussion about movement may be generated by watching video or live performances of rock or jazz drummers, gymnastic floor exercise routines, music videos featuring movement, or sports and fitness activities. If physically possible, the teacher should participate in or model the movements. Physical education and music classes can begin with warm-ups to music to provide a regular period for the development of motor skills, coordination, and skill in the audiation of rhythm.

Pantomime is a useful tool for experimenting with movement. Students and teacher can observe, discuss, and pantomime the specific body movements, preparation and release, and flow of energy involved, for example, in delivering a bowling ball, in serving the ball and swinging the racket in tennis, in throwing or kicking a ball, in long jumping, in rowing, and in shooting a basketball. Partners or small groups of students may be formed to pantomime a sports activity.

Students' basic comfort level during movement activities is important. Fear of ridicule by peers, lack of self-confidence, and lack of experience all contribute to anxiety on the part of the student. Individuals must be allowed time to find their comfort level. Activities should begin with "low visibility" movements. For example, the teacher might begin by having students raise and lower their heels while seated, and then ask them to "walk" their feet in place. Parallel arm movements might be used next, and then added to the foot movements. Having elicited that much movement from the students, the teacher might model a sequence of movements that the students will associate with aerobics or with music videos. When most of the students have imitated that sequence with some degree of comfort while seated, the teacher might ask them to stand behind their chairs and hold onto the backs of them. This puts students in a position to walk, bend or rock, so that the routine may include, for example, walking around the chair. (Note that the wishes of the student who refuses to move out of the chair must be respected.)

Gradual weaning of students from the chair can be accomplished by giving each one a prop such as a frisbee, a small racket, or a small instrument, to be used in some designated way while walking. Students tend to concentrate on the props, so that they are less self-conscious about moving. The teacher may accompany the movement with chant (using a neutral syllable), the playing of a drum, or the use of a recording. As students begin to synchronize their steps with the macro beat, a "conga line" can be formed. A boys' line and a girls' line can be formed separately if that eases anxiety. (The most exposed formation, and consequently one to be avoided until students are very comfortable with movement, is a circle formation.)

The use of balls is generally associated with fun and with socially accepted activities. Tennis, yarn, nerf, paper, or inflated balls can be passed, bounced, thrown, and caught to help develop coordination and beat competency. The guideline for appropriateness of an activity is simple: the focus in rhythm readiness activities must be on the kinesthetic, so that students eventually acquire a sense of consistency of tempo and an ability to divide macro beats into either two or three micro beats, depending upon meter.

Learning Sequence Activities: Rhythm

When students are no longer in rhythm babble, they can begin rhythm learning sequence activities. Learning sequence activities are designed to develop the students' audiation, reading, writing, improvisation, and composition skills. Every other week, each music class should begin with a five-to-ten minute rhythm learning sequence activity routine of chanting, moving, and audiating. (Alternate weeks should be reserved for tonal learning sequence activities.) Movement readiness and other classroom rhythm activities should be taught concurrently with learning sequence activities.

The teaching of learning sequence activities presents unique challenges for the teacher of middle school students, because those students have entered the stage of abstract and symbolic learning and they will tend to resist rote and drill. Middle school students are stimulated and challenged by the higher-level thinking skills such as drawing inferences, using intuitive thinking, creating, and improvising.

Learning sequence activities require intense concentration; the teacher must be sensitive to the danger of exceeding the attention span of the class. That attention span can be lengthened if the intensity of the activity can be combined with musicianship and with a controlled sense of play. Rigidity, fear, and boredom are obviously counterproductive, and must be avoided. Students who are new to learning sequence activities will tend to participate in the chanting of rhythm patterns more readily than they will participate in the singing of tonal patterns. For that reason, the teacher may choose to use only rhythm patterns for the first few weeks of instruction until trust in the routine has been established.

When students begin to chant patterns using a neutral syllable, "bah" may appear too juvenile. The teacher might experiment with "tah" or "bop" or other syllables, but must avoid "doo," as "du" (pronounced "doo") will be associated with the macro beat at the verbal association level of learning. Whether a neutral syllable or rhythm syllables are being used, rhythm patterns should always be chanted with vocal inflection and with a variety of dynamics, but without the involvement of specific pitches. For other valuable recommendations within this book related to the delivery of rhythm patterns during learning sequence activities, the reader should refer to the two articles written by Robert Harper. Once the teacher and students are both comfortable with the process for learning rhythm patterns, it may be helpful for the teacher to send home with the student a cassette tape of the patterns, chanted by the teacher, with a blank space after each pattern in which the student can practice responding privately.

When a class is ready to be introduced to the rhythm syllables used at the verbal association level of learning, the teacher might want to consider having the students listen to and discuss skat singing as a readiness activity. Also, quick reaction games with friendly competition among teams can be used when learning the terms "macro" and "micro," or "duple" and "triple."

Some students will begin to make inferences about the meter of music in their everyday lives. Of course, new content (unusual or combined meters) must be introduced through classroom activities before that content can be applied to learning sequence activities. The Jump Right In song collection (1985), and A Nichol's Worth (1978) contain songs that are appropriate for introducing combined and unusual meters in classroom activities. And just as content must be introduced in classroom activities, skill must be introduced in learning sequence activities.

If taught in the proper sequence, music reading skills can be acquired readily by students of this age. Furthermore, the ability to read music will give them a sense of concrete musical achievement. Each student should be given a personal staff book in which he can notate patterns that he has learned to read. Music writing activities can be facilitated by providing each student with a "magic slate."

Middle school students will be intrigued and challenged by creativity/improvisation units. During those units, the students may invent games to practice their skills. Students in well-disciplined classes could work in small groups or with partners, echoing each other's improvised or created patterns.

Readiness for Formal Learning: Tonal

The voice is personal, and it is deeply connected to one's emotional and physical well-being. Approaching singing with the adolescent in a straightforward, honest, and caring way may persuade students to explore and expand their own vocal awareness and vocal performance.

Singing performance is not an accurate measure of music aptitude. Students who sing well will appear to have (and likely will have) a high music aptitude. On the other hand, the non-singer may be in tonal babble, may have low aptitude, may have a physical deformity, may have a psychological block, or may have never experienced the singing sensation.

Boys who appear to be non-singers may be experiencing such a drastic physical change that they cannot control pitches. Such students need to learn to use their singing voices before they will be ready to sing tonal patterns in the learning sequence activities. Mis-labeling the music aptitude of students can be avoided by administering the Musical Aptitude Profile (MAP), which was cited earlier in relation to rhythm aptitude.

Exploration of the phenomenon of the voice can take any of several forms. The class could view and discuss a "voice print" and its uses as a means of identification of the individual (Palmer, 1974, p. 37-38). An oscilloscope might be borrowed from the science department so that students can see the sound waves produced when they deliver various vowel sounds, noises, and pitches into a microphone. If no oscilloscope is available, students can tape record their voices and re-play them for analysis and discussion.

Few students, including those who sing, will have developed a wide range of vocal sounds by the time that they are in middle school. Improvisation games and chants might be used as a means of exploring voice range and quality. Following is a list of examples.

1. Use a subject such as "winter" or "darkness" to stimulate the building of a vocal vocabulary that includes a variety of pitches, timbres, and durations. Use those sounds to create a sound piece, complete with silences and solos (Gordon and Woods, 1985, Activity Card 321: Paynter and Aston, 1970, p. 157).
2. Play and discuss the singing of Bobby McFerrin, jazz vocalist, using his album "Spontaneous Inventions."
3. Listen to and discuss recordings of avant-garde choral music.
4. "Pass" vocal sounds around the room or circle as quickly as possible by having each person improvise one sound (Gordon and Woods, 1985, Activity Cards 1457/1458).
5. Alter vocal sounds through tape manipulation as part of a music concrete composition.
6. Create an aleatory composition by numbering vocal sounds to be performed by chance methods.
7. Improvise in unison vocal sounds that depict specific feelings or ranges of feelings such as "deep and sad" or "agony to laughter" (Schafer, 1967, p. 18).
8. Respond vocally in unison to graphic notation invented by class members.

9. Chant poetry, rhymes, runes, and incantations.
   a. Listen to and talk about contemporary street chanting or "rapping," and give students an opportunity to compare raps. "Vista," (Gordon and Woods, 1985, 4A, pp. 74-75) is a chant familiar to many students.
   b. Create a talking blues, and perform it for the class with vocal inflection.
   c. Play and discuss a tape or video of black work-songs and chants.
   d. Read aloud from contemporary poems such as "Street Cleaner's Lament," (Marsh, Rinehart, & Savage, 1980, p. 20) or the poems of Shel Silverstein.
   e. Create speech ensembles and have them perform famous sayings, poems or speeches (Nash, 1972).

Learning Sequence Activities: Tonal

When students are no longer in tonal babble they can begin tonal learning sequence activities. Tonal learning sequence activities involve, among other things, the singing of tonal patterns in solo and in ensemble. The hurdle of having middle school students sing alone can be overcome with patience, understanding, and a few "tricks of the trade." Students in middle school who have had little experience with solo singing in the classroom, or who view general music class as a waste of time, will often refuse to try the solo patterns. The teacher must gain the trust and respect of those students before using learning sequence activities. That can be accomplished during the readiness activities cited in the preceding section.

If students are still reticent to sing despite their experiences with readiness activities, there are gimmicks that the teacher can employ to encourage participation. For example, students who are hesitant to sing alone might be willing to hum into a home-made or dime store kazoo. Another useful device is the audio pipe, a plastic tube with a funnel-like end that can be used to link two persons in a relatively private singing/listening partnership. A student can sing into the funnel end while another student or the teacher listens at the opposite end.

Singing class patterns as vocal warm-ups for a few weeks will establish a routine. When the high aptitude students seem confident, the teacher can ask one of them to sing a solo pattern. A correct response from that student will assure others that success is possible. The teacher should always allow a student to indicate reluctance or refusal to sing in solo. That student should be given the opportunity to sing patterns with the teacher and with high aptitude partners. Also, a "singing buddy" might accompany the reluctant singer to a private session with the teacher. A cassette tape, prepared with tonal patterns and a space for echoing those patterns could be used in a practice room or at home.

The use of tonal learning sequence activities with middle school boys and girls presents vocal problems that the elementary general music teacher does not encounter. The keyality of the tonal patterns should be transposed to accommodate the different voice ranges. The keyality of B is suitable for baritones, the keyality of F is suitable for most changing voices, and the keyality of D or E is suitable for treble voices. Once the keyality has been transposed, only students who use that keyality should be asked to sing in solo for a period of time, perhaps for the rest of that class period. For example, only the students with changing or changed voices might be asked to sing in solo on a particular day. (Some students with changing voices will be able to echo the patterns an octave below the rest of the class.) Even though the range will not be ideal, all students might be invited to sing class patterns in all keyalities so that everyone audiates and remains attentive throughout all tonal learning sequence activities. Strong singers and high tonal aptitude students should be seated next to students whose voices are changing to prevent other students from becoming confused when hearing the lower pitches.

The teacher must always establish the tonality and keyality of tonal patterns before they are echoed. The teacher should use a neutral syllable, such as "bum" or "loo," to establish tonality and to sing the patterns.[6] At first the teacher should echo the pattern with the student for teaching purposes. After students have echoed correctly with the teacher they should be asked to sing the pattern in solo for evaluation purposes. The teacher should wait for approximately eighty percent of the students to respond correctly to their assigned patterns before moving on to the next criterion in the section.

Oftentimes closing one ear allows a singer to hear his own voice in a new way, helping his pitch-matching. If a particular tonality is troublesome for more than a few students, the teacher should have students sing rote songs in that tonality. As with rhythm patterns, other recommendations related to the delivery of tonal patterns during tonal learning sequence activities - including the teaching of symbolic association - can be found within this book in the two articles written by Robert Harper.

Classroom Activities: Rhythm

Rhythm games help children to develop coordination, audiation, beat competency, and musicianship. Quick reaction games can be found in Rhythm Games for Perception and Cognition (Abramson, 1973) and in Rhythm and Movement (Findlay, 1971). Each student may be given a ball to bounce into a hoop, to a partner, or against a wall while the teacher chants, using a neutral syllable, or plays an instrument. The students may be helped to synchronize the bounce of the ball with the macro beat if they chant the neutral syllable on the beat or if the teacher employs Weikart's (1982) four-step language process (pp. 15-19).[7] Singing or chanting words while handling a ball or performing body movements may confuse students. Other games using a ball may include passing the ball around a circle to either audible beats, silent beats, or an alternation of the two. For variation, the passing of the ball could be stopped during the silent beats, the direction of the ball-passing could be changed upon a signal, a different meter could be used, or a different number of audible and silent beats could be designated.

The creative teacher can invent many other variations using the Dalcroze movement games, the pre-dance activities by Weikart (1982), and the activity cards from Jump Right In: The Music Curriculum (Gordon and Woods, 1985). Additional activities for developing coordination may include the bean bag toss, jumping over a bean bag, scarf juggling, the balloon toss, pulling stretch fabric scarves, and circle games using elastic loops.

Following are additional games that are appropriate for middle school students.

1. Use a chance or aleatory device, such as a large cube or "Wheel of Fortune" spinner, to determine the sequence for a series of rhythmic movements (Gordon and Woods, 1985, Activity Card 294).
2. "Pass the beat" from student to student through a side clap, a hand squeeze, or a jump.
3. Walk to the macro beats, using the lower register of the piano as a rhythmic model and pat to micro beats, using the upper register of the piano as a rhythmic model.

4. Assign one group of students the task of performing the macro beat and another group the task of performing the micro beat, each group performing only when its type of beat is heard.
5. Tap or pass a block or stone on the floor to the beat when it is audible, and remain silent when the beat is inaudible.
6. Flash a flashlight to the beat against a wall in a darkened classroom.
7. Play small percussion instruments that have been placed on chairs in a circle on silent beats and walk to the sound of another instrument on audible beats.

After the students have chanted rhythm patterns in learning sequence activities, they can use those patterns in a variety of games and other musical situations. The following are examples.

1. The teacher or a student leader can "call" (dictate) patterns and the group can echo those patterns as they walk the conga line.
2. Students can "pass" patterns around a circle, following the teacher's guideline for dynamics, form, or another element of musical performance.
3. Students can bounce or pass a ball as they chant patterns. A signal may be given by the teacher for students to reverse the direction of the ball.
4. Each student can extend patterns performed by the teacher or by other students by adding two macro beats up to a total of eight.
5. Each student can choose a partner and play a question and answer game with that partner. The first student can chant the pattern and the second student can answer by performing the pattern with a different inflection.
6. The students can use rhythm patterns and movement in canon.
7. The student can use rhythm patterns as ostinati when playing instruments or creating tape loops. The teacher and student first should chant the pattern within the context of the meter and tempo. Then the students should be taught how to manipulate the instrument and should be given time to explore the instrument before being asked to transfer specific patterns to the instrument.
8. Students can perform in classroom instrumental ensembles, one group playing macro beats, another group playing micro beats, and a third group playing an ostinato. Those classroom performances can be taped so that the students can learn not only

from creating and performing, but also from watching and listening to the tapes of their performances.

When students have acquired a vocabulary of movements with which they feel fairly comfortable, the teacher can expect them to create movement pieces. Creative movement in the general music classroom can be based upon a variety of sources, including poetry, musical form, electronic compositions, and program music. Contemporary poetry can be found that generates movement images and that appeals to middle school students. The poetry should be chanted while it is accompanied by instruments and movement.

To create a movement piece based upon musical form, students may work in cooperative learning groups. A cooperative learning group consists of a leader, an encourager, a recorder, a reporter, and a materials-gatherer. If the composition upon which the movement piece is to be based is familiar to the students, the teacher should lead a general discussion about tempo, style, and form that focuses on how the body might be used to communicate those elements. The students might make a list of locomotor and non-locomotor movements that would be helpful. The wearing of simple costumes can be visually pleasing. For further variety, the students can create shadow pieces in which they move between a light and a sheet hung across part of the room. The room should be darkened so that the viewers see a shadow image of the students who are moving.

Weikart (1982) believes that rhythmic competency and basic comfort with movement must precede sequenced movement such as dance. She states, "Beginners are beginners at any age when it comes to rhythmic movement. And all beginners need to develop similar basic competencies in order to be successful with more complicated rhythmic activities" (p. 5). Because students have difficulty decoding visual clues and mirroring movement, the most successful dances are those that are group-oriented and that allow some flexibility and freedom of form. To be avoided at first are the formation of a circle, hand-holding, and insistence upon "right" and "left" movements. Dances such as the "Birdie Dance" and the "Bunny Hop" allow everyone to try the movements without pressure to conform. The teacher may find it necessary to choreograph sequences when the original folk dances are too difficult.

Classroom Activities: Tonal

Teaching singing in the middle school is complicated by the diversity of adolescent voices. Boys whose voices are unchanged feel socially pressured not to sing "like a girl." A typical configuration of voice ranges for middle school boys is shown in the graph in Figure 1 (Swanson, 1973, p. 186, Fig. 13-2). That diversity of voice range combined with the social dynamics of adolescence will have a devastating effect on the quality of singing and on overall classroom progress in the general music class unless the teacher finds ways to neutralize those problems.

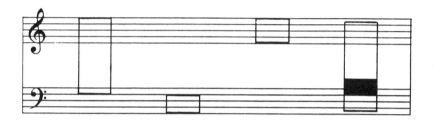

Figure 1. Diversity of Voice Ranges Among Middle School Boys

Many music educators would probably agree with Swanson (1973) that a boys' class should be scheduled separately, at least for a time, to allow for private discussion about the voice change and vocal experimentation without embarrassment in front of the girls (p. 195). That type of class may be more crucial in grades eight and nine that in the earlier years. If mixed classes are unavoidable, Marple (1975) believes that they "are only successful if the major characteristics [social and personality] of the boy are considered since the girl will be moving toward those characteristics as she matures" (p. 192).

Song literature for classroom singing in the middle school and junior high school should be suited to the students' maturity and to their vocal needs. Folk songs may appeal to students in grades six and seven and will be accepted by the older students who are interested in the revival of pop-folk artists such as Bob Dylan and Simon and Garfunkel. Songs in all tonalities should be used. Popular songs in various tonalities include, "Hard Day's Night" (mixolydian) by the Beatles, "The Sound of Silence" (minor) by Simon and Garfunkel, "Yesterday" and "Eleanor Rigby" (multi-tonal) by the Beatles, and "Love Me Tender" (multi-tonal) by Elvis Presley (Gordon and Woods, 1985). Songs from the Slavic and Yiddish cultures and folk songs of the British Isles and Appalachia also encompass a wide variety of tonalities. The voice graph in Figure 1 indicates that the range of a fifth between B and F in either octave may be an acceptable range for most voices. Ostinati to accompany those songs can be created. The teacher should be careful to keep both songs and ostinati within the voice ranges of the students.

Vocal chording as an accompaniment for rounds, canons, and songs requiring only tonic and dominant harmonies, can be sung by students using tonal syllables if those students are at the verbal association level of learning. For example, for the round, "Make New Friends," one group can sing "do ti do," a second group can sing "mi fa mi," a third group can sing "so so so," and a fourth group can sing the melody. For one-chord songs, several groups can perform a rhythm pattern, each on a different pitch of the tonic triad, while another group performs the melody of the song.

Conclusion

As a result of audiating, moving to music in a variety of meters, chanting rhythm patterns, singing songs in a variety of tonalities, and singing tonal patterns, students will acquire a thinking vocabulary that will allow them to make sense of music. When those skills are applied to the listening lessons, songs, dances, and compositions that have always been a part of the general music curriculum, those experiences will take on new meaning for both teacher and student.

NOTES

[1] Within this book, see "Informal Music Instruction as Readiness for Learning Sequence Activities" for more information about music babble.

[2] For a more complete explanation of the term "beat competency," refer to Teaching Movement and Dance (Weikart 1982).

[3] Within this book, see "Rhythm Learning Sequence" for more information.

[4]Within this book, see "The Measurement and Evaluation of Music Aptitudes and Achievement" for more information.

[5]Within this book, see "Coordinating Learning Sequence Activities and Classroom Activities" for more information.

[6]Within this book, see "Teaching a Rote Song" for more information about establishing tonality and meter through the use of preparatory sequences.

[7]The students first say the movement words, then say and do the movements, next whisper and do, and finally think and do.

REFERENCES

Abramson, R. M. (1973). Rhythm Games for Perception and Cognition. Miami, FL: Columbia Pictures Publications.

Bennett, P. (1986, September). "A Responsibility to Young Voices". Music Educators Journal, pp. 34-38.

Crook, E., B. Reimer, & D. S. Walker (1985). Silver Burdett Music. Morristown, NJ: Silver Burdett Company.

Findlay, E. (1971). Rhythm and Movement. Princeton, NJ: Summy-Birchard.

Gordon, Edwin E., & David G. Woods (1985). Jump Right In: The Music Curriculum. Chicago: G.I.A. Publications, Inc.

Marple, H. D. (1975). Backgrounds and Approaches to Junior High Music. Dubuque, IA: Wm. C. Brown Company.

Marsh, M. V., C. A. Rinehart, & E. J. Savage (1980). Music U.S.A. New York: Macmillan.

Nash, G. C. (1966). Music with Children: Rhythmic Speech Ensembles. LaGrange, IL: Kitching Educational.

Nichol, Doug (1978). A Nichol's Worth. Buffalo: Tometic Associates Ltd.

Palmer, M. (1974). Sound Exploration and Discovery. New York: The Center for Applied Research in Education.

Paynter, J., & P. Aston (1970). Sound and Silence. London: Cambridge University Press.

Schafer, R. M. (1967). Ear Cleaning. Scarborough, Ontario: Berandol Music Ltd.

Swanson, F. F. (1973). Music teaching in the Junior High and Middle School. New York: Appleton-Century-Crofts.

Weikart, P. S. (1982). Teaching Movement and Dance. Ypsilanti, MI: High/Scope Press.

Weikart, P. S. (1987). Round the Circle. Ypsilanti, MI: High/Scope Press.

MUSIC LEARNING THEORY APPLIED TO CHORAL MUSIC PERFORMING GROUPS

James M. Jordan

Introduction

The application of Music Learning Theory to a choral program adds depth by providing the conductor/teacher with music learning feedback from his students. That feedback allows the conductor/teacher to make more efficient use of rehearsal time by creating an effective teaching/learning process. This article contains suggestions for the use of Music Learning Theory in all aspects of the choral program. Of course individual teaching style will affect the applicability of some suggestions, and no one should try to implement too many new ideas at once, but by implementing a few of the more comfortable suggestions at first and gradually adding others, teachers will soon find Music Learning Theory to be a vital part of their choral curriculum.

K-4 Choral Performance

It is difficult to justify the existence of choral performance groups at the K-4 grade level. The major thrust of the school music program K-4 should be the maintenance of developmental music aptitude through efficient classroom teaching. Too often, the general music classroom degenerates into another chance for the music teacher to prepare for the upcoming school performance program at the expense of structured and sequential music learning experiences that could have a lifelong impact upon a child's stabilized music aptitude. For that reason, it is recommended that choral performance groups be started at grade 5, at which time music aptitude levels stabilize.

Informal Instruction: Tonal and Rhythm

The value of informal tonal and rhythm instruction for choral ensembles cannot be overemphasized.[1] A sense of resting tone and a sense of consistent tempo are crucial to the development of ensemble skills, whether for the high school select chamber choir or for the fifth grade unauditioned choir. In short, the musical growth of any ensemble will take place more rapidly if a foundation for music learning is built upon informal instruction. For example, an ensemble plagued by intonation problems may need informal tonal instruction, e.g., establishment of the audiation of a resting tone,[2] and an ensemble that cannot maintain a consistent tempo may need informal rhythm instruction, e.g., based upon Laban/Dalcroze movement activities to establish audiation of the macro beat and micro beat. The conductor/teacher should be aware that ensembles can become especially adept at echoic response, by which means they can echo an entire work without being able to audiate a single aspect. The results of that approach to performance are questionable intonation, a lack of consistent tempo, and a general lack of musical sensitivity. Teachers using Music Learning Theory in some form in the choral setting have found informal tonal and rhythm instruction to be critically important to music learning and to music performance.

Even after a choir has stabilized in terms of intonation and consistency of tempo, informal instruction techniques must be reapplied occasionally to refresh veteran singers and to prepare new singers to participate at an acceptable level. It is not uncommon for choral directors to recruit singers "out of the halls," the recruitment being based solely upon the student's vocal timbre and desire to sing. One of the strengths of Music Learning Theory is that it provides a means for teaching music skill. Before beginning to learn music formally, each student should be able to maintain a consistent tempo and reproduce a resting tone in a given tonality (Jordan, 1987). Choral music can be rehearsed concurrent to informal instruction, but the teacher is cautioned to select materials that are in familiar tonalities and meters.

Teaching to Individual Differences

Teaching to the individual music differences of students in a choral ensemble can have a profound effect upon the choral curriculum. Choral directors who conduct ensembles without knowing the individual potential of their singers may unknowingly frustrate low and average aptitude students, and may frequently bore high aptitude students. Discipline problems within a rehearsal are often caused by those elements of frustration and boredom. Both high aptitude students and low aptitude students are likely to leave the program. In contrast, the conductor, with music aptitude information in hand, can teach to the specific abilities of average and low students while continually challenging high aptitude students. He will no longer inadvertently ask students to sing in solo during rehearsal using materials that are inappropriate to their abilities.

In order to teach to individual musical differences, the teacher should administer a standardized measure of music aptitude that yields a tonal score and a rhythm score. For students in grades K-4, the Primary Measures of Music Audiation (PMMA) or the Intermediate Measures of Music Audiation (IMMA), measures of developmental music aptitude by Gordon, are recommended. For students in grades 4-12, the Musical Aptitude Profile (MAP), a measure of stabilized music aptitude authored by Gordon (1988/1965), is recommended.[3]

Use of Aptitude Scores for Working with the Changing Voice and the "Non-singer"

Working with the changing voice problems of male students is difficult at best. Many teachers assume that because a male student is having difficulty "matching pitch" he is not "musical." That is not always the case. It is possible that a student who can not match pitch has a high tonal music aptitude, but is unable to physically control his vocal mechanism. A teacher would handle the changing voice problem differently if he knew that he was working with a student who has a high tonal aptitude. Many young men having high music aptitude choose not to continue singing in their high school choirs because they know that they are not able to match pitch and may believe that they are "tone deaf." Those students do not know that their tone-matching deficiencies stem from a repairable vocal technique problem, and not from a problem with their audiation. The teacher can offer appropriate encouragement and persistent instruction to the young male student with a changing voice if that teacher is equipped with the objective information that a valid aptitude test provides.

The problem of the "non-singer" is similar to the problem of the changing male voice, in that teachers commonly misdiagnose physiological problems as musical problems. Many conductor/teachers continue to classify students as "non-singers" without having given themselves the benefit of knowing aptitude scores. The labeling of a student as a "non-singer" based upon opinion rather than aptitude scores could be considered malpractice in choral music education.

I have yet to discover a "non-singer!" All students can learn to sing at least at a level that is commensurate with their tonal aptitude. Most who are classified as "non-singers" are high or average aptitude students who have severe vocal technique problems. Those students, unaided by a knowledgeable teacher of vocal technique, continually compound their problem because they have the aptitude to know that they are not matching pitch. They often resort to improper vocal technique in an attempt to administer music first aid to themselves. If the teacher were armed with aptitude scores, he could tailor vocal instruction to focus upon a balance between the technical needs and the musical needs of the student, rather than confounding problems of technique with problems of audiation.

Use of Aptitude Scores for Seating Arrangements

Using music aptitude scores as a basis, the choral conductor can develop seating plans that will facilitate the music learning process. For example, when a new work is being introduced, the teacher should distribute students having high tonal aptitude throughout the ensemble to assist in the learning process. If a work is rhythmically complex, the teacher should distribute students having high rhythm aptitude throughout the choir. It is helpful also to know the tonal aptitudes of students when devising seating arrangements for a section. Students having a high tonal aptitude, distributed throughout a section, can help maintain pitch within the section and within the choir. In many instances, severe intonation problems can be eliminated by strategically seating students who have high tonal aptitude within a section. Knowledge of aptitude scores also makes possible a thumbnail sketch of each section. For example, if the average tonal aptitude score within a tenor section is low, the teacher will be forewarned that considerable instructional time may need to be spent with that section. Conversely, if the average tonal aptitude score within that section is high, the teacher should not tolerate pitch problems that are simply a result of a lack of attention or poor musicianship.

Use of Aptitude Scores for Selection of Appropriate Literature

The selection of appropriate choral literature for performance is difficult. While conductor/teachers take many factors into consideration, usually the music aptitude of the ensemble is either ignored or is considered subjectively. In the latter case, the conductor's opinion of the aptitude level of his group usually either masks the musical potential of the group with literature that is too simplistic, or frustrates the students with the literature that is beyond their musical means.

While the vocal technique required to perform a specific piece of music is certainly one criterion to be considered in choosing literature, it is safe to assume that if the members of a choir can audiate a piece of music, they probably will be able to execute that piece of music if given proper vocal instruction. Conversely, a choir whose members do not have the aptitude to audiate a given piece of music can never be taught enough technique to sing the piece well. When audiation and technique are pedagogically confounded, a group is prohibited from achieving outstanding performance. The quality of a music performance, in terms of both vocal technique and musicianship, is directly related to audiation, and audiation is directly related to aptitude.[4]

Use of Aptitude Scores for Grading

It may be possible for the teacher of a large ensemble to schedule individual times in which to hear each student perform in solo the patterns from the tonal and rhythm units that were taught in rehearsal. Students should be graded idiographically, i.e., in relation to their own aptitude. Students are enthusiastic about such a grading procedure, because it allays the fear that they will be graded in comparison to the "star" of the choir. By teaching to individual differences and grading idiographically, the teacher can help every student to feel that he is being challenged, taught well, and graded fairly. Frustration with music learning is nearly eliminated, and a wonderful atmosphere for music making is created.

Audiation, Breath Technique, and Artistic Choral Phrasing

Audiation and its relationship to musical phrasing is a fascinating topic. We can speak to friends for hours on end without ever thinking about where or how to breathe. Looking at the other side of the coin, why must we have breath marks in our vocal or instrumental music notation? Why did Hemingway not include breath marks in his texts to help the reader? While punctuation marks in literature do indicate some appropriate places to pause, we do not teach a course in elementary school entitled "breathing after periods."

Consider the following. Recite the lyrics of "My Country 'tis of Thee." Where did you breathe? Were you conscious of the need to breathe in specific places? Probably not. Why? The answer to that question, I believe, is crucial to artistic choral singing.

The reason that you do not recall the points at which you breathed is that the passage was familiar to you. The words were familiar, as was their order and their meaning. Breaths occurred as naturally as did the words. The process might be called "natural recitation," or "natural reading," depending upon whether you spoke from recall or from the printed page. Because you audiated the language, you were able to phrase naturally.

Consider the application of the same natural principles to choral performance. Is it possible that phrasing is unnatural for most singers because they simply cannot audiate the music that they are performing? All the breathing technique in the world is useless to a singer who cannot audiate.

The issue of phrasing is too complex to be covered thoroughly within this chapter. To summarize, if students do not have a thorough understanding of the materials they are singing - tonally, rhythmically, and harmonically at the very least - all the breathing technique and instruction in the world will not permit natural phrasing. One must be able to audiate in order to phrase. Natural choral phrasing is the natural by-product of audiation.

The Development of Choral Sight-Reading according to Music Learning Theory: Sound before Sight

Perhaps no other comprehensive objective is shared by so many choral music educators as is the objective of teaching students to "sight-read." While many choral programs use several methods and techniques to teach sight-reading with varying degrees of success, we must consider whether there is an approach to sight-reading that will be both more effective and more efficient. Music Learning Theory offers an efficient process for teaching sight-reading skills.

Like language, music has five vocabularies: hearing, speaking, reading, writing, and thinking. For a person to read and write a language, he needs to have hearing, speaking and thinking vocabularies in that language. The same is necessary for a person to be able to read and write music. Why then, do so many music educators stress the reading and writing of music before helping students to acquire hearing, speaking, and thinking vocabularies in music? It is actually more important for the members of a choral ensemble to have a hearing and speaking music vocabulary than for them to have a reading music vocabulary. The ability to read music is a by-product of an approach that efficiently teaches hearing, speaking, and thinking music vocabularies, in that order. Music Learning Theory is such an approach.

It may be important to examine the fact that "sight-reading" is a flawed term. Do we "sight-read" language? That is, do we read novels in which every word is unfamiliar to us? Of course not. While reading a novel, we come across occasional unfamiliar words embedded in the context of many familiar words. Because we have learned language efficiently, i.e., we have acquired hearing, speaking, and thinking vocabularies, we can infer the meaning of the unfamiliar word from its relationship to the familiar words. Just as "sight-reading" does not exist in language reading, it should not be expected to exist in music reading. If students have acquired the appropriate readiness vocabularies in music via Music Learning Theory activities, the process for reading music can be expected to be similar to the process for reading language. That process might be most accurately described as "sight-recall." Music Learning Theory can be applied to the development of sight-recall skills in members of a choir. The use of learning sequence activities materials from Jump Right In: The Music Curriculum is the most obvious and effective means of developing a tonal and rhythm pattern vocabulary, i.e., of providing the necessary readiness for sight-recall.

Use of the Tonal and Rhythm Register Books from Jump Right In: The Music Curriculum

The procedures for using the tonal and rhythm register books of <u>Jump Right In</u> have been described in detail in the publisher's materials.[5] The choral director should take five to ten minutes at the beginning of each choral rehearsal to teach tonal patterns by the use of those materials. While a great amount of calendar time will be needed to teach the tonal and rhythm units in a large ensemble, the material will be well-taught and the time well-spent. The tonal and rhythm register books can be used as designed for small ensembles, but record keeping poses some organizational obstacles if the ensemble is large. The teacher may choose to use the tonal and rhythm register books as they are designed, regardless of the size of the ensemble, or he may make adaptations. For larger ensembles, I have designed a large record sheet that resembles the right side of the register book and contains approximately 70 spaces for student names. That sheet can be mounted on a clipboard for use in rehearsals, but a more efficient approach is to pre-select the students to be heard in solo before rehearsal and prepare a "mini-register" for each of those students. The mini-registers can be printed on index cards, brought to rehearsal, used to record achievement, and deposited into a box. Later, the records of achievement can be transferred to the master register. A sample of the "mini-register" that I use is shown in figure 1.

Name_____

Date_____

Tonal Unit_____ Rhythm Unit_____

Criterion_____

Patterns Correct:

     E   M   D

_____   _____   _____

Figure 1: Mini-Register for use in large ensembles

Sight-Recall: Developing and Encouraging the Music Hearing and Music Speaking Vocabularies of Members of Choral Ensembles

It is important to support the Music Learning Theory teaching from Jump Right In by applying a sight-recall procedure to the rehearsing of choral literature. Specific recommendations follow. Adherence to those recommendations will dramatically raise the performance level of an ensemble, regardless of the amount of supplemental learning sequence material taught, e.g., material from the Jump Right In tonal and rhythm register books.

1. Use a neutral syllable for rehearsal. When a new work is first rehearsed, the objectives of the teacher should be an accurate and musical learning of the music and an open, free, singing style. Both can be accomplished by having students use a neutral syllable in place of the text. By using a neutral syllable, students enjoy three advantages: they work at the aural/oral level of skill learning, which is basic,[6] they are more focused on music elements than they would be if they were associating music with text, and they can use a syllable that facilitates good vocalization. While vocal pedagogues differ about which vowels should be used, vowels should be chosen that keep the voicebox low and relatively free. My preference is for "doo," "dun," and "dah," with special cautions concerning the latter. Voiced consonants should be used for works with a legato style. Only if vocal technique is correct will the teacher be free to conclude that poor intonation is a result of poor audiation, and he must be able to draw that conclusion in order to spend rehearsal time efficiently.[7]

2. Delay combining the text with the music until proper vowel modifications have been taught to the choir. After using a neutral syllable to rehearse a work in its initial stages, for the reasons cited above, the director should modify the vowel sounds associated with that syllable to reflect the vowel sounds that will be necessary when the text is added.[8]

3. Delay combining the text with the music until all musical elements of the work are mastered, i.e., correct pitches and rhythms, good tone quality with necessary vowel modifications, and appropriate style. All melodic and rhythmic aspects of the score, in addition to phrasings, vocal technique,

intonation, and consistent tempo, should be taught using a neutral syllable (Jordan, 1987). The addition of text before those elements are learned retards the development of music skills within an ensemble.

4. Rehearse at a soft dynamic level when initially learning a work. While intonation may suffer temporarily, rehearsing at a soft dynamic level allows the student to audiate more accurately not only individual parts, but the relationship of individual parts to other parts and to the whole. Ideally, the soft-dynamic level technique should be used throughout the introductory teaching of each unfamiliar work. Thereafter full voice should be used so that intonation problems are limited to problems of audiation.

5. Return to the soft dynamic level and the use of a neutral syllable as needed. It is wise to return to the soft dynamic level and the use of a neutral syllable when problems are encountered at any stage of the rehearsal process. In essence, that takes the choir back to the aural/oral level of learning, and allows the students to hear the problems more accurately within their section and the ensemble. If the problem remains unsolved, the teacher must return to appropriate informal rhythm or tonal instruction.

6. Focus teaching upon the vocal technique requirements of the work. While familiarizing a choir with a choral work, the teacher must identify clearly the sequential vocal techniques that need to be applied in order to allow the audiation of the students to be demonstrated. Specific vocal techniques explained in Ehmann and Haasemann (1982) and Haasemann and Jordan (1989) include diaphragmatic activity, support, support for legato, support for martellato, resonance, register consistency, staccato, legato, martellato, vowel modification, range extension, idiomatic problems among voice type, approach to the lift or break in each voice, crescendo, decrescendo, leaps, and appropriate choral sound for each music style period.

7. Rehearse each part individually to teach idiomatic vocal technique and phrasing. Each part in each piece of choral music contains problems unique to that voice type, and more specifically to the shape and execution of that line. Until a student has an understanding of the vocal/technical and musical demands of his line, he cannot produce an accurate vocal representation of what he audiates.

8. <u>Make sure that ensemble members can hum the resting tone and move to the macro beats and micro beats of the section of the work being rehearsed</u>. The teacher should establish the tonality and meter of a work or sections of a work to be rehearsed. In a given rehearsal, it is preferable initially to rehearse works of related tonalities and meters.

9. <u>Be tolerant if some students do not look at their scores; have the students write vocal technique suggestions in their scores</u>. The extent to which a student looks at his score will tend to be directly related to that student's music achievement. A student whose level of music achievement is low will avoid looking at his score much of the time, because to look would inhibit and confuse him in terms of audiation and music learning. That is, for the student to look at music notation while trying to initially audiate a new pattern or series of patterns, will keep him from learning. The tolerant teacher will find that each student uses the score as he deems appropriate. That is, after the student has audiated a given segment of music, he will look to see how that music appears in notation. In effect, the student is instinctively aligning his own learning experience with good skill learning sequence. As a result, he will be able to bring meaning to the notation rather than have to struggle to take meaning from it, as is often necessary when notation is used prematurely. In the initial stages of music learning, the teacher can enhance the value of the score to the student by asking the student to mark the score with vocal technique information.

10. <u>Hear students sing their choral music in solo, using a neutral syllable, preferably in private</u>. The teacher should meet with students individually at least once each semester, and perhaps more, to hear each student perform in solo the tonal patterns and rhythm patterns that have been taught at the beginning of rehearsals. During those sessions the teacher should also assess each student's progress in relation to vocal techniques and musicianship. Accurate records should be kept of each session by the teacher. Only through solo testing can the teacher be assured that the student is mastering the materials presented at a level commensurate with his music aptitude.

Imbedding Tonal Pattern and Rhythm Pattern Learning within Vocalises

Most choral conductors rely on the use of vocalises to teach various aspects of vocal technique to their ensembles.[9]   Some choral conductors then devote another portion of the rehearsal to the teaching of music reading. Those comprehensive objectives can be achieved simultaneously through the application of principles of Music Learning Theory. The tonal and rhythm content of the units of the Jump Right In curriculum, designed to develop audiation skill, can be introduced and taught as vocalises. Because young singers will be unable to sing what they audiate unless they have an understanding of basic vocal technique, the teacher needs to teach simultaneously the use of the diaphragm, the execution of the other aspects of vocal technique, staccato, legato, martellato, range extension, and vowel modification. The teaching of vocal technique helps audiation skill to be realized in practice, and vocal technique and audiation together give the student the readiness for reading notation.

Choral Curriculum Design Based Upon Music Learning Theory

Music Learning Theory provides the opportunity for a unique approach to choral curriculum design. Instead of organizing a choral curriculum based upon style characteristics and textures, the teacher can now organize curriculum around tonalities, meters, and vocal technique objectives. The classification of various tonalities (major, minor, dorian, etc.) and meters (duple, triple, combined, unusual paired, etc.) can be found in the Gordon taxonomies (Gordon, 1988, pp. 91 and 155). The vocal technique objectives can be based upon the work of Ehmann and Haasemann (1982) or the handbook by Haasemann and Jordan (1989). Finally, the teacher should collect and categorize choral literature that represents a cross-section of tonalities and meters, and that is appropriate for the level of technical instruction. Classroom activities (vocalises and choral literature) should be used to introduce new music content to members of the choral ensemble. That content should then be specifically taught at sequential skill levels through the use of Jump Right In materials (learning sequence activities), and all that is taught in learning sequence activities should be reinforced through more advanced work with the choral literature.[10] Choral literature should be selected for the curriculum upon the basis of vocal principles that it will help to impart and musical experiences that it will help to provide, not because of the music content that the teacher believes it will help to teach. Choral literature then assumes its proper role in the school curriculum.

Summary

When applying Music Learning Theory to the choral performing organization, the conductor/teacher should consider the following. (a) The teacher should measure each student's tonal and rhythm aptitude in order to use those scores for the purpose of teaching to the students' individual music differences. (b) Tonal learning sequence activities and rhythm learning sequence activities should be taught in the first five to ten minutes of the choral rehearsal, regardless of the size of the ensemble. (c) Vocal technique should be taught simultaneous to learning sequence activities, using tonal and rhythm content from the learning sequence activities. (d) Choral literature should be categorized and indexed according to its content (tonality, meter, etc.). (e) Choral literature should be used to introduce and to reinforce tonal and rhythm concepts taught in the learning sequence activities portion of the class. (f) Performance materials for the ensemble should be selected upon the basis of technical and music difficulty. (g) The teacher should meet with each student individually to measure progress toward vocal technique objectives and audiation skill objectives. (h) Grading should be determined idiographically, meaning that each student should be graded according to his achievement in relation to his music aptitude.

NOTES

[1]Within this book, see "Informal Music Instruction as Readiness for Learning Sequence Activities" for more information about informal instruction.

[2]Within this book, see "Audiation: The Term and the Process" for more information about audiation.

[3]Within this book, see "The Measurement and Evaluation of Music Aptitudes and Achievement" for more information.

[4]Both the teaching of audiation and the teaching of group vocal technique must be taken into consideration when constructing a choral curriculum. For comprehensive and sequential vocal technique objectives in addition to techniques of teaching vocal technique to choirs, the reader is referred to <u>Group Vocal Technique: A Video</u>, by Frauke Haasemann and James Jordan.

[5]Some of the publisher's materials are complimentary, and available upon request. Several articles within this book also offer guidance for the use of <u>Jump Right In</u> materials.

[6]Within this book, see "Skill Learning Sequence" for more information.

[7]Because of the importance of correct vocalization to teacher feedback, it is important that the teacher know techniques for avoiding undesirable chest register qualities in young singers, and for providing those singers with vowel modifications appropriate to the male and female voice in the middle and upper register. Further, caution should be used when the "ah" vowel is sung by amateur singers. The reader is referred to <u>Voice Building for Choirs</u>, by Ehmann and Haasemann and to <u>Group Vocal Technique: A Video</u>, by Haasemann and Jordan.

[8]The teaching of proper vowel modifications to the choir is of the utmost importance if good intonation is desired. Most choral intonation problems are not a result of poor audiation, but are, instead, the result of a lack of vowel modification that should be taught to the choir. Further, many choral directors teach vowel modifications, but teach the same modifications to the men as they do to the women. Vowel modifications are different for male and female voice types. For further information concerning vowel modification, see <u>Voice Building for Choirs</u>, by Ehmann and Haasemann, and <u>Group Vocal Technique: A Video</u>, by Haasemann and Jordan.

[9]Frauke Haasemann and Wilhelm Ehmann advocate the use of carefully designed group vocalises within the choral rehearsal. The reader is referred to the works by Ehmann and Haasemann and by Haasemann and Jordan for more detailed explanations.

[10]Within this book, see "Coordinating Learning Sequence Activities and Classroom Activities" for further information.

REFERENCES

Ehmann, Wilhelm and Frauke Haasemann (1982). Voice Building for
    Choirs. Chapel Hill: Hinshaw Music, Inc.
Gordon, Edwin. (1982). Intermediate Measures of Music Audiation.
    Chicago: G.I.A. Publications Inc.
Gordon, Edwin E. (1988). Learning Sequences in Music. Chicago: G.I.A.
    Publications, Inc.
Gordon, Edwin. (1988). Musical Aptitude Profile. Boston: Houghton-
    Mifflin.
Gordon, Edwin. (1979). Primary Measures of Music Audiation. Chicago:
    G.I.A. Publications Inc.
Haasemann, Frauke and James M. Jordan (1989). Group Vocal Technique
    for Choirs: An Instructional Video. Chapel Hill: Hinshaw Music, Inc.
Haasemann, Frauke and James M. Jordan (In Preparation). Group Vocal
    Technique for Choirs: the Vocalise Cards.
Jordan, James M. (1981). "Audiation and sequencing: an approach to score
    preparation." The Choral Journal, 21/8, p. 11-13.
Jordan, James M. (1987). "Choral intonation: a pedagogical problem for the
    choral conductor." The Choral Journal, April, p. 9-16.
Jordan, James M. (1986). The Effects of Movement Instruction Based upon
    the Theories of Rudolf von Laban and Their Effects upon the Rhythm
    Discrimination and Performance of High School Students. Ann Arbor:
    University Microfilms.
Jordan, James M. (1984). "False Blend: A Vocal Pedagogy Problem for the
    Choral Conductor." The Choral Journal, 24/10, p. 25-26.
Jordan, James M. (1987) "Informal Rhythm Training Derived from the
    Theories of Rudolf von Laban: Implications for the Teaching and
    Learning of Rhythm". Proceedings of the Southeastern Music
    Symposium. Athens: University of Georgia.

MUSIC LEARNING SEQUENCE ACTIVITIES IN THE PRIVATE VOICE LESSON

Diane M. Clark

Because the vocal mechanism does not begin to mature until the middle teen years, students often do not realize until they reach high school or college age that they have good singing voices, enjoy singing, and want to take voice lessons. If that is the first time that they have shown a serious interest in music, they will come to vocal study with no previously-acquired instrumental or theoretical skills to assist them in their learning. Therefore, high school and college vocalists often compare poorly in music skills to instrumentalists of the same age who have had numerous years of musical study. The old insult, "Singers have resonance where their brains are supposed to be," accuses vocalists of being poor musicians, but the reason for such weak musicianship is usually a lack of training rather than a lack of music aptitude.

It is certainly possible to teach a person who cannot read music how to sing with a more beautiful tone quality, but that person will be forever hampered by having to learn everything by rote and will have difficulty mastering any but the simplest music. Therefore, though it may seem somewhat tedious to teach the rudiments of music in the private voice lesson, the long range benefits are well worth the effort. As the singer develops music understanding and improves his music skills, doors will be opened to ever-greater music achievement. That is satisfying to students and teacher alike.

The two most basic elements of music are pitch and rhythm. Pitch is heard, and rhythm is heard and felt. Consequently, both the aural and kinesthetic senses are engaged. The visual sense, on the other hand, is not necessary (or desirable) to achievement at the elementary stages of music learning. Persons from primitive cultures can express themselves in music and dance, despite the lack of a system of music notation. To carry the thought one step further, babies sing and move in their cradles. It should appear obvious, then, that music is an art best and most naturally learned through aural and kinesthetic experiences. Still, teachers often attempt to teach music through the visual sense, by asking students to read notation, before those students can actually perform music. Music Learning Theory, as developed by Edwin Gordon (1988), completely reverses that process by training the ear and the body first, thereby enabling the student to bring meaning to music notation when it is encountered later (p. 4).

According to Gordon's Music Learning Theory, persons ideally should receive training in tonal and rhythm skills from infancy. However, in reality that seldom happens, and few persons are gifted enough to make significant progress in music on their own. Thus, we find many untrained children, teenagers, and adults labeled as "tone deaf" or as having "two left feet." In truth, those people are still in the tonal or rhythm babble stage, because they have never learned to audiate either tonality or meter (Gordon, 1984, pp. 23-25).[1] Such a person, if he is willing to make the necessary effort, can usually be helped to improve his music skills under the guidance of a patient and competent teacher.

In an effort to use Music Learning Theory as an aid in improving the music skills of voice students at Rhodes College in Memphis, Tennessee, this author applied learning sequence activities from Jump Right In: The Music Curriculum to private voice lessons during the 1986-1987 academic year. For thirteen students, including both music majors and non-music majors, the first ten minutes of each voice lesson during the entire year were spent in learning sequence activities. The remainder of each lesson was spent in learning the standard vocal repertory appropriate for each student.

Because there was no opportunity to administer a music aptitude test to the vocal students, it was necessary to assume that all students might have high music aptitude. Consequently, all were given the opportunity to perform the easy, moderate, and difficult patterns in each unit. That assumption appears to have been reasonable in light of the fact that no students failed to master the patterns at all three levels of difficulty during the period of instruction.

At the beginning of the year, the author presented an overview of Music Learning Theory to the students and explained that the purpose of using the learning sequence activities was to improve the students' abilities to audiate pitch and rhythm. The students were excited about the experiment and felt that it would meet an important need for them. The non-music majors were especially pleased that they were going to have the opportunity to work on basic music skills, since most of them had never had such an experience.

The students were told that they would engage in discrimination (rote) learning, much as they had as young children, and they were asked to accept the exercises at face value without probing for deeper understanding. To practice the exercises was more important than to understand the principles behind them. Theoretical concepts were explained only when greater understanding was absolutely necessary to avoid confusion.

Students were asked to bring a cassette tape recorder to each lesson. The author sang or chanted the patterns and the student echoed, while the entire process was being recorded on tape. Alternating tonal and rhythm units were taught in their entirety, one section per week. Part of the student's assignment was to practice the taped exercises at least once a day during the following week until he had achieved complete mastery.

In thirty weeks, the students mastered Tonal and Rhythm Units 1 through 4. Since those units contain only major and minor tonalities, (tonic and dominant functions), and duple and triple meters, there was no need to seek unusual repertory to use in conjunction with those learning sequence activities. The standard repertory studied by each student contained the material needed to reinforce the musical concepts being studied.

In the early weeks, the students proved to be good at echoing single tonal patterns, at remembering the first pitch of single patterns, and at finding the resting tone associated with one or two tonal patterns. However, some had trouble when they were asked to echo a series of two patterns, especially when one was tonic function and the other was dominant function. It was obvious that many students' abilities to hear and remember (to audiate) were weak. A few students were able to echo a series of up to three patterns immediately, but most had to take their tapes home for further study during the week. Students reported at the next lesson whether they had successfully mastered all of the patterns from the previous lesson. As the year progressed, all students improved in their ability to perform the longer, more complicated patterns.

Also during the early weeks, it became immediately evident that some students were naturally better at performing the tonal patterns, while other students were naturally better at performing the rhythm patterns. Of course, initially each student preferred to perform exercises from the dimension that was easier for him personally, and complained about performing the exercises that he found to be more difficult. But in the end, all admitted that performing the exercises that were more difficult for them caused them to improve their skills significantly. At the end of twelve weeks, the students were asked to evaluate their experiences to date, and they commented candidly:

Student A (senior piano major): The <u>Jump Right In</u> system was fun. It was a nice, relaxed approach to ear training.

Student B (senior voice major): This often seemed simplistic, but after a few weeks, I began to understand the true value of this simplicity. This reiteration of basic skills and covering of some things I never learned was beneficial. The melodic segments helped me more than the rhythmic.

Student C (junior music/theatre major): I noticed improvement in theory lab because of <u>Jump Right In</u>. The rhythm exercises improved my ability to keep a constant tempo and to be aware of both macro and micro beats. I found <u>Jump Right In</u> very beneficial.

Student D (freshman voice major): <u>Jump Right In</u> tonal and rhythm exercises proved to be very rewarding. The tonal exercises were much more difficult than the rhythm pattern exercises. Personally, I believe the tonal exercises were more beneficial to my vocal training. These exercises helped teach what students should have learned in early childhood. All voice students should be required to learn the <u>Jump Right In</u> techniques.

Student E (senior non-music major): I liked the <u>Jump Right In</u> exercises, although I found them difficult at times. With practice, the first several lessons became much easier. The last several lessons (with three-note groups to repeat) are still giving me trouble. I definitely believe that <u>Jump Right In</u> exercises should be continued.

Student F (junior non-music major): I feel that my pitch has been improved by the <u>Jump Right In</u> exercises. Also I find that I am a much better sight-reader than before, and that I am less likely to make mistakes on certain intervals. I am much better at correcting mistakes, too. I feel more comfortable with music now.

Student G (sophomore non-music major): The <u>Jump Right In</u> tonal and rhythm patterns were not only enjoyable, but they were very helpful to my techniques. I personally liked the tonal patterns more, because they offered more of a challenge. The exercises can also be frustrating, but I have noticed personal improvement in my tonal and rhythm techniques.

Further comments about the students' progress came from the professor of theory, who reported that the vocal students in his classes all showed definite improvement in their ear training work throughout the year.

As most teachers know, it is one thing to be able to perform exercises properly, but quite another to transfer the principles learned in those exercises into the performance of literature. The author was pleased to discover that on numerous occasions the principles mastered in the learning sequence activities could be easily applied to the students' learning of music, and that their learning was definitely facilitated by that application. The following are selected samples of specific situations in which the skills learned in learning sequence activities were applied to specific musical problems and helped the students to conquer those problems.

Rhythm Examples

Figure 1. Excerpt from "Widmung"

A student who was weak in rhythm skills was trying to sing the middle section of Schumann's "Widmung" (Figure 1), and was having difficulty singing duplets against the triplets in the accompaniment. The author had the student chant her part using rhythm syllables. Then the student listened while the author played the accompaniment and chanted the corresponding rhythm syllables. Finally, the student was instructed first to chant, then to sing the syllables that correspond to the melody, while the author played the accompaniment and chanted the syllables that correspond to the accompaniment. When the student was able to perform that task successfully, she sang using the German text and was able to perform the rhythm without error.

Figure 2. Excerpt from "Standchen"

Another rhythmically weak student was trying to sing the Richard Strauss "Staendchen" (Figure 2), in which many of the vocal phrases end on unaccented beats within a measure. The student had been unsuccessful at counting with numbers, but as soon as she chanted the rhythm syllables, she found it easier to sing the melodic line correctly. Once she had mastered the melodic line with the use of rhythm syllables, she returned to singing the German text and continued to sing the rhythm correctly.

Figure 3. Excerpt from "Casta Diva"

A student was trying to count the complicated melismas in the opening slow section of Bellini's "Casta Diva" from <u>Norma</u> (Figure 3), but was unable to perform the thirty-second notes in the correct rhythm. When she began to chant each phrase using rhythm syllables, she found that the familiar syllables were much less intimidating than the complex notation on the page. She soon succeeded in mastering the difficult phrases.

Tonal Examples

Figure 4. Excerpt from ''Divinites du Styx''

A student singing Gluck's "Divinites du Styx" from <u>Alceste</u> (Figure 4) was having trouble hearing the modulation in measure 34 and consequently persisted in singing an E-flat instead of the E-natural of the new key. The author had the student sing the F-major scale pattern on tonal syllables, and the student had no trouble audiating and singing the E-natural. The melodic fragment from measure 34 was also sung using tonal syllables without difficulty. The preceding fragment from measure 33 going into measure 34 was also sung using tonal syllables, and the relationship between the two fragments in different keys was noted. After mastering the entire phrase using the tonal syllables, the student never again had difficulty with the phrase. When the E-natural was an isolated pitch, she could not sing it in tune. When she audiated it as "ti" in a major scale pattern, she was able to sing it correctly.

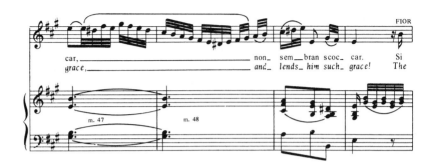

Figure 5. Excerpt from ''Ah guarda sorella''

A student singing the role of Dorabella in the duet "Ah guarda sorella" from Mozart's Cosi fan Tutte (Figure 5) was having difficulty singing in tune the melisma in measures 47 and 48. The author had her sing the notes in short pattern groups first using neutral syllables, then using tonal syllables. After that exercise, the student was able to sing the entire phrase in tune.

Figure 6. Excerpt from ''The Lord is My Strength and My Song''

A student singing the Soprano II part in "The Lord is My Strength and My Song" from Handel's Israel in Egypt (Figure 6) had trouble singing her part when the two voices crossed in beat three of measure 37. After learning the phrase, using tonal syllables so that she understood the nature of the patterns within the context of a tonality, and after repeating the process singing the Soprano I part to provide an understanding of the relationship of the two parts to one another, she was able to sing either part accurately against the other.

Though efforts were made to have the students accept learning sequence activities at face value, as children would do in rote learning, it was not possible to do so all of the time. Because music majors had already had several years of music theory, they had "lost their innocence" as far as musical concepts were concerned. Therefore, it sometimes seemed expedient to explain the relationship between ideas and terminology used in learning sequence activities and those used in their classes, so that they could connect the new concepts to things with which they were already familiar. It seemed reasonably easy to do that without causing confusion, and in fact, in some cases the Music Learning Theory terms helped to clarify concepts that had not previously been understood. Perhaps, in a sense, that was a way of having "the best of both worlds."

It should be noted that the author, a professor of voice and a competent musician who holds a doctoral degree in music, had only minimal experience using tonal syllables (major tonality only) and no experience using rhythm syllables. In the process of using learning sequence activities with students, her own facility has improved greatly, and she has enjoyed applying her new skills to the learning of her own performance repertory.

Because of the success experienced in this first year of experimentation, the author plans to continue the process for another year, resuming with Tonal Unit 5 and continuing to alternate tonal and rhythm units. She has also developed a plan for applying the techniques used in Music Learning Theory to the learning of complete songs, instead of merely working out trouble spots in the music. This plan can be used to encourage students to learn music aurally more than visually and to teach reliance on the ear more than on the eye. That should, in turn, cause students to be more confident about performing without music notation in front of them. Of course, learning can always be supported visually after it has first taken place aurally.

Song Preparation

I. Music
   a. Divide the melody of the song into short tonal patterns (non-rhythmic), play them, and record them on tape. Practice with the tape, listening, audiating, and singing those patterns, using a neutral syllable.
   b. Divide the melodic rhythm of the song into short rhythm patterns (non-melodic), perform them, and record them on tape. Practice with the tape, listening, audiating, and chanting those patterns, using a neutral syllable.
   c. Sing the tonal patterns (from a. above), using appropriate tonal syllables.
   d. Chant the rhythm patterns (from b. above), using appropriate rhythm syllables.
   e. Perform and record the entire melody of the song (with appropriate rhythm); then listen to, audiate, and sing that melody, using a neutral syllable.
   f. Audiate and learn to sing the song entirely without music, using a neutral syllable.

II. Text
   a. Read the text aloud as a monologue (divorced from the musical rhythm), and record it on tape. Practice with the tape, listening, audiating, and speaking the words with as much dramatic expression as possible.
   b. Audiate and memorize the text.

III. Combination
   a. Speak the text using the melodic rhythm of the song; perform with appropriate vocal inflection, facial expression, and body language (gestures).
   b. Sing the song, using the text; perform with appropriate vocal inflection, facial expression, and body language (gestures).
   c. Perform the song from recall (audiation).

In addition to continuing to use learning sequence activities regularly in private lessons, the author plans also to use learning sequence activities occasionally when all of her private students meet together in a studio class. That will give opportunity for the students to receive reinforcement from each other in their work with tonal patterns and rhythm patterns, and should greatly facilitate the learning process.

Other creative ways to apply the techniques cited in this writing should be forthcoming as teachers and students continue to work and grow through the use of learning sequence activities.

NOTES

[1]Within this book, see "Audiation: the Term and the Process" for more information about audiation, and see "Informal Music Instruction as Readiness for Learning Sequence Activities" for more information about music babble.

REFERENCES

Gordon, Edwin E. (1984). Learning Sequences in Music. Chicago: G.I.A. Publications, Inc.

Gordon, Edwin E. (1988). Learning Sequences in Music. Chicago: G.I.A. Publications, Inc.

MUSIC LEARNING SEQUENCE TECHNIQUES IN BEGINNING INSTRUMENTAL MUSIC

Richard F. Grunow and Denise K. Gamble

Beginning instrumental instruction based upon Music Learning Theory differs significantly from traditional approaches. Traditional approaches are typically characterized by the decoding of music symbols and the teaching of theoretical understanding. Instrumental instruction based upon Music Learning Theory is characterized by an emphasis upon the development of audiation and executive skills in combination with rote instruction, singing, movement, and improvisation.[1] Music reading is necessarily delayed to allow for the development of those skills. In addition, Music Learning Theory functions as a guide to "what" to teach, "when" to teach, and "how" to teach. "What" to teach and "when" to teach relate to appropriate method. "How" to teach relates to teaching techniques. The purpose of this paper is to discuss appropriate techniques for teaching beginning instrumental music in light of practical experience and research in Music Learning Theory.[2]

While some students, especially those with high aptitude and achievement, benefit from exposure to the literature and the executive techniques typically associated with private lessons, all students benefit from group instruction in the early stages of music instruction. When taught by a knowledgeable and skillful teacher, group instruction is more beneficial than a private lesson because students can learn from each other as well as from the teacher. As a part of group instruction, students learn to audiate with increasing precision because they have opportunities to compare their performances with those of other students. Also, acceptable tone quality and musical phrasing are more easily learned in a group setting because of the adjustments students tend to make in response to daily comparisons. That same phenomenon, coupled with the influence of more and better literature, is responsible for the fact that musicianship is best developed in an ensemble.

Homogeneous group instruction (instruction in which students play like instruments) is desirable because students benefit from hearing others perform on instruments like their own. Heterogeneous group instruction (instruction in which students play unlike instruments) is also desirable because students benefit from hearing different instrumental timbres.

Therefore, beginning instrumentalists should meet at times in group lessons of like instruments, and at other times in group lessons of unlike instruments.

The younger the student is when he begins to study a music instrument, the more he can ultimately learn. Although there is no correct chronological age at which all children should begin the formal study of a music instrument, there is a correct musical age. A child passes through a language babble stage in the process of learning how to speak a language. A child also passes through a music babble stage in the process of learning how to sing in tune and how to move his body in a consistent tempo. Just as we would not ask a child to speak in complete sentences before he has emerged from language babble, we should not expect him to perform in a meaningful way on a music instrument until he has emerged from music babble. A child has emerged from the music babble stage when he can sing in tune and move his body in a consistent tempo. At that time, he is ready to learn to perform on a music instrument. Some children achieve those readinesses by age two or three, and most by age nine or ten. However, some individuals remain in a music babble stage as adults.[3]

Classroom (general) music instruction usually helps students to emerge from the music babble stage. If students are still in the music babble stage when they are about to begin instrumental instruction, it is of paramount importance that the instrumental teacher help those students out of music babble. Students cannot be expected to demonstrate audiation when playing an instrument until they can demonstrate audiation without an instrument.

To help students emerge from music babble, the instrumental teacher should teach by rote a collection of short songs, representing an equal distribution of major and minor tonalities and duple and triple meters. The songs should be performed in a comfortable singing range, i.e., D to B above middle C. Accompaniment may be used only after the song has been learned. Because a principal goal of song instruction is for students to acquire the ability to maintain the tonality and meter of the song when they sing it in solo, the teacher should provide the stability needed to achieve that goal, i.e., he should establish the same tonality, keyality, meter, and tempo each time a given song is taught and reviewed.

The teacher should demonstrate and encourage movement to the macro beat when teaching songs. That movement is facilitated, especially for students who have low rhythm aptitude, through structured movement without song. Structured movement without song and rote songs should be taught within the same class period.

A reasonable beginning technique is to have students mirror the movements of the teacher. First, the teacher should demonstrate parallel arm movement in pairs of opposing directions, e.g., up/down - 8 times, in/out - 8 times, to one side of the body/to the other side of the body - 8 times. All movement should be performed by the teacher in a consistent tempo. If a student has difficulty mirroring the teacher, he can be asked to say aloud the directions in which his arms are to be moving as he attempts to participate. After most students have become competent at parallel arm movement, the teacher should have the students mirror him while he moves his arms alternately in the now-familiar directions, e.g., right arm up and left arm down changes to right arm down and left arm up, and so on. The teacher can add variety to the alternating arm movements by touching various body parts such as head, shoulders, nose, mouth, knees, waist, etc. The teacher may also choose to have students perform alternating movement with their legs. In many cases, speech movement will help students internalize consistent tempo. That may be accomplished by using the following three-step process: a) speak a neutral syllable while moving, b) whisper a neutral syllable while moving, and c) think a neutral syllable while moving. When students have become familiar with the previously described types of movement, the movement activities may be led by individual students rather than by the teacher. Students may also enjoy moving to a recorded, musical background. However, they should first engage in movement without a recorded, musical background. The goal of such movement activities is for the students to acquire the ability to synchronize movement with the beat of music (achieve beat-competency).[4]

During singing and movement activities, students should not be corrected in their performance. Rather, they should be encouraged and provided with an appropriate model. That model may be the teacher or, in many cases, high aptitude students in the class.

Students will benefit from singing tonal patterns and chanting rhythm patterns. Tonal patterns should be sung by the teacher using a neutral syllable, such as "bum," and students should echo those patterns using the same neutral syllable. Tonal patterns should be sung without rhythm. That is, all notes in the pattern should be of the same length. Major tonality should be taught before minor tonality. The teacher should first establish the tonality by playing characteristic chords of that tonality, e.g., tonic, dominant, and tonic in major or minor, in an appropriate singing range for the students. Then, the teacher should sing a tonal pattern. After a short pause, the class should echo that pattern. Immediately, without a pause, the teacher should sing the next tonal pattern. After a short pause, the students should echo that tonal pattern, and so on. The same procedure should be used for teaching two-note, three-note, four-note, and five-note tonal patterns. No more than two tonal patterns of one function (tonic or dominant) should be performed in succession. Each series of patterns should begin and end on the resting tone. When students can sing tonal patterns using a neutral syllable, they should learn to sing the same patterns using tonal syllables.[5] "Do" is the resting tone in major tonality, and "la" is the resting tone in minor tonality. After students have gained confidence in singing tonal patterns using a neutral syllable and using tonal syllables, they should be encouraged to sing those patterns in solo.

After students have achieved beat-competency with macro beats, they should add the micro beats with smaller body movements. Finally, they should move to both the macro beats and micro beats while chanting rhythm patterns. Rhythm patterns should be chanted without melody. Duple meter should be taught before triple meter. Students should move their feet (heels only) to the macro beats and their hands (on lap) to the micro beats. To begin, the teacher should establish meter and tempo by chanting the appropriate pattern from among those shown below.

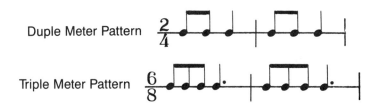

Next, the teacher should chant a rhythm pattern using a neutral syllable, such as "bah." The students should echo that pattern using the same syllable, beginning on the next macro beat. There should be no pauses between the teacher's and the students' chanting of rhythm patterns. Each rhythm pattern should be four macro beats in length. Students should not clap rhythm patterns. When students can chant macro and micro beat patterns using a neutral syllable, they should learn to chant those same patterns using rhythm syllables.[6] After the students have gained confidence in chanting rhythm patterns using a neutral syllable and using rhythm syllables, they should be encouraged to chant those patterns in solo.

Additional tonal and rhythm patterns (representing different functions) should be taught in the same manner after students have become proficient with the original patterns. For example, subdominant patterns should be taught next in major and minor tonalities, and division patterns should be taught next in duple and triple meters. If time is not sufficient to allow tonal patterns to be taught on one day and rhythm patterns to be taught on another day, tonal patterns should be taught at the beginning of a period and rhythm patterns at the end of the same period, or the reverse.

If executive skills are developed appropriately, students will perform musically and with acceptable tone quality in the early stages of instrumental instruction. Finger dexterity, embouchure, articulation, instrument position, posture, and breathing are executive skills. In the process of achieving executive skills, students will engage in instrumental babble. That allows them to experience the physical sensations associated with playing an instrument. The following procedures are suggested for teaching instrumental babble leading to the development of executive skills.

While the teacher demonstrates correct instrument position with a particular instrument, students should "make believe" that they are holding that instrument. All eyes should be on the teacher. The teacher should guide the students in holding the imaginary instrument and in moving their fingers in a manner similar to that of the teacher. Fingerings for pitches that the students will encounter in future lessons should be introduced as students improve their fingering dexterity. When students appear to have acquired facility on the imaginary instrument, they are ready to engage in the same and more advanced activities on the real instrument. The teacher should monitor closely the students' instrument position.

Students should learn both the connected and separated styles of articulation for a wind and a stringed instrument. (Wind instrumentalists will first need to follow a step-by-step approach to forming the appropriate embouchure. Teacher demonstration or pictures of appropriate embouchures will facilitate that process.) The syllables "doo" and "too" are associated with the connected and separated styles of articulation, respectively. The teacher should perform vocally the patterns shown below with connected and separated styles of articulation.

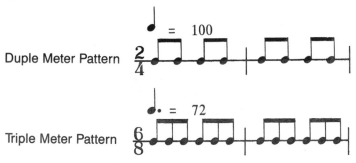

After the students echo those patterns with their voices, they should echo the same patterns with the air stream only. Next, they should perform both styles of articulation with the head joint (flute), reed (oboe and bassoon), mouthpiece and barrel/neck joint (clarinet and saxophone), or fully assembled instrument (all brass instruments), as they form the appropriate embouchure. Students should play a steady pitch or crow when performing on woodwind mouthpiece assemblies and reeds. However, when performing on the fully assembled brass instruments, students should not buzz on the mouthpiece at first. Rather, they should blow air through the entire instrument in a connected and separated fashion without buzzing. Although stringed and percussion instrument performers do not articulate with their tongue, they will benefit conceptually from the vocal and articulation procedures. Stringed instrument players should perform the same exercises on an open string, using various sections of the bow, i.e., tip, middle, and frog, with connected and separated styles. Percussionists should perform similarly with matched grip on a mallet instrument.

Appropriate posture for performing on a music instrument is best accomplished by asking the students to stand in front of the chair that they are using and then seat themselves without bending at the waist. As a result, students will sit in an erect fashion on the front of the chair. If posture becomes incorrect, the students should be asked to stand and repeat the process.

The process of breathing correctly to perform on a wind instrument is similar to the process that occurs when one speaks correctly. Rather than teaching students to breath correctly in the early stages of instrumental instruction, time is better spent in teaching them to audiate what they are going to play before they play it. As one develops the art of speaking, his own anticipation of what he needs to say functions as a guide for the physiological apparatus to prepare an adequate air supply. Similarly, audiation skill will allow the instrumental performer to anticipate what he needs to play as a guide to the physiological apparatus to prepare an adequate air supply.

To assist students with home practice related to developing executive skills, the teacher should prepare guidelines in the form of pictures, text, or both. Other guidelines should be prepared to remind students of what the teacher has taught them regarding instrument care and maintenance. Recorded examples on a cassette tape will also help to establish concepts of tone quality, articulation, and phrasing. Fingering charts for several pitches can assist in the development of executive skills. Neither music notation nor letter names should be associated with the fingerings. Each chart should comprise the same skeletal picture of the instrument with the appropriate darkened holes, keys, or strings for a specific pitch. As students develop a sense of tonality, the resting tone and tonal syllables associated with those fingerings, e.g., "Bb-do," "ti," "re," "mi," should be presented to the students.

When providing students with instrumental readiness, it should be understood that younger students learn audiation skills more quickly than do older students. However, older students learn executive skills more quickly than do younger students.

When students can audiate major and minor tonalities and duple and triple meters and can demonstrate the aforementioned executive skills, they are ready to begin playing patterns on their instruments. Instruction will be efficient if all students playing wind and mallet instruments begin on "Bb-do" (concert pitch). "D-do" or "A-do" is recommended for stringed instrument players. After students have sung familiar tonal patterns using tonal syllables in those keyalities, they should be asked to audiate and then sing "do." While they continue to audiate "do," the teacher should ask the students to place their fingers on the instrument in the appropriate place for "do" and echo-play immediately the rhythm patterns performed by the teacher on his instrument. Those patterns should be single pitch patterns that are rhythmically the same as the patterns they previously articulated on the head joint or mouthpiece, etc. Because the students are audiating the resting tone, the pitch they perform is in a musical context. The students are giving musical meaning to their first performance.

Soon, students should begin to perform melodic patterns (tonal and rhythm patterns combined) involving other pitches that they know, e.g., "Bb-do" and "ti;" "Bb-do," "ti," and "re;" and "Bb-do," "ti," "re," and "mi." At first, stepwise patterns of macro and micro beats in duple and triple meters should be used for best results. When performing melodic patterns, the teacher should turn his back, move behind the students, or ask the students to close their eyes. The students should not see the teacher's fingers, because if they do, they may imitate finger placement rather than audiate patterns. Similarly, all visual cues that might impede audiation should be avoided, e.g., tape should not be placed on the fingerboard for string players and note names on percussion instruments should be covered. Also, students should not be told the letter names of the pitches other than the resting tone ("Bb-do"). They should audiate the other pitches, using tonal syllables as tools for aural retrieval.

After students can perform melodic patterns from a simple folk song, e.g., "Hot Cross Buns," they should perform the entire song. Solo performances should be encouraged. The teacher may also add harmonic accompaniment. When students can perform a song on the original "do," they should learn to perform a different song, e.g., "Pierrot's Door," on a different "do," e.g., "Eb-do." Next, students should perform the first song using the new "do." Students soon realize that they can perform any song based on any "do." All of that should be done without the use of music notation. The use of fingering charts that do not include names of pitches other than the resting tone will encourage the aural approach to performing. Fingerings for pitches other than "do" should be labeled with tonal syllables. After students have performed songs in "Bb-do" and "Eb-do," they should learn to perform a song in the relative minor of "Eb-do," i.e., "C-la." The procedures for teaching the minor song are the same as for teaching the major song.

The rhythm dimension of learning needs to be balanced in the same way that the tonal dimension has been balanced. Songs in duple meter should be learned first, and songs in triple meter should be learned soon after.

When students can perform simple folk songs in major and minor tonalities and in duple and triple meters, they should be encouraged to sing and perform other songs they have heard on records, radio, TV, and so on. They should also be encouraged to listen to professional performers who play instruments similar to theirs. The students should learn that "if they can sing it, they can find it on their instrument." As a result, they will learn many new fingerings while establishing a concept of acceptable tone quality and phrasing. In time, they will also be able to notate those songs and make up their own songs.

As students become proficient at singing tonic and dominant patterns using tonal syllables, they should learn the words major, minor, tonic, and dominant. Following is an explanation of how students should be taught to recognize tonality and tonal pattern function within a tonality.

The students should be asked to listen and audiate while the teacher, using tonal syllables, establishes major tonality. The teacher should then sing a series of major patterns ending on "do." He should explain, by singing on "do," that the pitch he is singing is called the resting tone and its name is "do." He should explain that when the resting tone of the patterns is "do," the tonality is major. The students should be asked to audiate and then to sing the resting tone. Next, the students should be asked to listen to the teacher sing tonal patterns and respond by singing only the resting tone. The teacher should drill the students by asking them what the resting tone is called in major and what the tonality is if the resting tone is "do." Then, the teacher should explain to the students that when they hear a pattern that consists of any combination of "do," "mi," or "so," it is called a tonic major pattern. The students should be asked to listen to the teacher sing familiar patterns and respond by saying "tonic" after they hear a tonic pattern or "no" when the pattern is not tonic. Finally, the teacher should explain to the students that when they hear a pattern that consists of any combination of "so," "fa," "re," or "ti," it is called a dominant major pattern. The students should be asked to listen to the teacher sing familiar patterns and respond by saying "dominant" after they hear a dominant pattern or "tonic" after they hear a tonic pattern. Because there are only two possible responses, the teacher should investigate whether a student is guessing by asking that student why his response was correct. Minor tonality and tonal pattern functions in minor tonality are taught in the same manner except that "la" is the resting tone. Tonal patterns may be performed by the teacher in any keyality. However, if major and minor are taught in the same day, relative tonalities, e.g., G major and E minor, should be used.

After students can recognize tonality and tonal functions, they should apply those skills to their instruments. As a result of having developed executive skills by performing melodic patterns, they will already know the fingerings for several pitches. The following suggestions can be used to teach students to perform tonal patterns on their instruments, using those pitches and other pitches. It is advisable to use two-note patterns until the procedures are established.

First, the teacher should tell the students that they are about to learn to play a major tonic pattern. The students should then be asked to listen and to audiate while the teacher establishes tonality. Next, the teacher should sing the first pitch of the pattern using the appropriate tonal syllable while demonstrating the correct fingering for that pitch. The students should audiate and sing that pitch using the correct tonal syllable while placing their fingers correctly on the instrument. The teacher should sing the second pitch of the pattern using the correct tonal syllable while demonstrating the correct fingering for that pitch. Again, the students should audiate and sing that pitch using the correct tonal syllable while placing their fingers on the instrument. The teacher should establish tonality again and repeat the process as necessary. Next, the teacher should sing the correct syllables for the two pitches consecutively while demonstrating the correct fingerings. The students should echo by singing the tonal syllables while they move their fingers to the correct places. Finally, the students should be asked to listen to and to echo-play the entire pattern after the teacher plays it. The technique of combining echo-singing with finger movement should be taught for all familiar tonic and dominant patterns in major and minor tonalities.

As students become proficient at chanting macro and micro beat patterns using rhythm syllables, they should learn the words macro, micro, duple, and triple. The following is an explanation of how students should be taught to recognize macro beats and micro beats in duple meter. A similar procedure should be used for triple meter.

The students should be asked to listen and to audiate while the teacher, using rhythm syllables, establishes duple meter. The teacher should explain to the students that "du" is the macro beat name in duple meter. He should explain that when they hear a pattern in which only the syllable "du" is used, the pattern contains all macro beats. The students should be asked to listen to the teacher chant patterns in duple meter and respond by saying "all macro beats in duple meter" after they hear that pattern or "no" when the pattern includes micro beats. The teacher should explain that "du de" are the micro beat names in duple meter. He should explain that a pattern in which "du de" is always repeated is a pattern containing all micro beats in duple meter. The students should be asked to listen to the teacher chant patterns in duple meter and respond by saying "all micro beats in duple meter" after they hear that pattern or "no" when the pattern includes macro beats. The students should move to the macro and micro beats as they learn to recognize the words macro, micro, and duple.

Tonal patterns and rhythm patterns become familiar to the students as a result of those patterns having been taught by rote. Many students acquire a readiness to improvise unfamiliar tonal patterns and rhythm patterns with their voices and with their instruments. Such activities will serve to strengthen the students' understanding of familiar patterns.

To teach a simple tonal improvisation, the teacher should sing a tonic major pattern using tonal syllables, e.g., "do mi so," and ask the students to audiate a tonic major pattern that is different from the pattern sung by the teacher. The students as a group should sing their patterns. Individuals should be encouraged to respond in solo. Activities incorporating tonic patterns should be followed by the same activities incorporating dominant patterns. After students have improvised patterns with specific tonal functions, they can be asked to respond by alternating those functions. Students can also improvise on their instruments, but they should sing their improvised patterns using tonal syllables before playing them.

To teach simple rhythm improvisation, the teacher should chant a macro and micro beat pattern using rhythm syllables in duple meter and ask the students to audiate a macro and micro beat pattern that is different from the one chanted by the teacher. The students as a group should chant their patterns. Individuals should be encouraged to respond in solo. Improvisation activities may be expanded by adding new functions, e.g., divisions, and by alternating functions. Students can also learn to improvise rhythm patterns on their instruments, but they should chant their improvised patterns using rhythm syllables before playing them.

Before students engage in music reading, they should be taught to recognize the tonality of series of familiar tonal patterns that are performed by the teacher using a neutral syllable. Without establishing tonality, the teacher should sing or play a series of familiar major tonal patterns using a neutral syllable and remind students that if they are audiating the resting tone as "do," the tonality is major. Then, in the parallel keyality, the teacher should perform a series of familiar minor tonal patterns using a neutral syllable and remind students that if they are audiating the resting tone as "la," the tonality is minor. Finally, the teacher should perform using a neutral syllable, or play other series of familiar tonal patterns and ask the students whether they are audiating major tonality or minor tonality. The students should respond by saying "major" or "minor." They should be asked to respond in solo.

Also, before students engage in music reading, they should be taught to recognize the meter of series of familiar rhythm patterns that are performed by the teacher using a neutral syllable. Without establishing meter, the teacher should chant using a neutral syllable, or play a series of familiar duple rhythm patterns. He should remind students that if they are audiating "du de," they are audiating duple meter. At the same tempo, he should chant, using a neutral syllable, or play a series of familiar triple rhythm patterns. He should remind students that if they are audiating "du da di," they are audiating triple meter. Finally, the teacher should chant, using a neutral syllable, or play other series of familiar duple and triple rhythm patterns and ask the students whether they are audiating duple meter or triple meter. The students should respond by saying "duple" or "triple." They should be asked to respond in solo.

When students can recognize major and minor tonalities and perform a variety of tonal patterns on their instruments, they are ready to learn to read tonal patterns. To teach students to read tonal patterns, the teacher should first establish tonality and keyality. Next, the teacher should sing a familiar pattern using tonal syllables. After a short pause, the students should echo that pattern. Then, the students should be shown that pattern in music notation. An arrow should point to the line or space on the staff that is "do." The placement of the other syllables on the lines and spaces of the staff in relation to "do" should be explained. Then, the students as a group should sing that pattern aloud. Next, they should be reminded how to place their fingers on their instruments for "do" and the other pitches in the pattern. Finally, as they audiate that pattern, they should perform it on their instruments. The same procedure should be used for teaching other familiar tonal patterns.

When students can recognize duple and triple meters and perform a variety of rhythm patterns on their instruments, they are ready to learn to read rhythm patterns. To teach students to read rhythm patterns, the teacher should first establish meter and tempo. Next, the teacher should perform a familiar rhythm pattern using rhythm syllables. Without a pause, beginning on the next macro beat, the students should echo that pattern. Then, the students should be shown that pattern in music notation using the measure signatures 2/4 or 6/8. The teacher should explain that the patterns written in 2/4 are in duple meter and the patterns written in 6/8 are in triple meter. An alternative form of writing those measure signatures, as shown below, indicates how many macro beats are in a measure and what type of note is a macro beat.

Duple Meter $\frac{2}{\text{♩}}$ Triple Meter $\frac{2}{\text{♩.}}$

Then, the students should read those patterns using rhythm syllables. Finally, they should perform the patterns on their instruments, on a single pitch designated by the teacher, as they audiate the patterns. The same procedure should be used for teaching other familiar rhythm patterns.

After students can audiate and perform individual familiar tonal patterns seen in notation, they should learn to audiate and perform series of familiar tonal patterns seen in notation, without tonal syllables. When teaching students to read a series of tonal patterns, the teacher, using a neutral syllable, should establish tonality and sing the series of familiar tonal patterns, with pauses between the patterns. After a further pause, the students should echo that series of patterns with pauses between the patterns. Again, they should be shown those patterns in music notation and the teacher should remind them that the arrow points to "do" on the staff. The students, as a group, should then read aloud that series of patterns using a neutral syllable, pausing between each pattern. Finally, they should perform those patterns on their instruments in the same manner.

After students can audiate and perform individual familiar rhythm patterns seen in notation, they should learn to audiate and perform series of familiar rhythm patterns seen in notation, without rhythm syllables. When teaching students to read a series of rhythm patterns, the teacher, using a neutral syllable, should establish meter and tempo and chant the series of familiar rhythm patterns. Without a pause, i.e., beginning on the next macro beat, the students should chant that series of rhythm patterns. Next, the students should be shown that series of patterns in music notation. The teacher should remind them that the patterns in 2/4 are in duple meter and that the patterns in 6/8 are in triple meter. The students, as a group, should then read aloud that series of patterns, using a neutral syllable. Finally, they should perform those patterns on their instruments, on any pitch, in the same manner.

After students can read series of familiar tonal patterns by singing them using a neutral syllable and performing them on their instruments, they are ready to read (sight-read) series of patterns that combine familiar and unfamiliar tonal patterns. They should learn to sight-read tonal patterns by audiating them and then performing them on their instruments. If they experience difficulty in reading one or more of the patterns while using their instruments, they should sing those patterns using movable "do" syllables, and then perform them on their instruments.

After students can read series of familiar rhythm patterns by chanting them using a neutral syllable and performing them on their instruments, they are ready to read (sight-read) series of patterns that combine familiar and unfamiliar rhythm patterns. They should learn to sight-read rhythm patterns by audiating them and then performing them on their instruments. If they experience difficulty in reading one or more of the rhythm patterns while using their instrument, they should chant the rhythm patterns using rhythm syllables, and then perform them on their instruments.

Finally, students should be ready to read familiar and unfamiliar solo and ensemble music that combines tonal and rhythm patterns. In addition, they should read familiar and unfamiliar tonal patterns in new keyalities and familiar and unfamiliar rhythm patterns with new measure signatures. It is also appropriate at this time to teach theoretical understanding (names of lines and spaces, time value names of notes, etc.), as the students will need that information in order to communicate with other members of an ensemble or with the conductor. At the same time they are developing their music reading skills, they should continue to play by ear, notate familiar songs in many tonalities and meters, and engage in improvisation.

Music Learning Theory provides an organized structure for students to learn to audiate on a music instrument. When a student has developed audiation skill, he has the potential not only to perform with meaning on a music instrument, but also to understand and appreciate all types of music during and beyond his formal education.

NOTES

[1]Within this book, see "Audiation: The Term and the Process" for more information about audiation.

[2]For a thorough discussion of Music Learning Theory, read Edwin E. Gordon, Learning Sequences in Music: Skill, Content, and Patterns (Chicago: G.I.A. Publications, Inc., 1988). For further information about the application of Music Learning Theory to beginning instrumental instruction, read Richard F. Grunow and Edwin E. Gordon, Jump Right In: The Instrumental Series (Chicago: G.I.A. Publications, Inc., 1989).

[3]Within this book, see "Informal Music Instruction as Readiness for Learning Sequence Activities" for more information about the music babble stage.

[4]For further information about sequential rhythm instruction, read Phyllis Weikart, Teaching Movement and Dance: A Sequential Approach to Rhythmic Movement, 2nd Edition (Ypsilanti, Michigan: High Scope Press, 1984).

[5] Within this book, see "Tonal Syllables: A Comparison of Purposes and Systems" for more information about tonal syllables.

[6]Within this book, see "Rhythm Syllables: A Comparison of Systems" for more information about rhythm syllables.

MUSIC LEARNING SEQUENCE TECHNIQUES IN INSTRUMENTAL PERFORMANCE ORGANIZATIONS

Scott C. Shuler

The application of Music Learning Theory to instrumental ensemble instruction is both possible and desirable. Music Learning Theory provides the ensemble director with the means to improve his students' performance skills while broadening their music understanding. Unfortunately, some instrumental music teachers who do not understand the nature and purpose of Music Learning Theory have failed to take advantage of the benefits it offers. Some of those teachers fail to see the applicability of Music Learning Theory to the ensemble setting, mistakenly believing that it is strictly an elementary general music method. Others are prevented from incorporating Music Learning Theory into their teaching by fears, either of the inadequacy of their own skills or of their students' response to learning sequence activities. Still others would like to apply Music Learning Theory to their ensembles, but lack role models from whom to glean appropriate techniques.

In this article, each of the above concerns is addressed, and a rationale is presented for incorporating Music Learning Theory into the instrumental music setting. Specific procedures are recommended for the instrumental music teacher who wishes to make use of Music Learning Theory in the ensemble setting. A model of the ensemble performance process is presented, and the implications of that model for rehearsing the ensemble are discussed. Finally, traditional approaches to common problems encountered by school ensemble directors are re-examined in light of Music Learning Theory, and more appropriate solutions to those problems are proposed.

Resolving the Conductor/Teacher Dilemma

The school ensemble director juggles two responsibilities, that of teacher and that of conductor. The two are often viewed as contradictory rather than complementary. In order to satisfy the expectations of the educational community the director must produce educational results, helping his students achieve measurable objectives that are linked to the broad goals of the school. For most instrumental ensemble members their band or orchestra is the only music class in which they participate after elementary school. It is therefore essential for the director to function as a teacher, developing broad music understandings in his students that will enable them to be discriminating consumers of music. On the other hand, many less enlightened parents and school administrators attach primary, even exclusive, importance to the quality of the performances the director produces. That latter role, in which the director functions as a professional conductor, is too often the role that generates the greater public approbation, and therefore expands to dominate the director's priorities. The director who places primary emphasis on his teacher role tends to view his conductor colleagues as having abandoned their real purpose in the schools, while the director who has adopted the attitude of a professional conductor views the teacher role as unrealistic or impractical, except as it contributes to polishing the next performance. The director who seeks to be successful in both aspects of his job must find the common ground that links the roles of teacher and conductor. Music Learning Theory provides such a link.

The usefulness of Music Learning Theory in the ensemble setting is typically more obvious to the teacher than to the conductor. As a method that approaches music appreciation through music understanding and provides sequential and measurable performance outcomes, Music Learning Theory fits readily within the teacher's broader educational perspective. From the conductor's point of view, on the other hand, a surface examination of Music Learning Theory may lead to the conclusion that the method is not relevant to his needs. Such a rejection is premature, born of flawed understanding. Music Learning Theory is a performance-intensive approach, one that emphasizes sound over theory, and it can be used to great advantage in the ensemble setting. Through Music Learning Theory the director may produce better performing groups by developing in each student a higher level of musical skill and understanding.

Music Learning Theory and the Conductor

Rarely, if ever, does one hear a conductor complaining of having too much rehearsal time with his ensemble. On the contrary, the complaints one hears are of insufficient time to correct performers who are missing key signatures or distorting rhythms. "I would love to teach my students to play more expressively, but I have to spend all of my time just teaching them to play the right notes," is a common refrain. Faced with such problems, the effective conductor/teacher constantly looks for ways to classify and solve musical problems as quickly as possible, and in a manner that enables his students to apply what they have learned to new music. The outstanding conductor/teacher is an innovator, willing to deviate from the way he has been taught - radically, if necessary - in order to achieve his objectives. How will Music Learning Theory help?

The answer to that question becomes clear once the performance problems mentioned above are correctly classified. A clarinetist who fails to notice that he is flatting "ti" in major tonality lacks the tonal skills necessary to hear his mistake; a trumpeter who transforms duple meter patterns into triplets lacks a clear sense of duple meter; a saxophonist who cannot sight-read a technically simple melody lacks the ability to generalize from the tonal and rhythm patterns he has already learned to the new patterns encountered in the melody. Those problems are therefore appropriately classified as tonal, rhythm, and notational generalization problems, respectively. If Music Learning Theory is truly the process through which persons most efficiently learn tonal, rhythm, and notational skills, then it follows that the application of Music Learning Theory to instruction will enable the conductor to solve those problems most rapidly. In short, the most effective conductor will be one who applies knowledge of Music Learning Theory to the rehearsal setting. Music Learning Theory is not only an effective method for elementary general music teachers, it is an effective method for all music teachers.

Learning Sequence Activities
in the Instrumental Ensemble

Classroom activities in the instrumental ensemble setting consist of the traditional activities of the rehearsal, during which literature is introduced and polished. The director who uses Music Learning Theory effectively will also set aside regular time for learning sequence activities, which will supplement and support the classroom activities. Learning sequence activities provide ensemble members with sequenced tonal and rhythm experiences that insure their steady progress in literacy and understanding, progress that is too often neglected by school ensemble directors in favor of technique. When the director gives understanding and literacy priority over technique during the learning process, he provides his students with the motivation and the means to master the technical problems encountered in repertory. If students can audiate and read the music they are expected to master, they will be willing and able to practice intelligently any troublesome passages in their music. Through home practice of genuinely musical content, content that is much more motivating than contrived mechanical exercises, the students' technique will inevitably expand.

There are several possible approaches to using learning sequence activities in the ensemble setting. With small groups, use of the register books from Jump Right In: The Music Curriculum provides students with carefully sequenced experiences, and provides the director with objective feedback on the students' progress. However, the director of a larger ensemble may need to adjust the content and procedures of learning sequence activities to fit his particular situation. For example, although it is essential that the director measure his students' music aptitude and use the information obtained to individualize instruction, it might prove disruptive to seat students according to their tonal or rhythm aptitude for the beginning of the rehearsal (learning sequence activities) and then reseat them by instrument for the remainder of the rehearsal (classroom activities).[1] A second problem encountered by the director of a large ensemble is that there is insufficient time to hear every student perform patterns during a single rehearsal. The director who uses the Jump Right In register books may therefore wish to evaluate individuals during weekly sectionals, and devote learning sequence activities during full rehearsals primarily to class patterns. The learning sequence activities conducted prior to full rehearsal could be followed by a traditional ensemble warm-up.

A second approach to using learning sequence activities is to incorporate them into the ensemble warm-up. Such a warm-up fosters careful listening and the development of music understanding, while still allowing students to warm-up physically. In order to serve as a complete warm-up, learning sequence activities must be organized so as to include performance on instruments. That may require the inclusion of more than one skill level in a single learning sequence activities session. One possible procedure is as follows.

1. The director may lead aural/oral, verbal association, and/or partial synthesis activities, as dictated by the students' level of attainment. Those

activities may often be completed while the students quietly assemble their instruments, thus making optimal use of rehearsal time.

2. Once the students have attained the partial synthesis level of learning using a set of patterns, the director may have them echo the patterns on their instruments. For rhythm patterns, the director must first establish the meter and tempo; for tonal patterns, the director must first establish the tonality and the keyality. The director must also identify the concert pitch of the resting tone or, if the musicians have not learned to transpose, the resting tone for each instrument pitch group. The director should then perform each pattern exactly as he wishes the students to echo it, and the students should respond by playing the pattern on their instruments, either individually or as a group. During that process the students and director, having no notated music to follow, are free to focus their attention on appropriate tone quality, phrasing, dynamics, and style. To insure that students imitate what they hear rather than merely watching the director's fingerings during tonal echoes, the director should make certain that his hands are not visible. He may stand behind the group or behind a music stand, cover his hands with a handkerchief, or ask the students to close their eyes. Having students close their eyes often offers the additional advantage of increasing their aural concentration.

3. During learning sequence activities at skill levels beyond partial synthesis, after each student has successfully performed a pattern or set of patterns by singing or chanting he should repeat the skill activity by performing on his instrument. For example, after a student has demonstrated the ability to chant a single rhythm pattern from notation using rhythm syllables (symbolic association), he should perform that pattern from notation on his instrument.

In order to teach the lower skill levels while still making sure that his students play their instruments during the warm-up, the director may adopt one of two approaches. The first approach is to take a single set of patterns through several skill levels in a single day. In that approach the director may attempt to teach steps one, two, and even three during a single warm-up session, teaching the same content at each skill level. Such an approach is generally less effective, because it moves the students through the skill levels so rapidly that the content can not be fully mastered. The second approach is to overlap content, so that the students are dealing with different patterns during each step of the warm-up. In that approach students first participate in lower-level skills activities on a less familiar set of patterns, then perform on their instruments a set of patterns learned in previous rehearsals. The second approach is preferable, because it provides variety and a physical warm-up during learning sequence activities while still providing students with the repetition of content over a period of days that is necessary for enduring mastery of each set of patterns. For example, on Monday the director may first have his students participate in learning sequence activities through the partial synthesis level using new pattern set B (step one). Then he might present a set of notated familiar patterns A, perhaps by means of an overhead transparency, and have his students perform individual patterns on their instruments (step three). On Tuesday he may begin by teaching learning sequence activities which carry his students through the verbal association level using new pattern set C (step one), then ask his students to take out their instruments and perform echoes using pattern set B (step two). On Wednesday he may begin by leading partial synthesis activities using pattern set C. He might then have his students read chains of notated patterns from set A, first by chanting or singing and finally by performing the patterns on their instruments (step three). Of course, it is possible that each of the warm-ups described above, which were compressed into one day for purposes of illustration, may actually require a week or more of repetition before the majority of students has attained mastery of each set of patterns at the indicated skill levels. Limiting the number of patterns in each set will facilitate steady progress.

Once the majority of the group is comfortable with notation, the director will find that having students write patterns from dictation provides an accurate and efficient means of measuring their mastery of skill and content. Time may be saved by having the students either exchange papers or correct their own papers, comparing them to an overhead transparency prepared in advance by the director. When the students are ready for improvisation, individual students may provide the patterns to which the rest of the group responds.

A third approach to using learning sequence activities in the ensemble setting is to compromise between the two approaches mentioned above. The director might use the <u>Jump Right In</u> register books for individual evaluation in each weekly sectional, and reinforce those learning sequence activities by integrating class patterns into the ensemble warm-up before each full rehearsal. Alternatively, he might alternate learning sequence warm-ups with more traditional warm-ups in full rehearsals. For example, learning sequence warm-ups might be used on Tuesdays and Thursdays, and traditional warm-ups on Mondays, Wednesdays, and Fridays. Whichever approach is selected, the director should remember that for optimal growth the students should participate in learning sequence activities at least twice, and preferably three times, per week.[2]

Roadblocks to Effective Use of Learning Sequence Activities

Some directors who see the merits of using learning sequence activities in their rehearsals are reluctant to do so because they lack confidence in their own tonal and rhythm skills. It is true that the director must provide a model through both the accuracy of and his attitude toward what he is presenting. On the other hand, he must be willing to accept his own inevitable errors, thus establishing an environment in which students are also free to make mistakes. If the director devotes regular time to practicing the skills and content that he plans to present in class, he will have little trouble remaining at least one step ahead of the students, and he will at the same time strengthen the very audiation and movement skills that are necessary for successful conducting. Generally such practice involves only minor changes in the usual procedures for preparing a score. For example, many directors regularly sing each part in scores that they plan to conduct. Adding the additional step of singing in solfège troublesome tonal patterns extracted from the score will prepare the director to lead tonal learning sequence activities; practicing problematic rhythm passages using rhythm syllables will prepare the director to lead rhythm learning sequence activities. Participation in ballroom or folk dance classes and movement workshops will help the director overcome any inhibitions he may have toward leading rhythmic movement.

Some directors may feel timid about playing their instrument while leading echoes in the learning sequence warm-ups described above. All instrumental music directors devote years to mastering an instrument, but many allow their performance skills to erode once they begin teaching. One of the advantages of those warm-up procedures is that the director uses the instrument he has devoted years to mastering, thus providing his students with a model both of musical elements and of an adult who has continued to play his instrument after graduation. The power of such a model is great. The most important musical elements to model are accuracy in pitch and rhythm and appropriate tone quality, style, and phrasing. Fortunately, it is not necessary to have "peak chops" to achieve such musicality in echoes, so even the director who has allowed his valves to corrode a bit should be able to regain sufficient skill to perform echoes creditably. A gig stand located near the conductor's podium will facilitate ready access to his instrument, which can and should also be used to provide a model during classroom activities.

Other directors fear that their instrumental music students will not respond positively to singing and movement. Although students may initially show resistance to singing and movement activities, such resistance typically stems from shyness and insecurity rooted in lack of practice rather than from animosity toward the activities themselves.[3] If the teacher leads those activities comfortably and matter-of-factly, with no hint of tension in his face or voice, his students will eventually adopt the same attitudes. In fact, students who are accustomed to participating in learning sequence activities will complain when the director does not include learning sequence activities in rehearsal.

The director will find that he has many opportunities in rehearsal to demonstrate the positive results of learning sequence activities. For example, the director may point out patterns that the students have mastered through learning sequence activities when those patterns are encountered in repertory. The elementary tonic and dominant patterns commonly encountered in the bass lines of marches provide a logical starting point. The satisfaction that students experience as they sense themselves becoming musically literate will prove highly motivating, and the thrill they experience when they discover that they can sight-sing even simple music is often intense.

Coordination of Learning Sequence Activities and Classroom Activities

The director may find it necessary to adjust the content and procedures for learning sequence activities to accommodate the repertory chosen for classroom activities. He may sequence content for learning sequence activities as in the Jump Right In register books, or may extract content from literature currently being prepared. In the latter case the patterns will be chosen to hasten mastery of troublesome passages in the repertory, and will generally be more difficult.

As mentioned earlier, attempting to carry the same content through several skill levels in a single class warm-up is normally not desirable. However, a director in a new job often finds that he has inherited musically illiterate students who are accustomed to performing literature that is beyond their reading level. In that case the director may, at first, find it necessary to teach a large amount of new content in a short span of time. He may choose a set of unfamiliar patterns from the literature that he plans to rehearse during classroom activities, and teach that content stepwise from the aural/oral skill level through the symbolic association skill level during a single session of learning sequence activities. Mastery under such accelerated circumstances is difficult to achieve, so the director should adjust his approach as soon as possible to a more reasonable pacing of learning sequence activities. In order to make that adjustment the director may need to choose repertory for classroom activities that contains fewer unfamiliar patterns, at least until his students have mastered more content.

Ideally, the director should plan repertory sufficiently far in advance to be able to build a vocabulary of appropriate patterns one skill level at a time. If, for example, the director plans to introduce dorian tonality in an instrumental work in May, he should begin to prepare his students during the preceding fall. He should first have his students listen to dorian music. In order to save rehearsal time, recordings of dorian music may be played as the students enter the classroom and assemble their instruments. The director should then teach the students to sing dorian songs by rote. The songs sung may be folk songs, may be taken from popular contemporary literature familiar to the students, or may even be melodies extracted from the repertory to be played and sung using a neutral syllable. The director should then begin to teach dorian tonal patterns during learning sequence activities. He will probably not have sufficient time to teach all of the tonal patterns in the work before his ensemble plays it for the first time, but such thoroughness is not essential. The primary objective is for students to learn a sufficient number of patterns to develop a clear sense of dorian tonality. From that foundation the students will generalize (generalization-symbolic) as they sight-read the dorian instrumental work. After the first reading of the work, the director may identify patterns with which the students struggled and teach those patterns during subsequent learning sequence activities.

The same preparation process is equally valid for introducing new rhythm content. For example, if the director wishes to introduce unusual meter through an instrumental work written using a 5/8 time signature, he should prepare his students well in advance. He should start by having his students listen to music in 5/8 (or 5/4, etc., as the notation is irrelevant), then teach them to sing simple rote folk songs in the same meter.[4] Then the director should begin to build a vocabulary of rhythm patterns in that meter. Once the group has sight-read the work in rehearsal, the director may target additional problem patterns that can be taught during learning sequence activities.

In music, as in medicine, an ounce of prevention is worth a pound of cure. The appropriate application of learning sequence activities provides readiness that prevents many potential rehearsal problems from occurring. The director who fails to provide careful preparation for dorian tonality is fated to spend a great deal of rehearsal time correcting raised sevenths and thirds, as students try to fit the music into the more familiar minor or even major tonality. The director who fails to prepare his students for unusual meter will find himself going through unmusical contortions such as beating unnaturally large beats, overcueing, and subdividing to such an extent as to slow tempi, in an attempt to obtain a rhythmically precise performance. Such directors may also face the difficult task of "selling" the work to students who are reluctant to accept it because they cannot aurally understand it. On the other hand, the director who provides appropriate readiness through learning sequence activities insures a satisfying experience from the outset, and eliminates a great deal of frustrating "detail" rehearsal. His students will be able to hear what they play before they play it, and therefore will be able to shape their music appropriately. Most important from an educational standpoint, the teacher/conductor who completes the processes described above will have given his students the understanding necessary to enjoy literature in dorian tonality or unusual meter as performers and consumers.

The procedures outlined above for preparing a work in dorian or unusual meter are illustrations of how learning sequence activities may be designed on the basis of the literature to be performed. From an educational standpoint it is obviously preferable to maintain sequential tonal and rhythm learning to as great an extent as possible. In fact, students should not attempt to perform literature in dorian tonality until they have a clear sense of major and minor, nor should they attempt unusual meter until their sense of duple and triple meters is secure. For that reason, the director who wishes to make the most effective use of learning sequence activities will consider carefully the skill and content levels of his students, and will plan his repertory accordingly. A fine math teacher would not select homework problems that are so advanced that most of the students in his class would have to solve them by rote imitation. He would limit content to that for which his students had appropriate readiness, so that the students could work with conceptual understanding. Neither should a music teacher select literature that most of the students in his ensemble are unable to understand, read, and practice individually. The level of content that students have mastered during learning sequence activities should influence the literature selected for classroom activities, rather than vice versa.

Classroom Activities (Rehearsal)

The proper application of Music Learning Theory not only reduces the number of problems encountered in rehearsal, but it also provides both directors and students with the ability to solve musical problems more efficiently. Music Learning Theory provides a framework within which a director can readily diagnose and solve problems encountered during rehearsal, and do so in such a way that students may transfer their learning to new material. In order for learning to be efficient and educationally valid, the director must help his students learn to solve as many of their own problems as possible. That can be accomplished through the consistent use of Music Learning Theory methodology in both learning sequence activities and classroom activities. Developing music literacy and skills will not only save rehearsal time, but will also carry the class beyond the traditional teacher-centered rehearsal and empower the students to be independent learners who can continue their music-making beyond graduation, thus fulfilling one of the primary goals of music education.

In order to solve rehearsal problems most effectively, the director must be aware of the processes that a member of any performing ensemble must master in order to perform musically. From a Music Learning Theory point of view, an effective instrumental performer follows these basic steps while sight-reading.

1. The performer reads the notation and audiates the appropriate sound.[5]
2. The performer notes the conductor's gestures and derives appropriate interpretive clues.

3. The performer adds his own interpretive ideas based upon music previously stored in audiation, both from the portion of the work already performed and from earlier works in a similar style.
4. The performer translates the sound that he has audiated into performance on his instrument. [Note: this is the step during which technique is applied.]
5. The performer monitors and adjusts his performance in comparison to his original audiation, the performance of other members of the group, and the continuing gestures of the conductor.

The effective performer follows a similar process when playing familiar music, except that during step one the sound audiated is influenced by what the musician has heard during earlier readings, including the other instrumental parts; during step two the musician will be freer to watch the conductor's gestures, and will be able to anticipate the gestures more accurately based on previous experience; and during step four, the musician will have established physical movement patterns in previous performances that should, if disciplined by accurate audiation, enable him to perform the music more accurately.

It is common for student musicians to experience problems at one or more steps of the performance processes described above. The nature of the appropriate solution for each problem varies according to the step of the process at which the problem occurs. Therefore, in order for the director to provide the most efficient remedy, he must first identify the problem step.

Problems in step one are best remedied through learning sequence activities. Students must learn to audiate before they have "heard how it goes." Sight-reading without audiation is, at best, musical typing. The performer who has technique but does not audiate before playing will see notation and press keys (type the notes). Then, if he is capable, he will adjust the sound to fit what is occurring around him. He will bend or even change pitches, and will perform rhythms too late for precise ensemble. When several members of an ensemble resort to typing, the result is the amorphous imprecision typical of the mediocre ensemble. Furthermore, the result of such a process can not be expressive. Just as the office typist often types thousands of words mechanically, with no inkling of verbal meaning, so also the musical typist fingers thousands of notes mechanically, with no inkling of musical meaning. It is impossible for the conductor to shape every musician's performance of every part; he must teach his students to audiate, so that each can contribute individual musicianship to the group effort.

Problems in step two are best addressed by improving communication between conductor and musician. The first part of the solution is, of course, to make sure that the students watch the conductor. The second part of the solution is to make sure that students understand the meaning of the conductor's gestures, which include both movements and facial expressions. That may be accomplished through insisting, initially using words, that various exercises or passages selected from the music be performed exactly as the conductor indicates through his gestures. Once students learn to perform isolated passages in compliance with the conductor's gestures, the process of "reading" the conductor can be generalized to other passages and, eventually, to complete works.

It is common for a conductor to mistakenly analyze a problem as originating at step two when the difficulty really lies elsewhere. Such misdiagnoses can waste a great deal of time. For example, simply asking for attention will not result in improved communication if the musicians are struggling with the reading process; the conductor who desires expressive performance must first make sure that his students possess sufficient music literacy to audiate what is placed before them. Similarly, students who are struggling with technical demands cannot be expected to follow their conductor's every nuance. Under such circumstances, either more careful preparation or the selection of less demanding repertory is in order.

Perhaps the most frequent diagnosis that school conductors make of problems encountered in rehearsal is to place them at step four. It is true that students encounter many technical difficulties in the performance of literature, but it is inaccurate to attribute such a large percentage of problems to technique alone. For example, a director who hears students slow the tempo on a passage that contains many notes may assume that the problem lies in the students' inability to finger their instruments rapidly enough. However, it is entirely possible that the students lack a secure sense of consistent tempo, or that they have heard the passage played with an inappropriate ritard so many times in rehearsal that they have begun to audiate the flawed performance as correct. Such problems really lie at step one, and it is therefore unrealistic to expect students to correct the passage until they have been taught to audiate it correctly. A problem should be diagnosed as technical only when students are audiating a passage accurately, but are still unable to produce the sounds that they are audiating on their instruments.

When a technical problem is encountered, solving the problem during full rehearsal is rarely an efficient use of rehearsal time. First, such a problem is often limited to a small portion of the ensemble; to solve it while the remainder of the group waits is to invite boredom. Second, most technical problems are more quickly solved on an individual basis, during home practice, once students are able to audiate the desired result and are familiar with appropriate practice procedures. To help students learn such procedures, the director may take rehearsal time to describe or model the best procedure to follow in approaching a particular technical problem, then instruct the students to work on the problem during home practice. Finally, after allowing an appropriate number of days for the students to solve the problem, the director may appropriately use rehearsal time to combine the individual performances into a precise and expressive ensemble sound.

Common Rehearsal Problems and Solutions

The best procedure for identifying the step at which problems lie is a combination of scientific method and experience. The source of a problem must be identified through a process of hypothesis testing, beginning with the most likely. Once the cause of the problem is identified, an appropriate solution can be applied. The experienced teacher will recognize symptoms more quickly than will the inexperienced teacher, and will have had more opportunities to experiment with appropriate remedies. He will also encounter fewer surprises, as he develops the ability to anticipate problems and prepare solutions in advance. However, it is important that the veteran teacher remain critical of his own methodology, lest he fall into the habit of using corrective procedures that are inappropriate and therefore inefficient.

Following are examples of a few common rehearsal problems to which Music Learning Theory provides non-traditional solutions. Two problems that are primarily tonal are discussed first, followed by a problem that is primarily rhythmic. At least one traditional solution is identified for each problem, after which at least one Music Learning Theory solution is described.

One of the most common performance problems encountered by young musicians is the incorrect fingering of notes. Missing a note once may be due to mere carelessness on the part of the student, and therefore might be ignored during sight-reading, but missing a note repeatedly suggests that the problem lies at one of the first two steps in the performance process. The most expedient traditional solution to that problem, i.e., telling the student the name of the correct note, is rarely the most effective long-term solution, as it simply reinforces and perpetuates the student's dependence on the teacher. Asking the student to look at the key signature of the passage involves slightly more thought on the part of the student, but still neglects the student's more fundamental process, which is aural.

In most cases, the student should be able to <u>hear</u> that a misfingered note is incorrect. If he cannot hear the problem, he cannot be expected to correct it independently. Hence, the director must determine first whether the student is aware that a note is incorrect. Asking him to listen to and evaluate his own playing is an important first step. If he is unaware of his error, then he must be taught to audiate the passage correctly. If he is aware that the note is incorrect, but is unable to correct it, then the problem lies at step four of the performance process, and must be corrected accordingly.

Another common problem for directors is that young players often play out of tune. Some directors mistakenly feel that to help each student match a single pitch at the beginning of rehearsal is important, regardless of the method by which that matching is achieved. The rationale is that the matching of one pitch will automatically make the others better in tune. From that misconception stems such common procedures as relying exclusively on a visual strobe tuner during the tuning process. It is true that each instrument should be adjusted to achieve a compromise in pitch so that notes that tend to be either sharp or flat, due to the physical characteristics of the instrument and reed, can be humored into correctness. It is also true that a player who knows the tendencies of each note on his instrument will be able to anticipate and correct notes with a minimum of audible scooping and bending. However, a director-centered tuning process will prevent students from achieving independence in tuning. Few students have a visual strobe at home to use in correcting pitches. Furthermore, the process of visual matching bears little resemblance to the aural process of matching and blending with other musicians in an ensemble, which should be the director's goal.

The most important purpose of tuning one or more pitches, whether pursued at the beginning of rehearsal or elsewhere, is to teach the process itself, the actual physical approach to humoring pitches. When accompanied by accurate audiation, the mastery of that physical process will result in impeccable intonation. Intonation therefore involves both steps one and four; it is the technique of adjustment guided by tonal audiation. The teacher must provide a model of in-tune playing, and must help his students internalize that model. A musician who can audiate the sound of in-tune playing and has control of his instrument will discover the intonation tendencies of each pitch for himself, and he will begin to correct his intonation automatically. The director who teaches tonal audiation in combination with the technique of adjustment will be freed from the frustrating task of repeatedly telling his students what should be obvious, i.e., that there are pitch inaccuracies that must be corrected.

Even more misguided than visual or one-note tuning is the practice adopted by many string teachers of tuning each instrument for their students before every rehearsal. Again, that practice is born of expediency. Such a director assumes either that the students are incapable of tuning their own instruments, or that the students would take too much time to tune them. The practice perpetuates students' dependence on the director for tuning, takes more time over the course of many rehearsals than would teaching students to tune their own instruments, and encourages the kind of aural atrophy in students that accounts for the nerve-jarring intonation encountered at many concerts performed by young orchestras.

The string instrument or trombone performer has an even more obvious need for tuning skills than does the musician who plays a keyed instrument. Some directors, recognizing that fact, try to help by taping or marking in chalk lines on the string instrument fingerboard, or pencil marks on the trombone slide, to indicate where the "correct notes" are located. Tape on a fingerboard during the first week or two of instruction may help the student develop a feel for the correct stretch in his finger position. However, the continuing use of such a crutch encourages the student to become dependent on his visual or tactile senses and, again, inadvertently discourages his aural development. For example, a string student taught in that fashion will not acquire the aural skills needed to adjust his strings so that they are in tune relative to one another. Consequently, his pitch during home practice will inevitably be inaccurate. If a particular harmony, the pitch of his classmates, a slip in his tuning peg, or temperature conditions dictate that the performer should place his finger on a spot other than where his teacher has placed the tape or chalk mark, the string player who is dependent upon those crutches will happily continue to play out of tune. Likewise, the trombonist trained merely to find pencil marks will resist using the so-called "short second" position or the "long first" position that is necessary to play certain pitches in tune, denying the evidence of his ears in order to adhere to slide positions that are, at best, averages.

Recalling the performance process outlined above, the director who wishes to teach intonation should teach each student to do the following.

1. Audiate the correct pitch(es), either from notation or memory.
2. Audiate the pitch(es) he is producing.
3. Audiate the pitch(es) performed by other ensemble members.
4. Determine whether he should adjust his pitch(es) to match the ensemble.
5. If necessary, adjust his pitch(es).

Note that the first four steps involve audiation, that the second and third also involve listening, and that only the final step involves technique. The primary emphasis of the director must therefore be on the student's aural development, and the secondary emphasis should be on appropriate techniques for adjusting pitches to match those which are being audiated. Visual and tactile aids to tuning may be used, but should be approached as multisensory reinforcement for a concept that is ultimately aural in nature. The director should also keep in mind that it is easier to audiate patterns than to audiate individual pitches, so that in the process of developing intonation he should emphasize groups of notes rather than, for example, B-flat concert.

Many young performers struggle with the performance of syncopation, such as an eighth-quarter-eighth pattern in duple meter. That problem clearly lies at step one of the performance process. One common approach to solving the problem is to start by having the student perform a quarter-half-quarter pattern and then increase the tempo. That approach is inappropriate because it doubles the number of macro beats over which the syncopation takes place, thus creating an entirely different kinesthetic feeling in the pattern. The director may find evidence of the failure of that traditional approach by watching the foot tapping of students as he increases the tempo of the quarter-half-quarter pattern. Rather than making the transition to the new macro beat in the syncopated pattern, students often attempt to accelerate their foot tapping with the tempo until they tap their feet on each eighth note. When that proves physically impossible, they distort the rhythm or decrease the tempo. The end result is unmusical, and usually unrhythmic.

A second common approach to solving the problem of syncopation is for the director to write a series of four eighth notes on the board and then tie the middle two notes together. That approach has the dual advantages of maintaining the correct macro beat and emphasizing the importance of the underlying micro beat pulse. The problem with that approach is that it begins visually and emphasizes the intellect as a means of mastering a physical, movement-based task. As evidence that movement lies at the root of the problem, the director should watch the foot tapping of a student who is unable to perform the syncopation. Typically, such a student will temporarily lose the macro beat, tapping or moving instead on the syncopated quarter note.

The Music Learning Theory approach to mastering the syncopation problem described above is to work backward through the skill and content sequence to determine the level that the student has failed to master. A student who shows the errant tapping behavior described above may first need to develop a secure feeling for both macro beats and micro beats in duple meter, after which the teacher may begin to teach the syncopated (elongation) pattern at the aural/oral level. Until the student has mastered macro beats and micro beats as a foundation, the best he is likely to accomplish is a rough approximation of the pattern. On the other hand, once a student can imitate the syncopated pattern while maintaining a consistent movement to the macro beat, it is a relatively simple matter to introduce the notation for the pattern.

Conclusion

The instrumental ensemble director should embrace Music Learning Theory as a means of providing his musicians with more efficient and enjoyable learning experiences in rehearsal. The techniques and procedures outlined above are only a sampling of the improvements that can be made in the traditional rehearsal when the process of music learning is better understood. The wise director will continue to experiment and learn, drawing upon every innovation of method and technique that will improve his effectiveness. In the process he will help train a generation of adults who will support music and will participate actively in music-making.

NOTES

[1]Within this book, see "The Measurement and Evaluation of Music Aptitudes and Achievement" for more information about measuring students' aptitudes in order to individualize instruction.

[2]Each percussionist should participate in tonal activities by playing mallet instruments, and at the beginning level should be required to rent or purchase a bell set along with the drum or pad. To allow a percussionist to lose the opportunity to develop tonal musicianship by letting him sink into the unidimensional syndrome of drummerhood is educational malpractice, and perpetuates the bored drummer syndrome.

[3]One technique that has proven effective for encouraging many shy students to vocalize is to begin by allowing them to hum. Such students often find vocalizing with the mouth closed less threatening than singing. Once they feel comfortable humming, those students often begin to sing of their own volition in imitation of the director.

[4]Within this book, see "Rhythm Learning Sequence" for more information.

[5]Within this book, see "Audiation: The Term and the Process" for more information.

MUSIC LEARNING THEORY TECHNIQUES IN JAZZ PERFORMANCE ORGANIZATIONS

Robert Schilling

"Play it by ear." To no other style of music is that pedagogical philosophy more intrinsic than to jazz. Jazz is an art form based upon an aural tradition. The very existence of jazz as an art form has depended on the aural imitation of jazz masters. Consequently, it seems wrong to approach the pedagogy of jazz from a theoretical, rather than an aural perspective. Why have so many jazz educators disregarded the very center of their art form, the aural experience, and adopted a theoretical approach to teaching? Teaching jazz by teaching theory ensures that only those students with high aptitudes and strong motivation will have the opportunity to acquire the skills needed to improvise and perform jazz, while the remaining students are relegated to sectional parts of the school big band or jazz choir. The theory of chords, progressions, scales, style, and so on, is usually taught before and even in place of aural training. Perhaps that is because some educators find it easier to teach jazz theory based upon the common philosophy that "they either have it or they don't," than to address the problem of teaching aural skills.

In short, a missing element in much of jazz education today is the aural experience. That is, the development of audiation skill is ignored.[1] Audiation skills are fundamental to performing, composing, arranging or listening to jazz, and serve as a readiness for learning jazz theory. Music Learning Theory provides the framework for effectively and efficiently teaching audiation. The purpose of this article is to present suggestions for the effective use of Music Learning Theory with jazz performance organizations.

Defining Goals

Before discussing goals for the jazz performance organization, educators must first define what they are attempting to teach. That is, comprehensive and sequential educational goals must be established. Unfortunately, many directors of high school big bands and swing choirs define their comprehensive goal as "winning the first place trophy." Jazz education must be more than that. It must provide the jazz band and jazz choir participant with an understanding of jazz music. That should be the comprehensive goal of jazz education - the understanding of jazz. How can jazz educators, given the limited contact time of jazz band or jazz choir rehearsal, address the goal of teaching an understanding of jazz? The answer is simple: teach audiation.

Audiation is taught most efficiently through the careful combination of skill learning sequence[2] and content learning sequence,[3] as defined within Music Learning Theory. Advanced audiation skills are needed to perform jazz. Jazz improvisation, the "heart and soul" of jazz, requires particularly advanced audiation skills. For example, the jazz musician must audiate tonality and meter as a basis for what he is hearing and performing. In addition, he must audiate style, effects, articulation, phrasing, complex harmonic structures, and harmonic progressions that are often changed at the discretion of the players, as well as patterns or "licks" that he has just played and is about to play. Furthermore, he is expected to communicate an emotion through his solo. At a fast tempo, all of those demands on the jazz performer may occur within a matter of seconds. It becomes understandable, then, why theoretical understanding precedes or replaces audiation development in most jazz education curricula, even though that is inadvisable. Theoretical information is easier to teach than audiation skill, and the teaching of it produces some immediate, albeit limited, achievement, e.g., correct chord scale choices.

How is the achievement of our students evaluated? An examination of an adjudication form used at National Association of Jazz Educators (NAJE) festivals reveals some basic criteria for the jazz educator to consider. Those criteria are presented in Figure 1.

Balance/Blend	Intonation
Quality of sound	Phrasing
Attacks/releases	Dynamics
Time	Jazz style/feel
Musical sensitivity	Musical taste
Improvisation	Articulation

Figure 1. Criteria From an NAJE Adjudication Form

To choose two of the more basic criteria, musical sensitivity and musical taste are worthy comprehensive goals for all music students. However, a case could be made that skill in improvisation is also a noteworthy comprehensive goal for all students of jazz. Why should only the select few be given an opportunity to take a solo in jazz band or jazz choir? Yet that is exactly what happens. Only the high-aptitude students teach themselves to audiate, and consequently to improvise jazz.

By this point, many readers may fear that if they teach audiation, they will not be able to rehearse a reasonable amount of music. I assure you, that is not the case.

Skill Learning Sequence
and Jazz Content Learning Sequence

Music Learning Theory is based upon a combination of skill learning sequence and content learning sequence. Skill learning sequence should remain intact for jazz pedagogy, because a firm foundation in aural/oral and verbal association skills is a necessary readiness for generalization, and ultimately for creativity and improvisation.

The basic tenet of a content learning sequence is that some content serves as a readiness for other content, and consequently should be taught first. That tenet holds true for a jazz content learning sequence as well. The criteria presented previously in Figure 1 serve as a guide for establishing the jazz content learning sequences presented in Figure 2.

STYLE-FEEL

Swing 8th notes
Jazz Articulation
    staccato/jazz staccato
Jazz Phrasing
    upbeat/downbeat "push"
    "Ghost" notes
Special Effects
    doits
    glisses
    rips
    growls
    fall offs
    shakes/trills
    turns

HARMONIC QUALITIES

Diatonic major chords:
    Imajor 7 / V7
    IIminor 7 / IV major 7
    I6 / IV6
    IIIminor7 / VIminor7
    VIImi7(♭5)

Diatonic minor chords:
    Iminor (maj7) / V7(♭9)
    IImin7(♭5) / IVmin7
    Iminor6 / IVminor6
    ♭III+maj7 / VImin7(♭5)
    VIIo7

Extended structures:
    major 9, minor 9, dominant 9
    major 9(#11), minor 11,
        dominant 9 (sus)
    major 13, minor 13,
        dominant 13
    altered dominant 7 chords
        (#5, ♭5, #9, ♭9, #11, ♭13)

HARMONIC PROGRESSION

Major-Diatonic
    I IV V I
    I II V I
    I VI II V I
    III VI II V I
Minor-Diatonic
    I ♭VI II V I
    I ♭III II V I
    I VI ♭VI V I
    I ♭III ♭VI V I
Mixed Tonalities
    I #I II V I
    I VI II ♭II I
    I VI ♭VI ♭II
    I ♭III ♭VI ♭II I
    I   V7/IV IV6 UVmi6

MODES-PATTERNS

    Blues scale
    Dorian-Mixolydian
    Lydian-Ionian
    Aeolian-Phrygian
    Locrian-Jazz Minor
    Diminished Scale
    Lydian Dominant
    Whole tone

FORMS

    Blues
    Modal
    Rhythm Changes
    Contemporary Jazz

Figure 2. Jazz Content Learning Sequences

The series of jazz content learning sequences presented in Figure 2 is extensive, but not comprehensive. It is intended to serve as a guide for teachers who want to develop a personal jazz content learning sequence that meets the needs of their performing ensembles. Each heading represents a different dimension of jazz content, and each dimension serves as a readiness for improvising jazz. Should style be taught before harmonic structures? Should progression be taught before articulation? Those questions need to be answered on an individual basis as they apply to each teacher's ensemble needs. For example, if a jazz ensemble is not articulating jazz staccatos accurately, the teacher may want to teach articulation content. Or a teacher who is trying to teach improvisation on the blues form may want to teach the dominant harmonic structure, the blues scale, the root progression I IV V I, and the blues form. If the ensemble does not perform with a swing feel, the teacher and the students should sing or play jazz rhythm patterns that include swing eighth notes. Appropriate content, combined with skill learning sequence, will provide a framework for a logical and efficient jazz curriculum.

It should be remembered that all jazz content must be introduced at the aural/oral skill level if learning is to be efficient. After sufficient experience with the aural/oral skill level, students should be taught the same content at the verbal association skill level. If new content is introduced, the teacher must return students to the aural/oral level of learning. That kind of constantly changing and sequential combination of skill and content produces a challenging, efficient curriculum for the jazz student and educator. By starting at the aural/oral level of learning, the student will acquire the aural experience of jazz. Consequently, jazz will once again become "ear music" rather than "eye music."

Learning sequence techniques require the teacher and student to sing. Students in the jazz band may be reluctant to sing, but they must if learning is to be optimal. To break the ice, the teacher may want to introduce the activity of echoing by playing several rhythm patterns (initially easier than tonal patterns) and having the students echo those patterns on their instruments. A student is not necessarily audiating while playing a music instrument. Still, if the goal is to play a music instrument with good intonation, in the proper style, and with good rhythm, it is necessary for a student to audiate while playing. The reason that chanting and singing are necessary is that it is easier for the student to "hide" his inability to audiate while playing an instrument than while chanting and singing. To encourage students to sing, it may prove helpful to discuss some of the jazz masters who have sung jazz, e.g., Louie Armstrong, Ella Fitzgerald, and George Benson.

Specific Learning Sequence Activities

Learning sequence activities should take place during the first ten minutes of rehearsal. The teacher should begin by selecting content from the Jazz Content Learning Sequence (Figure 2), and by selecting the appropriate skill level at which to teach that content. The rehearsal may begin either with the teaching of tonal patterns, with the teaching of rhythm patterns, or with the teaching of a specific jazz content.

It is advisable to begin teaching the swing feel as early as possible. The swing feel is an abstract concept that defies definition. It can not be taught through the visual representation of swing eighth notes as the notation shown below.

To do so is to ask students to engage in eye music, not ear music. The swing feel can be taught most efficiently through imitation. Because jazz rhythm patterns incorporate eighth-note syncopation and "stretching" of the pulse, they "feel" different than "straight" eighth notes. The teacher should compose several jazz rhythm patterns or select patterns from the literature, and then sing (or play) those patterns to the ensemble members in a swing feel and in a "straight" feel. The students will hear the difference. At the aural/oral skill level the students should echo the patterns. Again, initially playing rather than singing the patterns will help students to get involved, but optimal learning is accomplished through singing. In addition to class patterns, solo patterns need to be performed in order to assess the individual achievement of students. The teacher can not be sure that a student is audiating unless that student performs the pattern in solo.

The same patterns that are used to teach the swing feel can be used to teach articulation in the jazz style. The jazz staccato and the classical staccato, shown below, are often played alike, much to the detriment of the music.

Jazz Staccato   **Classical Staccato**

Nothing makes a jazz ensemble sound more "square" than articulations that are played in a non-jazz style. Students must first learn the articulations at the aural/oral level of skill learning. Then names are given to the different articulations at the verbal association level. If the ensemble is performing music that includes the articulations and rhythm patterns being studied in learning sequence activities, the teacher should remain conscious of the fact that specific attention should not be given to the reading of music (symbolic association) until the students have had sufficient aural experience. In other words, the teacher should remember to retain skill learning sequence.

Jazz phrasing can be taught by using short melodic jazz patterns found in a number of improvisation books. Also, a list of jazz special effects can be found in any good arranging text.[4] The students should imitate the teacher before they learn the names of the effects or before they see the effects in notation. Every student in the ensemble should be able to sing a variety of jazz effects, including doits, flips, glisses, fall-offs, ghost notes, half-valves, and flutter tongue. If students can sing an effect, they can hear it, and if they can hear it, they can play it. If they can hear, sing, and play it, they can easily learn to recognize it in notation. That holds true for all jazz content.

The responsibility for teaching harmony is often assigned to the music theory teacher. If a student is fortunate enough to take a class in music theory, it is usually classical theory, and rarely (if ever) taught through learning sequence.

Ensemble directors have an opportunity to teach jazz theory as a part of the ensemble rehearsal. During the first ten minutes of rehearsal, students might be taught, for example, to echo diatonic seventh chords sung by the teacher. The teacher would establish tonality and then sing an arpegiated I major 7 chord in root position. The students echo the pattern by singing. Then the teacher would sing and the students echo an arpegiated II minor 7 chord in root position, an arpegiated III minor 7 chord, and so on. The teacher might also create and sing tonal patterns, void of rhythm, that are based upon those chords. The teacher and students would use a neutral syllable for all singing if the activities were carried out at the aural/oral level of learning. Later, at the verbal association level of learning, movable "do" ("la" based minor) syllables should be used.[5] In addition, proper names would be given to the chords at the verbal association level. Eventually, student capabilities can be elevated to the point that the teacher can begin every rehearsal with all students singing and playing diatonic seventh chords in a variety of keys as a warm-up exercise.

Another important part of the content of jazz education is harmonic progression in the jazz style. To begin teaching harmonic progression, the teacher should have students sing root progressions, using a neutral syllable (aural/oral skill level). The most common root progression in jazz is I II V I, (unlike in the classical style, for which the most common progression is I IV V I). Next, I VI II V, III VI II V, and so on, can be added to the basic vocabulary of patterns based upon root position chords. At the verbal association level of learning, solfège syllables should be used by the student and teacher. Eventually, students can combine the root progression patterns with the harmonic structures, producing complete diatonic and non-diatonic standard chord patterns. That process should commence with chords in root position and later should progress to a variety of voice-leadings. Once that point has been achieved, the students will be well on their way to acquiring a musical understanding of jazz harmony.

Modes and jazz patterns based upon modes are also an important part of jazz content. Modes are often explained theoretically and practiced in a scalar manner in traditional jazz education programs. That process contributes little to the development of audiation skill. Familiarity with modes should be acquired through the hearing and singing of patterns at the aural/oral level of learning. Cadential harmonic patterns are particularly effective for establishing the modal tonalities.[6] In addition, jazz patterns in various modes are readily available. Students need to audiate the sound of dorian, mixolydian, lydian, and the other tonalities before they learn the names and the notation of those tonalities.

Certain musical forms are common to jazz music. The Blues form is an example that has gone virtually unchanged since its beginning. Jazz forms should be introduced through directed listening, playing, and singing. For example, the rhythm section might play the basic 12-bar blues form while the other students sing the roots of the I IV V I chords at the appropriate measures. Later, other harmonic changes could be added and taught in the same manner within the Blues form, and other forms could be taught in similar ways. Standard jazz repertoire is an excellent source for teaching form, phrasing, progression, etc.

Classroom Activities

Classroom activities (instrumental/vocal activities) in jazz performance organizations include the rehearsing of jazz arrangements. In other words, classroom activities for instrumental performance organizations are the kinds of instrumental activities common to rehearsals, combined with some less traditional activities such as critical and analytical listening.

Listening to recordings is an excellent classroom activity. It is not necessary to play a recording of the specific arrangement being rehearsed. It is important only that the students hear the appropriate style of the music being rehearsed (jazz, pop, rock, etc.). A chosen recording may display a general style, such as Bossa, Jazz Samba, or easy Swing, or it may display a particular style, such as a Basie Ballad, a Maynard Ferguson rock chart, or an Ellington swing tune. The ability to audiate and perform in an appropriate style is paramount to musical performance. One needs only to hear large numbers of student jazz ensembles, e.g., by adjudicating festivals, to become aware of the general lack of instruction in jazz styles.

Students can be directed in their listening skills. For example, the students should be guided in listening to the tone of individual instruments, e.g., old saxophone sound versus a contemporary sound. In addition, careful listening to articulation, control, ranges, blend of sections and ensemble, phrasing, and emotional content will prove beneficial to a student's playing. Rhythm section players will benefit by attending to the "role" of each instrument within the section, and to the various comping styles of each performer.

Another important "classroom activity" is the sight-reading of new material. When a new arrangement is passed out, it is a good idea for the band or choir members to chant the rhythms of their parts throughout the entire arrangement, using a neutral syllable. That will help the students to initiate the proper stylistic feel, and it will familiarize them with the articulations, effects, and so on contained in the arrangement. The audiation of the correct rhythm helps considerably in sight-reading.

When rehearsing "old" material, the teacher should isolate problems and sing the correction to the students. Students from the ensemble as a whole or from the appropriate section should echo the teacher's "solution." When the students can sing a part correctly, the teacher should have them perform it. The students will gain additional valuable insight into the subtleties of jazz by hearing the teacher's performance.

The following is a summary of suggestions for incorporating learning sequence activities in jazz ensemble rehearsals.

1. Rehearsals should be planned to include sequential goals.
2. Learning sequence activities should be taught during the first 10 to 15 minutes of each rehearsal.
3. Jazz content should be chosen to meet the needs of the ensemble, and should be presented sequentially.
4. The audiation of jazz feel and style is a requisite for all jazz performance.
5. All content should be introduced at the aural/oral level of learning.
6. Jazz is an "ear music" not an "eye music." If students can hear, sing, and play "it," they can learn to recognize "it" in notation.
7. Content taught by rote, through skill learning sequence, serves as a readiness for generalization learning.
8. Rehearsal activities should be a learning experience, and should complement learning sequence activities.

Jazz educators must recognize and accept the fact that without the ability to audiate, a student can not learn to understand jazz. It is the responsibility of educators to teach audiation, and consequently to provide students with the opportunity to understand.

NOTES

[1]Within this book, see "Audiation: The Term and the Process" for more information.

[2]Within this book, see "Skill Learning Sequence" for more information.

[3]Within this book, see "Tonal Learning Sequence" and "Rhythm Learning Sequence" for more information.

[4]For jazz patterns, see Patterns for Jazz (Coker, 1970) For jazz effects, see The Contemporary Arranger (Sebesky, 1975).

[5]For more information about movable "do" syllables with jazz harmony, see "A Case for Movable 'DO'," Thom Mason, NAJE Research Proceedings, 1987.

[6]For more information about modal cadences, see Gordon, Learning Sequences in Music, G.I.A. Publications, Inc., 1988.

THE APPLICATION OF MUSIC LEARNING
THEORY TO RECORDER INSTRUCTION

Sally C. Weaver

When one performs music on a recorder, audiation is basic.[1] An instrumental performance, whether that performance is a single tone, a pattern, or a melody, is a demonstration of the performer's audiation.[2] Tonal audiation and rhythm audiation are essential and basic, but are not sufficient. The audiation of timbre and style (including articulation differences) are also important to a musical performance. The purpose of this article is to discuss the relationship of audiation skill development to recorder instruction.

Although it is possible to learn to "cover the holes" by rote and produce music on a recorder (with extensive repetition), merely training the student's fingers, breath support, and tongue is the least efficient way to train the musical mind. In appropriate instrumental instruction and performance, manipulative and embouchure skills are viewed as a demonstration of the student's audiation of tonality, meter, timbre, and musical style. Only then are manipulative and embouchure skills learned musically, and not merely mechanically.

Audiation skill instruction without the instrument needs to precede the transfer of that audiation skill to an instrument. The teacher should hear and see evidence of the student's audiation skills during singing, chanting, and movement activities. Specifically, to sing songs and echo tonal patterns, to perform chants and echo rhythm patterns, and to listen to recorder performances before working with the instrument will create in audiation the foundations for a musical, instrumental performance. Once instrumental instruction has begun, any new music content to be played on a recorder should be learned first through singing and movement activities to insure that the instrumental performance will be a true demonstration of the student's audiation.

Given the above, it can be seen that a learning sequence of audiation skills as demonstrated through singing, moving, and playing the recorder will support the development of each student's instrumental musicianship. Few recorder teachers implement such skill development on their own, and few instructional texts written for recorder contain exercises designed to develop audiation skills. More often than not, students learn by rote only to produce music from notation based upon the correct fingerings for single notes, rather than to first learn to make sense of music in audiation. Students who do not receive sequenced audiation instruction in conjunction with instrumental instruction may struggle to take steps toward more advanced audiation skills as best they can without the benefit of more effective instruction. Frequently, those students abandon music as an aural art and conclude that music is merely a mathematical/logical system of fingerings and notation.

As is true in playing any music instrument, playing the recorder is a complex mental and kinesthetic operation. Audiation is the mental activity; embouchure and manipulation skills, e.g., hand position and fingerings, are the kinesthetic activities of instrumental music.[3] Audiation of the tonal, rhythm, timbre, and style elements of music are converted to manipulative and embouchure skills in order to achieve the audiated result in performance. Although sequential steps toward such a conversion need to be taught, a trained musician transforms audiation to performance without belabored, conscious thought.

As soon as a beginning student has an instrument in his or her hands, the priority of the typical teacher becomes one of teaching embouchure and manipulative skills. In order for the student to make sense of the tone quality produced from an embouchure, the sequences of pitches produced by fingerings, and the rhythms produced by articulation, audiation must have been developed prior to those beginning stages of kinesthetic instruction. When audiation instruction precedes kinesthetic instruction, the development of kinesthetic instruction is quick, sequential, and self-motivating for the student.

By way of analogy, if a student who is learning an unfamiliar language has never seen the objects or understood the context for the words he is learning, his progress will be slow, frustrating, and highly dependent upon rote instruction from the teacher. For example, in trying to learn the terms and concepts for an unfamiliar science, such as electronics or quantum physics, in an unfamiliar language, the learner will lose the logic of the terms and concepts necessarily taught by rote because he will have few mental tools with which to grasp, categorize, and retain the new information. On the other hand, if a student is familiar with the objects to be learned and has an understanding of the context of those objects prior to learning the labels for them in an unfamiliar language, he is more likely to learn efficiently from the teacher and also to use his own knowledge to teach himself conceptually. As compared with the first student, the second student's learning will be accomplished more quickly, more independently, and more thoroughly.

It is simple to make analogies such as the one above in relation to something that can be seen or written, but rarely is such logic applied to that which is heard. When a student understands with his ears and musical mind the aural "objects" and context of music (as sound, not as notation), music learning is optimal. Once an aural understanding of the context of music (that is, audiation) is developed, it may be efficiently transferred to an instrument. Although the sequence of learning cited here is efficient, efficiency is not the point. The point is that each student's understanding of music and self-motivation toward achievement in music stems from appropriately sequenced music learning.

Considering the need to develop both audiation and kinesthetic skills in initial instrumental instruction, an instrument that requires less of a student kinesthetically may provide an appropriate transition from audiation to the playing of an instrument as an audible demonstration of that audiation. Although performance on the recorder is complex, it is less complex than performance on most instruments. The kinesthetic demands for the recorder are less than those for other instruments young children learn, e.g., the flute, piano, or violin. The manipulative and embouchure skills required to play the recorder are simple enough for the student to master relatively quickly, thereby allowing the focus of instruction to be placed on the transfer of audiation skills to performance skills. Breath control, embouchure, articulation, fingerings, and hand position are simpler, more logical, and more naturally achieved on the recorder than on other instruments. More specific technical benefits of beginning instrumental instruction on the recorder are outlined in the following paragraphs.

The embouchure for the recorder is relaxed and natural. The act of producing a pleasing tone quality is easy for even a young child.

Articulation on the recorder is easily audiated and produced. That is, there are no complex thought processes required to convert the audiation of articulation from the mind to performance, as there might be when playing the piano or a percussion instrument.

Many styles of articulation may be produced readily on the recorder. For example, it is relatively easy for the performer to produce articulation styles such as a staccato or separated legato once those styles have been audiated.

Fingerings on the recorder are logical enough for a beginner to master a wide range of tones, i.e., d to d', and several keys and tonalities relatively quickly. That range of tones is important for several reasons: it is within most children's natural singing range and it is wide enough to allow the child to master arpeggiated patterns on the instrument early in instruction.

Although breath control is important, the student can produce a good tone quality without elaborate explanations or practice in breath control; correct initial instruction with occasional reminders is usually sufficient. Also, the recorder is almost self-reinforcing to a young trained ear in that an unpleasant tone quality can be easily identified and corrected by the student.

Hand position on the recorder is natural, and most young children can cover the holes on a soprano recorder without difficulty after basic instruction. The instrument is small enough for a young student with small hands to finger properly.

A recorder that can be played in tune and with an excellent tone quality is inexpensive and durable. Also, a recorder does not require as much maintenance as most other music instruments.

All of the above factors allow the student to focus on audiation more readily in recorder instruction than is possible with most band and orchestra instruments. Even piano instruction, despite its requiring primarily hand positions and fingerings in early kinesthetic instruction, does not facilitate the student's use of audiation in the same way that recorder instruction does. Because the student has more kinesthetic control over pitch on the recorder than he has over pitch on the piano, and because the sound of the recorder differs more when played improperly, the student may participate more actively and more independently in the musical process when playing the recorder than when playing the piano.

Once manipulative and embouchure skills have been mastered by the recorder student as a demonstration of audiation skills, many of those same skills can be transferred to the playing of more complex music instruments. Specific skills that are transferable from the playing of the recorder to the playing of other instruments are fingering skills, embouchure development, articulation skills, breath support, and the skill of converting audiated sounds into instrumental performance. On the other hand, the transfer of recorder skills to the playing of another instrument is not necessary for the attainment of advanced musicianship, because the repertoire for recorder is sufficiently complex and vast to maintain the interest and music development of an advanced student.

Two important questions for the recorder teacher are "at what point is recorder instruction appropriate in the music development of a student?" and "what are the readinesses for instruction on the recorder?" To answer those two questions, one needs information about the music development of young children.

The first period of music development begins at birth (or perhaps prenatally) and ends when the child leaves music babble.[4] During that time, informal instruction, e.g., exposure to various tonalities and meters through singing, chanting, and movement activities, is appropriate. Formal music activities, including instrumental instruction, are inappropriate.

The second period of music development begins when the child leaves music babble and ends when the child's music aptitude has stabilized.[5] Although a child's music aptitude will stabilize at approximately age nine, there is no set chronological age at which a child leaves music babble. In a musically unstimulating environment, it is possible for a child not to leave the music babble stage before his music aptitude stabilizes. Therefore, it follows that not every child goes through the second period of development. At the other extreme, appropriate informal instruction may lead to a child's leaving the music babble stage before age four.

The third period of music development begins when the student's music aptitude has stabilized (approximately age nine) and ends when the student leaves high school. It is possible for a student to still be in music babble after his music aptitude has stabilized. For the purpose of this discussion, however, the author assumes that by the time the student's music aptitude has stabilized, instruction has been sufficient to lead him out of music babble.

When a student is out of music babble, he is musically ready to begin formal music instruction, which should include formal audiation skill development activities prior to any instrumental instruction. Because there is no set chronological age at which a student leaves music babble, the music teacher should assess each student's music development before beginning formal instruction.

Once it has been determined that a student is out of music babble, the sequenced presentation of pre-instrumental audiation activities may be directed toward one of two music objectives: minimal readiness or overall musicianship. For the first objective, only those select audiation activities that are the minimal readinesses necessary for instrumental instruction would be included in pre-instrumental instruction. For the second objective, more comprehensive activities that are sequenced toward the advancement of the student's overall musicianship would be included in pre-instrumental instruction.

The intent behind the first objective is to begin instrumental instruction as soon as the student is minimally prepared in audiation. To that end, the music content to be audiated prior to instrumental instruction is limited. Most often, the content is limited either to those multiple tonal patterns that are taught first according to traditional instrumental instruction or to a modicum of patterns from several tonal and rhythm content levels. With pattern study limited in those ways, Music Learning Theory is necessarily compromised. Skill learning sequence may be preserved, but content learning sequence is either disregarded or is sufficiently compromised as to inhibit the development of the students' audiation. The assumption that additional music content can be taught in conjunction with subsequent kinesthetic activities seems unlikely because of the amount of time required to develop and reinforce embouchure, articulation, tone quality development, breath support, hand position, fingerings, and articulation skills.

If the objective of overall musicianship is pursued, the extent of audiation skill development prior to instrumental instruction ideally would be as follows. Students will be well grounded in at least major and minor tonalities (tonic, dominant, and subdominant functions) and duple and triple meters (macro beat, micro beat, and division functions). That is, they will have begun symbolic association-reading activities for the content listed above in learning sequence activities. Classroom activities will have included songs and activities in tonalities other than major and minor and in meters other than duple and triple. It is particularly important that instrumental instruction begin after students have completed a tonal partial synthesis lesson in major and minor tonalities and a rhythm partial synthesis lesson in duple and triple meters. It does not seem beneficial to give only aural/oral and verbal association instruction and then proceed immediately to instrumental activities. To ensure an understanding of music and a musical performance, a student's foundation in audiation must be strong prior to the transfer of that audiation to the primary kinesthetic skills involved in the playing of an instrument.

Regardless of whether instrumental instruction is based upon minimal readiness or overall musicianship, that instruction should not begin until the student is musically ready. It should be noted that the objective of developing overall musicianship provides each student with a firmer foundation in tonal and rhythm understanding than does the minimal readiness approach. Also, when a more thorough approach is used for pre-instrumental instruction, the decision to begin instruction on an instrument is not hurried; instead, it becomes a natural outgrowth of that student's audiation skill development. Although the minimal readiness approach is an improvement over methodologies that ignore audiation development, the overall musicianship approach is plausible and much preferred.

In addition to being musically ready, a student must be physically ready to begin instrumental instruction. Although most students are not physically ready to play a band or full-sized orchestra instrument until they are in the third period of music development, students in the second period of music development may be physically ready to play the recorder, a small-scale violin or cello, a flute with a curved head-joint, the piano, or some melodic and non-melodic percussion instruments.

The physical readinesses for the recorder include the student's having finger tips large enough to cover the holes of the instrument, hands large enough to reach all of those holes, and the capability of independent, controlled finger movement. (It is the opinion of the author that small children should not be started on the smaller sopranino recorder, because children benefit more in early instruction from playing an instrument that sounds in their natural singing range.)

Of the instruments that a student is physically and musically ready to play during the second period of music development, the recorder is one of the best in terms of allowing the instructor to monitor the progress of tonal and rhythm audiation. Beginning tonal and rhythm instruction on the recorder is a close approximation of, and in fact an extension of, the tonal and rhythm instruction experienced previously through the development of singing and moving skills. A student who is out of music babble, who has acquired basic audiation skills, and who has the physical readinesses to play a recorder, may begin recorder instruction appropriately as early as the second period of music development.

After musical and physical readinesses have been assessed, questions concerning the basics of instruction are foremost. For example, what instrumental and vocal activities are appropriate in recorder instruction? Which activities are best used at what levels of learning to optimize each student's music achievement?

The complex instrumental skills involved in learning to play a music instrument are easy to identify. Minimally, they are tonal, rhythm, manipulative, and embouchure skills. Tonal skill instruction would include learning proper breath support to play in tune and echoing tonal patterns using the voice, the recorder, or another instrument. Rhythm skill instruction would include movement activities, articulation instruction, and echoing rhythm patterns using the voice, the recorder, or another instrument. Manipulative skill instruction would include fingering and hand position instruction. Finally, embouchure skill instruction would include setting up, reinforcing, and adjusting the embouchure to produce appropriate tone qualities.

The establishment of an effective sequence for the teaching of tonal, rhythm, manipulative, and embouchure skills, that is, the establishment of the best combination of kinesthetic and audiation activities, is important in recorder instruction. The principles of Music Learning Theory are valuable in both raising questions about and proposing answers for a proper instructional sequence.

Should audiation activities always precede kinesthetic activities (such as the fingering of tonal patterns)? Can instrumental activities replace vocal audiation activities at some levels of learning, or is it best to sing or chant all patterns to be audiated prior to performing them on an instrument? What is the value of instrumental (without vocal) inference activities? Once instrumental instruction begins, should learning sequence activities be sung, played on the instrument, or both? If both, what is a desirable balance? Extensive research is needed to address the coordination of learning sequence activities and instrumental kinesthetic instruction. Meanwhile, the following guidelines may be inferred from Music Learning Theory for the coordination of learning sequence activities and instrumental instruction.

Gordon has established that skills should be introduced in learning sequence activities and content should be introduced in classroom activities. Although it is not common for recorder instruction to include singing and movement activities, recorder instruction will be more effective if the content of the recorder lessons (minor tonality, triple meter, etc.) has been introduced previously in vocal and movement classroom activities. Once the content is introduced in classroom activities, that content may be presented in learning sequence activities and then, finally, in instrumental activities. Once a content level, such as minor tonality or triple meter, has been introduced in instrumental activities according to the above sequence, subsequent instrumental activities may include unfamiliar patterns within that content level, as allowed by bridging rules in Music Learning Theory. As tonal and rhythm skills are introduced in learning sequence activities, so should instrumental skills be introduced in instrumental activities.

The integration of Music Learning Theory with instrumental instruction continues to pose many interesting research questions. How can instrumental educators assess previous music instruction to determine objectively the best techniques for beginning instrumental instruction? How much skill and content should a beginning student master in music learning sequence activities prior to beginning instrumental activities? Once instrumental activities begin, should a student be able to bridge levels of skill learning sequence in instrumental performance that have been accomplished in audiation through singing and moving? Or is it better to have a student sing or chant and play all levels of content learning sequence at all skill levels of learning in some form of instrumental learning sequence activities?

Despite many unanswered research questions, there is one recorder method, Jump Right In: The Instrumental Series, that has been developed based upon Music Learning Theory. The authors, Richard F. Grunow and Edwin E. Gordon, have had to make compromises in its design to accommodate students whose general music background has not provided them with all of the readinesses that a Music Learning Theory curriculum would offer. Those compromises not withstanding, Jump Right In: The Instrumental Series, offers vast improvements over texts whose authors ignore principles of Music Learning Theory, and also over other texts whose authors have attempted to incorporate constructs of Music Learning Theory. Some of the specific assets of the Jump Right In Soprano Recorder Book are a series of pre-instrumental assessment criteria and materials that accommodate instrumental readiness activities, rote song instruction (singing), executive skill development (playing), melodic pattern instruction (playing), and tonal and rhythm pattern instruction (singing and chanting).

Many questions remain open to further inquiry. Still, the importance of nurturing audiation skill development in tandem with instrumental instruction cannot be overlooked when educating instrumental musicians.

NOTES

[1]Within this book, see "Audiation: The Term and the Process" for more information about audiation.

[2]In the context used here, an instrumental performance does not refer to a concert performance, but instead refers to any audible sound from an instrument, performed by a player of any ability.

[3]In music instruction, kinesthetic activities can include many types of large and small muscle movement activities. In the context used here, kinesthetic activities refer only to the muscle movements (fingers, hands, arms, mouth, tongue, and respiratory system) that are required to perform on a wind instrument.

[4]Within this book, see "Informal Music Instruction as Readiness for Learning Sequence Activities" for more information about music babble.

[5]Within this book, see "The Measurement and Evaluation of Music Aptitudes and Achievement" for more information about developmental and stabilized music aptitude.

THE APPLICATION OF
LEARNING SEQUENCE TECHNIQUES
TO PRIVATE PIANO INSTRUCTION

Mary Veronica Ranke

To accomplish the goal of applying Music Learning Theory to private piano instruction, one needs to answer the question, "What sequential steps are necessary to enable piano students to bring meaning to music notation rather than to try to take meaning from it?" Stated another way, "What sequential steps are necessary to enable students to audiate, and thus to understand music more profoundly than is possible through emphasis on the development of instrumental technique?"[1] Too often piano students have no concept of audiation as a part of the performance process, and by default simply play from the written page without "hearing" or "feeling." When given a new piece of music to learn, they make mistakes because of their lack of aural skill and aural awareness.

Before applying Music Learning Theory to teaching a private piano lesson, the teacher should focus upon the following facts.

1. Discrimination (rote) learning is the forerunner of inference (concept) learning. Perception and sensation are taught during discrimination learning.

2. Inference learning is a matter of listening to that which is unfamiliar and giving it meaning based upon its similarities to and differences from that which is familiar.

3. One gives syntax to music by audiating, the most fundamental requisites being the audiation of tonality in relation to a resting tone and the audiation of meter in relation to macro and micro beats.

4. When teaching a student of any age, the teacher must determine whether his student is out of the music babble stage.[2] If the student is still in music babble, the teacher should focus on helping him out of babble. A student is out of tonal babble when he can accurately echo simple tonic and dominant tonal patterns in major and minor tonalities

after the tonality has been established by the teacher. A student is out of rhythm babble when he can accurately echo simple macro and micro beat patterns in duple and triple meters after the meter has been established by the teacher.

5. Music is assimilated much in the same way that language is assimilated.

Traditionally, note-reading is introduced in the first piano lesson, along with hand position, the names of the notes on the keyboard, and some basic note values. The task of assimilating all of that new knowledge gets in the way of audiation.

Traditionally, the piano student arrives at subsequent lessons, sits at the keyboard, plays his assignment, and then leaves to go home and practice for the next lesson. Singing and physical movement are not encouraged. As a result, the student may never leave the music babble stage rhythmically and/or tonally. How many students do you know who cannot keep a steady beat after four or five years of what seems to be diligent practice? How many students do you know who, after years of practicing, still have problems playing elementary rhythm patterns within a piece of literature? How many students do you know, again after several years of study, who leave out prime accidentals like the F sharp in the key of G Major? Those are classic examples of students who are not "hearing" what they are playing. Such students may have an abstract understanding of theoretical relationships, but they have not yet developed audiation skills.

If the teacher applies Music Learning Theory to instruction, the same students can be taught to audiate, thereby solving some of the problems in their playing. However, in doing so, the teacher will need to incorporate additional activities into his lesson plans. He can use the same musical compositions, but his approach to those compositions will be different. For example, when the student does not feel a consistent tempo, large motor activities like swaying or walking should be used. Only if the student has a sense of consistent tempo will he be able to perform a musical composition with a consistent tempo.

Before lessons actually start, the teacher should have an interview/evaluation with the prospective student. An evaluation is advisable whether the student is a rank beginner or has studied for several years, as it is an opportune time to get to know the student's personality and to evaluate his special needs. During that time, the teacher should evaluate the hand structure of the student to see if his hand is developed enough to begin to study and to explore the keyboard. More fundamental, however, is the need for the teacher to determine whether the student is out of the music babble stage. Following are some recommended techniques for accomplishing that.

1. Play games that require physical activity to reveal the coordination skills of the student.

2. Have students echo simple rhythm patterns in duple and triple meters.

3. Have students echo simple tonal patterns in major and minor tonalities.

4. Have students sing a couple of simple songs that are well-known to them, preferably representing duple meter and triple meter and major tonality and minor tonality.

If a student is in the music babble stage, a pre-piano class should be recommended for the purpose of bringing that student out of music babble before private study is begun. During the pre-piano classes, the student should sing rote songs and should do basic movements without, and then with, music.

Only after a student has been brought out of music babble will he be able to audiate as he plays at the keyboard. Before beginning private piano study, the student should also have accomplished some of the exploration skills and should be able to recognize the different note groupings represented on the keyboard. He should also have strengthened his fingers through use of some basic finger games away from the keyboard.

The structure of the private lesson is important. Each lesson should include learning sequence activities. Tonal patterns and rhythm patterns should be taught on alternate weeks so that one dimension is taught without the other every week, and so that each dimension is given approximately equal attention. Those patterns should be taught for about five minutes during each half-hour lesson and for no more than ten minutes for an hour lesson. If the student attends repertoire classes or other group classes in which he receives instruction a second time during the week, learning sequence activities can be alternated between the group class and the private lesson or can be taught entirely in the group class.

When teaching tonal patterns in a private lesson, the teacher must first sing the patterns for the student, then echo the patterns with the student, and finally, for the purpose of evaluation, have the student echo the patterns in solo. Tonal pattern cassettes should be made available to students for home study. All directions for using the cassettes should be written clearly and given to the parent and student.The student may listen to more patterns than the teacher assigns, because familiarity with the different sounds can enhance the learning process. At the aural/oral level of learning, the teacher and student should sing the patterns using a neutral syllable. At the verbal association level of learning, the teacher and student should sing the patterns using tonal syllables.

When teaching rhythm patterns in a private lesson situation, the teacher must first chant the patterns for the student, then echo the patterns with the student, and finally, for the purpose of evaluation, have the student echo the patterns in solo. If the student has trouble keeping a consistent tempo while performing the patterns, the teacher should have him swing his arms or sway to the macro beat as he chants the patterns. Rhythm pattern cassettes should be made available to students for home study. As with the tonal pattern cassettes, all directions should be written clearly and given to the parent and student. The student may listen to more patterns than the teacher assigns, because familiarity with different sounds can enhance the learning process. At the aural/oral level of learning, the teacher and student should chant the patterns using a neutral syllable. At the verbal association level of learning, the teacher and student should chant the patterns using rhythm syllables.

After the student has acquired a small vocabulary of tonal patterns and rhythm patterns in learning sequence activities, the teacher should incorporate that vocabulary into instruction at the keyboard. For example, when the student can audiate tonic and dominant tonal patterns, the teacher should show the student how to perform tonic and dominant patterns on the keyboard. Patterns should be played first with one hand, then with the other, and finally with the two together in parallel motion. The student should use that skill as a readiness for learning to perform the accompaniment of such songs as "Mary Had a Little Lamb," "Merrily We Roll Along," and "The Dreidel Song".

The classroom activities portion of the lesson consists of rote song instruction, hand exercises, exploration of the keyboard, and the performance of repertoire.[3] Incorporated into the classroom activities is periodic reinforcement of audiation skills learned during learning sequence activities.

Rote song instruction should include songs in at least major and minor tonalities. Each song should include at least tonic and dominant patterns. In the first three or four months of lessons, all songs should start and end on the resting tone. Later, when the student can reliably audiate the tonic triad, songs can be used that start on "do,""mi," or "sol" in major tonality and "la," "do," or "mi" in minor tonality. The last note of the song should still be the resting tone. It is unnecessary to coordinate the patterns contained in the song with the patterns presented in learning sequence activities. At the aural/oral level of learning, the student benefits from hearing and becomes familiar with many types of patterns that he will later be learning in the learning sequence activities portion of the lesson. For additional reinforcement of listening skills, the student might be provided with a rote song practice tape.

Singing is indispensable to the development of audiation skills. Animal and marching songs interest young children, as do songs with nonsense words or funny sounding syllables. Children have an insatiable appetite for repeating songs that they enjoy, and that repetition is important to learning. Children can improve their sense of tempo and meter by moving to songs in different ways during those repetitions, and finally they can transfer their audiation skills to the keyboard by playing those songs. The teacher should introduce, teach, and review songs in a variety of ways, but always in ways that are efficient and educationally sound. Specific techniques that will be useful to all teachers, including teachers of piano, can be found elsewhere in this book in Gail Waddell's article, "How to Teach a Rote Song."

Movement activities, an important part of the private lesson, can take one of many forms. The following are examples. (a) The teacher may play a familiar folk song while the student moves freely to the music. (b) The teacher may play march music and have the student respond to the beat of the music through a large motor activity such as swaying. (c) The teacher may play a song such as "Gallop Quickly" to demonstrate a faster tempo, and have the student move to that new tempo.

During the technique portion of the lesson, the teacher should focus on strengthening the muscles in the student's hands and making them more flexible. There are many different methods of teaching technique, written by such renowned composers as Liszt, Corteau, Phillipp, Herz, and Czerny. The method one decides to use should be determined by the student's capabilities, hand size, coordination, flexibility, etc. The teacher should incorporate elements of learning sequence activities into the finger exercises. For example, with a young child the teacher may use "The Bear in the Cave" exercise, an exercise that is performed away from the keyboard. Some students fondly call that exercise the "Coffee-Table Exercise." The student should place his arm on the coffee table, relax his arm, and form a good hand position. The cavity of the hand creates the cave. The bear that sleeps in that cave is just waking up from a long winter's nap. As the bear stretches, the doors of the cave open. The student should lift one finger slowly, as high as he can, while maintaining a good finger position. The student should repeat that with each finger and should decide which door is higher, or which door the gigantic bear will leave from to find his food. When the student's fingers become strong enough, he should lift two fingers in alternation, e.g., fingers number two and three, and should perform a familiar rhythm pattern from learning sequence activities using those two fingers. The teacher should encourage the student to do this and other finger games away from the piano. The student needs to reinforce those technical activities at home, allowing the teacher more time in the lesson for the development of music and audiation skills.

The "Coffee Table Exercise," "Finger Rotations," "Landing on a Penny," and "Create Your Own Story" (around the finger movements you are doing) are all ways to strengthen the fingers away from the keyboard. "Finger Rotations" involve the same hand position as the "Bear in the Cave," but the finger development is different in that the student develops skill in alternating finger movement. The student should alternate his first and second fingers, then his second and third fingers, etc. while maintaining a consistent tempo. Once that has been accomplished, the teacher should have the student perform, with alternating fingers, four beat rhythm patterns that are already part of the student's audiation vocabulary. After the student has accomplished performance of four-beat patterns, he should begin to work toward performing six-beat patterns and then eight-beat patterns.

If a student has difficulty moving his finger up and down in the same spot, the teacher can use the "Landing on a Penny" game. The teacher should place five pennies on the table in a configuration that matches the student's hand size. The student should lift his finger, as with the "Bear in the Cave," hold, and then slowly let the finger down, landing on the penny without moving the position of the penny. That will help develop a strong, accurate finger attack on the piano keys.

Many students need to be creative, and they enjoy pretending. Rather than telling them the story about the "Bear in the Cave," the teacher might have them create their own story, basing it on how the hand position is supposed to be when they are playing the piano. Students will come up with stories about a bird's nest, the bunnies home, etc. This is one of the ways that the teacher can allow for the individuality of the student to be exercised.

Exploration at the keyboard should be taught concurrent to beginning finger games. A portion of each lesson should be used for exploration at the keyboard for perhaps six weeks or more. However, it should be paced according to the student's needs. During that portion of the lesson the student should become familiar with all of the keyboard and with the sounds of the different octaves. The sequence for the exploration series should be the following: (a) The student should be taught to recognize the black and white keys, look inside the piano, and experiment with the pedals. (b) He should learn to recognize the groups of two and three black keys. He should play the groups of two black keys up and down the keyboard. Depending upon the strength of his fingers, the student may use the second and third fingers, striking the two black keys simultaneously. Next, the student should play each note separately while concentrating on good finger position. (c) The student should repeat the same exercise, this time playing the groups of three black keys using fingers two, three, and four. If the student has the necessary readiness, the teacher should have him play those exercises hand over hand while maintaining a consistent tempo. Using only one hand and increasing the tempo will present an even greater challenge. Also, the student should learn to alternate between groups of two and three black keys. The young student should stand and walk the length of the keyboard as he plays the patterns, because stretching can damage both hand position and consistent tempo. (d) The student should learn to recognize the positions of the white keys of the keyboard. He should play each C hand over hand, while maintaining a consistent tempo. That process should be repeated for each of the remaining six white notes of the keyboard. Children might like to say nonsense words such as "drip-drop" while they play the exercise. The student should play the selected notes using his second or third finger. Using the strongest fingers first at the keyboard facilitates good hand position, which, in turn, makes good tone quality possible.

After the student can audiate tonic patterns, the teacher should introduce ascending and descending tonic triads at the keyboard. It is generally easiest for the student to reach the white key triads (C-E-G, G-B-D, and F-A-C). A story that works well for teaching tonic triads to students at the keyboard is the sad tale of "My Red Balloon." "I have a beautiful red balloon. When I let go of the string it goes up in the sky." (Have the student play the C Major tonic triad hand over hand ascending the keyboard. The student should crescendo as he plays the ascending triads.) "When the balloon reaches the top, it hits the limb of the tree and goes POP! Sadly, it comes tumbling down to the ground." (As the balloon is falling, have the student play the C Major triad hand over hand descending the keyboard. The student should decrescendo as he plays the descending triads.) The teacher should encourage the use of fingers one, three, and five. The same activity can be used in minor tonality when the student is able to audiate minor tonic patterns. The teacher may change the color of the balloon or even change the story, and use the notes A,C, and E.

When approached by the student about the "other" names for the notes the teacher might answer, "Some people use letter names A, B, C, D, E, F, and G. I find it easier to sing do-re-mi, which is solfège. (The teacher should sing, not speak the syllables.) So in the piano lesson, let's use solfège." If a student persists, the teacher might tell him the letter names as they relate to the piano, and then move on to the content scheduled for the lesson.

The content of the entire lesson should be preplanned. Goals and objectives should be set for each student, and records should be maintained. Maintaining a basic record sheet for each student is a method of keeping track of which tonal patterns and rhythm patterns the student can perform, which rote songs he has learned, what he has technically accomplished, and what pieces he has performed.

After the student has learned to sing tonal patterns at the verbal association level of learning using tonal syllables, the teacher should help reinforce those patterns by having the student sing them and play them on the piano. During that activity, the teacher also should reinforce good hand position, proper fingering, and good tone quality. As patterns are reinforced at the keyboard, the teacher should introduce ways to play the same patterns in different keyalities. For example, the teacher should introduce the pattern "do-mi," with C as "do," move to G as "do," and then perform the pattern with D as "do." If the student is audiating well, he will hear that D to F is not the "right" sound. He will make the necessary adjustment to F sharp without knowing that the note he is playing is a sharp. Eventually, the student will learn the terminology of sharp and flat at the theoretical understanding level. That terminology is unnecessary information at the verbal association level of learning.

As the student progresses, the teacher should sing several familiar tonal patterns using a neutral syllable, and the student should be able to audiate those patterns and play them at the keyboard. Of course, alternate lessons involve chanting and playing rhythm patterns rather than singing and playing tonal patterns. When the student plays rhythm patterns, he should apply one of the finger exercise activities. As was the case with tonal patterns, rhythm patterns should be played first with one hand, then with the other, and finally with the two together in parallel motion. The teacher can reinforce the learning of patterns by teaching a new song that has familiar rhythm patterns and tonal patterns in an unfamiliar order. If the student is audiating those patterns well at the partial synthesis level of learning, he will be able to play that song on the piano without any difficulty.

Finger training at the keyboard can also reinforce the rhythm patterns worked on during the learning sequence activities portion of the lesson. Once the student is able to chant four beat rhythm patterns at the aural/oral level using neutral syllables, the teacher should reinforce those same patterns at the keyboard. For example, after chanting a simple macro and micro beat pattern using neutral syllables, the student should play that pattern using fingers one, two, and three on any three white keys. As the student's hand gets stronger, he can perform that same pattern as a five finger exercise.

After the student has sung tonal patterns using tonal syllables and chanted rhythm patterns using rhythm syllables, and has played those patterns on the keyboard, he is ready to be introduced to those patterns in music notation at the symbolic association level of learning. Because the student is able to audiate the patterns that he is seeing in notation, he will be able to bring meaning to the music notation.

The practice of technical exercises is not a part of Music Learning Theory. However, to achieve in the art of keyboard playing, one must practice scales. The piano player needs to practice warm-ups and to develop the muscle structure of the fingers and arms, just as an athlete practices warm-ups and muscle-building exercises before he plays a particular event. Practicing scales increases the flexibility and strength of the hand. Skill at playing scales and arpeggios eliminates many technical problems that might otherwise occur while a student is learning to perform a piece of music, because familiarity with scales and arpeggios outside of a musical context serves as a readiness for successful performance of scales and arpeggios within a musical context. That readiness allows the student to concentrate on the musical elements of the composition, resulting in a more musical performance. That is not to say that the exercises themselves should be played mechanically. Any keyboard exercise should be audiated before it is played, and the student should concentrate on good tone quality and musicality even when practicing scales.

Scale playing can be introduced as soon as the student is able to audiate "do-re-mi-fa" at the aural/oral level. The small child should divide the major scale between his two hands as four notes plus four notes, e.g., left hand C,D,E, and F, and right hand, G,A,B, and C. The teacher should tell the student to start on a particular note, point to that note, and give the directive, "Now play the pattern that I sing." The teacher should gradually incorporate scales other than C major. The student, if audiating well, will make the necessary adjustments at the keyboard on the basis of what he is audiating.

As the child's technique improves and his fingers strengthen, he should play scales with each hand independently, using the standardized scale fingerings. He should play the scales in a smooth and connected style. Later the word legato can be introduced. Then he should play the scales in a detached style while maintaining good tone quality. Eventually, the student should play ascending scales with a crescendo and descending scales with a decrescendo, and the reverse. The act of phrasing scales helps the students to think in terms of longer musical lines. Success in playing a longer musical line depends upon the capability of predicting the longer line through audiation. When a student is capable of predicting through audiation, he will perform all music, including that which is seen in notation, more easily and more musically.

Next, the student should play scales using both hands together in contrary and parallel motion. The student should practice equal voicing between the hands, forte versus piano, two-note phrases, and crossed hands (left over right). Any form in which a scale could occur within a piece of music should be practiced separately. An important distinction is that, when a Music Learning Theory approach is used from the beginning of instruction, audiation is functioning as the guide for everything that is played.

The use of Music Learning Theory principles encourages the teacher to adapt lessons to the needs of the individual student. The strengths and weaknesses of each student are different, and the teacher needs to be flexible enough to adapt to specific needs. The level of a child's music aptitude, for example, is of paramount importance, and should be measured.[4] Then, depending upon the aptitude, age, hand size, maturity, and creative personality of the student, the teacher can plan and select the appropriate musical compositions and exercises that will best suit the needs of the student.

The following is a sample lesson and a summation of the process of adapting Music Learning Theory to private piano instruction. The sample lesson includes learning sequence activities and the classroom activities portion of the lesson. The lesson is appropriate for a four to six year old child who is already out of the music babble stage. It would be approximately the fifth lesson and would be half an hour long. Practice procedures would be clearly explained to the student and the parent. The student would have the tonal and rhythm tapes as well as the rote song tapes. The student would tape the lesson, and the parents would be encouraged to incorporate "listening" into the student's daily routine.

SAMPLE PIANO LESSON

Opening song	Sing "Hello, Somebody Hello."
Tonal Patterns	Sing tonal patterns at the aural/oral level of learning from Unit 3, Section A, Criterion 1. All pattern cards can be found in Jump Right In: The Music Curriculum.
Rhythm Patterns	none this week
Rote Songs	Teach "Twinkle, Twinkle." Check off rote songs in the student's lesson book ("Engine, Engine," "Alley, Alley-O," "Mr. Hippo," and "Hot Cross Buns").
Technique	Use the "Bear in the Cave" Exercise.
Exploration Series	Explore the white keys, hand over hand, using C as "do."
Play	Have the student play E and C (identified through demonstration at the aural/oral level of learning), while the teacher plays or sings the "Marching Song."
	Have the student play E and C and sing "Marching Song."
	Remind student of the check-off for the Repertoire List. (Repertoire List includes songs that the student has learned and that the student is capable of performing.)
Closing Song	Sing a song of the teacher's choice.

SUMMATION OUTLINE

I. DISCRIMINATION LEARNING
   A. Aural/oral
      1. Sing rote songs.
      2. Sing (echo) tonal patterns in major tonality and minor tonality, and chant (echo) rhythm patterns in duple meter and triple meter.
      3. Move to enhance understanding of tempo, meter, and style.
      4. Play patterns on the keyboard.
      5. Explore the keyboard.
   B. Verbal Association
      1. Attach tonal and rhythm syllables to the patterns that have already been learned at the aural/oral level of learning.
      2. Play the patterns on the keyboard, hands separately and then together.
      3. Learn the terms micro beat and macro beat.
      4. Play three-note finger exercises.
   C. Partial Synthesis
      1. Combine tonal patterns in scales and triads.
      2. Extend rhythm patterns to six or eight macro beats. Use five-finger exercises, hands separate then hands together.
      3. Play rote songs at the keyboard.
   D. Symbolic Association
      1. Learn to read familiar tonal patterns and rhythm patterns.
      2. Practice writing familiar tonal patterns and rhythm patterns.
      3. Create new tonal patterns and new rhythm patterns based upon familiar patterns. (Bridge to Creativity/Improvisation.)
   E. Composite Synthesis
      1. Audiate and read series of familiar tonal patterns and rhythm patterns in a familiar and unfamiliar order.
      2. Read, write, and play familiar songs.
      3. Create songs, using familiar tonal patterns and rhythm patterns in an unfamiliar order.
      4. Introduce "Mystery" tunes (Songs familiar to the student, written out in musical notation with no title. The student must identify the title of the song after audiating it.)
      5. Practice scales and triads.

II. INFERENCE LEARNING
  A. Generalization
    1. Aural/oral - Identify tonal patterns or rhythm patterns as being same or different.
    2. Verbal - Echo, using rhythm syllables or tonal syllables, patterns that were performed by the teacher using a neutral syllable.
    3. Symbolic - Read, write, and play tonal patterns or rhythm patterns.
  B. Creativity/Improvisation
    1. Aural/oral - Play or sing tonal patterns and play and chant rhythm patterns in response to different tonal patterns or rhythm patterns sung or chanted by the teacher.
    2. Symbolic - Write, then play, the tonal patterns or rhythm patterns from the creativity-aural/oral level of learning.
  C. Theoretical Understanding
    Learn the terminologies related to discrimination learning.

NOTES

[1]Within this book, see "Audiation: The Term and the Process" for more information about audiation.

[2]Within this book, see "Informal Music Instruction as Readiness for Learning Sequence Activities" for more information about music babble.

[3]The term "classroom activities" is more appropriate for describing an elementary general music class than a private piano lesson, but it is used here for its connotation as a counterpart to learning sequence activities.

[4]Within this book, see "The Measurement and Evaluation of Music Aptitudes and Achievement" for more information.

REFERENCES

Agay, Denes (1981). Teaching Piano: A Comprehensive Guide and Reference Book for the Instructor, Volumes I and II. New York: Yorktown Music Press, Inc.

Bastien, James W. (1977). How to Teach Piano Successfully. Illinois: General Words and Music Co.

Booth, Victor (1982). We Piano Teachers. London: Hutchinson & Co. Ltd.

Briggs, Dorothy Corkville (1970). Your Child's Self-esteem. New York: Doubleday & Company, Inc.

Choksy, Lois (1974). The Kodaly Method: Comprehensive Music Education from Infant to Adult. Englewood Cliffs, NJ: Prentice-Hall, Inc.

Choksy, Lois (1981). The Kodaly Context: Creating an Environment for Musical Learning. Englewood Cliffs, NJ: Prentice-Hall, Inc.

Gieseking, Walter and Karl Leimer (1972). Piano Technique. New York: Dover Publications, Inc. pp 9-12.

Gordon, Edwin E. (1988). Learning Sequences in Music: Skill Content and Patterns. Chicago: G.I.A. Publications, Inc.

Gordon, Edwin E. (1982, 1983, 1984, Summer). Music Learning Seminars. Philadelphia: Temple University.

Landis, Beth and Polly Carder (1972). The Eclectic Curriculum in American Music Education: Contributions of Dalcroze, Kodaly and Orff. Washington, D.C.: Music Educators National Conference.

Suzuki, Shinichi (1969). Nurtured By Love: A New Approach to Education. New York: Exposition Press.

MUSIC LEARNING THEORY AND THE SUZUKI METHOD

Barbara Hanna Creider

One of the most important changes in the approach to teaching music that has emerged in the latter half of the twentieth century has come from the thinking of Shinichi Suzuki of Japan. According to his approach, children first listen to music and later learn to play the music that they have first learned by ear.

Suzuki calls his method the Mother Tongue Approach because he models music study on the way that children learn to speak. There are many similarities between Suzuki's work and Edwin Gordon's work concerning the way children learn to process musical data. Gordon's Music Learning Theory is an attempt to show teachers how they can teach music to children based upon the levels of understanding that children develop as they learn musical syntax, a process that is similar to learning language syntax.

One of the problems with intelligently assessing the differences between Suzuki's Mother Tongue Approach and Gordon's Music Learning Theory is that both are complex. The problem is compounded by the profound linguistic and cultural differences involved in comparing a Japanese philosopher-teacher's thought with an American academic's empirical research. Both their methodology and their conceptual framework are so radically different that even when they use a common language apparently clear to both, they may, in fact, not be communicating.

Each approach is richly complex, but in ways that do not parallel each other. Gordon's writings describe a highly technical construct of hierarchical mental functions. Suzuki's writings, on the other hand, seem almost childish in comparison; they are rambling, autobiographical, and filled with inspirational aphorisms that at first seem to have little to do with music education.

Suzuki is a philosopher-educator whose most pressing concerns are with creating a sensitive heart in the child. Moral virtue and musical sensitivity are closely connected in Suzuki's thought. "When talking about the start and development of a talent, the most basic desire should be the search for truth, goodness, beauty and love..." (Suzuki, 1981, p. 71).

Throughout Suzuki's writings, the terms "ability" and "talent" are used in a broader and more profound sense than they would have been had he limited his writing to the purely musical. It is helpful to look at Suzuki's writings within the context of the Buddhist tradition out of which he is working. One aspect of this tradition is the use of a physical discipline, such as archery in Zen Buddhism, as a means of spiritual advancement. Suzuki has adapted aspects of this to learning the violin, and considers violin study as a discipline that can be used to shape the growing personality of the child. A student might study Suzuki violin from age three through high school, master the three Mozart violin concerti, and put the violin away forever, having accomplished the purpose of the violin study.

In Journey Down the Kreisler Highway (1987), a journal of an American violin teacher studying at the Suzuki School in Matsumoto, Craig Timmerman describes a curriculum for teacher trainees that included elements borrowed from Zen monastic practice: calligraphy classes aimed at deepening self-knowledge and the use of koans, a type of nonsense aphorism used by Zen masters to instruct their disciples in spiritual growth. (Perhaps the best known example of a koan in the West is the phrase, "If you meet the Buddha on the road, kill him" [Edwards, 1981, p. 823]). Timmerman describes his own struggles with Suzuki's statement that he wished students to repeat a phrase ten thousand times. He concludes that the statement is a kind of koan, and describes his own process of coming to terms with what Suzuki could possibly mean by such a statement (Timmerman, 1987, p. 42). In another journal entry, Timmerman describes Suzuki asking him what he thought of what he had seen that day. This happened day after day, with Timmerman growing increasingly uncomfortable with his own answers. Finally, he answered the question with "nothing," the classic Zen response. This seemed to be the answer Suzuki was waiting for, and he chuckled, bowed, and never asked the question again (Timmerman, 1987, p. 43).

Suzuki happened to play the violin, so he applied his discoveries to teaching violin to children. But the goals of the Suzuki method encompass much more than learning to play the violin. Suzuki talks about teaching joy through music. He means the joy of mastering a piece of music and the great pleasure of being able to play well, but he may also mean something deeper. The process of learning to play the violin shapes who the child will become, directing his developing mind and soul in the direction of beauty, goodness, and ultimately, joy.

In contrast, Gordon is a scientist, not a philosopher. Gordon wastes little time on speculation. His writings are terse, concrete, and rigorously logical. The chapters are laid out with beautifully scientific precision. Each branching of the logic tree is dealt with succinctly and thoroughly and this logical parallelism of his thought means his analyses fit nicely into charts and tables. His choice of how to describe reality is radically different from Suzuki's mode of description.

Gordon has chosen to pursue his ideas within the academic community, and thus his thought is tied to and shaped by the western academic tradition of research and scholarly publication. That tradition requires specialization and the fragmentation of broad fields into smaller, more manageable disciplines and minute topics for research. The fields of investigation become further limited by consideration for other researchers' areas of specialty. The whole tradition of western academic thought mediates against any kind of extra-disciplinary synthesis. The need for precision works in both directions and has the effect of limiting the vision of the researcher to explore only what can be precisely defined.

Gordon's research is in how children learn music, and does not extend to any other aspect of their development. Thus, unlike Suzuki, Gordon would not make pronouncements about how to teach a child to become a fine human being, as that is not within his discipline. So what is at the core of Suzuki's whole purpose in teaching music to children, that is, creating fine hearts and sensitive human beings, is not addressed in Music Learning Theory in any way.

Instead, Gordon's answer to the question, "How do children learn music?"comes from statistical analysis of groups of American school children in controlled experiments that can be verified by replication. In doing so, he has clearly improved our understanding of the learning process and made teaching music an easier task. He measures aptitude for music by the child's ability to perceive and understand groups of sounds in two basic dimensions that he defines as "tonal" and "rhythm." Learning to audiate tonal and rhythm patterns is central to Gordon's system of measuring aptitude in children, so that the more skilled a child is in audiating differences in two tonal patterns, the higher the child's tonal aptitude will be.[1] While the ability to audiate is clearly basic to any other ability in music, such as producing a beautiful tone or playing with expression, those elements are not researched to the degree the more basic quantifiable elements of tonal and rhythm audiational skills are studied. Gordon speaks of his knowledge as deep, but narrow.

Music Learning Theory and the Mother Tongue Method are governed by different assumptions about value and the nature of reality. Direct comparisons between Gordon's and Suzuki's discoveries are therefore difficult to make and probably not very useful. However, when one begins to examine each approach as it relates to the practical issues of how to teach a child music, some interesting possibilities emerge for combining the two. Both approaches start with the understanding that it is good to include music in the child's world from the beginning. Suzuki sees this as a necessary component to the child's adapting to his birth culture. If it happens that the child sees playing the violin as a normal behavior for his birth culture, he will play the violin, too. Listening to music and making music with the child as the child grows from infanthood to school age is necessary in the same way that listening to speech and speaking is. The Mother Tongue Approach involves first hearing music and then learning to "speak" it in the same natural way that a baby listens to and then learns to speak English or Japanese.

Gordon explains that same phenomenon in a different way. His research has demonstrated that a very young child goes through a phase for music similar to the speech babble that precedes learning to talk.[2] To the extent that the child is exposed to music, the child has the material available to work through that phase and mature to a point where he can accurately audiate and reproduce pitch and beat. Until children reach the age of nine, their music aptitude scores are highly volatile. Children who participate in music tend to have scores that remain higher than children who receive no musical stimulation. It seems to be a case of "use it or lose it." The potential for some level of achievement in music is universal, but that potential atrophies in children who receive little or no exposure to music.

Both Suzuki and Gordon believe that a child's ability to learn music can be increased by early exposure to hearing and making music, both stress hearing as a prerequisite to learning to perform on a music instrument, and both believe that rote learning should precede learning to read music.

While there are philosophical differences between the two approaches, they can be used together. Gordon speaks of inborn aptitude and Suzuki believes that environment determines ability, but those differences do not affect the way that a child is taught. In Suzuki's system, because of his belief that ability breeds ability, music study is carried out so that the child will develop musical sensitivity and talent. In Gordon's system, one exposes the child to music study at an early age so that the child's music aptitude will stabilize at the highest level possible. One could argue that those may be two ways of expressing similar things. Gordon's is a finite, measurement-based, academic view, while Suzuki's is a more open-ended, spiritual view.

Suzuki says, "Any child can learn." So does Gordon, but he speaks of children with high, average, and low aptitude. That is, he has found that the potential for learning is greater in some children than in others. A superficial judgement again would be that the two statements conflict, but deeper examination reveals agreement. For example, children involved in Suzuki instruction are never tested for ability or formally measured against each other. "Any child can learn" means that any child will benefit and will develop in "ability" if lovingly taught in a "no failure" environment. I do not believe that even Shinichi Suzuki would say that all children are capable of achieving the same level of artistic sensitivity in performance. He would say only that all children will achieve more if taught correctly. In fact, examples of successes with Downs Syndrome children are often cited to prove that all children are capable of learning. The point of Suzuki instruction is not a competition to see which child is best; rather, the goal is to allow each child to develop his or her abilities as much as possible.

Similarly, it would be a misinterpretation of Gordon's research to use any of his tests as a screening tool to determine which students are talented enough to receive music lessons. Aptitude is not the same thing as performance ability; a highly motivated child of lesser aptitude might become a better player than a high aptitude child who cares little about music study and does not practice. Music aptitude is measured so that each child can be given the opportunity to achieve as much as possible. Knowing music aptitude test scores, a teacher can know approximately what to expect from each child. That teacher then can tailor the classroom exercises so that all children in the class are challenged to accomplish what they are capable of accomplishing without being either intimidated or bored. Both Suzuki and Gordon are committed to allowing each child to develop through correct teaching so that all children, not just the so-called gifted ones, benefit from instruction.

Perhaps the aspect of Music Learning Theory that is most significant for Suzuki teachers working with preschool children is Gordon's research into the phenomenon of music babble. If Suzuki teachers are aware of the existence of music babble, and if they can identify children who are in the music babble stage, they can save those children and their parents trouble and frustration by recommending that informal instruction be given until the child comes out of babble and is ready for formal instrumental study. A child still in music babble will have great difficulty audiating the Suzuki repertoire, and will make very slow and painful progress in Suzuki study.

We know that the neurological development of an infant is incomplete at birth. Slowly the brain begins to master control of limbs, head, neck, etc., and muscle tone develops to support the work of the brain (Leach, 1986, p. 160). That process continues for several years as more subtle functions begin to operate. A good example is the child's knowledge of left- and right-sidedness. If a teacher faces a young child and raises the right arm, the child will typically raise the left arm to mirror the action of the teacher. Conversely, an older child whose neurological development is more complete will typically raise the right arm in response to the raising of the right arm by the teacher. Gordon's research has made us aware that a similar "wiring in" process takes place for the ear and the brain before the child can make sense of music. Most of us are familiar with a baby's speech babble as a natural precursor to using words, but music babble as a precursor to formal music learning is not so widely recognized. By drawing an analogy between the way in which speech babble is understood to operate and the way in which music babble might operate, we can better understand what is appropriate for teaching music to small children.

We know that babies begin making expressive sounds at about one month of age. The pre-language process evolves from grunts and sighs into vowel sounds. Consonants are added and an expressive nonsense language emerges. Over time, that language is refined to sound more like the language the baby hears. I have seen children in speech babble tell jokes and then laugh, complain, deliver stern pronouncements, ask questions and answer them, and carry on convincing sounding monologues, all in a language that was the child's own. A child can begin to learn the language spoken by the adult caregivers in his environment only after he has created a framework for language learning through babbling. Babble can neither be skipped nor rushed. A seed must establish roots before it can grow leaves, and the child must go through speech babble before he can learn language. If the seed were to sprout leaves before establishing roots, there would be no way for it to sustain growth, and the plant could not flourish.

Babble seems to take place instinctively. Even deaf babies babble to some extent (Kent, 1980, p. 41). The direction in which babble develops is colored by the environment. Babies of English-speaking parents learn to discriminate and produce the sounds needed to speak English in the same way that babies of Japanese speaking parents learn to discriminate and produce the sounds needed to speak Japanese.

By having music as a natural and active part of his cultural environment, a child becomes an early and natural musician in much the same way that he becomes an early and natural speaker. That process is the basis of the Suzuki approach. However, there is no mention of the babble phase of learning a language in any of the Suzuki literature. If Suzuki is correct in modeling the learning of music performance after the way that a child learns to speak, the phenomenon of music babble needs to be taken into account within the Mother Tongue Approach.

A child in music babble will not be able to keep a consistent tempo. Suzuki teachers who ask three-year-old children to participate in rhythm games in group lessons will see many children move and clap randomly, showing little sense of the pulse of the music. Similarly, a group of young children will be unable to carry a tune. Pitch levels will be only approximate. Children in music babble simply do not process music in the same way that adults do.

A child in speech babble has the advantage of a world filled with language models, and usually with loving, eager caregivers who are thrilled and delighted with each step of progress that the child makes toward speaking. With those environmental aides, the child teaches himself to progress through the stages of babble, and eventually to speak.

A typical child's experience with music babble is a different story. Before the current emphasis on early education, babble went largely unnoticed and little harm was done by beginning before children were ready for formal instruction. But with the rise in popularity of Suzuki, more children are being asked to play music instruments before they have exited the babble phase. There is a tendency for adults to misunderstand what is needed and to insist upon correct performance when a child does not sing correct pitches or rhythms. But it is inappropriate to correct a child still in babble, and worse to give the child the impression that he cannot sing. Music babble is not a negative stage, nor is it an indication that the child is not musical. It is only an indication that the child is not musically mature. It is not possible for a child in music babble to learn music in the same way that a child out of music babble learns music. We can give the child a negative experience if we insist upon formal, structured music lessons for a child not yet out of music babble. On the other hand, a child in music babble must have access to specific music experiences in order to come out of babble. We do not isolate a child in speech babble from language, but we often decide to wait to involve a child in music until after he can demonstrate the ability to perform correctly.

In addition to listening to music, children in music babble need activities that involve singing, moving, dancing, and experimenting with instruments. Motion and thought are closely bound together for small children; children will understand beat better if they can feel it in their bodies through movement. It is best if teachers and parents understand that the child in babble needs informal instruction in the form of enrichment, without adult-imposed expectations of what kind of responses will be deemed correct.

The Temple University Children's Musical Development Program is a program designed to help children work through the music babble stage. Children as young as eighteen months are enrolled in classes with their parents, and those children are allowed to study Suzuki violin only when it is clear that they have come out of music babble. I taught the children Suzuki lessons in a classroom in which several children wait and take turns, so that although lessons are individual, children can observe each other informally. All children in my Suzuki classes should have passed through music babble, but inevitably there were a few children still in babble who had been admitted because of parent pressure. In my experience, children who have not yet passed through babble have done poorly with Suzuki instruction. There have been no exceptions, and age does not seem to be a factor. Children in music babble have been unable to link together the various four note sections of "Twinkle, Twinkle, Little Star," the foundation piece for all Suzuki instruction and the first piece that children learn to play. They do not seem to be able to feel the rhythms of the four variations of "Twinkle," and are not only unable to move the bow to play the rhythms on the violin but are unable to sing them back to the teacher as well. Intonation on the instrument seems to be accomplished visually rather than aurally by those children. If they can see colored tapes marking the location of the various finger placements on the violin fingerboard, they can place their fingers approximately correctly, but they have no aural sense of right- and wrong-sounding placement. If they are asked to concentrate on something other than finger placement, intonation becomes poor without the child noticing.

Often a child in music babble is placed for group instruction with children who are out of music babble. A child in that circumstance inevitably falls painfully behind the other children. Suzuki instruction, which has as its goal to give children an experience that will build self-esteem and self-confidence through a "no failure approach," becomes tedious and defeating for that child. He sees others do easily what is impossible for him. It seems senseless to enroll a child in a program that will only lead to frustration and failure, when waiting until the child is clearly out of babble will permit easy success. For children out of music babble, starting violin lessons at age three is a wonderful idea; they have fun and they succeed. But for the three year old child who is still in music babble, the same instruction can be a mistake. Ideally, teachers should inform parents of what rate of progress to expect, so that they can make intelligent decisions about whether to enroll a child in Suzuki instruction before that child is out of music babble.

Once a child is out of music babble and enrolled in Suzuki instruction, further enrichment outside of instrumental instruction should still take place. To limit the child's listening to the cassette tape of the Suzuki repertoire reflects a misunderstanding of Suzuki's intent. Children need to listen to a variety of styles of music in addition to the music that is included in the Suzuki Book One repertoire.

The Suzuki violin repertoire has frequently been criticized for being harmonically and rhythmically limited. There is no question that that is the case. One needs to understand, however, that the repertoire is selected and ordered so as to be precisely suited to teaching the physical and kinesthetic aspects of violin playing. The Book One repertoire is exclusively in major tonality and duple meter. The first half of the book is limited to A major. There are sound pedagogical reasons for that, but they have to do with the way that the child's hands and arms need to be developed to accomplish the physical playing of the violin, not the way that the child's ears and brain need to be developed for aural accomplishment. The pieces in Book One introduce a series of precisely graded string crossings of increasing difficulty in such a subtle way that only the teacher is aware of their purpose. Similarly, left hand finger dexterity and independence develop remarkably as a result of learning to play precisely those pieces in the order in which they are presented. The teacher who is Suzuki trained will understand how to use the repertoire, and his students will make progress without the use of etude books and boring exercises. Much of Suzuki's genius as a violin pedagogue is evident in the selection and ordering of his repertoire.

I would not interfere with the Book One repertoire in any way from a playing standpoint, as it has been carefully planned and works well. Once children have mastered Book One, however, they will have acquired enough physical technique to begin to study diverse material. New keys are introduced in Book Two, and new tonalities and meters could be introduced as well.

The violin is a complex instrument to play. A piano student can place his hands anywhere on the keyboard, and even before studying, produce sounds merely by depressing the keys. The whole range of tonalities and keyalities is available to the child from the beginning. That is not so with the violin. Merely learning to hold the instrument requires weeks of study. An untutored child can only pluck the four open strings and perhaps scrub the bow across them. Many months of practice are needed before the child has acquired enough skill to play anything at all, much less music in minor or dorian tonality, or unusual meter.

The necessary slow beginnings in violin study should not prevent the child from proceeding with his music education. He can still listen, sing, move, and dance. The broad spectrum of musical development can and should still be nurtured away from the violin. Many music resources are available to children in our society. Does the family attend any sort of collective worship services regularly in which music making is a part? Do members of the family play musical instruments? Do they listen to the radio in the car? Do they go to parades, picnics, or ethnic festivals? In addition to music available on record, cassette, and compact disc, music is played in every elevator, shopping mall, waiting room, airplane, etc., in the country. We must not, and in reality can not, limit the child to Suzuki Book One repertoire. We should encourage him to participate in a wide variety of other music experiences while the Book One repertoire is being learned. The child can certainly learn to dance and move to music in triple meter and unusual meter and sing songs in minor tonality or phrygian tonality while mastering the physical skills needed to play music in A major and duple meter.

The Suzuki teacher can facilitate the total learning process for children in two important ways. First, parents need to be encouraged to seek beneficial music experiences for their children. The teacher might offer a certificate for the child who attends three concerts, or organize a lending library of cassettes for parents, or suggest a class outing to a Bluegrass festival. Gordon would urge parents of Suzuki students to enroll their children in some kind of supplemental musicianship class that involves opportunities to sing, dance, and move their bodies to music that represents a variety of tonalities, meters, and styles. One cannot assume that parents will do those things without encouragement from teachers.

A second, more direct way for Suzuki teachers to help their students is to include Gordon's learning sequence activities in the Suzuki group lessons. It seems that there is a lot of potential for integrating Gordon's work with patterns into Suzuki group lessons, as a natural outgrowth of tonalization work.

Once the children can hear and imitate a two note group, I can begin teaching tonic and dominant patterns in A major. When the children have learned a small repertoire of tonic and dominant patterns in A major, I can begin to ask individual children to play or sing patterns after I play them. Once that becomes easy for the children, I ask them to sing or play the first note of a patterns that I played. Rhythm patterns can be played by the teacher on an open string and can be chanted or played by the children. I rarely spend more than five minutes of the group lesson on learning sequence activities and I try to alternate between rhythm units and tonal units from lesson to lesson.

Conclusion

Much creative work remains to be done to adapt the Music Learning Theory materials so they are immediately accessible to practicing Suzuki teachers. The differences between the two approaches are profound, however, and this work should be undertaken only by people who understand both methods. One of the strengths of the Suzuki movement is its openness to successful ideas from other sources. There is an ongoing process of learning, experimentation, and adopting what is good within the umbrella philosophy of the Suzuki movement. Within that process, there is definitely room for an exploration of Music Learning Theory.

Music Learning Theory is not an approach that is easy to grasp, but I think that it has a great deal to contribute to Suzuki programs. It works well as a support to instrumental study and is particularly well-suited to the rote learning emphasized in the Suzuki movement. While the merging of those two methods is hardly something a teacher can accomplish quickly, the results will be well worth the time spent.

NOTES

[1]Within this book, see "Audiation: The Term and the Process" for more information about audiation.

[2]Within this book, see "Informal Music Instruction as Readiness for Learning Sequence Activities" for more information about music babble.

REFERENCES

Edwards, C.W. (1981). "Dogen." Abingdon Dictionary of Living Religions. Nashville: Keith Crim, ed. Abingdon.
Edwards, C.W. (1981). "Zen." Abingdon Dictionary of Living Religions. Nashville: Keith Crim, ed. Abingdon.
Gordon, Edwin E. (1980). Learning Sequences in Music. Chicago: G.I.A. Publications, Inc.

Kent, Raymond D. "Articulatory and Acoustic Perspectives on Speech Development." (1980). The Communication Game: Perspectives on the Development of Speech, Language and Non Verbal Communication Skills, Abigail Peterson Reilly ed. Pediatric Round Table, 38-43. Johnson and Johnson.

Leach, Penelope (1986). Your Baby and Child from Birth to Age Five. New York: Alfred A. Knopf.

Suzuki, Shinichi (1981). Ability Development from Age Zero. Athens, Ohio: Ability Development Associates, Inc.

Suzuki, Shinichi (1983). Nurtured by Love. Athens, Ohio: Ability Development Associates, Inc.

Timmerman, Craig (1987). Journey Down the Kreisler Highway Memphis, Tennessee: Ivory Palaces Music.

INTEGRATING MUSIC LEARNING THEORY INTO AN ORFF PROGRAM

Nadine Cernohorsky

Music Learning Theory and Orff-Schulwerk: Descriptions and Comparisons

One of the more popular approaches to teaching general music in the elementary school is that of Carl Orff, an approach known as Orff-Schulwerk. Music teachers who use Orff techniques make music fun for students. The students actively participate in and enjoy a variety of music experiences such as singing, moving, playing instruments, and improvising. Moreover, the teachers take pleasure in the success of their students, and are consequently motivated to continue to guide each student's music development. It is easier to teach students who enjoy music than to teach students who dislike it.

If Orff-Schulwerk is successful and the teachers and the students enjoy it, then why should music teachers implement Music Learning Theory into an Orff program? Would Orff teachers using Music Learning Theory have to change the way they think and teach? How would music teachers coordinate learning sequence activities and Orff activities in the elementary general music class? The purpose of this article is to answer those questions.

Although Carl Orff and Edwin Gordon have different ideas about what to teach and how to teach it, both approaches to teaching music are intended to lead to the same goal - to develop music understanding. The two approaches will be compared and contrasted briefly in the following paragraphs before suggestions are made for combining the two.

Orff's elemental approach to teaching music is based upon the abilities of children to experience, imitate, explore, and create music. Aural experiences precede visual experiences. In other words, by the time a student learns the symbol for a musical concept, he has developed an understanding of that concept by experiencing it. According to Orff, the basic element of music is rhythm because it is inherent to both movement and speech. Characteristic of Orff-Schulwerk music instruction is the use of speech patterns and rhymes, melodic and rhythmic ostinati, the pentatonic scale, pitched and unpitched percussion instruments, and melodic and rhythmic improvisation.

Unlike Orff-Schulwerk, Music Learning Theory is based upon objective research. Through research, Gordon has developed both a skill learning sequence and a content learning sequence. The sequence of skills in Music Learning Theory is similar to the order of activities proposed by Orff. For example, aural/oral precedes verbal association, which precedes symbolic understanding (visual), which precedes creativity and improvisation. Gordon's content learning sequence includes both tonal and rhythm content. Gordon believes that "in order to fully understand music, one must be aware of its basic aural elements, which are a sense of tonality and a sense of meter" (Gordon, 1984, p.2). Though the general categories of tonal content and rhythm content are used also in Orff, the specific patterns and the sequencing of those patterns according to their difficulty levels are unique to Gordon. Gordon believes that audiation is the key to all music learning.[1] According to Gordon, the audiation of a variety of tonalities and meters is the readiness for music literacy, and is therefore the basis for teaching music according to Music Learning Theory.

"Orff-Schulwerk is not a method; rather, it is an indicator, a signpost" (Keller, 1974). A method, according to Gordon, is "why" we teach "what" we teach"when" we teach it (Gordon, 1984, p.9). The principles of Orff-Schulwerk may be understood and applied in a variety of ways, and Orff-Schulwerk can come close to functioning as a method when applied in some of those ways. For example, belief in the need for an ontogenetic[2] development of melodic skills provides answers to "what" to teach and "when" to teach it. "So-mi" is taught before "so-mi-la" and "so-mi-la" is taught before "so-mi-do." The shortcoming of the Orff-Schulwerk approach is in the lack of an answer to the question "why." Why teach "so-mi" before"so-mi-la," and so forth? Is it easier for a child to sing "so-la-so-mi" than to sing "so-mi-do?"

Music Learning Theory, on the other hand, is a method specifically because it answers the questions "why," "what," and "when." Sequential objectives are defined in terms of skill and content. "What" to teach includes music skills (aural/oral, verbal association, etc.) and tonal and rhythm content (major tonality, tonic function, duple meter, macro and micro beats, etc.). "When" to teach the content and skills is determined by readiness hierarchies based upon research. For example, before a child learns the verbal association for "so-mi-do," he must sing that major tonic pattern in solo using a neutral syllable while audiating the resting tone in major tonality. Within that illustration, the "what" is the verbal association for a major tonic pattern and the "when" is the appropriate time to teach verbal association of patterns, i.e., after those patterns have been taught at the aural/oral level. "Why" teach at the aural/oral level of learning before teaching at the verbal association level of learning? The answer to that question is that the child will be able to develop an understanding of music syntax, and consequently give meaning to music more easily, if aural/oral learning precedes verbal association learning in relation to a given piece of content.

The combining of Music Learning Theory and an Orff program strengthens the sequence and direction of Orff classroom activities. Reciprocally, appropriate Orff techniques aid the teaching of appropriate method through Music Learning Theory. Without the motivational activities of Orff-Schulwerk (or comparable classroom activities), the sequential objectives of Music Learning Theory will appear less interesting and attractive to students.

Orff-Schulwerk has been successful in the development of children's music understanding for decades. Unfortunately, the progression of activities applied within the Orff approach to music instruction is not always logical and efficient. The sequence of content and skills must be justified if the Orff approach is to become a method as opposed to being simply a series of activities and techniques. Both appropriate method and appropriate techniques are essential in the development of music literacy. The Orff process is thus enhanced and intensified through the application of method as defined by Music Learning Theory.

The implementation of Music Learning Theory into an Orff program enables Orff teachers to teach to students' individual musical differences both efficiently and effectively. Orff believed that all children have musical ability (music aptitude) and that they all should be given the opportunity to participate and experience success in music. Gordon agrees that all children are born with music aptitude, but he recognizes that some children have high aptitude, some children have low aptitude, and most children have average aptitude. A teacher can measure a student's music aptitude through the administration of a valid music aptitude test appropriate to the age of the student.[3] By use of valid aptitude measures, a teacher is better able to adapt instruction to the individual differences of students (Gordon, 1984, p.224). Consequently, students are more likely to experience success in music. Gordon's music aptitude research provides a means by which Orff teachers can enrich their teaching by making it more responsive to the individual and more thorough.

In order to create a successful union between Orff-Schulwerk and Music Learning Theory, music teachers need to understand the concept of audiation. The term audiation, often referred to by Orff teachers as "inner hearing," means to hear music when the sound is not physically present. Gunild Keetman said "the inner ear must hear the sound before it is played" (1974, p.90). Orff teachers incorporate audiation into their teaching in many ways, and may therefore be able to apply Music Learning Theory to their curriculum without dramatically changing the way in which they teach. For example, an Orff teacher may be audiating a nursery rhyme while chanting rhythm patterns to the class for imitation. When asked to play a specific rhythm pattern on an unpitched percussion instrument, the student may audiate familiar words that correspond to that pattern. Following is an example.

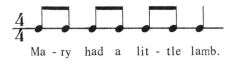

Ma - ry   had   a   lit - tle   lamb.

Orff-Schulwerk provides further opportunity for audiation through echo-clapping, echo-patting, singing, improvisation, instrument playing, listening, and creative movement.

The important distinction between the kinds of audiation activities cited above and the kinds of audiation activities associated with Music Learning Theory is that Gordon considers the audiation of tonality and meter to be the basis for music literacy. Therefore, it is necessary for teachers to teach students to audiate tonality and meter. That can be accomplished through the use of learning sequence activities. By devoting the first five to ten minutes of each class period to learning sequence activities, a teacher can develop students' audiation in a way that will enrich the Orff classroom activities that follow.

The Orff process of experience-imitate-explore-create is similar to skill learning sequence in Music Learning Theory. While Gordon and Orff believe that exploration, creation, and improvisation are necessary to develop music understanding, their use of those terms differs. Experience and imitation in Orff-Schulwerk are similar to the aural/oral skill level in Music Learning Theory. In each case a student must hear and experience the music aurally before he is asked to imitate or perform orally through singing and movement. Exploration precedes the experience/imitation, or aural/oral level of learning. A child begins to explore sounds and movement from birth. That period of early exploration is referred to in Music Learning Theory as the music babble stage.[4] After a child has developed a vocabulary of tonal patterns and rhythm patterns through exploration, experience, and imitation (by means of audiation), he will be able to create and improvise music.[5]

The term explore literally means to investigate, examine, seek, and search (Webster, 1979, p.400). To explore in music is to experiment with familiar and unfamiliar sounds and to become aware of how they interact and fit together in patterns, but to do so without giving those patterns musical meaning. Exploration and creation are not the same. Exploration provides a basis for creation. A child explores when he has not yet developed a vocabulary of tonal patterns and rhythm patterns in various tonalities and meters that can be recalled in audiation and used in creativity. Exploration does not necessarily involve audiation. Perhaps students with low music aptitude need to explore more than do students with high music aptitude.

In the Orff music classroom, exploration is frequently associated with playing instruments. Students experiment with different sounds, timbres, and ways of playing barred (pitched) and unbarred (unpitched) percussion instruments used individually and in combination. That exploration familiarizes the child with instruments and their characteristics. A common Orff technique is to explore timbres and sounds that may represent or symbolize a specific object, mood, or event. Orff teachers believe that without the necessary exploration of sounds through the use of instruments, a student's creativity will be inhibited.

An Orff teacher who incorporates Music Learning Theory into his program needs to understand how Gordon defines improvisation and creativity. Gordon considers creativity and improvisation to be distinct but related. Gordon believes that a child creates when he organizes familiar and unfamiliar material into something new, with no external restrictions having been imposed. For example, if a teacher performs a series of four macro and micro beat patterns in duple meter, a student may respond with a series of rhythm patterns of any function in duple meter. In improvisation, external restrictions are placed upon the student. For example, the teacher might perform a phrase in major tonality, using the functions tonic-tonic-dominant-tonic, and ask the student to respond with a phrase using the same tonality and functions, but different patterns. Creativity is easier than improvisation because of the lack of restrictions. To that extent, creativity is a readiness for improvisation.

Creation/improvisation, for the two terms are often used synonymously in Orff-Schulwerk literature, is an important component of the Orff approach to music instruction. Students are encouraged to create/improvise rhythmically and melodically (tonally) through singing, chanting, moving, and playing instruments. To avoid discouraging the student, Orff teachers begin with short exercises that involve familiar material and gradually progress to longer exercises that involve both familiar and unfamiliar material. Initially, group improvisation protects the individual from exposure and serves as a transition to individual improvisation (Keetman, 1974, p.89). Beginning exercises include improvising tonal and rhythm "answers" to the teacher's tonal and rhythm "questions" and improvising ostinato accompaniments. The teacher may restrict the student to use of the pentatonic tonal system in singing, the octave and the fifth in bordun accompaniment, and other criteria that he deems appropriate.

Orff-Schulwerk and Music Learning Theory represent two different approaches to the teaching of tonal content. A teacher using the Orff approach begins tonal pattern instruction with pentatonic patterns. A teacher using the Music Learning Theory approach begins instruction with diatonic (major and minor) patterns. Proponents of both approaches endorse the teaching of rote songs in many different tonalities.

The Orff approach to music instruction is based in elemental music making. In the introduction to Elementaria, Werner Thomas describes elemental music making as "an effective, preliminary study that leads to the understanding of great music in its entirety... and opens the way to all kinds of style" (Keetman, 1974, p.12). The "elements" are patterns based upon the pentatonic scale. Students begin singing with the two-note "cuckoo" call ("so-mi"), which is deemed natural for students to sing. That is followed by three-note tonal patterns. Making music within the pentatonic tonal system has one great advantage. When students sing or play pentatonic music on tonebar instruments (such as the xylophone), anything they perform will sound pleasing because it will be free of dissonance. Thus the pentatonic scale provides students with the necessary tools to play pleasant-sounding music on the instruments.

According to Music Learning Theory, it is important for students to learn two tonalities concurrently, such as major and harmonic minor or dorian and mixolydian. A student does not know what one tonality is until he has another to compare it to. A sense of tonality is essential to music understanding. A student has developed a sense of tonality when he can sing relatively in tune in major tonality and in harmonic minor tonality. Although students are taught patterns first in major and harmonic minor tonality, they perform rote songs in all the tonalities. As instruction progresses, they should be taught tonal patterns in the other tonalities as well. The larger the vocabulary of tonal patterns a student can audiate, the better able he will be to understand a piece of music.

Diatonic patterns are not difficult for students to perform as long as the students learn to sing arpeggiated patterns before stepwise patterns. The leading tone helps to establish the resting tone and contributes to the development of a child's sense of tonality. The half-step interval, considered by some to be difficult for children to sing, is difficult to sing only if it is audiated and sung in isolation, without reference to a tonality (Gordon, 1984, p.88). If a half-step is audiated and sung in relation to a tonality, such as in the cadential pattern "ti-do" in major tonality, it is easier to perform in tune.

Pentatony, which contains no half-steps, has no leading tone. Gordon calls it a "floating" tonality, because any tone may be used as the resting tone (Gordon, 1984, p.87). Gordon believes that the performer or listener imposes major or minor tonality on pentatonic music by audiating "ti" or "si" as the subjective leading tone. "Even if pentatonic might be considered a tonality with one of its five tones accepted as a resting tone, that resting tone would duplicate a resting tone of an already existing tonality, thus relegating pentatonic to a variation of the latter" (Gordon, 1984, p.86). The lack of a definite leading tone and resting tone in the pentatonic tonal system makes it a subjective tonality. The performer or listener may identify any tone as the resting tone. On the other hand, diatonic tonalities are objective tonalities because they each have a specific resting tone. It is important for a student to be able to audiate objective tonalities, such as major and minor, before he is expected to audiate subjective tonalities, such as pentatonic. Otherwise the child will not learn to audiate properly (Gordon, 1984, p.87).

Coordinating Orff-Schulwerk and Music Learning Theory in the Music Classroom

When used together in an organized music curriculum, Music Learning Theory and Orff-Schulwerk complement each other. The classroom activities, which can be taught incorporating Orff techniques, provide the initial readiness for the sequentially organized learning sequence activities of Music Learning Theory. In turn, learning sequence activities reinforce what is learned in classroom activities. Learning sequence activities are extended and enriched through Orff techniques. Most important, Orff-Schulwerk gains sequence and direction through the use of skill and content learning sequence.

Learning sequence activities should be taught for no less than five and no more than ten minutes at the beginning of each music class. The remainder of the class period should be devoted to classroom activities in the Orff-Schulwerk style. Skills should be introduced through learning sequence activities and should be reinforced through Orff activities. Content should be introduced through classroom activities and should be developed through learning sequence activities. The interaction between Orff-Schulwerk classroom activities and Music Learning Theory learning sequence activities is based upon the interaction between skill and content.[6]

It is impossible within the scope of this article to discuss every possible way to coordinate Orff activities and learning sequence activities. Therefore, some popular techniques that are typically associated with Orff-Schulwerk will be discussed in relation to Music Learning Theory. Those techniques are imitation, the use of movement (specifically body percussion), the use of tonebar instruments, and the use of rhythm speech.

Imitation is a natural response for children. A child may repeat words or phrases, spoken or sung, that he hears. He may imitate body movement that he sees. Imitation is a natural skill, and it can contribute to the development of other skills, such as audiation skills and motor skills. The term echo is often used synonymously with the term imitation in Orff-Schulwerk to describe activities such as echo-play, echo-clap, and echo-sing.

In learning sequence activities, students echo tonal patterns and rhythm patterns in solo and in groups in order to develop audiation skills. In Orff-Schulwerk activities, students echo tonal patterns and rhythm patterns through instrumental performance, through movement, and through singing and speaking. Echoing is used often as a game. Children enjoy games, and games enable children to learn while having fun. Keetman believes that "echo-play trains accurate listening, quick reaction, memory and feeling for form" (1974, p.27). In Elementaria (1974), Keetman provides many examples of how echo-play may be used in the form of games. Three examples follow. First, students may echo-play or echo-sing phrases that were performed by the teacher while moving to the beat. Second, a student may be the leader instead of the teacher. Third, the teacher and class may echo-clap the same pattern together. The class must follow the teacher or student leader as he changes patterns and movement. In learning sequence activities and in Orff classroom activities, the teacher must always establish tonality and/or meter before he begins the activity to enable the students to audiate the resting tone and/or meter.

Instruction in movement should be an important part of classroom activities. Just as it is important for a student to develop a vocabulary of tonal patterns and rhythm patterns, it is important for him to develop a vocabulary of locomotor and nonlocomotor movements. Keetman agrees that "no Schulwerk lesson should be without movement exercises" (1974, p.107). Some of those exercises include guided exploration of movement, reaction training, structured and unstructured movement, creative movement, movement improvisation, and traditional dances.

Movement instruction during classroom activities is an important adjunct to rhythm learning sequence activities. Teachers must provide opportunities for students to move their bodies to a steady beat. (Classroom activities in which students move their bodies in a manner not synchronous with a steady beat are also desirable.) Only after a student is able to move his body to a steady beat and in a consistent tempo is he ready to begin instruction in rhythm learning sequence activities, i.e., to effectively begin the formal development of rhythm audiation. The teacher should develop coordination skills separate from rhythm audiation skills at first. Coordination skills should be developed through movement during classroom activities, and rhythm audiation skills should be developed through the chanting of rhythm patterns during learning sequence activities. If a student is asked to do both simultaneously before he is ready, he will not be successful.

Students may be asked to combine coordination activities and rhythm audiation activities when they are ready. An example of combining coordination and audiation is the chanting of a rhythm pattern while stamping the macro beat with the feet and tapping or clapping the micro beat with the hands. The teacher could enrich the movement environment for the student by incorporating into the many fine Orff-Schulwerk activities other movement activities, such as those devised by Dalcroze, Laban, and Weikart.

A popular movement activity used by Orff teachers is known as body percussion. When using body percussion, the students use their bodies to create different sounds. Four common body percussion movements are stamping feet, patting knees, clapping hands, and snapping fingers. In an Orff program those body sounds should eventually be transferred to their respective instruments. For example, stamps should be transferred to the bass xylophone and snaps should be transferred to the soprano glockenspiel. Echoing rhythm patterns with body percussion is difficult because it requires both coordination and rhythm audiation. Echoing rhythm patterns through chanting, using a neutral syllable such as "bah," is less difficult and more desirable. That does not require coordination, but it does develop rhythm audiation. Performing rhythm patterns with body percussion is more difficult than performing a steady beat with body percussion. For example, it is more difficult to pat a rhythm pattern on the knees than it is to chant that rhythm pattern while patting the steady beat. To perform rhythm patterns with body percussion using more than one level, e.g., stamping and clapping, is more difficult than to move at one level, e.g., stamping or clapping. Body percussion can be a useful and motivational classroom activity if it is taught with respect to the children's current audiation and movement skills.

The ability to play pitched and unpitched percussion instruments requires aural and kinesthetic skills. If a child cannot move his body in a coordinated manner, he will not be able to play instruments in a coordinated manner. If a child cannot audiate meter and tempo, he will not be able to maintain a steady beat and a consistent tempo while playing percussion instruments. An instrument should function as an extension of the body, and that is possible only if the development of coordination skills and rhythm audiation skills through movement instruction and learning sequence activities precedes instruction on the instrument. To give meaning to the playing of pitched percussion instruments requires tonal audiation skills in addition to rhythm audiation and coordination skills. Those skills should be taught without instruments, and then should be transferred to the playing of instruments. Tonal audiation, rhythm audiation, and movement must be taught separately before they are combined in instrumental performance. That does not mean that the use of instruments should be delayed until a student is completely coordinated and can audiate in every tonality and every meter. It means only that unless a student can audiate a particular meter or tonality and move in a coordinated manner without an instrument, he will not be able to exhibit skills in that tonality or meter while playing an instrument.

Once a student is able to sing tonal patterns and chant rhythm patterns in solo in learning sequence activities, he may be asked to perform those familiar patterns on the tonebar instruments in classroom activities. For example, assume that a student is able to sing specified tonic patterns in major tonality using a neutral syllable. The alto xylophone might be set up in a major tonality, e.g., C Major. Depending upon the aptitude and experience of the student, the instrument may include all of the tonebars or only those representing the tonic triad, C E G. After the teacher establishes tonality, he should ask the student to echo-sing a specific tonic major pattern, such as "do-mi." The teacher may show the student which bar (C) to start on. The student should try to play the pattern on the xylophone while singing and/or audiating the pattern. The teacher should offer help as needed. The teacher should not use the terms resting tone, C is "do," major tonality, or tonic function until the student has learned those terms at the verbal association level, and of course all tonal patterns should be performed without rhythm.

The same procedure may be followed with rhythm patterns. Before performing rhythm patterns on barred percussion instruments, the student should develop playing skills through the performance of steady beat patterns. He should learn to play with one hand alone, with both hands simultaneously but on different pitches (right hand plays A and left hand plays D), and with hands alternating either on one pitch or on two different pitches (left hand plays D then right hand plays A). Because the performance of steady beat patterns develops technique, it should be considered a readiness for the playing of rhythm patterns and melodic patterns. When performing rhythm patterns on tonebar instruments, only one tone should be used. As always, the student should chant the pattern before playing it.

Melodic patterns are an amalgamation of tonal patterns and rhythm patterns. They include macro beats, micro beats, divisions, and elongations; they also include more than one tone. When performing melodic patterns on tonebar instruments, the student should first sing the melodic pattern using a neutral syllable. If he has tonal problems performing the pattern, he may sing the pitches without rhythm, using tonal syllables (if he has learned those syllables in learning sequence activities). If he has rhythm problems performing the pattern, he may chant the durations without melody using rhythm syllables (if he has learned those syllables in learning sequence activities). If a student has difficulty performing melodic patterns on the instruments, it is a result of a deficiency in coordination skills, tonal audiation skills, rhythm audiation skills, or any combination of those skills.

The final Orff classroom activity to be discussed here is the use of rhythm speech. Orff believed that children's rhymes provide a natural starting point for the study of rhythm. Small rhythmic units are extracted from children's rhymes, songs, and names to form "rhythmic building blocks" (Keetman, 1974, p. 24). Those building blocks are simply rhythm patterns. The process of using words to express rhythm patterns is known as mnemonics. Deriving rhythms from words and finding words to fit rhythms can be fun, as well as a learning experience. However, without the prior development of aural/oral and verbal association skills, rhythm speech can be difficult and confusing.

Rhythm patterns combine to form a meter. Rhythm understanding is developed only if a student learns to audiate rhythm patterns within the context of a meter. Once a student can chant a rhythm pattern in solo using a neutral syllable, he should learn the rhythm syllables and proper names for those patterns and their meters. According to Gordon, each rhythm pattern must be assigned one set of logical syllables.[7] Following is an example of a rhythm pattern and its corresponding rhythm syllables.

The rhythm syllables are indicative of the meter and function of the pattern. The pattern is in duple meter. The "du" is the macro beat, the "de" is the micro beat, and the "ta" is the division. If that pattern were to be represented by the word "strawberry," the student would not draw the same conclusions. He may become confused by the verbal association of "strawberry" when he finds out that the same pattern may be represented by the words "blueberry," "bicycle," and "hamburger." An older student or a student with high aptitude may make the necessary connections, but a young student or one with low aptitude usually will not. Mnemonics may be used, but only as an extension of rhythm syllables after rhythm syllables have been mastered.

Following is an example that incorporates Music Learning Theory into Orff rhythm speech. The students chant the rhyme, "Humpty Dumpty sat on a wall" while moving to the beat. Next, they chant the rhyme using a neutral syllable while audiating the words and moving to the beat. The students move first to the macro beat and then to the micro beat. The teacher asks the students to identify the meter of the chant. "How do you know that it is in triple meter?" The students should be audiating the rhythm syllables in triple meter. The teacher may then ask the class if they know another rhyme that is in triple meter. A student may respond with "Jack be nimble, Jack be quick."

Individual rhythm patterns may be extracted from the rhymes to form instrumental ostinati. A student will perform rhythmic ostinati more accurately if he is audiating meter and rhythm syllables than if he is repeating a word or phrase while playing its rhythm. For example, if a student plays the rhythm pattern shown below on the xylophone, he will perform it more accurately if he audiates duple meter and the appropriate rhythm syllables than if he audiates the words "and going home."

In the latter case, he will not be audiating meter, and will thus be more likely to perform unrhythmically. He will also be less able to generalize what he has learned to the same rhythm pattern used in a different song in conjunction with different words.

Conclusion

Orff-Schulwerk provides music teachers with a wide variety of ideas and activities. A few of those ideas have been described to illustrate how Music Learning Theory can be integrated into an Orff program. Both Music Learning Theory and Orff-Schulwerk are successful and respected approaches to music instruction. Each can gain significantly from the other. By integrating Music Learning Theory into Orff-Schulwerk, one naturally integrates Orff-Schulwerk into Music Learning Theory. A music curriculum that incorporates both processes would be ideal.

NOTES

[1]Within this book, see "Audiation: The Term and the Process" for more information.

[2]Ontogenetic is related to the development of small, individual elements into larger forms and structures.

[3]Within this book, see "The Measurement and Evaluation of Music Aptitudes and Achievement" for more information about music aptitude testing.

[4]Within this book, see "Informal Music Instruction as Readiness for Learning Sequence Activities" for more information about the music babble stage.

[5]To proceed from the aural/oral level of learning to the creativity/improvisation level of learning within the dictates of Music Learning Theory requires a"bridging" movement, i.e., a temporary skipping of levels within the stepwise skill learning sequence.

[6]Within this book, see "Coordinating Learning Sequence Activities and Classroom Activities" for more information about the interaction of skill and content.

[7]Within this book, see "Rhythm Syllables: A Comparison of Systems" for more information about rhythm syllables.

REFERENCES

Choksy, Lois, Robert M. Abramson, Avon Gillespie, and David Woods (1986). Teaching Music in the Twentieth Century. Englewood Cliffs, N.J.: Prentice-Hall.

Gordon, Edwin E. (1984). Learning Sequences In Music: Skill, Content, and Patterns. Chicago: G.I.A. Publications, Inc.

Gordon, Edwin E. (1987). The Nature, Description, Measurement, and Evaluation of Music Aptitudes. Chicago: G.I.A. Publications, Inc.

Gordon, Edwin E. and David Woods (1986). Jump Right In: The Music Curriculum. Chicago: G.I.A. Publications, Inc.

Keetman, Gunild (1974). Elementaria. London: Schott and Co. Ltd.

Keller, Wilhelm (1974). Introduction to Music For Children. New York: Schott Music Corp.

O'Brien, James P. (1983). Teaching Music. New York: Holt, Rinehart and Winston.

Orff, Carl and Gunild Keetman Music For Children: Vol. I Pentatonic. London: Schott and Co. Ltd.

Orff, Gertrud (1980). The Orff Music Therapy. New York: Schott Music Corp.

Wheeler, Lawrence and Lois Raebeck (1985). Orff and Kodaly. Dubuque, Iowa: Wm. C. Brown Publishers.

Woolf, Henry Bosley, editor in chief (1979). Webster's New Collegiate Dictionary. Springfield, Mass.: G. & C. Merriam Company.

INTEGRATING MUSIC LEARNING THEORY INTO THE KODALY CURRICULUM

John M. Feierabend

Zoltan Kodály believed that music instruction should not be for the select few alone, but that music literacy is the right of every citizen. He was dedicated to elevating the quality of music education in Hungary in terms of both appreciation and understanding. Kodály wished for all Hungarian children to come to know their musical mother tongue, Hungarian folk songs, as well as to know music considered to be masterworks of recognized composers. At the same time, he suggested that a cappella singing should be the means by which children develop music understanding. He believed that the voice is the most natural instrument to man, is accessible to all people, and enables one to develop inner musicianship that will later allow him to express musical thinking through an instrument rather than to try to derive music meaning from an instrument.

As a result of his beliefs and convictions, Kodály inspired a group of Hungarian music theorists and educators to survey exemplary systems of music education and develop a method for Hungarian music educators. That research resulted in the acquisition of pedagogies from Sarah Glover and John Curwen in England, John Weber and Fritz Jode in Germany, Emile Chevé in France, and Emile Jacques-Dalcroze in Switzerland.

The system of music education developed by the Hungarians has served as an inspiration and model to teachers in many other countries. Each country in turn has adapted the Hungarian model to accommodate cultural differences and recent research. As American music educators strive to develop an appropriate adaptation of the Hungarian model, they will do well to investigate the work of Edwin Gordon for the insight that it has to offer.

Gordon's Music Learning Theory supports many of the tenets that Kodály teachers advocate: the use of relative solfege, the use of rhythm syllables, sequenced instruction, singing before playing instruments, and a goal of music literacy, to name a few. However, the similarities between the approaches of Gordon and Kodály are balanced by the differences between the two. It is the differences that provide a feast of relevant thinking for Kodály teachers.

Music Learning Theory consists of three sequences that parallel the organization of the Kodály curriculum; those are a skill learning sequence, a rhythm learning sequence, and a tonal learning sequence. The skill learning sequence is similar to the process known to Kodály music educators as preparation, presentation, and practice. The tonal and rhythm sequences are more distantly related.

The Kodály rhythm and tonal sequences are based upon the patterns Kodály found to be most natural for Hungarian children to sing and that occur regularly in Hungarian folk songs. The Gordon rhythm and tonal sequences were derived from experimental research that investigated American children's ability to aurally discriminate between patterns that had been paired on the basis of similarities and differences. That Kodály and Gordon developed different rhythm and tonal learning sequences by investigating different abilities, i.e., singing and aural discrimination (both of which are important), should encourage the teacher to integrate the Kodály approach and Music Learning Theory.

Combining Gordon's Music Learning Theory with the Kodály curriculum can be as easy as setting aside five to ten minutes for learning sequence activities at the beginning of each period. However, more thorough integration is also possible. Whether a teacher attempts a thorough integration or adapts only the learning sequence activity aspects of Music Learning Theory into a Kodály approach, the students will benefit. The next section of this article will give details about the less thorough approach, and the section following that will give information about the more thorough approach.

Combining Learning Sequence Activities with the Kodály Curriculum

The ease with which Gordon's learning sequence activities can be integrated into a Kodály curriculum may be surprising. During the first five to ten minutes of each music class, the teacher should lead the students in rhythm and tonal dialogue (learning sequence activities)[1] in accordance with their rhythm aptitude and tonal aptitude.[2] Following the learning sequence activities, the remainder of the lesson should proceed as the teacher desires. Both the learning sequence activities and Kodály lessons are accommodated in that arrangement.

During approximately the first year of learning sequence activities, students echo a variety of rhythm patterns and tonal patterns, using a neutral syllable or solfège or rhythm syllables. No reading or writing is introduced initially. Students who are taught through learning sequence activities will echo rhythm patterns and tonal patterns that they may not study in a Kodály sequence for a year or two. Those aural and verbal experiences seem not to confuse students. To the contrary, learning sequence activities enable students to bring a far deeper understanding of major and minor tonalities and duple and triple meters to the Kodály sequences when those concepts are later presented

In the early years, the student's aural and oral abilities are challenged without the teacher demanding notational understanding of the content presented. As a result, students develop a deeper and more intuitive understanding of tonal and rhythm content. The reading and writing of patterns studied in the learning sequence activities (symbolic association) is not introduced until two to four years of instruction have taken place, the exact time dependent on frequency of class meetings and other factors. Rhythm reading is introduced earlier than is tonal reading. By the time Kodály-trained students experience learning sequence activities that include symbolic association, they will be ready to integrate the reading and writing of rhythm patterns into their vocabulary of Kodály reading and writing skills.

Tonal Differences

The teaching of tonal learning sequence activities begins with the students echoing tonic and dominant patterns in major tonality and minor tonality, using a neutral syllable. At first, the patterns are arpeggiated so that students are not required to sing semitones. That experience provides students with an aural preparation that will complement the pentatonic material presented during Kodály lessons. The benefits of combining pentatonic and diatonic patterns are shown in the research of Catherine Jarjisian (1981). She concluded that singing both pentatonic and diatonic patterns resulted in improved singing ability when compared with singing either pentatonic or diatonic patterns exclusively.

As students progress in tonal learning sequence activities, they will begin to use solfège syllables in the echoing of tonic and dominant patterns and later subdominant, multiple, and cadential patterns, in major and minor tonalities. Those syllables will not have been studied yet in a Kodály curriculum. In learning sequence activities, the syllables are simply sung by rote in echo response to the teacher. The students are not required to answer questions concerning intervallic relationships or to identify those patterns in notated form. The objective in echoing tonal patterns sung with solfège syllables is to build associations between syllables and sound, and consequently increase the student's vocabulary of tonal patterns. That vocabulary will later function as the foundation for making tonal generalizations. A traditional Kodály sequence, building specific intervallic relationships, can be taught concurrently without confusing the student.

By the time the students are introduced to reading and writing in learning sequence activities, they are likely to have completed approximately four years of a Kodály curriculum, during which time they will have learned how to read and write many tonal patterns that include the diatonic tones of the major and minor scales. The extra aural and verbal training that will have taken place during learning sequence activities will enhance the student's preparation for music reading and writing in the context of either Kodály or Gordon activities.

The tonal sequences used in the learning sequence activities and in the Kodály approach coincide frequently during the elementary years. Each approach to a given tonal sequence reinforces the other approach and deepens the student's understanding of the material. During the learning sequence activities, students will be introduced to dorian, mixolydian, lydian, and phrygian tonalities through their primary harmonic functions. The harmonic understanding of those tonalities is a welcome complement to the introduction of the modes in upper levels of a Kodály curriculum.

Rhythmic Differences

The differences between the Kodály approach and the Gordon approach to teaching rhythm center around the different rhythm syllables used in each approach. One way to explain the rationale for using Gordon's rhythm syllables rather than the traditional Kodály rhythm syllables is through an analogy to the classic solfège controversy between the proponents of a moveable "do" system and the proponents of a fixed "do" system. The justification for using the moveable "do" is to discover aurally the relationships of tones to the resting tone and to each other. Conversely, the premise supporting the use of fixed "do" is that each tone should reflect the absolute letter name regardless of key or tonality: a tonal pattern will be sung with different syllables depending upon the keyality. Gordon's rhythm syllables more closely reflect the logic of the moveable "do" system in that they are derived from the aural/kinesthetic relationship that rhythm durations have to the beat and to each other. Patterns that sound and feel the same are labeled with the same rhythm syllables, regardless of measure signature.[3] Conversely, the Kodály rhythm syllables reflect the time value name of each rhythmic duration (ta=quarter note, ti=eighth note), regardless of meter. When Kodály rhythm syllables are used, rhythms that sound and feel identical are associated with different rhythm syllables if they are written in different meters. An example of two visually contrasting but aurally parallel series of rhythm patterns is shown below.

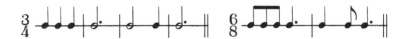

The integration of a Kodály approach to rhythm and a Gordon approach to rhythm would be difficult without adoption of the rhythm syllables used in learning sequence activities. While a Kodály teacher may find it awkward to learn a different rhythm syllable system, the effort is justified by the logic of Gordon's rhythm syllables, the ease with which students learn them, and the benefits of integrating learning sequence activities and a Kodály approach. Teaching learning sequence activities using Kodály's rhythm syllables would require students to learn two sets of rhythm labels for each rhythm pattern. Therefore, the use of both rhythm syllable systems is not recommended. The set of rhythm syllables used by Kodály teachers is not critical to the objective of teaching according to Kodály principles. Therefore, the rhythm syllables can be adopted from learning sequence activities and rhythmic integration between learning sequence activities and a Kodály approach can be successfully accomplished.

Early rhythm instruction in learning sequence activities consists of students echoing macro and micro beat patterns in duple and triple meters, using a neutral syllable, while maintaining a consistent pulse with their hands and/or feet. The study of macro and micro beat patterns in duple meter coincides with the study of quarter notes and pairs of eighth notes in early Kodály-based lessons. The study of macro and micro beat patterns in triple meter during early learning sequence activities provides a rich preparation for later Kodály lessons that incorporate triple meter.

As students progress through learning sequence activities, they chant progressively more complex rhythm patterns, first using neutral syllables and later using rhythm syllables. While it is true that students echo rhythm patterns that they will not learn in a Kodály curriculum for a few years, there appears to be no confusion because students are not required to understand those patterns symbolically. By the time students are introduced to rhythm notation in learning sequence activities, they will have learned to symbolically recognize those rhythm patterns in the Kodály curriculum.

An advantage of using learning sequence activities within a Kodály rhythm curriculum is that in learning sequence activities, patterns in both duple meter and triple meter are learned from the first lessons. The early introduction of patterns in triple meter is needed in an American Kodály curriculum, because our culture's folk songs are based equally on duple meter and triple meter. Learning sequence activities help to fill that gap.

The later levels of rhythm learning sequence activities provide experiences with advanced rhythm patterns. Students will not read and write all of the patterns that they study aurally, but they will experience through echoing, using neutral syllables and rhythm syllables, more complex rhythm patterns than are generally a part of a Kodály curriculum.

Thoroughly Integrating Skill Learning Sequence Into the Kodály Curriculum

Most Kodály teachers have encountered the learning sequence of "preparation, presentation, and practice" (The "Three P's"). Some have learned other terms to describe that sequence, but the concept remains the same. Before formally learning rhythm patterns or tonal patterns, the student should experience them informally through song and movement. When a class can perform rhythm patterns and tonal patterns with accuracy, those patterns can be identified and labeled. Finally, the newly learned rhythm patterns or tonal patterns are practiced through listening, reading, and writing.

Skill learning sequence in Music Learning Theory has many similarities to the "Three P's" used in the Kodály approach. The differences, however, are worth examining. What Kodály teachers refer to as "preparation," Gordon refers to as the "aural/oral" level of learning. By either term, it is a first experience with patterns that will be labeled later. Gordon suggests that students working at the aural/oral level first should sing songs that contain tonal content to be studied in learning sequence activities. They should echo rhythm patterns and tonal patterns, using a neutral syllable rather than text. The research of Mary Goetze (1985) supports Gordon's contention that neutral syllables should be used. Kodály teachers do a great deal of echo-singing with their students, most often using added texts. The use of a neutral syllable while echoing patterns appears to be valuable to learning, and should not be neglected.

Gordon's stepwise hierarchy of skill learning proceeds from aural/oral to verbal association, partial synthesis, symbolic association, composite synthesis, generalization, creativity/improvisation, and theoretical understanding, in that order.[4] However, in addition to stepwise movement, Gordon recommends bridging (formerly known as spiraling) movement, e.g., the temporary skipping of steps to reinforce learning. Readers familiar with Gordon's skill learning hierarchy and the concept of bridging will recognize the many bridging movements cited in the next few pages of comparisons of the Gordon learning sequence and the Kodály learning sequence.

Gordon suggests that a body of familiar patterns should be repeated for a period of time until those patterns are sung accurately. Then, new arrangements of previously learned patterns, in combination with unfamiliar patterns, can be sung. Unfamiliar patterns are echoed using a neutral syllable at the generalization-aural/oral skill level of skill learning sequence, a level that may be approached by bridging from the aural/oral level of learning.

Gordon suggests one further activity that Kodály teachers include in the preparation stage, and that can be approached by bridging from the aural/oral level of learning. Students are invited to engage in question/answer activities using neutral syllables. The teacher sings a tonal pattern or chants a rhythm pattern and the students respond with a different pattern. That level of learning in Music Learning Theory is called Creativity/Improvisation-aural/oral (without verbal association). Kodály teachers frequently engage in question/answer activities using rhythm syllables, solfège syllables, or text. According to Music Learning Theory, students should use a neutral syllable for question/answer activities before they use rhythm syllables or solfège syllables for that activity, and according to Music Learning Theory, they should never use text when creating patterns.

After they have completed instruction at the preparation level, Kodály teachers "present" patterns. Gordon suggests that "presentation" should involve only previously experienced (familiar) patterns, and that solfège syllables or rhythm syllables should be used. According to Gordon, visual crutches should not be used at the first presentation stage, which he terms "verbal association." At the verbal association level of learning, patterns are performed by the teacher, using solfège syllables or rhythm syllables, and are echoed by the students using the same syllables.

Before symbols are introduced, Gordon recommends participation in additional verbal stages through bridging and stepwise movement, stages that Kodály teachers would categorize as "practice." At the first such level, the generalization-verbal level of learning, the teacher performs unfamiliar patterns, using a neutral syllable, and students echo, using appropriate solfège syllables or rhythm syllables. That is equivalent to the skill that Kodály teachers call "practice listening." The important distinction here is that within Music Learning Theory, if the generalization-verbal level of learning is approached as a bridge from the verbal association level of learning, students will not yet have learned any form of notation. Kodály teachers frequently "present" verbal labels and symbols prior to the practice listening stage. Gordon believes that aural and verbal skills should be strengthened in the early stages of learning, and that if symbols are presented too soon they will serve as a crutch that retards the acquisition of aural and verbal skills. Symbols are presented to students only after those students have demonstrated proficiency with verbal syllables.

Another level of "practice" that can occur prior to the introduction of symbols if bridging movement is applied is creativity/improvisation-aural/oral (with verbal association). During that skill level the teacher presents a pattern, using solfège or rhythm syllables, and the student responds with a different pattern, also using solfège or rhythm syllables. This level is parallel to the Kodály question/answer activities, cited a few paragraphs above.

Gordon suggests that students should be taught rhythm and tonal concepts by echoing patterns rather than by simply singing songs. To give an aural context to those patterns he includes a level of learning called "partial synthesis" prior to the introduction of symbolic association. At the partial synthesis level of learning, students are asked to recognize the tonality or meter of a series of tonal patterns or rhythm patterns. The recognition of tonality and meter is not ordinarily taught until later levels in the Kodály approach, and then it is presented symbolically. At the partial synthesis level of learning students are required to recognize tonality and meter by sound, without relying on visual clues.

The skills discussed thus far are presented prior to the introduction of notation, which is accomplished next at the symbolic association level of learning. At that level students are shown how familiar tonal patterns and rhythm patterns appear on the staff, an activity that would probably have been included in the first (verbal) presentation stage in a pure Kodály curriculum. If learning theory is to be taken into consideration, verbal presentation and symbolic presentation must be separated by practice listening.

During the process of introducing music notation at the symbolic association-reading level of learning, the teacher sings or chants tonal or rhythm patterns using solfège or rhythm syllables while showing those patterns in notation to the students. The students echo those patterns, using the same syllables, while looking at them in notation. Practice reading can be pursued by bridging to the generalization-symbolic (reading) level of learning, during which students are required to read unfamiliar patterns in combinations with familiar patterns.

Another Gordon skill level that involves reading is called "composite synthesis-reading." As at the partial synthesis level of learning, students are expected at the composite synthesis level of learning to recognize the tonality or meter in a series of tonal patterns or rhythm patterns. Composite synthesis differs from partial synthesis in that students make that determination through the reading of notation. The three learning levels cited above, symbolic association, generalization-symbolic, and composite synthesis, would most likely be included in the practice reading stage in a Kodály curriculum.

It should be noted that Gordon discourages the use of any pre-symbolic systems for teaching the reading of rhythm patterns or tonal patterns. Students should not read iconic representations of the melody consisting of higher and lower pictures, letter representations of solfège syllables, or hand signs prior to reading notes on the staff. Nor should any pre-notational system for rhythm reading be used. Those substitute notations could conceivably be introduced at the symbolic association level of learning, but they are considered by Gordon to be inefficient. The only symbols recommended for use in Music Learning Theory are those from standard music notation.

There are four skill levels in Music Learning Theory that relate to the writing of music. The first skill level, "symbolic association-writing," consists of the teacher presenting familiar patterns, using solfège syllables or rhythm syllables, and the students notating the patterns on a blank staff. That would probably be introduced in the Kodály classroom as part of the presentation stage. Practice writing can then be pursued by bridging to the generalization-symbolic level of learning, at which time the teacher presents unfamiliar patterns, using a neutral syllable, and the class notates them. That reflects the type of activity used in the Kodály class during the practice writing stage. At a subsequent writing skill level approachable by bridging, creativity/improvisation-symbolic, the teacher presents patterns using a neutral syllable, and the students respond to each level by notating a different but complementary pattern. That is a logical extension of the question/answer activities that are included during verbal stages of the Kodály approach.

An important sequential writing skill level in Music Learning Theory is "composite synthesis-writing." While learning at that level, after writing several patterns through dictation, students determine the overall tonality or meter of those patterns. There is no counterpart for that activity in the Kodály stages of preparation, presentation, and practice. Kodály students are usually told the tonality and meter before they begin a dictation example.

To see better the relationship between the Kodály stages of preparation, presentation, and practice and Gordon's skill learning sequence, refer to the following chart.

Kodály	**Gordon**
Preparation	Aural/Oral
	bridge to generalization- aural/oral
	bridge to creativity/ improvisation-aural/oral (without verbal association)
Verbal Presentation	Verbal Association
Practice Listening	bridge to generalization-verbal
	bridge to creativity/ improvisation-aural/oral
	Partial Synthesis
Symbolic Presentation	Symbolic Association-reading
Practice Reading	bridge to generalization- symbolic (reading)
	Composite Synthesis-reading
Writing Presentation	Symbolic Association-writing
Practice Writing	bridge to generalization- symbolic (writing)
	bridge to creativity/ improvisation-symbolic
	Composite Synthesis - writing

In order to thoroughly incorporate Gordon's skill learning sequence into the Kodály curriculum, the Kodály educator must incorporate three separate presentation stages. They are (a) the presentation of solfège or rhythm syllables at the verbal association level, (b) the presentation of reading notation at the symbolic association-reading level, and (c) the presentation of writing notation at the symbolic association-writing level. Each is followed by the appropriate type of practice. Creative and improvisational activities should be included at the preparation, practice listening, and practice writing stages, as shown in the above chart.

The refinement of the "Three P's" learning sequence by use of Gordon's skill learning sequence helps teachers to focus on a single skill and to determine when students are ready to move on to the next skill level. With only one presentation stage, as suggested in the Kodály approach, teachers may innocently introduce the syllable name for a pattern (verbal), what the pattern looks like (symbolic-reading), and how the pattern is written (symbolic-writing) all in one class session. Further, practice stages for listening, reading, and writing in a Kodály approach become more specific when Gordon's skill learning sequence is followed. In short, Gordon's skill learning sequence insures that only one skill is developed at a time.

Integrating Gordon's Tonal Content Sequence Into the Kodály Curriculum

During various periods of history, Hungary has been dominated by other cultures, and those cultures have influenced the development of the folk music of Hungary. Kodály's dedication to the discovery and preservation of the folk music that could truly be called Hungarian led him to the music of the rural villages of Hungary. He worked to restore interest in the ancient pentatonic music, and he researched the music of many small villages. Later, as he became interested in music education, Kodály encouraged music educators in Hungary to use pentatonic music for two reasons. First, he wanted to return the ancient pentatonic music of Hungary to its people. Second, he thought the use of pentatonic melodies for music literacy was wise, because they contained no semitones. Kodály believed that young children had trouble singing semitones in tune (Kodály, 1974, p. 221). Still, Kodály did not suggest that all music cultures were rooted in pentatonic music. His approach to music education was designed for Hungary, and possibly for closely related cultures.

Gordon's research has led him to conclude that American children develop musical meaning in part through an informal understanding of tonality, which begins with a feeling for resting tone and is developed through experiences with music in major and minor tonalities. Gordon does not suggest that music teachers should omit pentatonic music, but only that they should not omit music in major tonality and minor tonality.

Gordon also delays the singing of semitones, although for a reason different from Kodály's, by avoiding stepwise patterns in the early levels of his Music Learning Theory. He begins with arpeggiated tonal patterns based on tonic and dominant functions in major and minor tonalities. Gordon believes that stepwise patterns are not as beneficial as arpeggiated patterns in developing accurate audiation, since students can easily slide from tone to tone rather than sing distinct pitches.

One possible adaptation Kodály teachers could make in their tonal curriculum would be to begin with songs that outline major tonic and dominant functions. The American flavor of tonic and dominant functions occurs clearly in songs like "Paw Paw Patch," "Sandy Land," and "Little Red Wagon." Developing a collection of folk songs based upon tonic and dominant functions, and later upon subdominant and cadential functions, might be enlightening, and closer to our American folk song roots.

Integrating Gordon's Rhythm Content Sequence Into the Kodály Curriculum

With the adoption of Gordon's rhythm syllables, many possibilities exist for integrating the rhythm component of Music Learning Theory into a Kodály curriculum. Just as Gordon believes that tonal understanding is dependent upon a feeling for resting tone in both major and minor tonalities, he believes that rhythmic understanding is dependent upon a feeling for a consistent pulse and its division in duple and triple meters. As in the Kodály approach, Music Learning Theory suggests that the first content taught within a rhythm curriculum should be in duple meter, with patterns consisting of duple meter macro and micro beats. Unlike Kodály, however, Gordon recommends the concurrent learning of triple meter rhythm patterns that consist of triple meter macro and micro beats. By learning rhythm patterns that include triple meter macro and micro beats, students are prepared to derive maximum value from the American and English nursery rhymes and folk songs that can be included in the early levels of a Kodály curriculum.

After they have acquired a small vocabulary of macro and micro beat patterns in duple and triple meters, students might be introduced to what Gordon refers to as division patterns. Duple meter rhythm patterns with divisions, notated with 2/4 or 4/4 measure signature, might include the following.

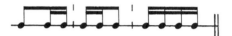

Triple meter rhythm patterns with divisions, notated with a 3/8 or 6/8 measure signature, might include the following.

After students have acquired an understanding of simple division patterns, they might be introduced to what Gordon refers to as elongation patterns. Elongation patterns contain elongations of macro beats, micro beats, or both. Duple meter rhythm patterns with elongations, notated with a 2/4 or 4/4 measure signature, might include the following.

Triple meter rhythm patterns with elongations, notated with a 6/8 measure signature, might include the following.

Later, students will be introduced to rhythm patterns that include both elongations and divisions. In duple meter, those patterns, notated with a 2/4 or 4/4 measure signature, might include the following.

In triple meter those patterns, notated with a 3/8 or 6/8 measure signature, might include the following.

An even more advanced study of rhythm will include rests, ties, and upbeats, all of which are derivations of rhythm patterns previously studied. The concept of enrhythmic notation could be introduced at any logical time. Enrhythmic notations would involve the transcriptions of 2/4 patterns into 4/4, 2/2, 4/2, 4/8, or 2/8, and 6/8 patterns into 3/8, 9/8, 3/4, 6/4, or 3/2.

General Lesson Suggestions

In a Kodály lesson, students are frequently invited to sing a song using either rhythm syllables or tonal syllables throughout. According to Music Learning Theory, that practice is not desirable. Gordon maintains that students should use only the song text or neutral syllables when singing a song in its entirety. If a difficult pattern is encountered students may rehearse that pattern using rhythm syllables or tonal syllables, but they should then return to singing the song as a whole with text (or neutral syllables). Gordon believes that when rhythm syllables or tonal syllables are used throughout a song, those syllables become substitute lyrics that limit the student's ability to use the tonal patterns of the song in conjunction with other rhythms and to use the rhythm patterns of the song in conjunction with other melodies. The same kind of damage is done when a given tonal pattern is sung with a particular rhythm rather than being sung independent of rhythm, and when a given rhythm pattern is sung with a particular melody rather than being chanted independent of melody.

The changes required to integrate Music Learning Theory into the Kodály curriculum do not seem nearly as radical as they might have seemed in the formative years of the Kodály movement. Kodály educators in America have already begun to adapt and refine the curriculum. A variety of rhythm syllable systems are being explored at the Kodály training centers. The de-emphasis of pre-symbolic reading crutches is being advocated by Hungarian pedagogues themselves. Recent Kodály publications include 2/4 and 6/8 patterns in the first grade classroom materials. It seems that Music Learning Theory provides information that can lead to the development of an even more refined Kodály approach that is right for America. Moreover, Kodály teachers will find the challenge of integration thought provoking, exciting, and rewarding, as new levels of understanding are achieved by the students.

NOTES

[1]Within this book, see "General Techniques for Teaching Music Learning Sequence Activities" for more information about learning sequence activities.

[2]Within this book, see "The Measurement and Evaluation of Music Aptitudes and Achievement" for more information about tonal and rhythm aptitude and testing.

[3]Within this book, see "Rhythm Syllables: A Comparison of Systems" for more information about Gordon's rhythm syllable system.

[4]Within this book, see "Skill Learning Sequence" for more information about Gordon's skill learning hierarchies.

REFERENCES

Goetze, Mary (1985). Factors Affecting Accuracy in Children's Singing. Ph.D. Dissertation, University of Colorado at Boulder.
Jarjisian, Catherine (1981). The Effects of Pentatonic and/or Diatonic Pitch Pattern Instruction on the Rote Singing Achievement of Young Children. D.M.A. dissertation, Temple University.
Kodály, Zoltan (1974). The Selected Writings of Zoltan Kodály. London: Boosey and Hawkes.

DALCROZE RECONSTRUCTED: AN APPLICATION OF MUSIC LEARNING THEORY TO THE PRINCIPLES OF JACQUES-DALCROZE

Patricia Shehan Campbell

Of all the international approaches to music learning that have been brought to the United States, the techniques of Emile Jacques-Dalcroze may be at once the most elaborate and the most elusive. Although the Dalcroze approach was conceived 90 years ago, making it the oldest of the classic methods of music education (which include Orff, Kodaly, and Suzuki), there remains a veil of mystery that shrouds much of the Dalcroze philosophy and practice.[1] While certified Dalcroze teachers are rare in public school music, most teachers of general music, choral music, and instrumental music classes are likely to have employed aspects of Dalcroze techniques in their teaching. In light of the pervasiveness and the staying power of Dalcroze principles, the newly recognized value of Gordon Music Learning Theory, and the common ground apparent between the two, it seems appropriate to consider the application of Music Learning Theory as a means of providing a sequence for the greater use of Dalcroze in the general music classroom.

Movement with a Mission

"Movement with a mission" is one description of the Dalcroze approach to music education. Dalcroze eurhythmics has been inaccurately described as dance, and its image has been one of young dancers in black leotards leaping to the rhythms of improvised piano music. In reality, the Dalcroze approach is three-pronged, including not only a unique form of rhythmic movement but also ear training (solfège and solfège-rhythmique) and improvisation. The key qualities that link accomplishment in each of the elements of the Dalcroze approach are imagination, a keen listening sense, and an immediacy of response to the musical stimulus.

Jacques-Dalcroze regarded music education as a holistic process that requires the integration of the entire person:

> Not only, then, should the ear and voice of the child receive adequate
> training, but in addition, every part of his body which contributes to
> rhythmic movement, every muscular and nervous element that vibrates,
> contracts, and relaxes under the pressure of natural impulses (Jacques-
> Dalcroze, 1921/1980, p. 4).

Jacques-Dalcroze maintained that the body was the mediator between
musical sound and its mental construct. He established an approach to
music instruction that coordinated the ear, the brain, and the kinesthetic self
in response to rhythm, pitch, form, and the expressive elements of music.
He saw physical experiences as a prelude to intellectual understanding.
Jacques-Dalcroze sought to awaken a feeling for natural bodily rhythms,
and to help students develop an agility and coordination that they could
apply to the realization of music rhythms through movement.   The
Newtonian laws of the mechanics of motion were given new meaning, as
Jacques-Dalcroze designed his eurhythmic and solfège exercises around the
concepts of time, space, and energy.

    While eurhythmics is the most unique and widely known of the
Dalcroze techniques, the Dalcroze triad of experiences in movement, ear
training, and improvisation is significant to his designation of "inner
hearing" as the foundation of music learning. Dalcroze training is designed
to develop in students an ability to internalize an aural sense and kinesthetic
feeling for beat, meter, rhythm, melody, and form, all of which are parts of
what Gordon calls audiation.[2] In short, the Dalcroze approach stems from
the mind-body connection, which interweaves physical and intellectual
experiences carefully throughout the course of instruction. The focus is on
the development of "inner hearing."

    The Dalcroze ideas originated in Switzerland at the turn of the century.
Emile Jacques-Dalcroze was then experimenting with approaches to ear
training in his post as professor of harmony at the Geneva Conservatory in
Switzerland. He astutely recognized that despite the advanced stages of
technical proficiency that his students demonstrated through the playing of
their instruments, there were notable gaps in their musical abilities. Simple
rhythms were wrongly rendered, and flaws in pitch and intonation were
frequent. Students often demonstrated mechanical rather than musical
understanding.

    For experienced performers and naive children alike, the Dalcroze
techniques lay the foundation for a thorough musicianship.   The
achievement of proficient eurhythmic movement requires a repertory of
complex kinesthetic reactions. The students' movement will include any

number of possibilities: in space and in place, locomotor and non-locomotor, isolated gestures using the hands, arms, head, shoulders, or a combination of body parts. Students may move independently, with partners, or in groups. Their movement is a personal and immediate response to the music, which sounds on the piano, on percussion instruments, vocally, or (rarely) on recordings. Students become proficient as they follow the tempo, rhythm, and meter of music with their bodies, learning to react quickly to changes in any aspects of the music, e.g., changes in meter, rhythm patterns, dynamics, or phrase length.

Ear training is at the heart of a Dalcroze education. Solfège and solfège-rhythmique entail the study of sight-singing and ear training in ways that again combine musical and muscular entities. In the initial stages, students are led to an understanding of tones and semitones and their relationships in scales, melodic passages, and selected songs. The fixed "do" syllable system is used in the Dalcroze practice in order to develop a sense of absolute pitch. Through the use of solfège, in combination with rhythm patterns, students learn to create musical renderings of scales and to respond to any changes in key spontaneously.

Kinesthetic experiences are associated with Dalcroze solfège in unique ways. Singing is accompanied by hand gestures that show the position of the pitch in space or by movement of the fingers on the arm as an imaginary keyboard. Scale degrees can be stepped or shown through the relationship of bodies to one another (leaning toward for half steps, standing upright for whole steps, and leaning away for augmented seconds). The hearing of harmonic progressions might be assessed through movement as well; the student may sing chord tones while executing designated movements for tonic, dominant, and subdominant chords. In those ways, the ear, the voice, and the body converge to sharpen listening discrimination skills.

Improvisation is the third part of the Dalcroze approach of music education, and exists as much in integration with eurhythmics and ear training as it does as its own entity. Improvisation allows students the freedom of expression that personalizes the musical experience, whether exercised through movement, in rhythmic speech, with instruments, or at the keyboard. Sounds become the inspiration for movement, and conversely, silent movement is interpreted musically. Beginning with precise imitation of the teacher's or a partner's melodies, rhythms, and movements in the manner of a mirror-image, students eventually acquire a repertory of movement and musical ideas from which they can draw for improvisation. They are taught to respond quickly and clearly to music in a particular style, rhythm, key, or form. The teacher must be skilled in keyboard improvisation to present eurhythmics instruction as it was originally conceived. Jacques-Dalcroze held that improvisation is the synthesis of musical experiences and the ultimate measure of sensation, imagination, and theoretical understanding.

The Dalcroze techniques call for a high degree of attention, concentration, and memory on the part of the student. The freedom needed for creativity, imagination, and musical expression are balanced by the discipline necessary for acute listening, analysis, and the immediacy of response to the music. The ear, the mind, and the body are fine-tuned and coordinated as a network of receivers and respondents to the essence of music - its time, space and energy. Jacques-Dalcroze initiated an important pedagogy that, when practiced well, can cause the human organism to reach beyond understanding and appreciating music, to the maximum - living music.

The Reciprocity of Dalcroze and Music Learning Theory

The Dalcroze approach to music education has important characteristics in common with Music Learning Theory. Those characteristics may well allow for the convergence of the two into a single pedagogy. The basic philosophical premise of each rests in the cultivation of aural skills for the purpose of building a music syntax, i.e., music literacy. The Dalcroze concept of inner hearing is similar to Gordon's concept of audiation. Both pertain to a sophisticated level of music understanding, in which musical sensation can occur internally without the physical presence of the sound itself. Whether the term "inner hearing" or the term "audiation" is applied, the result is that one using music notation "hears what he sees, and sees what he hears" once the skill has been developed (Gordon, 1984, p. 48).

Jacques-Dalcroze was distressed that children often learned music tactilely before they developed their hearing sense. He believed that early music education should be based entirely on hearing, and that instrumental lessons should be permitted only after a solid foundation of ear training has been acquired. He was troubled with the commonly-held attitude that playing piano marked one as a musician, when in fact the "sense of touch develops to the detriment of hearing" (Jacques-Dalcroze, 1921/1980, p. 53). His remarks are pointed:

...the dear mammas, with their naive candour, are convinced that musical development depends exclusively on learning the piano. What a mistake! Pianoforte lessons, unless preceded by training of the ear and by rhythmic movement, frequently damage the aural and rhythmic faculties.

Both Jacques-Dalcroze and Gordon support the adage "say it, then play it," in that both advocate that the experiences of singing, chanting, and hearing should precede instrumental study.

Like Dalcroze in regard to the importance of kinesthetic response to music, Gordon (1984) proposes that movement be employed "as an aid in maintaining a consistent tempo and in sustaining a meter" (p. 28). He affirms that young children "depend upon movements to grasp the meaning of steady beat, consistent tempo, and meter" (p. 29) and he recommends that children be encouraged to respond to music by using the large muscle movements required of walking, marching, swinging, or dancing.

Experience in eurhythmics and fundamental movement helps students to perform musically, e.g., to shape and phrase individual sounds into expressive units. That is the point at which performance is more than skill; it becomes art. Jacques-Dalcroze extended that concept further to underscore the importance of the kinesthetic sensation in its totality. Every movement in the playing of a musical instrument, according to the Dalcroze practice, can be divided into preparation, attack, prolongation, and return to preparation. The movement that occurs before and after the actual striking of a key is as vital as the attack itself.[3] Likewise, Gordon (1984) affirms that "the performer is as concerned with what happens within and between the notes as he is with what happens to the notes overall," or should be (p. 109). An artistic performance demands attention to psychomotor skill and to the overall feeling of the music, both of which are enhanced by eurhythmic experiences.

Within Music Learning Theory, Gordon has set improvisation as a particularly important level in the inference phase of the learning sequence. With the acquisition of a vocabulary of tonal patterns and rhythm patterns, creative composition and improvisation can readily occur. The Dalcroze approach to music education and Music Learning Theory are similar also in their emphasis on improvisation as both a process and a product. Improvisation is recognized by both as vital to musical growth in the early learning stages, and also as a skill that improves with experience and with focused attention to music syntax.

Points of Contention

Despite the solid pedagogical techniques that Dalcroze and Music Learning Theory jointly espouse, there are several points of contention between the two. One is the disagreement over which solfège system should be used. Jacques-Dalcroze adhered to the practice of using fixed "do," in which C is the starting note of the scale regardless of the tonic. For example, when the fixed "do" system is used, a G Major scale begins on C and contains an F#. Jacques-Dalcroze reasoned that children develop absolute pitch as the sense of C is impressed upon the ear, the muscles, and the mind. Furthermore, he felt that the interrelationship of the scales would become clear, with children able to aurally determine the order of tones and semitones that constitute each scale.

Gordon maintains that moveable "do," the tradition of British music educators Sarah Glover and John Curwen, more readily establishes aural relationships among tonalities. When moveable "do" is used, the tonic of the scale moves. For example, C is "do" in C Major and D is "do" in D Major. The use of moveable "do" creates a more efficient means of understanding the function of individual scale degrees in various keys by allowing the tonic of the key to provide an aural anchor for dominant, subdominant, and other tonal functions. Gordon's view is that fixed "do" works against the aural understanding of tonal relationships, that it is visually linked to the staff, and that it is consequently a damaging system to employ at levels of learning other than theoretical understanding. The disparity between the use of fixed "do" and the use of moveable "do" is a philosophical gap of considerable measure, yet the extent to which singing is promoted as a prelude to notation is a shared and overriding tenet.

A second major point of contention between Jaques-Dalcroze and Gordon is the emphasis of Music Learning Theory on the use of voice as the principal musical medium, to the initial exclusion of all other instruments. The use of piano as a motivation for students engaged in Dalcroze eurhythmics, and as a harmonic support in solfège exercises, is seen by Gordon as an encumbrance to the aural acquisition of tonal patterns and rhythm patterns so central to Music Learning Theory. While Dalcroze teachers regard the use of the voice as important in learning and retaining melodies, their frequent use of the piano as an accompaniment to movement and solfège exercises may impede the development of audiation skill in relation to both the tonal dimension and rhythm dimension. According to Music Learning Theory, music should be transmitted vocally in the early stages, and only after extensive vocal experience should patterns be produced through the use of an instrument.

Dalcroze and Gordon also hold different views of the process of symbolic association, at which time notes are introduced as visual representations of sounds experienced in earlier stages. While both practices emphasize extensive listening as a means of reinforcing the matter of "sounds before symbols," some proponents of Dalcroze introduce staff notation in small increments as opposed to the holistic approach recommend by Gordon. Beginning with a one-line staff, Dalcroze students are led through the singing of "do" pitches on the line, "re" pitches above the line, and "ti" pitches below the line as an introduction to tonal notation.

```
        RE
DO  ------------------------------------------
        TI
```

After the one-line staff has been mastered, a second line is added, thereby introducing two new pitches, "mi" and "fa." The third, fourth, and fifth lines of staff notation are added as the students become comfortable with the pitches presented with each new line.

In a similar manner, some students of Dalcroze instruction learn to read and write rhythm notation by employing a mapping procedure referred to as "Dash-A-Note."[4] Taking chalk in hand, students draw horizontal dashes from left to right to represent what is heard or performed; the longer the sound, the longer the dash. Those dashes are then converted to notes.

Gordon is opposed to pre-notational systems, claiming that they impede rather than facilitate the development of music reading skill. If children have internalized the sounds of tonal patterns and rhythm patterns through extensive aural experience, then the graphic display of those sounds can be readily learned through the introduction of the complete system of staff notation.

Despite the points of contention cited above, Dalcroze and Gordon share the goal of developing complete musicianship, including expressive performance, literacy, theoretical understanding, and the development of skill in audiation. Dalcroze instruction might be strengthened by the influence of Gordon while retaining its key focus on aural and kinesthetic development. Through the adaption of several techniques associated with Music Learning Theory - the use of the moveable "do" solfège system, the greater use of the voice as a vehicle for the acquisition and reinforcement of patterns, and the introduction of complete staff notation following sufficient aural experiences - Dalcroze may become an even more effective approach to music learning and to the development of musical sensitivity.

A Learning Sequence for Dalcroze

Dalcroze provides a three-way channel of eurhythmics, solfège and improvisation, with a wealth of experiences contributing to achievement in each. Dalcroze teachers are as creative as they are musical, with the ability to spontaneously determine a variety of approaches to a problem. The training in the Dalcroze approach is unique in its emphasis on creative problem-solving, e.g., how many ways can anacrusic feeling be demonstrated? For each Dalcroze teacher, the teaching method is a personal one, distinguished by the individual personality of teacher and students. There is no absolute learning sequence; rather, a series of techniques over an extended period of time are employed to provide for the development of students' innate musicality.

Music Learning Theory offers a logical sequence by which the use of Dalcroze techniques could lead to the development of music understanding. While consideration is given to developmental levels of the child within the Dalcroze approach, and to a progressive ranking of music concepts from introductory to the more advanced, there is no structured set of curricular guidelines. While nothing replaces the experience of Dalcroze training for teachers, the application of Music Learning Theory can provide a framework for the use of Dalcroze eurhythmics, solfège, and improvisation in school music programs. Each of the subheadings below is a progressively higher level of learning taken from Gordon's skill learning hierarchy.[5]

Aural/Oral

The aural/oral level of discrimination learning is critical to Dalcroze instruction. In maintaining the Pestalozzian view of "sound before symbol," which Jacques-Dalcroze embraced, the aural/oral preparatory period is at the crux of his practice.

Eurhythmic experiences require intensive listening to elements of music such as beat, divisions of beat, metric accents, rhythm patterns, tempo, and dynamic nuances. Children at the pre-literate level should be offered numerous experiences designed to open their ears and to develop the physical skills so vital to eurhythmics and to music understanding. Through kindergarten, development of the ability to listen and respond to music is a challenging feat in itself. Teacher expectations for movement at that age should include the ability to walk, run, skip, and gallop. To perform those movements in response to music is a complex skill, one that may come naturally to young children, but must be cultivated in most through instruction. An awareness of body parts, a control of balance, an ability to move backward, forward, and sideways, starting and stopping on command, are movements that, once learned, can be called upon even by young children as a response to musical events. Such kinesthetic responses are evidence that aural learning has occurred.

As children advance through the primary grades, they become able to listen with greater concentration, and their capacity to perform complex movement increases. The rate of advancement is dependent in large part on the quality of their music instruction. The ability to determine the appropriate movements for walking, running, and skipping music becomes more refined through the primary grades, indicating that aural and kinesthetic discrimination learning has taken place.

Before students are subjected to the intensity of sophisticated solfège exercises for which Dalcroze is well-known, they need to be taught rote songs at the aural/oral level of learning. After a repertory of rote songs has been learned, a concentrated learning process that Gordon refers to as "learning sequence activities" can be added to the rote song experience. Through learning sequence activities at the aural/oral level of learning, ·students acquire vocabularies of tonal patterns and rhythm patterns, and brief musical phases delivered by the teacher and sung or chanted, all or in part, by the teacher. The consequent learning becomes of significant value to Dalcroze eurhythmics activities.

The Dalcroze approach gives greatest emphasis to the aural/oral level of Gordon's learning sequence. The aural reception of music patterns, in particular rhythm patterns, is treated somewhat differently than in other music education practices, in that the sound is transformed into movement. Eurhythmics responses are derived directly from the sound stimulus. The oral presentation of tonal patterns and rhythmic patterns is somewhat suppressed, as the piano, rather than the voice, is the main instrument of transmission. Still, children are prepared to audiate as they are introduced to a repertory of melodies and rhythmic figures that are as diverse as the movements they learn to master.

The application of Music Learning Theory to the Dalcroze techniques emphasizes the voice as central to the acquisition of a vocabulary of tonal patterns and rhythm patterns. A Dalcroze teacher integrating Music Learning Theory into the Dalcroze curriculum might have students chant patterns before moving to them. The process need not completely eliminate the use of the piano, which is germane to classical Dalcroze practice. Instead, a sequence for learning a rhythm pattern, for example, might proceed as follows: (a) the teacher's chanting of the rhythm pattern, (b) vocal imitation of that rhythm pattern by the students, (c) the teacher's performance of that rhythm pattern on the piano, (d) rhythmic movement by the students, and (e) the combination of piano, movement, and student chant.

Verbal Association

The association of names with sounds should follow the extensive exposure of children to musical patterns and phrases. Scales, considered of primary importance within the theory and practice of Dalcroze, are seldom presented without solfège syllables. Scales are not necessarily taught intact. Rather, musical phrases are presented by isolating pitches, (trichords or tetrachords, for example) within the scale, and assigning rhythms to them. In this way, theoretical scales become musical phrases within the context of the scale. Music Learning Theory, on the other hand, calls for tonal patterns to be associated with syllables and to be taught separately from the rhythm dimension. Those patterns are based upon tonality and harmonic function. The use of scales is avoided.

Since rhythms are played by the teacher more frequently than they are vocally presented, and since they are usually moved to rather than chanted by Dalcroze students, there is not a common system of mnemonics to be found among Dalcroze teachers. When the teaching circumstance warrants verbal designations, Curwen syllables and rhythmic speech are frequently used. Gordon's system of rhythm syllables is relatively new, and one that is internally consistent and based upon beat function.[6] The Gordon rhythm syllable system can be fused readily with the Dalcroze approach as a means of verbal association. The creative Dalcroze teacher may also use improvisations of speech, movement, and melody to fortify a specific rhythm so that it becomes internalized in the ear and in the mind.

Partial Synthesis

Dalcroze eurhythmics are designed to review rhythms that were previously experienced, as an evaluation of learning that has occurred. In order to progress to the reading and writing of notation, there must be some assurance that children have had substantial aural and kinesthetic experience with meter, rhythm, tempo, dynamics, and pitch concepts, and that in the case of melody and scales, they are capable of attaching the appropriate solfège syllables. There is no logic in advancing to the reading and writing of music until experiences of the pre-literate phase has been extensively presented through partial synthesis learning. Dalcroze instruction is a continuous stream of checks and reviews throughout the daily lessons, assessing the abilities of children to listen and respond.

Symbolic Association

Through intensive listening and movement experiences, the Dalcroze practice provides a readiness for the reading of music notation. Solfège technique is used to introduce pitch and rhythm notation in gradual increments from notes grouped around one-line staves to the complete staff, and from dots and dashes to notes that indicate durational values. Through the application of Music Learning Theory, full-staff notation rather than pre-notational systems can be presented, provided that students have progressed successfully through the earlier levels of aural learning.

The reading and writing of music is an important objective of the Dalcroze approach. Eurhythmics activities develop physical sensitivity necessary to feel the musical flow, and solfège further activates the ear, but both are geared toward music literacy, or the ability to read music with efficiency and ease while also reading between the lines for the inherent musical expressiveness. The audiation or actual performance of familiar patterns that comprise simple folk songs or standard works of the repertory are possible for beginners of every age when Dalcroze techniques have been consistently applied.

Composite Synthesis

At the highest level of discrimination learning, composite synthesis functions as a second opportunity to evaluate and reinforce earlier stages of learning (the first stage having been partial synthesis). In the Dalcroze practice, students are observed and critiqued for their ability to read and write music. Beginning with familiar patterns, students are subjected to a progression of challenges: Can they write what they step? Can they read a series of patterns that they already learned by rote? Unfamiliar material is not often used at the composite synthesis level, because Dalcroze instruction is founded on aural-kinesthetic experience. Much of the music to be read or written is familiar, as notational experiences occur after the music has been heard, moved to, and/or sung.

Generalization

After having had the close guidance of the teacher in the early stages (discrimination levels) of music learning, the student has more independence in the acquisition of skills at inference levels of learning. At the generalization level of learning (the first of the inference levels), the student is required to identify new musical material based upon its relationship to familiar materials, and to do so without the rote learning processes that occurred at all previous levels of learning. Unfamiliar music should not be totally distant to the ear, but should relate to musical styles, rhythms, and melodies that were heard and acquired earlier.

A hoped-for consequence of Dalcroze instruction is greater musical autonomy. Dalcroze instruction is experiential and exploratory in nature, although students are gently guided by the teacher. In more advanced stages, students are presented with musical problems to solve that demand the application of the familiar to the unfamiliar. Can they listen for the new tonality and, based upon their past experience with tones and semitones in tonal learning sequence, can they identify the tonal patterns? Can they step and then write a rhythm pattern consisting of quarter notes and eighth notes in a different order than previously experienced? Can they sight-read a folk song, given that they have sung and moved to music with similar, but not the same, melodies? Those capabilities represent the musical independence that is the goal of Dalcroze instruction and of the generalization level of Music Learning Theory.

Creativity/Improvisation

Dalcroze practice is founded upon the principle that improvisation activates the mind in the most musically expressive manner possible. Obviously, the greater the musical training and experience, the more sophisticated will be the student's capability of creative music-making. When students have been presented with a selection of melodic and rhythmic possibilities that are learned well, those students are in the position to call them up for use in improvisatory ways. The same is true for creative movement. Even when earlier movement and singing experiences are freely creative, the Dalcroze teacher gives approval for those musical behaviors that are most appropriate and most genuinely musical, thus reinforcing the vocabulary that will be of greatest use in improvisatory lessons to come.

For some students, the prospect of free improvisation is at first inhibiting. Preschool children feel less inhibited than elementary children, who feel less inhibited than adolescents. However, the improvisations of young children will likely be less ordered than those of students with more musical experience. For the best results, experiences in improvisation should be built into early lessons, realizing that greater creative potential is generated with the internalization of each new musical idea. When improvisation occurs, there is a certain sense that the student has come to possess the pattern, the phrase, or the musical concept.

Dalcroze improvisation is experimental, giving students a chance to play with the possibilities of how a musical idea can be expanded, contracted, or changed through accent, texture, dynamics, or timbre. While the keyboard is the ultimate tool for improvisation, and one that teachers use frequently to motivate students to move, the use of speech, song, and instrumental and movement improvisation are also common within the Dalcroze approach. Ensemble improvisation, especially by older students with extensive training, is highly regarded by proponents of Dalcroze instruction.

Theoretical Understanding

The last tier of the learning sequence serves as a conclusion to the myriad of performance and listening experiences that have come before. Rather than place the cart before the horse by teaching note names, time values, and interval descriptions before the development of skill in "inner hearing" or "audiation," Dalcroze teachers encourage the orderly presentation of music and movement first, followed by the learning of terminology. Theoretical understanding is easily acquired if prior learning has been thorough. In fact, elementary concepts about the structure of music, a significant component of music theory, can be readily learned concurrent to earlier phases that entail concentrated listening and appropriate vocal and kinesthetic responses. When the physical self has been privy to music, the direct link to the intellectual self occurs easily. The final task in the learning sequence, theoretical understanding, requires that students employ the correct language to transmit their understanding to others.

Conclusion

A Dalcroze music education is a demanding course of study, and one that combines feeling with logic, art with skill, and the body with the mind. There is no occasion within that course of study for receiving or responding through the mental or the physical channels alone; rather, the student of Dalcroze becomes quick and correct of ear, brain, and body. Dalcroze instruction lays a musical foundation through its eurhythmics, solfège, and improvisation techniques, which together provide the students with a balance of experiences in listening, analysis, and response.

Whatever it may lack in learning sequence, Dalcroze distinguishes itself through its unusually creative and expressive approach to music learning. In essence, Dalcroze has underscored "music" in "music education." At the same time, Music Learning Theory provides the sequence that allows experiences to surpass the point of loosely-connected lessons, and to further its status of pedagogy with a purpose. The merging of the two perspectives can only strengthen the learning experience for the student. Music understanding and music appreciation on the part of the student are the inevitable results.

NOTES

[1]"Dalcroze" refers to the pedagogical techniques, while "Jacques-Dalcroze" refers to the man who established them.

[2]Within this book, see "Audiation: The Term and the Process" for more information about audiation.

[3]For an analysis of the totality of the kinesthetic experience, see Abramson, Robert M., (1986) in <u>Teaching Music in the Twentieth Century</u>, Choksy, Lois, Robert M. Abramson, Avon E.Gillespie, and David Woods Englewood Cliffs, N.J.: Prentice-Hall, Inc., p. 38-9.

[4]Lisa Parker, Head of the Dalcroze Department at the Longy School of Cambridge, Ma., coined this term.

[5]Within this book, see "Skill Learning Sequence" for more information about Gordon's skill learning hierarchy.

[6]Within this book, see "Rhythm Syllables: A Comparison of Systems" for more information about the Gordon rhythm syllable system.

REFERENCES

Jacques-Dalcroze, Emile (1921/1980 reprint). <u>Rhythm, Music and Education</u>. London: The Dalcroze Society.
Gordon, Edwin E. (1984) <u>Learning Sequences in Music</u>. Chicago: G.I.A. Publications, Inc.
Gordon, Edwin E. (1988) <u>Learning Sequences in Music</u>. Chicago: G.I.A. Publications, Inc.
Choksy, Lois, Robert M. Abramson, Avon E.Gillespie, and David Woods (1986) <u>Teacher Training in the Twentieth Century</u>. Englewood Cliffs, N.J.: Prentice-Hall, Inc.

LABAN MOVEMENT THEORY AND HOW IT CAN BE USED WITH MUSIC LEARNING THEORY

James M. Jordan

Introduction

The learning of style is central to the development of musicianship. Because style is built upon a framework of rhythm and rhythm is built upon images of motion, the music teacher needs a vocabulary of movements by which to teach rhythm imagery through both physical and mental pedagogies.

Good musicianship is dependent upon the ability of the performer to feel various styles through the rhythms he performs. Does a Verdi phrase have the same weight and flow as a Brahms or Palestrina phrase? No. But how have we learned that as music teachers? Perhaps we have learned with the help of recordings, performances, and countless hours of private study throughout our careers. Is there a more efficient way to sensitize students to the quality of music that defines style and musicianship? Can students be taught through movement to free their bodies, and subsequently to allow the skill of rhythm imagery to operate freely when they perform? Can they be taught to use a vocabulary of physical feelings related to rhythm, and to do so in a comprehensive manner so that a variety of feelings can be applied to the same rhythm? In short, are tools available that will allow music educators to help students acquire a vocabulary of physical sensations, and to recall those sensations in order to apply rhythm imagery to musical performance?

Audiate a performance that you have previously judged to be "unmusical."[1] Was the performer playing in tune? Was he technically proficient? Perhaps and perhaps not. Was the style executed well, i.e., did the rhythm have the qualities that were appropriate to the style? Probably not. Was Mozart sung like Verdi? Was Bach played like Brahms? Once a teacher realizes and accepts the all-encompassing importance of rhythm, his teaching effectiveness will improve dramatically. He will instill in his students a feeling of excitement about the simplest phrase. Movement will become central not only to the general music class, but to large performance groups. Students will understand music rather than merely imitate it.

The rhythm issues posed in this article are important. Music educators, however, have paid considerably less attention over the years to the correct sequencing of rhythm instruction than they have to the correct sequencing of tonal instruction. It is time to give the teaching and learning of rhythm the attention that it deserves. Rudolf von Laban's work with movement, applied to the principles of music learning sequences found in Gordon's Music Learning Theory, provides music educators with the necessary tools to do so.

Laban's Philosophy of Movement

One must have an understanding of Laban's philosophy concerning movement if he is to use Laban's principles effectively. For Laban, the act of moving was a link between the physical and mental experiences of life. He believed that through the act of moving, one experienced an interaction of mind and body. He also believed that movement was everywhere; movement could be seen, organized, and consequently appreciated in the still leaf, the crying baby, the child at play, and the young and the old.

To Laban, the central issue underlying the teaching of movement was that students needed to visually, physically, and internally experience the energy of movement, and then acquire the ability to sequentially recall movement experiences. He believed that after helping a student to recall experiences from his "movement thinking," the teacher could enrich that student's movement thinking by providing other similar experiences. For example, Laban believed that it was important for the teacher (a) to recall the experience of skipping, (b) to analyze the students' ability to skip, and (c) to provide a movement vocabulary for students having difficulty skipping so that they could learn to recall skipping movement. Laban believed that everyone experiences all of the subtleties and complexities of movement during early childhood, but that not everyone recalls all of those movements in later life.

It is the job of the movement teacher (music educator) to identify which specific movement experiences a student is not recalling, and then to provide sequential, prescriptive movement instruction to reawaken those movements in the student. Movement teachers must have experienced a comprehensive variety of movement themselves in order to effectively diagnose, prescribe, and teach movement. Moreover, to teach with meaning, the teacher must instruct through the use of sequential concepts, or movement themes.

Laban Effort Elements

Movement is more than a change of location of the body or a change in
position of the body limbs. There are changes in speed, changes in
direction, changes in focus, and changes in the energy associated with
different movements. There is consequently a constant fluctuation in levels
of exertion. Laban defined exertion in movement as the interrelationship of
Flow, Weight, Time, and Space, which he called the Effort elements. For
each of the four Effort elements, Laban identified a pair of extremes that he
called qualities, with the idea that the quality of each element of a given
movement can be described in relation to its placement on a continuum that
extends between those two extremes.

Flow is the variation in the quality of bodily tension that underlies all
the Effort elements. The extremes of Flow are free and bound. Free flow
allows the energy to flow through and out beyond the body boundaries.
Free flow movement is difficult to stop. A person experiencing total free
flow would be weightless and free of tension. Bound flow forces the mover
to contain energy within the body boundary. Bound flow movement is
restrained, and can be stopped easily. A person experiencing extreme
bound flow would be tense to the point of motionlessness. Between the two
extremes of free flow and bound flow are infinite gradations of tension.

Weight is the sensation of force or pressure exerted in a movement.
The extremes of Weight are light and heavy. Light movement is delicate
and overcomes the sensation of body weight. Heavy movement is forceful
and uses the sensation of body weight to make an impact. A person must
sense the quality of his movements as being either light or heavy. Central to
one's understanding of movement, and consequently to his understanding of
rhythm, is the ability to sense involuntary changes in one's own body weight
as well as to be able to change weight at will.

Time relates to the expenditure or duration of time in a movement. The
extremes of Time are sustained and quick. Sustained time is prolonging,
lingering, or decelerating. Quick time contains a sense of urgency and
rapidity. For musicians, the Effort element of Time is closely related to
tempo.

Space is the manner in which energy is focused in a movement. The
extremes of Space are direct and indirect. Indirect movement involves a
flexible but all encompassing attention to the environment. Direct
movement involves a channeled, singularly-focused awareness of the

environment. The element of Space is closely related to the concept of focus. Is the space in which a movement takes place focused or spread? Do all body parts focus to a central point, or are they dispersed?

Finally, one might think of the Effort elements of Flow, Weight, Time, and Space as the "how," "what," "when," and "where" of movement. Flow represents the "how," Weight the "what," Time the "when," and Space the "where." The Laban concepts of Flow, Weight, Time and Space not only contribute to the understanding of movement, but are crucial to the understanding of rhythm and style. Without experiencing Flow, Weight, Time, and Space in movement, or more directly, without sensing the elements of Flow, Weight, Time, and Space in rhythm patterns, one will be limited in his ability to audiate and perform rhythm.

Experiencing the Effort Elements in Combination

Once the teacher has grasped the concepts of Flow, Weight, Time, and Space, he will have become equipped with two skills: (a) observation, so that he can accurately observe the strengths and weaknesses of the students in his class, and (b) prescription. As a result of observation, he can improve movement and rhythm instruction by teaching to a student's weaknesses and strengths.

It is easiest to gain an understanding of the Efforts through their various combinations as suggested by Laban. It is difficult to experience Flow, Weight, Time, or Space separately. By adjusting the relative intensities of Flow, Weight, Time, and Space within an activity, one can create an infinite variety of movement possibilities. Laban assigned an action verb to each combination of three Effort elements. Central to his theory is simultaneous concentration on the three factors of Weight, Space, and Time taking over or predominating changes in Flow. Laban's action verbs, which describe combinations of Effort elements, along with movement examples for each verb, are shown in Figure 1. The experiencing of the movement that the action verb represents is crucial to one's ability to formulate an effective rhythm pedagogy and nurture accurate and stylistically appropriate rhythm performance in children and adults.

LABAN ACTION VERB	QUALITIES/ ELEMENTS	MOVEMENT EXAMPLES
FLOAT	indirect/(S) light/(W) sustained/(T)	treading water at various depths
WRING	indirect/(S) heavy/(W) sustained/(T)	wringing a beach towel
PRESS	direct/(S) heavy/(W) sustained/(T)	pushing a car
GLIDE	direct/(S) light/(W) sustained/(T)	smoothing wrinkles in a cloth, or ice skating
DAB	direct/(S) light/(W) quick/(T)	typing or tapping on a window
FLICK	indirect/(S) light/(W) quick/(T)	dusting off lint from clothes
SLASH	indirect/(S) strong/(W) quick/(T)	fencing, or serving a tennis ball
PUNCH	direct/(S) strong/(W) quick/(T)	boxing

Figure 1. Laban Effort Elements in Combination to Describe Actions

The reader should note that a variation of one or more of the qualities will result in a different intensity of the movement experience. After experiencing the Effort combinations shown in Figure 1, the reader is encouraged to complete the imagery exercise shown in Figure 2. Without pause, the reader should perform quickly each pair of movements shown. If the exercises are performed correctly, the mover will feel a sudden shift of energy between the two movements of each pair. Each exercise should be performed first with external body movement and then with no external body movement, so that the mover can internalize the various combinations of movements, and, more important, the changes in energy between the two movements in each combination. The quality of the Time element of each movement should be varied, as should the direction of each movement. The performance of the combinations shown in Figure 2 provides a basic readiness for the audiation of rhythm and rhythm style.

Punch/Press
Punch/Slash
Punch/Dab
Slash/Wring
Slash/Flick
Wring/Float
Wring/Press
Float/Flick
Float/Glide
Glide/Dab
Glide/Press
Dab/Flick

Figure 2. Movement Imagery Exercise

Application of Laban to the Music Classroom

Edwin Gordon (1984, pp. 250-253) has proposed a comprehensive rhythm curriculum that can be taught best through use of the Laban concepts of Flow, Weight, Time, and Space. Central to Gordon's rhythm curriculum are (a) an emphasis upon the need for informal movement before formal rhythm experiences begin, (b) an emphasis upon the need for informal exploration and development of the concepts of Flow, Weight, Time, and Space as readinesses for learning rhythm and rhythm styles, and (c) an emphasis upon the need for free body movement related to both usual and unusual meters so that the learner will be prepared to discriminate kinesthetically among meters. Also central to Gordon's rhythm curriculum is the understanding that the sensation of macro beats and micro beats is essential to the establishment of consistent tempo, which is in turn central to a person's rhythm development. Without a sense of consistent tempo, one cannot store rhythm patterns in audiation, nor can one sense meter.[2] In effect, one who lacks a sense of consistent tempo is constantly experiencing unusual meter. Therefore, to teach the rhythm dimension of music effectively, one must help students experience the macro beat through large body movement, divide that macro beat into micro beats through finer movement, and consequently develop a sense of consistency of tempo.

Although Laban was not interested in applying his theory to music education, it can be applied appropriately and effectively to informal and formal rhythm instruction. The ideas of Laban provide a strong pedagogical base for those who wish to understand the movement capabilities of their students and to apply to their teaching a logical, sequential movement curriculum that is supportive of Music Learning Theory rhythm instruction.

Informal Movement Instruction

While some rhythm learning can take place without sufficient informal movement experience having occured as a readiness, that rhythm learning will be greatly retarded and limited in scope. Students without sufficient informal movement experience cannot maintain a consistent tempo, cannot develop facility in unusual meter, and cannot improvise effectively. Informal instruction in movement as a rhythm learning readiness knows no chronological age; for example, one may need to begin rhythm teaching for a senior high school choir with informal movement activities. Most conductors would agree that consistent tempo is one of the crucial elements to the development of both personal musicianship and ensemble musicianship, yet few teachers and fewer conductors teach consistent tempo informally through body movement. Many choose marching, stepping to the beat, clapping, etc. to legislate a sense of ensemble tempo without having first awakened the individual student's physical feelings for rhythm and tempo.

Teachers must consider two modes of instruction when providing informal movement instruction to children and adults: (a) the coordinative aspect of movement, and (b) the Laban movement theme aspect of movement. Phyllis Weikart (1985) offers a good model for the former. In her approach to movement education she stresses the development of coordination as a prerequisite for formal movement activities, and she presents an effective means of measuring and evaluating coordination.

Each child should be presented a balanced informal movement experience. Through the use of Laban principles (all the Laban efforts should be used), the teacher can provide such an experience. Informal Laban movement instruction should require nothing of the student other than participation in real-life experiences (float, dab, flick, etc.) into which Laban elements can be later incorporated. The teacher should attempt to free the student from movement inhibitions, thereby providing him with a comprehensive vocabulary of kinesthesia, and with sensations that will form the foundation for all rhythm learning. Usual and unusual meters cannot be taught directly until the body is free to experience the unique kinesthesia of every style and every meter.

Laban's work in its complete form entails sixteen Effort themes. Details of those Effort themes can be found in <u>Modern Dance Education</u> (Laban, 1980).[3] For purposes of informal instruction, the most important themes from that source are awareness of body, awareness of Weight and Time, awareness of Space, awareness of the Flow of the weight of the body in Space and Time, use of the limbs of the body, combinations of the eight basic Effort actions, and elevation from the ground. Details of the pedagogy of the themes can be found in <u>The Mastery of Movement</u> (Laban, 1975, pp. 29-51). A model curriculum can be seen in a study by de Moura Silva (1983).

An individual movement profile such as the one shown in Figure 3, used in conjunction with the videotaping of student movements, will be an invaluable tool for the teacher. By assessing and recording the movement skills of each student, the teacher orients himself to the kind of instruction that is needed.

Name _____ Grade _____

Student Signature (On Reverse Side)

Instructions: The teacher should complete each of the following bar graphs based upon separate viewings of the videotape.

Student is able to demonstrate ease in moving using the following concepts. Particular attention should be paid to the Efforts of Flow and Weight.

    1 = not comfortable with Effort category
    5 = comfortable with Effort category

I. OVERALL EVALUATION

LOW (---) HIGH

	1	2	3	4	5
FLOW					
WEIGHT					
TIME					
SPACE					

II. SKIPPING

	1	2	3	4	5
WEIGHT					

III. SIGNATURE ANALYSIS

Which Effort or Efforts are mirrored in the student's handwriting?

	1	2	3	4	5
FLOW					

free (---) bound

	1	2	3	4	5
WEIGHT					

light (---) heavy

	1	2	3	4	5
TIME					

quick (---) sustained

	1	2	3	4	5
SPACE					

indirect (---) direct

IV. SUMMARY: (Circle One or More)

EFFORT STRENGTHS:	FLOW	WEIGHT	TIME	SPACE
EFFORT WEAKNESSES:	FLOW	WEIGHT	TIME	SPACE

Figure 3. Individual Movement Profile

The following sequential procedure should be applied to a selected movement activity to facilitate the recording of results on the Individual Movement Profile shown in Figure 3.

1. Place a video camera in a location from which all students can be seen for the entire activity.
2. Videotape the entire activity, making sure that the teacher has had an opportunity for interaction with each student (perhaps serving as each student's partner)
3. Using the video tape, evaluate each student's movement and record the results on the Individual Movement Profile (Figure 3) or a similar recording form.

Note that the separate activity of skipping needs to be observed and the results recorded on the Individual Movement Profile. A weakness in skipping may be indicative of a lack of body freedom (and control) that is necessary for rhythm performance. For example, a child who does not skip with height is not able to hold back his weight on the high point of the skip.

Note also that the student is asked to write his name in longhand on the reverse side of the profile form. A student's handwriting can provide clues to his use of Weight and Flow. For example, some students will sign their name very quickly, with sharp, angular penmanship. That writing style may be indicative of a child who is direct in his use of Weight and Flow, but weak in his ability to prolong the application of energy throughout a movement task.

After each student within a class has been evaluated, a class summary should be made so that the teacher can design informal movement activities to meet both individual and class needs. For each Effort circled in the Effort Strengths in item IV of the Individual Movement Profile, a tick mark should be recorded on a class summary sheet, such as the one shown in Figure 4, to indicate proficiencies. The teacher should select activities (sequential objectives) that will meet both the needs of the class and the needs of individual students who are deviant from class norms.

DATE _____

CLASS _____

CLASS LIST	FLOW		WEIGHT		TIME		SPACE	
High Aptitude	Strong (S)/Weak (W)		S	W	S	W	S	W
_____								
_____								
_____								
_____								
Average Aptitude								
_____								
_____								
_____								
_____								
_____								
_____								
Low Aptitude								
_____								
_____								
_____								
_____								

Jump Right In Activity Cards Selected to Improve Movement

Figure 4. Class Effort Summary Sheet

The teacher will need to select movement activities through which the Effort elements can be constantly presented in desirable combinations. While an infinite number of activities and many sources of activities are available, the Jump Right In activity cards listed in Figure 5 are illustrative of the kinds of activities that facilitate the teaching of Laban themes. The various themes should be experienced on a rotating basis.

LABAN THEME	ACTIVITY CARD NUMBERS
Awareness of body	763, 1452, 1454, 1460, 1474
Awareness of time	763, 1455, 300, 1470
Awareness of space	1454, 1467
Awareness of flow of the weight of the body in space and time	1465, 392, 405
Instrumental use of the limbs of the body	1474, 1468, 1456, 1452, 1454
Combinations of the eight basic effort actions (dab, flick, glide, etc.)	1468, 1470, 1460, 392
Elevation from the ground	300, 1467

Figure 5. Laban Themes addressed by Specific Activity Cards from *Jump Right In: The Music Curriculum*

An informal movement curriculum conceived from the above framework will result in significant improvement in the rhythm audiation skill of students. Skill in audiation is the single most important skill that students can possess when they engage in formal instruction in music.

Formal Instruction in Rhythm:
Aural/Oral and Verbal Association

We can infer from the work of Laban, Gordon, and others, that movement instruction must precede rhythm instruction. An essential part of aural/oral rhythm learning occurs through movement. Plainly stated, effective rhythm audiation cannot take place unless the body is free and is able to place accurately pulses of varying weights and flows at will.

The development of consistent tempo is imperative to the acquisition of skill in rhythm audiation. Whenever consistent tempo is lacking after formal instruction has begun, the teacher should return to informal movement to help the students free their bodies. A rigid body feeling is the major contributor to inconsistent tempi in individuals and in ensembles. The student must be able to freely and flexibly place macro beats accurately, and divide those macro beats into micro beats appropriate to the meter. Movement should accompany all rhythms taught at the aural/oral level. Further, a variety of styles should be explored through the use of the Laban Efforts. Students must be taught that a given rhythm can elicit a variety of feelings, each feeling being dependent upon the style and the meter of the music.

When teaching rhythm patterns using a neutral syllable, the teacher who has presented a comprehensive informal movement experience to his students will find new thrills in aural/oral rhythm teaching. He will find that students asked to vary the Weight and Flow of a given pattern will be able to apply hundreds of body feelings to that pattern. Subsequently, rhythm syllables should be used at the verbal association level of learning to solidify and organize the learning of rhythm patterns.

Edwin Gordon has developed a rhythm syllable system to use during formal rhythm instruction in music. That system is the most comprehensive rhythm syllable system available to music educators because of its internal logic.[4] Gordon's rhythm syllable system also provides the flexibility that is needed for musical expression. Some examples may help to illustrate the above points. Consider the following rhythm in unusual paired meter.

An understanding of Laban principles provides teachers with a comprehensive pedagogical view of this and other rhythms. First, "du be" feels different than "du ba bi" when performed correctly. Many teachers, however, teach students to sense that pattern with consistency of feeling among and between the eighth notes. Inconsistent tempi occur when all the eighth notes are audiated with the same feeling. In Laban terms, the Flow is different between the two groupings. The rhythm above can be audiated using any one of the Effort combinations shown in Figure 6. Each combination should be audiated while moving, speaking, and associating the appropriate body feeling with the rhythm.

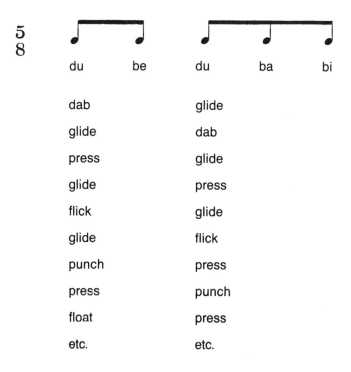

5 8	du	be	du	ba	bi

dab	glide
glide	dab
press	glide
glide	press
flick	glide
glide	flick
punch	press
press	punch
float	press
etc.	etc.

Figure 6. A Variety of Effort Element Combinations applied to the same rhythm pattern in unusual paired meter.

Consider another example, this one in unusual unpaired intact meter.

Once again, "du be," "du," and "du ba bi," elicit three distinctly different feelings. Audiate the rhythm pattern placing the same Weight and same Flow on each macro beat. Now change the Flows, but keep the Weights of the macro beats constant. An inconsistent tempo will likely result because of inaccurate placement of the micro beats between the macro beats. Now change both the Weights and Flows for the "du be," the "du," and the "du ba bi." Consistent tempo and style should result. Once again, consider a few applications of Effort combinations to the rhythm pattern, as shown in Figure 7. Each combination should be audiated while moving, speaking, and associating the appropriate body feelings with the rhythm.

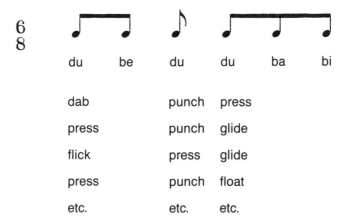

Figure 7. A variety of Effort Element Combinations applied to the same Rhythm Pattern in Unusual Unpaired Intact Meter.

The teaching and learning of music through the application of Laban principles in combination with Gordon's Music Learning Theory carries with it several advantages. First, students are given the necessary readiness for formal rhythm instruction through informal movement experiences. Second, the student acquires a sense of consistency of tempo through body movement. Third, music educators are provided with a movement vocabulary with which to accomplish the difficult task of teaching style through rhythm at an early age; style becomes the first, rather than the last concept taught in rhythm. And fourth, the teacher improves his own performance as a teacher, conductor, and musician.

NOTES

[1]Within this book, see "Audiation: The Term and the Process" for more information about audiation.

[2]Within this book, see "Rhythm Learning Sequence" for more information.

[3]Within this book, see "Informal Music Instruction as Readiness for Learning Sequence Activities" for more information.

[4]Within this book, see "Rhythm Syllables: A Comparison of Systems" for more information.

REFERENCES

Gordon, Edwin E. (1984). Learning Sequences in Music. Chicago: G.I.A. Publications, Inc.

Gordon, Edwin E. (1988). Learning Sequences in Music. Chicago: G.I.A. Publications, Inc.

Gordon, Edwin E. & David G. Woods (1985). Jump Right In: The Music Curriculum. Chicago: G.I.A. Publications, Inc.

Jordan, J. M. (1985). The Effects of Informal Movement Instruction Derived from the Theories of Rudolf von Laban upon the Rhythm Performance and Discrimination of High School Students. Doctoral Dissertation, Temple University.

Laban, Rudolf (1975). The Mastery of Movement. Lisa Ullman, ed. London: MacDonald and Evans.

Laban, Rudolf (1980). Modern Educational Dance. Lisa Ullman, ed. Boston: Plays.

de Moura, Silva, M. (1983). An Examination of Rudolf Laban's Theory of
    Modern Educational Dance to Derive Implications for Program
    Development in Elementary School. Doctoral Dissertation, Temple
    University.
Weikert, P. (1984). Teaching Movement and Dance. Ypsilanti, MI:
    High/Scope Press.

IMPLEMENTING MUSIC LEARNING THEORY WITHIN A COLLEGE CURRICULUM

Wayne Hobbs

Introduction

Ideally, there would be no need to implement Music Learning Theory within the college curriculum. Incoming music majors, having received instruction based upon Music Learning Theory since early childhood, would enter a college or conservatory with highly developed aural/oral and other discrimination skills. Even inference learning, including elementary theoretical knowledge, would be relatively well-developed. Under such ideal conditions, post-secondary music study could be considered higher education in the truest sense. The more abstract questions now primarily restricted to graduate study could be contemplated by undergraduate music theory students, music reading and dictation exercises could be drawn from scores of great complexity, and subtle style comparisons could be made with full confidence that students are hearing even minute differences with a genuinely musical understanding.

Unfortunately, such a utopian condition does not exist, and despite a growing acceptance of Music Learning Theory as a basis for the music education of children, major improvements in the overall preparation of incoming freshman musicians are unlikely in the near future. The reality is that in most post-secondary schools, including those of the highest reputation, a large number of new students arrive with inadequately developed audiation skills.[1] That is the case despite the advanced level of their instrumental technique, the beauty of their voices, their intellectual understanding of music rudiments, and even their advanced but mechanistic music reading ability. Of still greater concern to post-secondary instructors and administrators should be the fact that many of those aurally immature students leave our institutions with degrees in hand, but with little improvement in ear-related abilities. Because most music school graduates teach music to our children, and thus may perpetuate inadequate musicianship training, it is imperative that the college curriculum in music be designed to accommodate those aurally deficient students, in addition to the few students whose audiation skills are highly advanced.

The typical undergraduate music curriculum rests upon one or more of the following unstated assumptions concerning audiation skills:

1. Audiation skills are of relatively little importance.
2. Audiation skills cannot be taught; one either has them or he does not.
3. Audiation skills should be taught simultaneously with theoretical concepts.
4. Audiation skills are only marginally related to other music courses such as applied studies, introductory music literature courses, or keyboard skills.

Few college faculty members or administrators would lay claim to some of those assumptions, but the structure of curricula and the teaching practices of most schools of music support them by default if not by design.

According to Music Learning Theory, a secure aural/oral foundation is a necessary readiness for music reading, dictation, improvisation, composition, style comparison, and analysis. Yet few undergraduate music curricula require or even allow for sufficient aural/oral achievement prior to the undertaking of such studies. If the most fundamental premise of Music Learning Theory - the primacy of the aural/oral skills - is accepted, then there are fundamental errors in existing course sequencing.

The Freshman-Sophomore Theory Sequence

No component in the present college curricular structure is more antithetical to Music Learning Theory than is the traditional freshman-sophomore theory sequence. Few would deny its centrality and importance in the curriculum. Current practice calls for a four-to-six semester sequence in which ear training, sight-singing, and other musicianship skills are either integrated with "written" theory courses or separated into a parallel sequence of courses. Students beginning the sequence typically are placed into sections without benefit of scores on a standardized test of music aptitude. Instead, most institutions limit themselves to locally developed achievement tests of written theory that may or may not include sight-singing or dictation. While those tests may be valid for testing music achievement, they offer no guidance for predicting the relative ease with which the student may acquire audiation skills. For that reason, attempts to place new students into theory sections according to ability are often ineffective.

Within the college theory class, the effects of inadequate student audiation skills upon the learning of musically meaningful theoretical concepts frequently have been ignored. Instead of teaching analytical processes that originate in accurate and insightful aural perception and proceed toward musical-intellectual conceptualizations that inform and enlighten the student, quasi-musical games that allow circumvention of audiation have been invented. Examples include the practice of mechanically labelling vertical sonorities with chord symbols in response to the visual cues of the score, part-writing by means of numerous and robotic "rules," and a type of notation-based form analysis in which the student attempts to locate measure numbers that correspond to sections of a musical type as indicated in a text-book model. Most students can be taught to play those games successfully by means of intellectual processes and without the need to resort to aural information and musical inference. Ordinary computers have been "taught" to apply the same logic.

Meanwhile, "ear training and sight-singing" classes are engaged in their own games. In melodic and harmonic dictation exercises, the questionable practice of laboriously repeating an example again and again at a deliberate pace persists. Success in such an enterprise has yet to be positively correlated with any skill that is necessary or even useful to a musician.

In sight-singing instruction it is common for students to be assigned a given number of musical examples to learn. The diligent student manages to learn them with the aid of a piano, a friend, or a tape recorder. A few students with exceptionally high music aptitudes already are skilled sight readers, and consequently require no outside practice. Others simply fail when called upon in class. In none of those cases is any teaching or learning of sight-singing actually taking place. Most good teachers are aware of such inadequacies, but many have become frustrated to the point of abandoning hope of finding a solution.

Why does this problem persist in so many of our otherwise excellent institutions? In my opinion, it is because we have not yet discovered a genuinely successful approach to teaching audiation within the college curriculum. Our acceptance of the current curricula is based upon the assumption that we are in fact accomplishing our goals in skill development. We are motivated toward self delusion by the fact that our continued existence as institutions of higher learning depends upon a reasonable level of apparent student success. Since we cannot afford to have large numbers of students fail, we have devised substitute criteria - what I have characterized as games - which depend less, or not at all, upon genuine audiation skills.

Other Music Courses

Some of the problems in music literature courses, conducting courses, and many other music courses in our curricula are closely related to the failure of musicianship skills classes to develop adequately music inference skills that are based upon a firm foundation of audiation ability and the ability to associate that which is audiated with notation.

The audiation of music notation, for example, is a skill necessary to one's fully comprehending textbook examples and other materials drawn from music literature. Audiation ability is also a precondition for a genuinely musical understanding of stylistic differences (though students often become adept at comparing verbal descriptions of music despite an inability to actually hear the differences). The audiation of a score concurrent to performance is a skill central to the responsibility of a conductor. Composition requires advanced inferential audiation skills. The study of an instrument or voice demands adroitness with composite synthesis. It can be seen that most, if not all, courses in the music curriculum rely upon aural capacities. Those capacities can best be honed in an effective program of musicianship training that has been developed in accord with the precepts of Music Learning Theory. When audiation skills are lacking in a significant number of music students, music learning is substantially diminished and information about music must be substituted.

An Approach to Curriculum Reform

What then are the implications of Music Learning Theory for the college music curriculum? Principally, audiation abilities must be sufficiently developed before other types of music learning can occur with efficiency. That premise is in conflict with the general practice of concentrating music courses into the first two years of the curriculum.

Ideally, entering music majors should be tested carefully for audiational aptitude and achievement. Gordon's Musical Aptitude Profile (1965) and the Aliferis Music Achievement Test[2] (1954) are examples of appropriate instruments for that purpose. Students with low aptitudes should be denied immediate admission if other success indicators, such as applied auditions or ACT and SAT scores, are similarly negative. Those admitted to the program should then be placed in classes based upon the level of their need for learning sequence activities. Admission to the other traditional music major classes would be dependent upon reaching minimum achievement levels in the development of audiation skill. Those levels would be predetermined for each type of class.

Under such a plan, the first four levels of learning sequence activities classes would be considered remedial. Completion of level four would represent readiness for theoretical understanding of materials used in such typical Freshman courses as Theory I and Introduction to Music Literature. Subsequent learning sequence activities classes, through perhaps a level ten, would prepare students for more advanced traditional courses. Less advanced traditional courses would coincide with appropriate levels of learning sequence activities classes. In most instances the student could be expected to advance approximately two levels in one semester. A one-half to one hour period per day might be reserved for classes in all levels of the development of audiation skill to meet simultaneously. That would facilitate moving students to more advanced levels as their proficiencies improved. Students who must begin at level one would be allowed to enroll in other music courses only if those courses are designed to accommodate students with underdeveloped audiation skill. Examples would include an unauditioned choir or a piano class in which rote teaching is the principal method employed.

The following is a list of theoretical levels of learning sequence activities classes as they might relate to some of the traditional courses. It is expected that more precise and appropriate requirements will emerge over time.

Course	Pre-requisite Level (Completed)
Theory I	Level 4
Theory II	Level 6
Theory III	Level 8
Theory IV	Level 10
Form and Analysis	Level 10
Intro. to Music Lit.	Level 4
Music History	Level 10
Unauditioned Choir	Level 1

Some entering students who score high on aptitude and achievement tests will be deficient in the use of tonal syllables. Most will be unfamiliar with Gordon rhythm syllables. It is desirable to provide accelerated help sessions for those students through the use of Gordon's Jump Right In: Tonal and Rhythm Pattern Cassettes or a similar tape or computer program.

The objection may be raised that in many schools there will be a low percentage of students qualifying for normal freshman courses in the first year of college. Consequently, the large number of students required to spend an initial year engaged in learning sequence activities prior to commencement of "normal" courses would be disruptive to the typical music curriculum.

A possible remedy is to reschedule more general academic or core curriculum courses into the freshman year. In fact, substantial benefits may accrue to the student who studies European history, philosophy, or art history at the onset of the music curriculum while audiation skills are developing. After all, the typical music curriculum is unique among university undergraduate curricula in its high concentration of major courses in the freshman year. That anomaly has long been justified by the need for skill development over a span of many semesters. This proposal simply recognizes audiation skills to be basic and preeminent.

Other Approaches

For those who consider the proposal outlined above to be idealistic or impractical, there are less radical, if less effective ways of altering the traditional curriculum to take advantage of the precepts of Music Learning Theory.   These might be employed as intermediate steps toward a more complete reform.

One such approach would consist of devoting the first half semester of Theory I to learning sequence activities and appropriately related classroom activities. The more typical review of notational rudiments and beginning written harmony exercises would be delayed until the second half of the semester. While that approach would be less disruptive of the normal sequence of courses, it would not allow sufficient time for aurally deficient students to acquire the necessary skill levels prior to undertaking notationally based studies.

Another compromise is simply to introduce learning sequence activities into musicianship studies simultaneous with other traditional courses in the curriculum. That would require no alterations in course sequencing and alignment and thus would minimize the disruptive impact of the new program upon the curriculum. Unfortunately, it would also minimize the efficiency and effectiveness of learning sequence activities, because in other music classes the level of theoretical understanding would be engaged prematurely and without proper foundation.

Most music majors have developed at least some music reading ability prior to entering college, and many have been exposed to aspects of traditional theory and literature. But music reading skill that is not based upon a secure audiation ability is shallow and insufficient. If the student does not hear with his mind (audiate) what he sees with his eye, he is deprived. Instrumentalists in particular are susceptible to reading music in a mechanistic manner in which pitch symbols are associated directly with finger positions and motions, but not with an audiated pattern of pitches. The performer sees the notes, presses the correct fingers at the proper times, and the pattern sounds. The expectation or anticipation of the pitch is not present. Thus, the interpretation may be musically insensitive. Performers who read in such a way are likely also to be unaware of any pitch errors that they are propagating. It is essential to give as much attention as possible to enhancing and refining the audiation skills of incoming music majors.

Gaining Administrative and Faculty Support

It is necessary to secure the cooperation and support of colleagues to implement successfully any curriculum revision. For the revisions under consideration here, the music administrator, the coordinator of undergraduate theory, and those who teach the first two years of theory are of primary importance. Administrators generally are resistant to changes that are highly disruptive to the established schedule or that generate controversy. Theory professors understandably are reluctant to employ new approaches that require substantial retraining on their part. While the learning sequence activities included in Jump Right In: The Music Curriculum (Gordon and Woods, 1985) are usable at the college level, there are, at present, no published materials based upon Music Learning Theory that are specifically intended for college students. Therefore, learning sequence activities must be adapted, and appropriately supportive classroom activities must be devised by the professor. For the teacher who has a strong interest in musicianship training, that may represent a positive challenge; but if the class is merely a load-filling assignment, the unavailability of prepared and organized materials may be an impediment to the abandonment of more conventional approaches. Overcoming resistance based upon those legitimate concerns is dependent upon convincing colleagues that the improvements in student performance will be substantial enough to warrant the necessary adjustments and expenditure of professional time and energy.

Controlled research pertaining to the use of learning sequence activities at the college level does not yet exist in published form. It is of critical importance that such a program of scholarly investigation be undertaken soon. For now, research involving subjects of pre-college age, conducted by Gordon (1965, 1974, 1976, 1978, 1988) and others, must suffice. That research may be supplemented by the observations of those who have attempted implementation of such programs.[3] One might consider establishing a pilot program with a section of volunteer or randomly selected students. Music education faculty members or ensemble directors could devote five to ten minutes of each hour in their methods courses or rehearsals to learning sequence activities such as those found in Jump Right In. Upper-level undergraduate or graduate students in music education might well be encouraged to enhance their own audiation abilities by teaching learning sequence activities to children or peers, for one perhaps learns most effectively through teaching others. Successes in such limited applications might then be cited as justification for a more comprehensive program.

The administrator who wishes to implement curricular change based upon Music Learning Theory should consider sending key faculty members to seminars in which those precepts are introduced. While seminar attendance can involve a substantial expenditure, there is probably no more effective way to build enthusiasm, knowledge, and skills among faculty members.

Implications for Accreditation

An additional concern of the administrator could be whether such a novel approach would be acceptable to accrediting agencies, in particular the National Association of Schools of Music (NASM). Properly implemented, curricula based upon Music Learning Theory should encounter no difficulty with NASM or any other recognized accrediting body.

For many years, NASM has encouraged alternative instructional approaches. According to the NASM constitution, one purpose of the organization is "to establish and maintain minimum standards for the education of musicians, while encouraging both diversity and excellence"

(NASM, 1987, p. 6). Under the rubric, "General Standards for Graduation from Curricula Leading to Baccalaureate Degrees in Music; Basic Musicianship," an important precept followed in NASM evaluations is given: "the precise format and details of the curricula utilized to achieve this breadth of skills and understandings are best determined by the individual institution in ways that are commensurate with its unique goals and resources" (NASM, 1987, p. 45). Conversations with experienced NASM evaluators and members of the Undergraduate Commission confirm that as long as standards of excellence are not abridged, curricular diversity and innovation are generally approved by visiting evaluators and by the Undergraduate Commission, the body that is charged with recommending action on applications for initial or renewed accreditation.

It is important to NASM that all objectives and policies of the curriculum and its constituent courses be clearly stated, and that evaluative data be maintained to demonstrate that critical musicianship skills are being acquired by students. If the utilization of Music Learning Theory indeed produces superior results, there should be no adverse effect upon accreditation. Contrarily, one could reasonably expect commendation.

The application of the principles of Music Learning Theory as advocated by Gordon may result in radical changes to the traditional college music curricula. Changes of that magnitude inevitably generate opposition and resistance.[4] But the potential reward of greater excellence in the education of musicians and music teachers should be sufficient motivation to call us to the task.

NOTES

[1]Within this book, see "Audiation: The Term and the Process" for more information.

[2]The Aliferis and Aliferis-Stecklein Music Achievement Tests are available now only by direct order from Prof. John Stecklein, 2129 Folwell St., St. Paul, Minnesota 55108.

[3]The author conducted experimental musicianship classes using learning sequence activities at Western Kentucky University from 1984-86. Dr. Maureen Carr at Pennsylvania State University also has developed teaching materials based upon Gordon's theories.

[4]Within this book, see "Implementing Music Learning Theory in a School Music Curriculum" for more insight into impediments to change.

REFERENCES

Aliferis, James (1954). *Music Achievement Test: College Entrance Level*. Minneapolis: The University of Minnesota Press.

Gordon, Edwin E. (1965). *Musical Aptitude Profile*. Boston: Houghton-Mifflin.

Gordon, Edwin E. (1974). "Toward the Development of a Taxonomy of Tonal Patterns and Rhythm Patterns: Evidence of Difficulty Level and Growth Rate". *Experimental Research in the Psychology of Music: Studies in the Psychology of Music*. Vol. 9. Iowa City: The University of Iowa Press.

Gordon, Edwin E. (1976). *Tonal and Rhythm Patterns: An Objective Analysis*. Albany: State University of New York Press.

Gordon, Edwin E. (1978). *A Factor Analytic Description of Tonal and Rhythm Patterns and Objective Evidence of Pattern Difficulty Level and Growth Rate*. Chicago: G.I.A. Publications, Inc.

Gordon, Edwin E. (1981). *Tonal and Rhythm Pattern Audiation Cassettes*. Chicago: G.I.A. Publications, Inc.

Gordon, Edwin E. (1988). *Learning Sequences in Music: Skill, Content, and Patterns*. Chicago: G.I.A. Publications, Inc.

Gordon, Edwin E. and David G. Woods (1986). *Jump Right In: The Music Curriculum*. Chicago: G.I.A. Publications, Inc.

N.A.S.M. 1987-88 Handbook (1987). Reston, Va.: National Association of Schools of Music.

TEACHER EDUCATION
AND MUSIC LEARNING THEORY

Roger A. Dean

The Discipline of Music Education

It has been said that many students entering a music education degree program do so in order to perpetuate the "good times" they experienced as members of high school performing groups. While that sentiment is understandable, it exemplifies short-sighted, shallow, and immature thinking. Good times certainly are desirable outcomes of participation in a music program; they are remembered and have lasting value. But sound education (pun intended) is much more than a collection of good times.

While studying to become music teachers, music education majors need to be introduced to a model of music instruction that recognizes music as a discipline worthy of study and not merely a collection of activities. In the recent revision of The School Music Program: Description and Standards, we are reminded that

> Music is worth knowing. It is a field of study with its own special body of knowledge, skills, and ways of thinking. The ability to perform, to create, and to listen to music with understanding [underlining mine] is highly desirable for every member of society (MENC, 1986, P.13).

Unfortunately, that publication makes no mention of how music understanding could be systematically developed. Edwin Gordon's suggested purpose for music education is

> to provide students with music understanding [underlining mine]...so that they can learn to perform and to respond aesthetically and to use symbolic representations of their and others' aesthetic feelings to the extent that their music aptitudes will allow (1988, p. 21).

Fortunately, Gordon's Music Learning Theory provides music education majors, and indeed the music education profession, with a framework for systematically developing music understanding, and it does so without thwarting the traditionally enjoyable aspects of music activities.

Music and Academic Respectability

When Music Learning Theory is implemented in the instructional process, music as a K-through-12 school subject takes on academic respectability without losing its identity as an art form or as a desirable activity. Jump Right In: The Music Curriculum (Gordon and Woods, 1985) is based upon Music Learning Theory. Now, for the first time choral, instrumental, and general music teachers have available, through the learning sequence activities from Jump Right In, a music curriculum that provides a systematic means for developing a functional understanding of tonal relationships and rhythm relationships. It includes 53 sequential tonal units and 53 sequential rhythm units, each comprising (a) tonal patterns or rhythmic patterns of known audiation difficulty levels; (b) one of the eight essential skills that are connected to tonal units and to rhythm units; (c) a procedure designed to elicit group and individual responses from children; and (d) a procedure for evaluating and recording the progress of each child.

By engaging in learning sequence activities, students increase their chances for meaningful musical involvement in traditional classroom and rehearsal activities.[1] Also, students develop a more thorough understanding of tonal and rhythmic relationships and therefore can read music, create music, improvise music, and sing and play instruments with increased rhythmic integrity and better intonation.

The Introduction of Music Learning Theory in the Undergraduate Curriculum

While in the Navy, I served on an aircraft carrier that displaced 40 thousand tons, carried 3000 men and 100 aircraft, and traveled up to 30 knots on the open seas. I remember how astonished I was when I first observed how long it took the carrier to react to a command of speed or direction change. It was then that I experienced an old axiom in a rather dramatic fashion: INERTIA IS DIFFICULT TO OVERCOME!

Inertia is difficult to overcome wherever it is found - including in institutions of higher learning in which music teacher preparation programs exist. In the article "Why Teachers Fail," (Williams et.al., 1984) the authors quote David Imig of the American Association of Colleges for Teacher Education, who said, "Without a doubt, teacher education is and ought to be the next focus of those trying to improve the schools" (p.64). Subsequent to that admonition, several reports were published that offer suggestions for overhauling teacher education. Tomorrow's Teachers (1986), a report of the Holmes Group, and A Nation Prepared: Teachers for the 21st Century (1986), a Task Force report published by the Carnegie Forum on Education and the Economy, are two recent examples. Unfortunately, most reform movements in the education profession seldom, if ever, include the so-called "specialities," such as music education, in their deliberations. And it has been a long time since any substantive suggestions for reform in music education have been sounded by organized bodies from within the music education profession.

If reform in the preparation of public school music teachers is to take place, it must begin in institutions that carry the responsibility for the preparation of music teachers, inertia notwithstanding. An introductory course is needed in the music education curriculum that addresses basic issues common to general music, choral music, and instrumental music. Traditional undergraduate courses, such as "Instrumental Techniques" and "Music in the Elementary School," tend to define only that portion of music education reflected in the course title, often introducing contradictory approaches to skill and content acquisition. Undergraduate courses with titles such as "Foundations of Music Education" tend to emphasize general educational philosophy, educational psychology, and music education history. Tenuous connections between general learning and music learning are made by music education professors. While interesting, engaging in such speculation has limited value when compared to what now is known about learning the basics of music. Whatever the value of general learning theories may be, they do not provide a sufficient foundation for a music curriculum. It is no longer conscionable for those charged with the responsibility of educating future music teachers to ignore published research that reports on how and when children learn music most effectively. The introductory course that is needed is Music Learning Theory.

Music Learning Theory at Temple University

After considerable debate, Music Learning Theory became a required course in the music education undergraduate curriculum at Temple

University in 1983. Currently students enroll during either the first or second semester of the freshman year. The course begins by distinguishing between "music theory" and "music learning theory," because the word "theory" in both phrases causes confusion. Music learning theory is defined as a marriage between music (sound) and learning theory (a sub-heading under the discipline of education). Music Learning Theory, then, is a theory of how music is learned.

Next, students are asked to reflect on their own public school music experiences. Most report that they recall little to suggest a coordinated curricular plan used by their general, choral, and instrumental teachers. The discussion leads them to think about the difference between a curriculum based upon what the teacher thinks should be taught - typical of public school music - and a curriculum based upon students' readiness to learn - a basic tenet of Music Learning Theory. It intrigues them to imagine working in a school system that bases its music teaching upon a structure for music learning while preserving teacher individuality.

Students should know that Gordon's Music Learning Theory was not conceived in a vacuum. It has its roots in educational psychology and in music fundamentals. To that end, five psychological schools of thought are presented to the undergraduate students (Nye, 1983, pp. 11-33). Characteristics of each school and important persons associated with each school are discussed. The five schools are: (a) the Behaviorist-Environmentalist school, (b) the Normative-Maturationist school, (c) the Cognitive-Interactionist school, (d) the Psychosexual- Personality school, and (e) the Humanist school.

The course continues with the reading and discussion of the first nine chapters of Learning Sequences in Music: Skill, Content, and Patterns (Gordon, 1988). When applicable, connections are made between general learning theory and Music Learning Theory, but those chapters focus principally on issues specific to music content. Students begin to gain insight into some commonly underdeveloped music skills, such as the ability to audiate a resting tone while aurally discriminating between tonic and dominant triads in major and minor tonalities, the ability to maintain a consistent tempo while aurally discriminating between macro and micro beats in duple, triple, and unusual meters, the ability to audiate a page of music notation, and the ability to sing accurately that which is on the page.

As Temple music education majors study Music Learning Theory, they are drawn to the inevitable conclusion that "audiation" is central to the understanding of music development, and therefore it must be taught at all instructional levels.[2] Prospective elementary and secondary school music teachers need to grasp the complexities of audiation and how it can be taught systematically through the use of tonal and rhythm patterns.

Although building personal music skills is not the primary purpose of the course, some attention is paid to skill development. Students are asked to engage in a variety of activities aimed at skill building both in and out of the Music Learning Theory class. First, they are required to listen to and echo tonal and rhythm patterns on the <u>Tonal And Rhythm Pattern Audiation Cassettes</u> (Gordon, 1981), first using a neutral syllable and then using tonal or rhythm syllables.[3,4] Students record their listening experiences on a "listening log."

Second, a five-to-ten-minute learning sequence activity, either tonal or rhythm, is conducted by the instructor during most Music Learning Theory class periods. Because principles of skill learning sequence are observed, neutral syllables are used before tonal and rhythm syllables, aural material is synthesized before notation is employed, opportunities for creativity and improvisation are provided, and recognition of familiar material is practiced prior to attempting to identify unfamiliar material.[5]

Third, students are encouraged to recognize the tonality and meter of music compositions that they hear, study, and perform in private lessons, ensembles, and music history and literature courses. Opportunities to report findings are provided during Music Learning Theory class time.

Fourth, after students have learned to recognize the characteristic sound of each tonality, short melodic compositions are played for the class on the piano. Those melodic fragments (void of rhythm) begin in one tonality and modulate to another tonality, keyality, or both. Students are asked to name the initial tonality and the concluding tonality.

Fifth, after students have learned to recognize the characteristic feeling of each meter, short rhythmic compositions are played on one pitch on the piano. Those rhythmic fragments (void of melody) begin in one meter and modulate to another meter, tempo, or both. Students are asked to name the initial meter and the concluding meter.

Sixth, after students have had separate experiences with tonal modulations and metric modulations, they are asked to listen to short melodies that begin in one tonality and meter and modulate to a different tonality while maintaining the same meter, that modulate to a different meter while maintaining the same tonality, or that modulate to a different tonality and a different meter. Students are asked to identify the initial tonality and meter and the concluding tonality and meter.

Seventh, taped excerpts of music literature are played for the class. The compositions played vary in tonality, meter, and style. Students are asked to identify the tonalities and meters heard.

Eighth, students are asked to choose a partner in the class and practice the singing/chanting of tonal/rhythm patterns with each other, both in and outside of class.

Ninth, students are asked to compose short tonal melodies (void of objective rhythm) that modulate to different tonalities, and short rhythm compositions (void of melody) that modulate to different meters.

And finally, students are asked to compose a short melody (without words) that contains both tonal and rhythm elements, and modulates, both tonally and metrically.

The development of music skills that is begun in Music Learning Theory class at Temple University is not systematically reinforced in subsequent semesters through course work as would ideally be the case. Nevertheless, many students claim that the experiences in skill development employed in the Music Learning Theory course help them with the music learning process within other music courses, for it provides a syntax necessary to bring basic meaning to music that is heard or seen.

Are Traditional Theory Courses Doing the Job?

All too often, courses ostensibly designed to develop personal music skills fall far short of their goal. After successfully completing such courses, many students still are unable, for example, to aurally discriminate among tonic, dominant, and subdominant functions in major and minor tonalities. Many college music teachers charged with the responsibility for developing basic musicianship do not seem to know how to rectify that situation. As a result, many unproductive and counterproductive procedures are employed, a partial list of which follows.

a) Notation is used in an attempt to explain aural phenomena, thereby denying the independence of the ear from the eye.

b) Primarily diatonic passages are stressed initially in sight-singing and dictation exercises at the expense of developing the student's ability to discriminate among pattern functions.

c) Two-note intervals are emphasized at the expense of developing the student's vocabulary of two, three, four, and five note tonal patterns.

d) "Do" based minor instead of "la" based minor is used, masking the distinction between resting tone and tonic.

e) Counting systems based upon time value rather than beat function are used, delaying the establishment of a kinesthetic orientation to meter and rhythm.

f) Theoretical explanations are given to so-called "key signatures," which could be more accurately described as "do signatures," for neither key nor tonality (modality) is learned solely from the number of sharps or flats in the signature.

g) Theoretical explanations are given of so-called "time signatures" or "meter signatures," which could be more accurately described as "measure signatures," for neither tempo nor meter is learned solely from the numbers employed.

h) Tonal patterns and rhythm patterns are combined in initial dictation and in sight-singing exercises, resulting in proactive inhibition.

In light of those practices, it is not surprising that many music educators who have graduated from schools approved by the National Association of Schools of Music and who have been certified by state departments of education to teach music are deficient in personal music skills. It is unreasonable to expect deficiently trained music educators to effectively guide the musical development of their students.

Continuing Education for the Practicing Music Teacher

The report of the Task Force on Music Teacher Education states that

Music educators need to become mature persons and professionals whose ongoing development allows them to meet responsibilities effectively and creatively. Attention needs to be given to expanding the depth and breadth of knowledge, to demands of increased competence, and to newly developed instructional methods and technology systems (1987, p. 43).

Music Learning Theory falls into the category of "newly developed instructional methods," and is foreign to the vast majority of practicing music teachers. Therefore, graduate study and in-service sessions in Music Learning Theory for practicing music teachers are the logical vehicles for developing an understanding of the music learning process and the continued development of personal music skills.

Conclusion

Music teachers in training and veteran music teachers who have a genuine interest in the musical development of children owe it to themselves and to the profession to become knowledgeable about Music Learning Theory. With that knowledge, literally hundreds of music teachers have concluded that an educationally oriented, academically respectable, district-wide standardized music curriculum can become a reality. Perhaps we now have an answer for Mr. Mabbitt (1987) who decries"...colleagues in our profession who range from tyrannical contest moguls to sleepyheaded zombies who wander aimlessly from lesson to lesson..." (p. 24).

That practice should be based upon theory is a statement widely known and espoused by educators. That the practice of music education can have its basis in a theory of music learning slowly but surely is becoming known to music educators.

NOTES

[1]Within this book, see "General Techniques for Teaching Learning Sequence Activities" for more information about learning sequence activities.

[2]Within this book, see "Audiation: The Term and the Process" for more information about audiation.

[3]Within this book, see "Tonal Syllables: A Comparison of Purposes and Systems" and "Rhythm Syllables: A Comparison of Systems" for more information about tonal syllables and rhythm syllables.

[4]Those cassettes now are out of print. If the reader wishes to duplicate that activity, it is suggested that <u>Jump Right In Tonal and Rhythm Pattern Cassettes</u> be used.

[5]Within this book, see "Skill Learning Sequence" for more information.

REFERENCES

Gordon, Edwin (1981). Tonal And Rhythm Pattern Audiation Cassettes. Chicago: G.I.A. Publications, Inc.

Gordon, Edwin (1988). Learning Sequences in Music. Chicago: G.I.A. Publications, Inc.

Gordon, Edwin (1987). Jump Right In Tonal And Rhythm Pattern Cassettes. Chicago: G.I.A. Publications, Inc.

Gordon, Edwin and David Woods (1985). Jump Right In: The Music Curriculum. Chicago: G.I.A. Publications, Inc.

Grunow, Richard and Edwin Gordon (1987). Jump Right In - The Instrumental Series: Teacher's Guide-Soprano Recorder Book One. Chicago: G.I.A. Publications, Inc.

Holmes Group (1986). Tomorrow's Teachers: A Report of the Holmes Group. East Lansing Mich.: The Holmes Group, Inc.

Mabbitt, Larry. (1987). "A Response to Paul Lehman". Music Educators Journal, September.

Mark, Michael. (1986). Contemporary Music Education. New York: Schirmer Books, A Division of Macmillan, Inc.

MENC (1986). The School Music Program: Description and Standards. Reston, Virginia.

Nye, Vernice (1983). Music for Young Children. Dubuque: Wm.C. Brown Publishers.

Task Force on Education and the Economy (1986). A Nation Prepared: Teachers for the 21st Century: The report of the Task Force on Teaching as a Profession. Washington, D..C.: The Carnegie Forum on Education and the Economy.

Task Force on Music Teacher Education (1987). Music Teacher Education: Partnership and Process: A report by the Task Force on Music Teacher Education for the Nineties to the Music Educators National Conference. Reston, Virginia.: Music Educators National Conference.

Williams, Dennis A., Lucy Howard, Dianne H. McDonald, and, Renee Michael (1984, September 24). "Why Teachers Fail." Newsweek, pp. 64-70 .

THE IMPORTANCE OF SOUND BEFORE SYMBOL IN DEVELOPING INTUITIVE COLLEGE MUSICIANS

Maureen A. Carr

Introduction

If musicianship courses are to lead to the development of intuitive musicians at the university level, it is essential that students acquire the ability to bring meaning to music notation. Some students appear to have been "born" with the type of innate musicality that allows them to "hear with their eyes," while others are still in the process of developing that ability when they enter college. Students who have yet to fulfill their potential for associating sounds with symbols tend to treat the musical score as a visual phenomenon. Consequently, they are unable to arrive at a distinct aural understanding of the music that they are reading and the voice-leading exercises that they are writing. For those students, only certain melodic, harmonic, and rhythmic patterns are familiar to them in notation. Other patterns are totally unfamiliar to them. As a result, those students are not likely to achieve as high a level of musicality as that of their peers who are already able to associate sounds with symbols in a comprehensive way.

How can teachers lead all students to a reasonable level of sophistication in music reading and at the same time guide their progress through the music theory curriculum, which of necessity relies on notation?[1] Part of the solution is to have students learn tonal patterns and rhythm patterns aurally before they are asked to read and write them. That approach is similar to the way in which a native language is learned, i.e., by hearing and speaking before reading and writing. The purpose of this paper is to show how the Music Learning Theory of Edwin Gordon can be used to help students progress from the aural/oral level of learning to the symbolic association level of learning, a necessary progression in light of the importance of sound before symbol in developing musicianship.[2]

Tonal and Rhythm Patterns:
Taxonomy and Levels of Difficulty

Two aspects of Gordon's Music Learning Theory that are important to the teaching of aural theory are the taxonomies of tonal patterns and rhythm patterns and the criteria used for establishing levels of difficulty among the patterns. Gordon's categorization of tonal patterns and rhythm patterns as being easy, medium, or difficult is supported by extensive research. It is the depth of Gordon's research into the levels of audiational difficulty of the patterns that makes his theory so convincing.[3] However, the actual methodology that Gordon has devised involves more than the taxonomy of patterns. The learning sequence activities that he has devised for teaching those patterns are not arbitrary. Gordon's unified and coherent approach to the teaching of tonal patterns and rhythm patterns makes it possible for the teacher using learning sequence activities to provide students with an aural basis for understanding music notation.

Intuition (Dewey) and Inference Learning (Gordon)

Before showing how Music Learning Theory applies to the teaching of aural theory, it might be helpful to compare John Dewey's explanation of intuition with Edwin Gordon's definition of inference learning. In Art as Experience, Dewey writes the following.

'Intuition' is that meeting of the old and new....Oftentimes the union of old and new, of foreground and background, is accomplished only by effort, prolonged perhaps to the point of pain....the background of organized meanings can alone convert the new situation from the obscure into the clear and luminous (Dewey, 1934, p. 266).

That which Dewey refers to as "old and new," Gordon refers to as "familiar patterns" and "unfamiliar patterns" (Gordon, 1984, p. 11). The tonal patterns and rhythm patterns to be learned, as categorized according to audiational difficulty by Gordon, could provide the "background of organized meanings" alluded to by Dewey. It would follow that those students who are able to audiate tonal patterns and rhythm patterns will indeed have established a "background of organized meanings" for their own use. By acquiring a vocabulary of "familiar patterns," students will establish a context through which they can identify "unfamiliar patterns" when sight-reading "obscure" excerpts from music literature. In Dewey's terms, the students will have found a means of "convert(ing) the new situation from the obscure into the clear and luminous."

The analogies presented above are strongly supported by Gordon's conclusion that, "Inference learning takes place when we coordinate in audiation unfamiliar patterns with familiar patterns in a tonality or in a meter" (Gordon, 1984, p. 22). Thus the familiar patterns become the background for interpreting the unfamiliar patterns at the foreground.

Essential and Unessential Notes (Gordon), Background of Organized Meanings (Dewey), and Structural Levels (Schenker)

If one views tonal patterns and rhythm patterns as melodic and rhythmic reductions of a more elaborate musical texture, an analogy to Schenkerian theory may be added to the Gordon/Dewey insight. However, Schenker's concept of background differs considerably from Dewey's. It is more specific, and it has to do with the fundamental structure of an entire piece.

> [Here] Schenker viewed every well-composed tonal piece as being reducible to one of essentially three patterns, all based on the tonic scale and triad. While these patterns and the ability to recognize them are important, so are the details and the working-out of motivic and thematic ideas. These occur at the MIDDLEGROUND and FOREGROUND levels -- as the terms suggest, closer to the surface of the composition (Forte and Gilbert, 1982, p. 131).

Schenker's concept of middleground seems close to Dewey's concept of background. It is interesting to speculate that Gordon's hierarchical approach to essential notes within patterns, and larger patterns as reductions of what we are hearing, also might be thought of as middleground events in terms of Schenkerian theory.   Gordon defines essential notes within patterns as

> those notes that define the function of a pattern...Because the patterns that we are audiating include only essential notes, they generally are only abbreviations of the complete patterns that we are aurally perceiving (Gordon, 1984, p. 12)...We unconsciously place the unessential notes in the patterns of essential notes as the patterns of essential notes are being read (Gordon, 1984, p. 16).

Notational Audiation and Music Aptitude

The systematic study of tonal patterns and rhythm patterns should help all students to become comfortable with the audiation of unfamiliar repertoire. Innately musical students - those who seem to have been born "hearing with their eyes" - might have already started to develop a "background of organized meanings" through their previous experience with music literature. Still, even their achievement levels should improve through the use of learning sequence activities, since "...it is rare indeed to find a student whose achievement is as high as his aptitude" (Gordon, 1984, p. 224). Furthermore, students with high music aptitude might not be uniformly high in tonal aptitude and rhythm aptitude (Gordon, 1984, p. 228). It is not uncommon for a given student to have a low tonal aptitude and a high rhythm aptitude, or the reverse. Those students who have low tonal aptitude, low rhythm aptitude, or both, are in the greatest need of acquiring a "background of organized meanings" upon which to base theoretical understanding (Gordon, 1984, p. 22). While most properly taught students will become proficient "sight-readers," aptitude will have a direct bearing on the level of achievement that each attains.

The skill that is being focused upon here is notational audiation, which Gordon defines as ". . . audiating when reading familiar or unfamiliar music in performance or silently . . ." (Gordon, 1984, p. 19). Through notational audiation, students bring inferential meaning to the symbols on the page. Building upon the "background of organized meanings," students engaged in sight-reading should be able to reduce the "pain" referred to by Dewey in his definition of intuition.

Learning Sequences, Discrimination Learning, Inference Learning and Theoretical Understanding

Learning sequence activities consist of the study of tonal patterns and rhythm patterns taught first at the aural/oral level of learning as preparation for verbal association and all other levels of discrimination (rote) learning, including symbolic association. Discrimination learning in turn becomes the readiness for inference learning. Theoretical understanding is the highest level of inference learning (Gordon, 1984, p. 22).

At the aural/oral level of discrimination learning, the student imitates the teacher in chanting tonal patterns and rhythm patterns. Notation of the patterns is avoided at this stage in an effort to develop audiation.

The conflict between writing and audiation is not unique to the notation of music, but was recognized as long ago as the fifth century B.C. by the Egyptian King Thamus, who feared that writing could indeed interfere with memory.

> If men learn this [writing], it will implant forgetfulness in their souls; they will cease to exercise memory [audiation] because they rely on that which is written, calling things to remembrance no longer from within themselves, but by means of external marks (Plato, Phaedra, 1961 edition, p. 520).

Students are encouraged to associate sound with symbol at the level of symbolic association. At the point of symbolic association, students already should have developed a large repertoire of tonal patterns and of rhythm patterns through the earlier stages of discrimination learning. Using those familiar patterns as their "background of organized meanings" students will be able to read familiar patterns at the symbolic association level of discrimination learning and later read unfamiliar music notation at the generalization level of inference learning. Thus, skill in notational audiation ultimately serves as a pre-requisite for the highest level of inference learning, theoretical understanding (Gordon, 1984, p. 22).

Let us assume that a musical example, such as Haydn's <u>Piano Sonata</u> <u>XVI:23.2</u> (Figure 1) is unfamiliar to most music students. If they have already developed skill in notational audiation, and if they are able to group the essential notes of what they are "hearing with their eyes" into familiar and unfamiliar patterns, students will then be using discrimination learning (beginning with aural/oral) as the foundation for inference learning (ending with theoretical understanding).

Practical Application of Music Learning Theory to a University Music Theory Program

The question remains as to how the use of Music Learning Theory might help students to develop a background of organized meanings to enable them to audiate from notation, or to hear with their eyes, repertoire such as the Haydn excerpt shown in Figure 1. The application of learning sequence activities to the university music theory program gives students who have not yet developed a background of organized meanings an opportunity to do so.

At the School of Music of The Pennsylvania State University, learning sequence activities are being used in the musicianship courses of a Schenker-oriented undergraduate theory curriculum. We do not claim to have all of the answers, but we feel that we are asking the right questions. Undergraduate students are required to take four semesters of musicianship classes, which meet three times a week, for one credit each semester. (They also take four semesters of music theory [text by Aldwell/Schachter, 1978-1979], one semester of analysis, and one or more theory electives, depending upon the degree program.)

Since fall of 1986, freshmen in the musicianship courses have been grouped heterogeneously by music aptitude, each class representing a cross section of Musical Aptitude Profile scores. The purpose of the course is to help students to gain music understanding. There are four aspects to the course:

**Figure 1. Excerpt from Haydn Piano Sonata XVI: 23.2.
Heule Edition**

1. Gordon learning sequence activities from <u>Jump Right In: The Music Curriculum</u> (Gordon and Woods, 1985).

    The singing of tonal patterns and the chanting of rhythm patterns, first using a neutral syllable, and later using tonal syllables[4] or rhythm syllables,[5] serve as a preparation for reading patterns in notation and for creativity/improvisation.

2. Ottman melodies from <u>More Music for Sight-singing</u> (Ottman, 1981).

    The melodies from the Ottman book are sight-read in   class. Beginning in Fall of 1988, the 4th edition of Bruce Benward's <u>Sight-singing Complete</u> (Benward, 1986) will be adopted for use by freshmen.[6]

3. Benward dictation materials from <u>Ear Training</u> (Benward, 1987) and <u>Advanced Ear Training</u> (Benward, 1985).

    Exercises in melodic, rhythmic, harmonic, and contrapuntal dictation are introduced in class. Students are encouraged to do additional drill with the assistance of computer programs.

4. Fundamentals.

    The fundamentals emphasized in written theory are reinforced in musicianship classes.

The instructors follow a common syllabus, and give common sight-singing and dictation quizes at five week intervals. Students are evaluated continuously through   class participation as well as at the five week intervals.   At the end of each semester, each student sings for a sight-singing jury consisting of the instructor and the coordinator of theory/aural skills.

The musicianship courses meet for fifty minutes each on Monday, Wednesday, and Friday. At least ten minutes of each class are devoted to learning sequence activities. Shown in Figure 2 is a schedule of events for the first five weeks of Musicianship I as it was taught in the Fall of 1987. The schedule illustrates how the Gordon materials are presented in relation to Benward dictation exercises and Ottman sight-singing exercises.

	M	W	F
		W 8/26 MAP tests	F 8/28 MAP tests
Gordon Benward Ottman	M 8/31 Tonal 1 A 266-268	W 9/2 Rhythm 1 A-B Mel. 1 A-B	F 9/4 Tonal A-B 269-271
Gordon Benward Ottman	M 9/7 Holiday ' ' ' '	W 9/9 Rhythm 1 C-D Harm 1 A-B	F 9/11 Tonal 1 C-D 272-274
Gordon Benward Ottman	M 9/14 Rhythm 2A 275-277	W 9/16 Tonal 2 A-B Mel 1 C-D	F 9/18 Rhythm 2 B 278-280
Gordon Benward Ottman	M 9/21 Tonal 2 C-D 281-283	W 9/23 Rhythm 2 C Harm 1 C-D Rhythm 1 A	F 9/25 Tonal 2 E 284-286
Gordon Benward Ottman	M 9/28 review 287-289	W 9/30 quiz quiz	F 10/2 quiz

**Figure 2. "Musicianship I," Schedule for Fall of 1987:
8-26 to 10-2**

On the first day of class (8-31), the instructors sang the tonal patterns of Unit 1 A, using a neutral syllable, and students responded, also using a neutral syllable. The same tonal patterns recurred in Tonal Unit 2 A (9-16), the difference being that tonal syllables were used the second time. During the first semester of each school year, tonal patterns and rhythm patterns are taught on alternate days. In subsequent semesters greater emphasis is usually placed on tonal patterns, because students seem to progress more slowly with tonal skills than with rhythm skills.

In the Fall of 1986 students did not see any patterns in notation until December 1st. In the Fall of 1987, tonal pattern cards and rhythm pattern cards were made available for students to purchase. That facilitated drill outside of class and allowed students to assume leadership roles within the class. At the sophomore level, for example, students sometimes chant patterns to each other in and outside of the classroom setting. The availability of cassette recordings of the patterns allows the instructor to give students more responsibility for learning patterns. In the future, cards and tapes should make it possible for students to advance through the curriculum at a faster rate than at present. At the present time, Tonal and Rhythm Units 1-13 are taught during the freshman year, and Tonal and Rhythm Units 14-27 are taught during the sophomore year.

The tonal content and rhythm content of the Benward and Ottman activities (see Figure 2) are not necessarily related to the Gordon materials. In the earlier exercises, Benward and Ottman place more emphasis on scalewise passages, while Gordon places more emphasis on arpeggiated tonal patterns. That does not create a serious conflict if students are able to hear stepwise fragments as elaborations of arpeggiated patterns, but to do so requires students to differentiate between essential and unessential notes at an early stage of learning. In future years it might be beneficial to the learning process for beginning students if the Benward and Ottman materials are used in an order that will present arpeggiated fragments prior to scalewise fragments.

A format similar to that shown in Figure 2 is followed for all four semesters of the musicianship classes. In the fourth semester, an honors section is offered to encourage high aptitude students to audiate complex structures, including chromatic, multitonal (atonal), and serial-based tonal patterns. Those complex patterns are not included in the Gordon teaching materials, but are presented in his text within the intertonal and interkeyal classifications (Gordon, 1984). Research as to difficulty levels would have to be done if those patterns were to be incorporated into teaching materials. Knowing that Gordon considers his work to be evolutionary, there is every reason to believe that his research will result in the inclusion of additional patterns within future teaching materials.

Let us examine the analysis shown in Figure 1. Notice that the voice-leading is generated by the essential notes that outline the tonic triad (F, Ab, C), dominant seventh (C, E, G, Bb), tonic triad (F, Ab, C), augmented sixth (Db, F, Ab, B), and dominant triad (C, E, G). The highly ornamented line in the upper part of the Haydn excerpt is nothing more than an elaboration of those essential notes. The chord of the augmented sixth in measure three (Db, F, Ab, B) is prefigured in the "neighbor-note" motives of measure one (C, "Db," C and C, "B," C). The neighbor notes themselves, i.e., Db down to B, a diminished third, evolve in linear fashion in the second half of measure 3 to outline the interval of an augmented sixth (Db up to B). The goal of the augmented sixth interval (Db, Bn) is the dominant octave C.

Students who are able to hear the essential notes and patterns (or arpeggiations, in Schenker's terms [Forte/Gilbert, 1982, p. 32]) should be able to understand the dependency of the notes Db and B on C, whether in the context of measure 1 or 3.

In Figure 3, tonal patterns from Units 25 and 32 of Jump Right In: The Music Curriculum are shown along with a series of experimental tonal patterns. All patterns are transposed to f minor for the convenience of the reader.

**Figure 3. Two Series of Gordon Patterns and
a Related Experimental Pattern**

The patterns from Units 25 and 32 prepare students to hear the relationship of the diminished third (Db down to B) to the dominant pitch C. The third series of patterns is an experimental one that reorders the diminished third to form an augmented sixth. Although the foreground of the Haydn excerpt is highly complex motivically, students who have audiated a sufficient vocabulary of tonal patterns should be able to arrive at a theoretical understanding of its melodic and harmonic functions. Thus students can be led to a theoretical understanding of an unfamiliar piece of music as they are reading it in notation, provided that they are capable of audiating basic tonal patterns and rhythm patterns and of attaching sounds to symbols. There is every reason to believe that a background consisting of organized aural meanings will help students to interpret familiar and unfamiliar repertoire, thus helping them eventually to reach the highest level of theoretical understanding that they are capable of achieving.

NOTES

[1]It is interesting to note that Heinrich Schenker felt very strongly that students should be taught "to hear" before they study composition. "Is not learning to hear the first task, during which time the student might well dispense with composition?..no music school can be released from the obligation of teaching to hear correctly" (Schenker, 1979, p. 9).

[2]Within this book, see "Skill Learning Sequence" for more information about Gordon's levels of skill learning.

[3]Within this book, see "Audiation: The Term and the Process" for more information about audiation.

[4]Within this book, see "Tonal Syllables: A Comparison of Purposes and Systems" for more information.

[5]Within this book, see "Rhythm Syllables: A Comparison of Systems" for more information.

[6]The fifth edition of Benward's Sightsinging Complete, co-authored by Maureen Carr, is scheduled for publication in 1991. Melodic fragments from that edition are being used on an experimental basis.

REFERENCES

Aldwell, E. & C. Schachter (1978-1979). Harmony and Voice Leading. (Vols. 1-2). New York: Harcourt, Brace, Jovanovich, Inc.

Benward, B. (1985). Advanced Ear Training. Dubuque: William C. Brown Publishers.

Benward, B. (1987). Ear Training (3rd ed.). Dubuque: William C. Brown Publishers.

Benward, B. (1986). Sight-Singing Complete (4th ed.). Dubuque: William C. Brown Publishers.

Dewey, J. (1958). Art As Experience. New York: Capricorn Books, G. P. Putnam's Sons. (Original work published,1934).

Forte, A. & S. Gilbert (1982). Introduction to Schenkerian Analysis. New York: W. W. Norton and Co.

Forte, A. (1979). The Structure of Atonal Music. New Haven: Yale University Press.

Gordon, Edwin E. & David G. Woods (1985). Learning sequence activities from Jump Right In: The Music Curriculum. Chicago: G.I.A. Publications, Inc.

Gordon, Edwin E. (1984). Learning Sequences in Music: Skill, Content, and Patterns. Chicago: G.I.A. Publications, Inc.

Gordon, Edwin E. (1988). Learning Sequences in Music: Skill, Content, and Patterns. Chicago: G.I.A. Publications, Inc.

Gordon, Edwin E. (1985). Reference Handbook for Using Learning Sequence Activities. Chicago: G.I.A. Publications, Inc.

Haydn, J. (1972). Piano Sonata XVI:23,2. Munich: G.Henle.

Ottman, R.W. (1981). More Music for Sight-Singing. Englewood Cliffs: Prentice-Hall, Inc.

Plato. (1961). The Collected Dialogues. E. Hamilton & H.Cairns (Eds.). New York: Bollingen Foundation,Distributed Pantheon Books.

Schenker, H. (1979). Free Composition. (E. Oster,Trans.). New York: Longman. (Original work published 1935).

INTEGRATING MUSIC LEARNING THEORY INTO THE NON-MUSIC MAJOR COLLEGE CURRICULUM

Harry Semerjian

College students who are not music majors comprise a segment of music education that is nearly invisible in the literature and neglected by the leadership of the profession. Who are those students? Why is their music education important?

The students who are the subjects of this article may be enrolled in colleges with or without a music major or a music school. In any case, the college probably does have a music minor complementing its majors such as business administration, communication, special education, psychology, and others. Non-music majors are typically expected to elect from a medley of courses in art, languages, literature, music, philosophy, and other disciplines clustered under the rubric of "liberal arts" or "humanities." Music courses must compete with the other humanities offerings for their enrollments.

There are many reasons for students to enroll in music courses at non-music-major colleges. It is logical to think that students who have had piano, instrumental, or vocal training in high school would be eager to capitalize on their familiarity with the subject. One might also think that students want to learn more about music because it is so universally popular among the younger generation.

Based on extensive teaching experience at such an institution, I would say that those reasons are only partially true and may be self-deluding. Many high school musicians come to us "burnt out;" they have been in too many festivals, parades, and performances. They shun the music courses and performing groups in college with the fervor of a convert. While college students nearly universally "love music," they quickly learn (if they do not already know) that the professors of college music courses generally teach a "different kind of music."

Maybe students have registered for music courses for some of the reasons listed above. Often the reasons are far more mundane: the course is being offered at the right hour or has no Friday or Monday meetings; the course is the only one still open; the professor uses the same tests every semester and students already know the well-rehearsed answers for a good grade; the professor does or does not give essay exams or term papers; the course is considered an easy course in which everyone receives high grades. Teaching in the non-music-major, non-music-school setting is hardly rhapsodic or romantic. It has little of the glamour associated with teaching at one of the top music schools in the country.

Why should music be taught at such colleges, and why should one want to teach such music courses? Some leaders in higher education might rephrase and consolidate the questions, asking if the resources spent on music courses and music faculty in those colleges might not be spent more wisely on expanding the major offerings.

Others, myself included, believe that the resources spent on music courses open doors within an individual, adding an important dimension that enhances the quality of that individual's life. Teaching music to non-music-major students is essential to the growth of those individuals, and growth should be the principal goal of college education. Today's college students will be "consumers" of music for the rest of their lives. What they learn (or do not learn) about music while in college can either reinforce their prejudices or help them mature musically. Students leaving college will become bankers, lawyers, accountants, and others who may ultimately serve as members of school committees, finance boards, and personnel boards in the cities and towns across our land. If they have been poorly taught and have not experienced personal growth in music, they will reflect those experiences (and lack of experiences) when they make decisions as leaders. Either as consumers or as decision makers, those individuals will help to determine the quality of life in our country, which includes the quality of our music and music instruction.

Assuming that those who teach music in non-music-major colleges view their responsibilities and their students as important, then they must find the most effective means to teach music to the non-music-major student population in the short time that is available. A traditional three-credit undergraduate course spans a maximum of forty-five class hours, with about twice that amount of time expected in outside preparation. Since many students will have only one music course during their college tenure, it is important for the professor to be as pertinent, effective, and efficient as possible in communicating the subject. Added to the problem of time is the problem of diversity. Students may elect from a variety of music courses, e.g., a basic music theory course, a survey of music literature, or (for a fraction of the credit) a performing group.

The problems of limited time, diverse course offerings, and unpredictable levels of student motivation demand that music professors become as effective as possible if they are to accomplish any music education that will have a lasting effect on students. Many have overlooked or ignored Music Learning Theory in their search for ways to become more effective. Music professors who teach music courses and direct music groups for non-music majors, and who are sincerely concerned about being efficient and effective in the process, should adopt, adapt, and integrate the results of research made possible by the presence of Music Learning Theory. To do so will make music offerings more substantial in terms of the subject matter itself, and more meaningful in terms of the growth and understanding of students, and consequently more lasting in the overall positive effects.

The application of Music Learning Theory involves the use of specific learning sequences within each course of study. Learning sequence activities are structured in accordance with what is to be learned, how it is to be learned, and when it is to be learned.

The variety of music courses offered to non-music majors ranges from literature courses to performance groups to theory courses to music lessons. What is taught appears to be similar in scope to the offerings of a music school, but the offerings for non-music majors are similar neither in the depth nor in the number of courses available. It is important to note also that class members form a far less homogeneous group, ranging from those who have had extensive experience with music to rank beginners. The professor's task is to relate the material to all of those students. How might that be done within the context of the different types of courses?

Music literature courses form the bulk of the music courses offered to non-music majors. Logic would demand that some sort of music survey course, which includes information about the elements of music, be a prerequisite for other special courses like Baroque Music. That is not always the case. Thus it may be that every music literature course in a college may start with an "elements of music" component designed to develop the listening skills of the class members. The professor must develop those skills as best he can in five or six class meetings, which is a tall order. Music Learning Theory can help the professor to accomplish that task in as musical a manner as possible.

Within the component of a music literature course that is focused on the elements of music, special attention should be given to the feeling of a macro beat, to the differentiation between duple meter and triple meter, and to the differentiation between major tonality and minor tonality. Those characteristics apply to most of the selections heard in the music literature courses offered to non-music majors. Less common tonalities and meters might be handled on a case-by-case basis.

The first problem encountered by the professor may be that a few class members are still in the music babble stage.[1] The professor may identify students who are still in rhythm babble by playing a march and having all students march in place or sway from side to side to determine who can and who can not audiate a macro beat. The professor may identify students who are in tonal babble by having students echo simple tonic and dominant tonal patterns in major tonality and minor tonality (Gordon, 1984, pp. 144, 168). Remedial help may be required outside of the class meetings to prepare the "babblers" for full participation in the formal instruction during class time. Within the first two weeks of class, the students should be able to differentiate between major tonality and minor tonality, and between duple meter and triple meter. Beginning at the aural/oral level of learning, and proceeding through the verbal association and partial synthesis levels of learning, the professor may use the easy patterns as "rock bottom" references that students can use thereafter to differentiate among the most basic tonal and rhythm functions.[2] The students will have gained a formal, if simple, audiational reference after they have successfully experienced that portion of instruction.[3]

The same procedure also may help to improve musicianship among members of college ensembles and students enrolled in piano lab. To teach most effectively, the conductor/professor needs to know the extent to which students can audiate rhythmically and tonally. The conductor may rehearse works programmed for an ensemble by reviewing the principal tonal patterns and rhythm patterns of each piece in the keyality of that piece before beginning. That warm-up should help the students to audiate the tonality, the keyality, the macro beat, the micro beat, and some of the melodic rhythm of the piece.

Both the basic music theory course and the harmony course may also benefit from the application of Music Learning Theory if the professor organizes the course according to skill learning sequence (Gordon, 1984, pp. 11 - 61). In both courses, it has been traditional to stress music as a visual skill or to use a keyboard as a substitute for students learning aural concepts through audiation. If the principles of Music Learning Theory are applied to music theory instruction, the student will learn to audiate before learning to read or write music notation.

Just as the professor of the music literature course must limit the material taught, so must the music theory professor. Will all of the modes be taught? Will the more obscure meters such as unusual unpaired intact meter be taught? In one such course I have limited the material to tonic, sub-dominant, and dominant functions in major and minor tonalities and to macro and micro beat, division, and elongation functions in duple and triple meters

Within the first two weeks of a music theory course for non-music majors, the professor or those assisting should hear each student echo the easy tonic and dominant tonal patterns in major and minor tonalities and the easy macro and micro beat and division and elongation patterns in duple and triple meters (Gordon, 1984, pp. 144, 168). Some students may be able to learn moderate and difficult patterns as well in that amount of time. Starting at the aural/oral level of learning and proceeding through the verbal association and partial synthesis levels of learning, students will gain a common core of aural experiences that will function as a readiness for beginning reading and writing exercises. The student will be able to give meaning to those exercises at the symbolic association level of learning as a result of being able to audiate the patterns read and written. Success in reading and writing at the composite synthesis level of learning follows easily. And so the learning process continues in a logical and musically meaningful order.

The basic music theory course should be a prerequisite for the course in harmony. If students have learned to discriminate between duple meter and triple meter and between major tonality and minor tonality, the tasks of the harmony course may be varied. One task may be to develop the learning of additional meters, e.g., usual combined, and additional tonalities, e.g., dorian. Another may be to introduce additional rhythm and tonal functions, e.g., ties and upbeat patterns in rhythm learning and multiple patterns in tonal learning. The primary task, however, should be to apply the understanding gained from basic theory to harmony. As with more basic courses, the general rules of skill learning sequence should apply to the harmony course. Students must be able to audiate a chord or a chord progression before reading, writing, or constructing it. The first part of the course should be devoted to audiating the chords and functions that will be applied later at higher levels of skill. Of course, there will be fewer students who can or will want to take the harmony course as compared with more basic courses, but the students who do register for a harmony course will probably be the students with the most experience in music.

Finally, the most obvious course into which Music Learning Theory should be integrated is the music "methods" course. Many elementary education majors and special education majors must take either a course in music methods or a course in art methods. In some colleges, a combined course like "Arts in Elementary Education" might be required. The students in such courses are not going to be music teachers or art teachers. Rather they will use music and the arts to help teach other subjects. That concept is frequently referred to as "arts in education" to distinguish it from "arts education." In order to be able to use the arts in education, one must be somewhat knowledgable about the arts. Therefore, the music methods or arts course taken by the future elementary educator or special educator needs to provide a rigorous experience that will give the student the confidence needed to integrate music and the other arts into the general curriculum.

Music Learning Theory should provide the basis for either the music methods course or the music portion of the arts methods course. Students should be able to audiate easy tonal patterns in major and minor tonalities and easy rhythm patterns in duple and triple meters through the skill level of partial synthesis. Also, they should understand how to use movement in the classroom to help students to feel a macro beat. They should be able to create lessons that apply the feeling of macro beat to music, movement, and language arts. Those should be the minimal musical requirements, even in an arts methods course.

The ideas enumerated above can be even more cogent if the professor has gained insights into the specific potentials of individual students through the use of the Musical Aptitude Profile (MAP). MAP scores can be used to predict who will have more trouble and who will have less trouble in specific facets of the various courses. It is possible to administer selected subtests of MAP that relate most closely to the content of a particular course. For example, the subtests that relate most directly to the basic music theory course are probably Tonal Imagery Part I and Rhythm Imagery Parts I & II. MAP scores can help the professor to individualize instruction and to ensure that a given grade for a student represents not only his achievement in comparison with others, but also his achievement in comparison with his own potential.[4]

There are two factors that seem to work against the adoption of the ideas above. The first factor is that music professors tend to teach in the manner in which they were taught. Music Learning Theory was not a part of their college or pre-college experiences, and yet they learned music well enough to succeed. Of course professors teaching in accord with that view forget that they may have been born with high aptitudes, and that they were fortunate enough to have had those aptitudes fulfilled. Those professors believe that the traditional way in which they were taught helped them, and that it should therefore help their students. That attitude will be reinforced until major music schools integrate Music Learning Theory into all aspects of their curricula.

The second factor is the thought that a professor may look foolish and lose the respect of his or her peers by engaging in some of the activities advocated here. "Imagine! Time wasted administering MAP. And, the class will feel silly marching or swaying to a macro beat. None of my colleagues do things this way. I am a professional and I do not do this sort of thing. It's childish." Again, little will change until major music schools integrate Music Learning Theory into their curricula and a generation of new professors is educated by example.

The stakes in this game are high. I believe that they are nothing less than the future quality of life in our country. Those who are teaching music for the general college population must examine their goals. They are not educating professional musicians. They are teaching music for the enrichment of the lives of their students, and through them for the enrichment of society as a whole. If professors teaching non-music majors could enrich the lives of their students musically, students graduating from music schools might have an informed audience for their art. If professors are going to enrich the lives of their students musically, they must remain as informed as possible about how that can best be done.

Currently, Music Learning Theory provides the best means of supplying musical enrichment to the lives of non-music majors. The alternative is to continue to muddle along in the perpetual half-life that we have helped to create.

NOTES

[1]Within this book, see "Informal Music Instruction as Readiness for Learning Sequence Activities" for more information about the music babble stage.

[2]Within this book, see "Skill Learning Sequence" for more information about the levels of skill learning.

[3]Within this book, see "Audiation: The Term and the Process" for more information.

[4]Although Edwin Gordon does not recommend the use of MAP with college students, this author has found it helpful when working with non-music majors.

REFERENCES

Gordon, Edwin E. (1965). <u>Musical Aptitude Profile</u>. Boston: Houghton-Mifflin.

Gordon, Edwin E. (1984). <u>Learning Sequences in Music</u>. Chicago: G.I.A. Publications, Inc.

Gordon, Edwin E. (1988). <u>Learning Sequences in Music</u>. Chicago: G.I.A. Publications, Inc.

FACILITATING THE PROCESS OF CHANGE TO A SCHOOL MUSIC CURRICULUM BASED UPON MUSIC LEARNING THEORY

Richard McCrystal

Implementation of a new program (an innovation) and consequent changes in curriculum and teaching is a customary way to bring about improvement in school programs. Not only is the quality of the innovation going to be related to school improvement, but the degree that the innovation is implemented will also affect improvement. A high quality innovation, such as Music Learning Theory, that is poorly implemented is not likely to produce the desired results. This article will describe a process that has been developed to assess the degree of success in implementing an innovation, in this case, Music Learning Theory. What follows may help you to understand better the change process. It also may help you to facilitate the adoption of Music Learning Theory by your school system. At least it will alert you to the pit-falls encountered by one trying to effect change in others.

Assume that by adopting Music Learning Theory a school system forces teachers to make changes in how they teach music. Difficulties will be encountered. Of course, problems associated with change are not limited to school systems, music teachers, or the adoption of Music Learning Theory. Most of us have encountered the behaviors to be described in this article in a variety of organizational settings. Efforts to bring about curriculum reform in any discipline, not only in music, tend to have minimal effect. "To come through implementation with enough left to admire will require starting with a lot and doing well along the way" (Bird, 1986, p. 47).

Much of what will be covered in this article is based upon the research of Gene E. Hall and Shirley M. Hord (Hall and Hord, 1987). There are three major topics to consider: STAGES OF TEACHER CONCERNS, LEVELS Of USE, and the INNOVATION itself.

Bringing about change is difficult, because change is a process, not an event. To develop a process takes time and money. Typically, the introduction of change into a school system is attempted through inservice "events." Inservice is grounded in the belief that staff members can and will grow beyond the minimum expectations of initial employment, which is as it should be, but if inservice sessions are treated as isolated events rather than as part of a continuous process, and if individual differences among teachers are ignored, the expected change will likely join the mass of failed efforts to bring other changes into schools.

"Entertainers, politicians, advertisers, and others interested in gaining acceptance and support for their plans by a client group adjust the presentation of their messages so that they can be understood by their recipients" (Hall and Hord, 1987, p. 53). To help teachers accept Music Learning Theory, one should know and accommodate those teachers' viewpoints. Usually the management of change is approached from the viewpoint of the one who wants to bring about change rather than from the viewpoints of those asked to change. The reverse is needed. In the case of educational change, one must begin by assessing stages of teacher concern. The next section of this article contains specific information about the stages of teacher concern, and two subsequent sections contain specific information about levels of use and about the innovation itself.

Stages of Teacher Concerns

Hall has identified seven stages of concern about change. At the beginning of the change process teachers are typically concerned about acquiring information about the innovation. As the teachers progress through the stages of concern, their focus shifts from informational concerns to personal concerns, from personal concerns to managerial concerns, and from managerial concerns to implementational concerns. Typically, inservice programs begin at the implementational level and ignore the managerial and personal stages. That may be why there is little "left to admire" in most attempts at educational reform.

The first stage of concern is AWARENESS. At this stage there is little concern or involvement with an innovation, such as Music Learning Theory. One is simply aware that there is a "Gordon method."

The second stage is INFORMATIONAL. At this stage there is an interest in learning more details about the innovation. The individual is not yet concerned about personal consequences of adopting the innovation, especially if the actual adoption is still so distant as to be hypothetical. He is simply interested in the general characteristics of the innovation, its requirements for use, and the effect that it is intended to have.

The third stage is PERSONAL. The nonuser of Music Learning Theory, for example, will begin to have feelings of anxiety about the inadequacies of his musicianship or background in relation to teaching the new way. He will be concerned about the reward structure of the school system, about his role in decision making, and about the potential conflict between teaching the "new way" and teaching as he has in the past.

The fourth stage is MANAGEMENT. At this stage, attention becomes focused on the processes and tasks involved in teaching through Music Learning Theory, or through whatever the innovation might be. Questions become more intense regarding resources, scheduling, class load, record keeping, and the time demands to be made on the individual.

The fifth stage is CONSEQUENCE. At the consequence stage the intensity of the teacher's concern finally becomes focused on the potential impact of the innovation on the learner (client). The issue at this stage is one of how well teaching based upon Music Learning Theory will improve student competencies, performance, and attitudes. Many inservice programs are based upon the false assumption that everyone involved is already at the consequence stage, when in reality they are perhaps still at the management stage or the personal stage.

The sixth stage is COLLABORATION. The focus at the collaboration stage is on coordination and cooperation with others to the end that the innovation be used successfully. This is the stage common to those trying to bring about change. Their hope is to bring others to the collaboration stage with them.

The seventh stage is REFOCUSING. To reach this stage one needs to have been so imbued with the innovation that he is trying to find ways to improve upon it and to make its implementation more effective.

By knowing and remaining conscious of the seven stages of concern, one can readily gauge the placement of himself and others on that scale. Further, one who knows the stage of concern of a teacher will be encouraged to think of that teacher as an individual rather than as an abstraction, and will consequently be more effective in working with that teacher. The detailed techniques involved are beyond the scope of this article, but they can be found in the Hall and Hord book (1987).

Levels of Use

To ask whether one does or does not use Music Learning Theory is simplistic. In reality, one is likely to be functioning at a particular level of use, and it is expected that one's level of use will change with growth (or neglect). Of course individual differences will be seen in levels of use just as individual differences were seen in stages of concern. There are eight levels of use. As was true for the stages of concern, knowing the levels of use will help one to plan and monitor the change process through diagnosis of staff behavior.

The first level of use, ironically, is NONUSE. The teacher functioning at this level has little or no knowledge of Music Learning Theory. He is neither involved nor doing anything to become involved.

The second level of use, ORIENTATION, parallels the second stage of concern, information. At this level the potential user is acquiring information and determining what adjustments will be needed to get involved more deeply.

The third level is PREPARATION. It is at this level that the nonuser can be expected to become a user, e.g., to start using Music Learning Theory for the first time in his teaching.

The fourth level is MECHANICAL USE. The user functioning at this level is more concerned with his personal needs than with his students needs. His focus is on short term use of the innovation, a sort of living-from-day-to-day approach, as he adjusts his orientation and becomes accustomed to the process of teaching through Music Learning Theory.

The fifth level is ROUTINE. The teacher's use of the "new" has become stabilized. Few changes need to be made in its daily use. According to Hall and Hord, little thought is given at this level to improving on the innovation.

The sixth level is REFINEMENT. At this level the user begins to adapt aspects of Music Learning Theory to suit the specific needs of his students and the peculiarities of local conditions. That is possible only after the user has become knowledgeable about each of the factors involved, e.g., student abilities and other characteristics, local conditions, and the intricacies of Music Learning Theory itself.

The seventh level is INTEGRATION. This is the level at which the user combines his own efforts to use Music Learning Theory with the efforts of his colleagues. Through collective action, all parties will have greater impact upon the learning of their students.

The eighth level is RENEWAL. The user who has reached the renewal level has blossomed into an ideal of the "professional" teacher. He develops his own major modifications and innovations to increase the impact that his teaching has upon students. He is also likely to set new goals for himself, for the program, and for the school system.

The stage of concern and level of use of the person responsible for change in a school system is key to facilitating that change. Hall and Hord (1987, p. 215) reported that style of leadership has a profound effect on the success or failure of any innovation. The building principal plays a critical role in the process, but he needs help from a music supervisor or resource teachers and, to a somewhat lesser degree, from outside consultants. A principal, music supervisor, or resource teachers whose style is that of an initiator, will cause change to occur. One whose style is that of a manager will help change to occur. One whose style is that of a responder will merely allow change to occur. Hall and Hord established a Continuum of Change Facilitators: Overt Resistor --> Covert Saboteur --> Laissez-faire --> Responder --> Manager --> Initiator --> Despot (Hall and Hord, 1987, p. 243). The reader can probably supply names of persons who match each of those roles.

At first glance a linear relationship is apparent between stages of concern and levels of use. A person at the mechanical level of use might be expected to be at the management stage of concern. To date, the data that has been examined can be used to demonstrate a close relationship between the two at the extreme ends of the scales, but the parallels are much less clear toward the middle of the scales. Hall (1987) states that "the relationship between Stages of Concern and Levels of Use is not simple" (p. 338).

In an earlier publication about innovation in the schools, Hall had limited his focus to Stages of Concern (Hall and Loucks, 1979). The addition of Levels of Use helps the teacher and the supervisor to discriminate between the issue of teacher concerns regarding the change process and the issue of the extent to which a given teacher is involved in the change process, in this case the process of using Music Learning Theory.

Innovation Component Checklist

The third of Hall and Hord's three major topics regarding innovation and change in the school setting is the innovation itself. They address the fact that there is no such thing as a "teacher-proof" curriculum, and that teachers at the school level may tend to treat curriculum idiosyncratically, i.e., as a local "cottage industry" (1987, p. 116). Therefore, a checklist is needed to help counter tendencies to corrode the innovation over time. Hall and Hord's answer to that need is an Innovation Component Checklist

(1987, p. 115). For the purposes of this article it will be referred to simply as the Checklist.

The Checklist is a tool designed to help achieve consensus about what represents appropriate classroom use of an innovation. A scale is used that ranges from the ideal implementation of the innovation, through acceptable levels of implementation, and finally to the level of implementation that is considered minimally acceptable. The Checklist should accommodate the evaluation of the critical components of the innovation, and should also include examples of unacceptable variations of the innovation. That inventory process has been made easier, in the case of Music Learning Theory, by Gordon's detailed descriptions of the theory and its components, as found in <u>Learning Sequences in Music</u> (Gordon, 1988) and in the "Reference Handbook for Using Learning Sequence Activities" from <u>Jump Right In: The Music Curriculum</u> (Gordon and Woods, 1985). Rarely does the developer of an innovation provide such exact directions for potential users.

Four steps are needed to develop an effective checklist for the implementation of Music Learning Theory. First, one must learn the components of Music Learning Theory, specifically the components of learning sequence activities (in relation to skill, tonal content, and rhythm content) and the components of classroom activities. To accomplish that will require training. Persons familiar with Music Learning Theory will be helpful in learning and listing the components and their acceptable variations. Second, one must observe and interview a small number of users of Music Learning Theory. The more varied its use (including incorrect use) the more helpful to the observer, because one learns what something is both by observing what it is and by observing what it is not. Any variety in application will help one to sort out the acceptable from the unacceptable. Third, one must adjust the Checklist based upon observed practices. Fourth, one must observe and collect data from a larger sample of users than was done in step two. The Checklist will be valuable in helping staff to know what is acceptable. The Checklist will be valuable to the process of evaluating teacher performance as well as to the process of implementing Music Learning Theory.

The change process often is carried out with no clear and concrete description of the innovation (Hall and Hord, 1987, p. 125), but in the case of Music Learning Theory, that is not a problem because of the clear description that we do have. Problems in implementation are more likely to result from teachers' intense feelings of concern prior to their being brought to stage five of the stages of concern, and from teachers who are nonusers.

When consensus is reached among those involved with implementing Music Learning Theory within a given setting, an important step toward success will have been accomplished.

Recommendations

What conclusions might be drawn at this point? If you are teaching or supervising music in a school system that is not using Music Learning Theory and you are convinced that Music Learning Theory should be used, where do you start?

First be prepared to spend the needed time. Three years is minimal. Also, a budget will be needed to cover the cost of the inservice process, and to a much lesser extent, the cost of supplies. Rather than convert an entire school system at once, it may be wiser to start with small portions of the school system. While that will often increase the time needed for a total conversion, starting small and succeeding is preferable to starting large and failing.

At least one person on the staff needs to be thoroughly trained in the application of Music Learning Theory to teaching. A one-day or two-day workshop is not at all adequate for that person if he is to progress beyond the awareness stage. One possibility is to have the key person or persons participate in an intensive series of summer classes. (That may increase the time needed to accomplish the goal, because a number of summers will be needed for proper training.) Another option may be to arrange for a sabbatical leave or a paid leave of absence for the key person. Until Music Learning Theory is taught in more colleges and universities, training will not be easily accessible. The lack of training opportunities is ironic, considering that Gordon has been identified in the <u>Music Educators Journal</u> as one of five major influences on American music education over the last century (Shehan, 1986).

Testing the music aptitudes and music achievement of students is important to the application of Music Learning Theory in the classroom. Classroom teachers will identify with and support a music program that is as accountable as the three R's sooner than they will identify with and support an "extra-curricular activity." Measuring and evaluating instruction in music can help to tap that support at the same time that it dramatically taps elements of music learning that may have been overlooked by more traditional approaches to music instruction. Boards of education will also be better able to understand and appreciate the music program that they are asked to fund when the results of that program can be measured. Music Learning Theory contains components that lend themselves to accurate measurement.

Most school systems are supported by an equalized property tax base, but at the same time contain educational programs that vary from classroom to classroom. Variation will occur as long as there are individual differences among teachers, administrators, and students. The degree that such variations should be tolerated is open to question. Music Learning Theory allows for variation in teaching style, but not in skill and content presented. A Checklist is needed to manage the ever-present forces that work against providing all students with the best that a local school system resources can provide. A Checklist will be more easily developed on the basis of Music Learning Theory than on the basis of less structured, more traditional practices. That is because Music Learning Theory has an eloquent internal logic.

As difficult as change is to bring about, the task is well worth the effort needed when a marked improvement in education is the expected result. That is the case in the implementation of Music Learning Theory.

REFERENCES

Bird, T. (1986). "Mutual Adaptation and Mutual Accomplishment: Images of Change in a Field Experiment." A. Lieberman (Ed.), Rethinking School Improvement. New York: Teachers College, Columbia University.

Gordon, Edwin E. (1985). "Reference Handbook for Using Learning Sequence Activities." E. Gordon & D. Woods, Jump Right In: The Music Curriculum. Chicago: G. I. A. Publications, Inc..

Gordon, Edwin E. (1988). Learning Sequences in Music. Chicago: G. I. A. Publications, Inc..

Hall, G. E., & S. M. Hord (1987). Change in Schools, Facilitating the Process. Albany: State University of New York.

Hall, G., & S. Loucks (1979). "Teacher Concerns as a Basis for Facilitating and Personalizing Staff Development." In A. Lieberman & L. Miller (Eds.), Staff Development, New Demands, New Realities, New Perspectives. New York: Teachers College, Columbia University.

Shehan, P. K. (1986, February). "Major approaches to music education: An account method." Music Educators Journal, 72(6), 26-31.

CONTRIBUTORS

Betty Bertaux: B.S., University of Tennessee. M.M.E. with Kodály emphasis, Holy Names College. Vocal music teacher at the Spring Branch Independent School District, Houston, Texas.

Patricia Shehan Campbell: B.F.A., Ohio University. M.M., University of Akron. Ph.D., Kent State University. Studied Dalcroze technique at Kent State University and at the Longy School in Boston. Assoc. Professor of Music Education at the University of Washington.

Maureen Carr: B.A., Marywood College. M.F.A., Rutgers-The State University. Ph.D., University of Wisconsin-Madison. Professor of Music and Coordinator of Theory and Aural Skills at The Pennsylvania State University School of Music.

Nadine Cernohorsky: B.M., Susquehanna University. M.M., Eastman School of Music. Ph.D. in progress, Temple University. Orff Certification, Level 1, Hartt School of Music. Preschool music teacher at St. Thomas in Fort Washington, Pennsylvania, and in the Children's Music Development Program at Temple University.

Diane M. Clark: B.M., Rhodes College. M.M., Indiana University. D.M.A., University of Mississippi. Assoc. Professor of Voice and Chair of the Music Department, Rhodes College.

Barbara Hanna Creider: B.M., Oberlin Conservatory. M.M., M.M.A., D.M.A., Yale School of Music. Suzuki violin teacher at the Settlement Music School in Philadelphia, Pennsylvania.

Roger Dean: B.M.E., Wheaton College. M.M.E. American Conservatory of Music. D.M.A., University of Oregon. Professor of Music Education and Chairman of the Department of Music Education and Music Therapy at Temple University.

John M. Feierabend: B.M., Wayne State University. M.M. with Kodály Emphasis, cooperative program between Silver Lake College and the University of Wisconsin. Ph.D., Temple University. Assoc. Professor of Music Education at Hartt School of Music at the University of Hartford, summer Kodály faculty of Silver Lake College and Belmont College, and Coordinator of the Connecticut Center for Early Childhood Music Education in Music and Movement.

Denise Kath Gamble: B.M., Syracuse University. M.M., Ph.D., Temple University. Educational consultant for teachers using Jump Right In: The Music Curriculum and educational consultant for the New Haven Board of Education.

Edwin E. Gordon: B.M., M.M., Eastman School of Music. M.Ed., Ohio University. PhD., University of Iowa. Professor of Music and Carl E. Seashore Professor of Research in Music Education at Temple University.

Richard F. Grunow: B.M., University of Wisconsin-Plattville. M.M., Ph.D., University of Michigan. Assoc. Professor of Music Education at the Eastman School of Music.

Robert Harper: B.A., University of New York at Stony Brook. M.S., Long Island University. Elementary general music teacher at the William Floyd School District, Long Island, New York. Writer and advisor for the New York State Music Curriculum for Kindergarten through Grade 6.

Wayne Hobbs: B.M.E., Florida State University. M.C.M., New Orleans Baptist Theological Seminary. Ph.D., Tulane University. Director of the School of Music at Texas Tech University.

Linda Lee Jessup: B.M., State University of New York at Potsdam. M.M., West Chester University. Ph.D., Temple University. Asst. Professor of Music Education at Montgomery Community College. Director of the Young Children's Music Program and Microcomputer Software Applications Consultant at Ursinus College.

James M. Jordan: B.M., Susquehanna University. M.M., Ph.D., Temple University. Studied at the Laban Institute of Movement Studies. Chair for Music Education and Asst. Professor of Music Education and Conducting at Hartt School of Music of the University of Hartford. Music Director and Conductor of The Greater Hartford Youth Chorale.

Lili Muhler Levinowitz: B.M., Westminster Choir College. M.M., Ph.D., Temple University. Director of Research for the Center for Music and Young Children in Princeton, New Jersey.

Richard McCrystal: B.M., Eastman School of Music. M.Ed., University of Rochester. Ph.D. in progress, Temple University. Adjunct Professor of Music at Trenton State College.

Mary Veronica Ranke: B.M., M.M., Peabody Institute of the Johns Hopkins University. Coordinator of the Annapolis Branch of the Peabody Institute Preparatory School. Piano faculty member at the Peabody Institute Preparatory School and Arundel Community College.

Harry Semerjian: B.M., M.A., Boston University. D.Ed., University of Massachusetts, Amherst, School of Education, Center for the Study of Aesthetics in Education. Professor of Music and Chairperson of Graduate Arts in Education Programs at Fitchburg State College.

Robert Shilling: B.M., Berklee College of Music. M.M., Ph.D. in progress, Temple University. Education Planner for the New Jersey Department of Education.

Scott Corbin Shuler: B.M., University of Michigan. M.M. University of Illinois at Champaign-Urbana. Ph.D., Eastman School of Music. Music Consultant for the Connecticut State Department of Education.

Cynthia Crump Taggart: B.M., M.M., University of Michigan. Ph.D., Temple University. Asst. Professor of Music Education at Case Western Reserve University.

Gail Waddell: B.M., M.Ed., University of Cincinnati. Level 3 Orff Certification, University of Denver. Elementary general music teacher for the Forest Hills School District, Cincinnati, Ohio.

Darrel L. Walters: B.M., M.M., University of Michigan School of Music. Ph.D., University of Michigan School of Education. Asst. Professor of Music Education at Temple University.

Sally Weaver: B.M., University of Michigan. M.M., Ph.D., Temple University. Teacher of music classes for parents and young children and Program Coordinator for the Center for Music and Young Children in Princeton, New Jersey.

Coletta Wierson: B.M., Luther College. M.M., University of Colorado. Elementary music teacher in Hopkins, Minnesota.

INDEX

EDITORS

Darrel L. Walters is Assistant Professor of Music Education at the Boyer College of Music, Temple University. He taught public school music in Michigan for 16 years prior to joining the Temple faculty in 1986. Professor Walters has taught Music Learning Theory to graduate students at Temple University, conducts seminars in the application of Music Learning Theory, and has written manuals for teaching materials based upon Music Learning Theory.

Cynthia Crump Taggart is Assistant Professor of Music Education at Case Western Reserve University, effective September, 1989. She has taught school music for five years in Kenosha, Wisconsin and Ann Arbor, Michigan, and has taught undergraduate music education classes at Temple University. She has also served as coordinator of the Temple University Center City Children's Music Development Program.

AUTHORS

The twenty-six authors who have contributed to **Readings in Music Learning Theory** are music educators from universities and public and private schools in eleven states. Their combined expertise encompasses general, vocal, and instrumental music from preschool through the college level, the specific approaches of Dalcroze, Laban, Orff, Kodaly and Suzuki, university-level music theory and music pedagogy, private instruction, and, of course, Gordon Music Learning Theory. Reading this book may be the next best thing to having a discussion with each of them about their approaches to teaching music and their applications of the principles of Music Learning Theory to private and group music instruction.